NEW DEVELOPMENTS IN
CLINICAL PSYCHOLOGY

EDITED BY
FRASER N. WATTS

Published by
The British Psychological Society
in association with
John Wiley & Sons Limited
Chichester • New York • Brisbane • Toronto • Singapore

BL British Library Cataloguing in Publication Data

New developments in clinical psychology.
1. Clinical psychology
I. Watts, Fraser N.
157'.9   RC467

Distributed in the United Kingdom by
The Distribution Centre
Blackhorse Road, Letchworth, Herts. SG6 1HN.
ISBN 0 901 71528 X

Distributed outside the United Kingdom by
John Wiley & Sons Limited.
New York, Brisbane, Toronto, Singapore.
ISBN 0 471 90711 1

Printed in Great Britain by A. Wheaton & Co. Ltd., Exeter.

CONTENTS

PREFACE

When a publisher asks you to consider editing a book on 'new developments' in a field such as clinical psychology, it is only prudent to pause to consider whether there is enough that is new and significant to justify such a book. I decided that there was. Having read, with growing pleasure, the interesting and engaging chapters the contributors have prepared for this book, I feel amply vindicated in that judgment.

For each chapter, I looked for a topic that linked together recent scientific research with developments in professional practice. The balance between the two varies somewhat from chapter to chapter, but each achieves this integration in its own way. I hope this will help practitioners to see how research can underpin significant developments in the professional role, and help academics to see how their research can have important practical applications.

I have taken some liberty with the term 'new'. Some chapters are based on work done in the last two or three years (such as *group management of the handicapped*), others draw on work that has been available for longer but has not been as widely disseminated as it deserves (such as *interaction process recall*); yet others report a significant variation on an established theme (such as the increasing application of *small N designs* outside the context of behaviour therapy). But I believe each chapter has something to say, in terms of information or comment, that will appear fresh to many potential readers.

The work undertaken by clinical psychologists is becoming so diverse that we are in danger of splintering into groups of specialists who take little interest in each others' work. I hope that

i

despite this, the span of topics in this book is broad enough that every clinical psychologist will find several chapters of direct relevance (though I am conscious of some notable omissions such as the elderly). However, I also hope that many clinical psychologists will want to read the whole of this book, and find out how other areas of work are developing. It has been a pleasure to see how related themes have emerged in chapters concerned with different client groups. I have allowed some of these connections to determine the order in which the chapters appear, so that most chapters have something in common with the one (or two) that come before and after.

Editing this book has been an enjoyable task and I am grateful to the many people who have helped to make it so, to the many colleagues who generously suggested topics or authors (especially my colleague in the 'next door' office, Mark Williams, whose excellent advice is always generously available), to Joyce Collins and Christopher Feeney of the BPS publications department for their friendly and efficient help, and especially to the contributors, who have produced readable, informative chapters of the right length, on the topics requested, and delivered them by the required deadline. No editor can ask for more.

Fraser N. Watts
MRC Applied Psychology Unit, Cambridge

St Bartholomew's Day, August 1984

EATING DISORDERS

Peter J. Cooper

This chapter will be largely devoted to the newly identified eating disorder, bulimia nervosa. The defining features, epidemiology and clinical characteristics of the condition will be described, and a cognitive behavioural approach to its management outlined. The implications of applying this cognitive behavioural approach to the understanding and treatment of anorexia nervosa will be considered. The considerable body of contemporary research in the area of obesity and anorexia nervosa will not be considered, since a number of excellent reviews have recently been published (for example, Garfinkel and Garner, 1982; Stunkard, 1982).

BULIMIA NERVOSA

Defining features

For many years it has been recognized that distressing episodes of uncontrolled eating occur in some patients with anorexia nervosa and in a small proportion of those with obesity. However, it has only recently become apparent that such bulimic episodes constitute the central feature of a relatively distinct clinical syndrome. This condition has attracted a variety of diagnostic labels, but those which have gained widest acceptance have been 'bulimia' (American Psychiatric Association, 1980) in America, and 'bulimia nervosa' (Russell, 1979) in Britain. The diagnostic criteria for the latter are:

- patients suffer from powerful and intractable urges to overeat;
- they seek to avoid the fattening effects of food by inducing vomiting, abusing purgatives, or both;
- they have a morbid fear of becoming fat (Russell, 1979).

It is likely that the second criterion is unduly narrow, in that some patients who fulfil the other two criteria and compensate for having overeaten by extreme dieting rather than by vomiting or taking laxatives are in other respects indistinguishable from patients who fulfil Russell's criteria for bulimia nervosa (Fairburn, 1983).

Epidemiology

Russell's original description of bulimia nervosa was based on the clinical characteristics of a sample of 30 patients. It had taken him six and a half years to collect this patient series, suggesting that the condition was rare and seen only occasionally at specialist clinics. However, there is now evidence that many cases existed undetected during this time. In 1980, with the help of a popular British women's magazine, 499 women who fulfilled self-report diagnostic criteria for bulimia nervosa were identified (Fairburn and Cooper, 1982). In their demographic and clinical characteristics these women closely resembled Russell's series of patients, yet few had been provided with professional help. This study has since been replicated using a different sampling technique, and a further large sample of women fulfilling self-report diagnostic criteria for bulimia nervosa were identified (Fairburn and Cooper, 1984a). Both these studies pointed to bulimia nervosa constituting a major source of undetected psychological morbidity.

Studies of the prevalence of the syndromes of bulimia and bulimia nervosa and their constituent components have produced conflicting findings. These differences are largely attributable to the methodological weaknesses of much of this research (Fairburn, 1984a). However, some tentative conclusions can be drawn. In one British investigation, a self-report questionnaire was used to elicit information on weight and on eating habits and attitudes from women attending a family planning clinic (Cooper and Fairburn, 1983). It was found that 20.9 per cent had experienced a bulimic episode (defined as 'an episode of uncontrollable excessive eating') during the previous two months; and 2.9 per cent had used self-induced vomiting as a means of weight control. The point prevalence of bulimia nervosa was found to be 1.9 per cent. A similar survey has been conducted in America (Pyle *et al.,* 1983). A large group of college students were administered a questionnaire based on the DSM III criteria for bulimia, and using a criterion of weekly bulimic episodes and weekly self-induced vomiting or laxative abuse, a prevalence of 1.4 per cent for the bulimia syndrome was obtained.

These two epidemiological surveys indicate that the syndromes of bulimia and bulimia nervosa have a high prevalence. However, the resource implications of this finding are not clear, since not all people who fulfil research diagnostic criteria regard themselves as in need of help. The authors of the British study attempted to elucidate which factors were associated with individuals regarding themselves as having an eating problem (Cooper *et al.,*

1984). The most important were the presence of bulimic episodes, and a high score on the Eating Attitudes Test (Garner and Garfinkel, 1979) which reflects disturbed eating habits and abnormal attitudes to food, eating, body shape and weight. These findings require further investigation.

All the epidemiological work in this area has been based on responses to self-report questionnaires and, as such, the findings must be regarded as preliminary. Even when reputable measures of established validity have been used, the sole reliance on self-report data meant that complex behaviours and attitudes could not be explored and important individual differences were likely to have been obscured. Future research should employ standardized interview techniques, particularly for the assessment of the specific psychopathology of the disorder, about which least is known. Also, longitudinal research is required to provide information on the incidence and course of the condition.

Two clear findings about the distribution of the disorder have consistently emerged from epidemiological studies and clinical reports. First, bulimia nervosa appears to be virtually entirely confined to women. A review of the published series of patients with bulimia or bulimia nervosa reveals that around 1 per cent of these patients are men, a figure similar to that found in one community study (Fairburn and Cooper, 1984a). Second, the disorder appears to occur predominantly in young adult women rather than in adolescents, as is the case with anorexia nervosa. The great majority of patients with bulimia nervosa are in their twenties, although a wide age range may be affected. It has yet to be investigated whether bulimia nervosa is particularly prevalent in sub-groups of the population, as has been found to be the case with anorexia nervosa (Garner and Garfinkel, 1980).

Clinical features

Russell (1979) provided a detailed account of the eating habits, specific and non-specific psychopathology, and weight history of the 30 patients in his original series. He also outlined the physical complications of the disorder. The clinical features of a further 34 patients with bulimia were later described (Pyle *et al.*, 1981), largely confirming Russell's earlier findings. However, only recently has a description been provided of a patient series in which standardized recruitment and assessment procedures were used (Fairburn and Cooper, 1984b).

The principal complaint of patients with bulimia nervosa is of having lost control of their eating. The amount of food consumed in bulimic episodes varies greatly between patients, and quantity is not therefore a useful defining feature. What is common to such episodes is that they are *experienced* as excessive, unpleasant and outside voluntary control. Patients themselves have no difficulty in differentiating between such episodes and merely overeating

(Abrahams and Beumont, 1982). The frequency of bulimic episodes is also variable; however, at presentation, about 50 per cent of patients report that they occur at least daily (Fairburn and Cooper, 1984b).

The nature of bulimic episodes is fairly uniform in character. Typically, the patient's eating pattern consists of attempts to maintain a rigid diet, punctuated by episodes of loss of control. These episodes are almost invariably secret and usually consist of the consumption of items of food which the patient is attempting to exclude from her diet. The food tends to be eaten rapidly, with little or no enjoyment. Clinical reports suggest that circumstances which are likely to precipate bulimic episodes include dysphoric mood states, boredom, and having transgressed some dietary rule. Further research is required for a more detailed understanding of the psychological events and processes which lead to loss of control.

At presentation, the great majority of patients with bulimia nervosa have a normal body weight, reflecting a balance between their disturbed eating and compensatory behaviour. The most common method of weight control is self-induced vomiting. This is generally accomplished by inducing the gag reflex using fingers, although some patients learn to vomit spontaneously. The frequency of vomiting tends to be greater than the frequency of bulimic episodes. In one patient series three-quarters reported vomiting at least once a day and nearly half reported vomiting at least twice a day (Fairburn and Cooper, 1984b). Vomiting is almost always induced in secret and patients may escape detection for many years. At presentation, most patients with bulimia nervosa give a history of bulimic episodes with self-induced vomiting of four or five years' duration.

Laxatives are also used by some of these patients to control weight. Exercise as a method of weight control is also common, although it is not clear that it is used more frequently amongst these patients than amongst other weight-concerned groups.

The central disturbance in patients with bulimia nervosa appears to be cognitive in nature. They have beliefs and values about the importance of a particular body shape and weight similar to those found amongst patients with anorexia nervosa. They are profoundly afraid of becoming fat and extremely sensitive to any changes in weight or shape. One study (Fairburn and Cooper, 1984b) used a standardized clinical interview to assess the psychopathology of 35 patients with bulimia nervosa and found that the most prominent feature was a morbid fear of fatness, which was present in marked degree in 86 per cent of patients. This fear led to an intense preoccupation with thoughts about weight and shape and to frequent weighing. Less than a quarter displayed a pathological pursuit of weight loss of the degree one would expect in patients with anorexia nervosa. Indeed, the desired weight of these patients was no different from that of women of equivalent age in the general population. The precise nature of the specific psychopathology of patients with bulimia nervosa and its relation to particular behavioural disturbances requires further systematic investigation. Such work is currently hampered by the lack of appropriate assessment instruments.

People who experience bulimic episodes and control their weight by vomiting or taking laxatives are at risk of serious physical complications. Detailed accounts of these risks have been provided elsewhere (Russell, 1979; Fairburn, 1983). The most serious complication relates to the potassium loss caused by the vomiting and laxative abuse. Clinically significant hypokalaemia has been found in over 10 per cent of these patients (Mitchell *et al.*, 1983). This can result in cardiac arrhythmias which are potentially fatal. Tetany, peripheral paraesthesia, epileptic seizures, and, in the long term, renal damage may also occur. It would be prudent for psychologists referred these patients to have them physically assessed as a matter of routine, and during treatment to be on the alert for signs of physical problems.

Patients with bulimia nervosa have a high level of non-specific psychological disturbance. Two features dominate the clinical picture, namely anxiety and depression. One study (Fairburn and Cooper, 1984b), which used the Present State Examination (Wing *et al.*, 1974) to assess mental state, found situational autonomic anxiety to be present in nearly three-quarters of patients; anxiety on meeting people in nearly half; and both free-floating autonomic anxiety and panic attacks in about a third. Detailed enquiry revealed that most of these symptoms related to situations concerned with food and eating. The second important aspect of the non-specific psychopathology is the high level of depression. Many authors have commented on this, but only one study has compared the depressive symptoms of patients with bulimia nervosa with those of patients with a primary diagnosis of major depressive disorder (Cooper and Fairburn, in press). A number of superficial similarities were revealed, such as an equivalent level of depression on a global index of severity, as well as a similar frequency of a number of depressive symptoms. However, a discriminant function analysis revealed a clear bimodality, reflecting a different inter-relationship between symptoms for the two patient groups. Furthermore, detailed enquiry revealed that the depressive symptoms were also likely to be secondary to the eating disorder. Longitudinal studies are required to confirm this impression.

Aetiology

Bulimia nervosa is a disorder of unknown aetiology. Russell (1979) regarded the most important predisposing factor as being a previous history of anorexia nervosa. He found that 57 per cent of his sample had had 'unequivocal' anorexia nervosa and a further 27 per cent had had a 'cryptic' form of the condition. However, later work has not confirmed this finding. The two community studies (Fairburn and Cooper, 1982, 1984a), and two clinical series (Pyle *et al.*, 1981; Fairburn and Cooper, 1984b) found that well under half of those with bulimia or bulimia nervosa could ever have fulfilled diagnostic criteria for anorexia nervosa. Bulimia nervosa should not therefore simply be regarded as a chronic complication of anorexia nervosa.

Two factors of possible aetiological importance have emerged from epidemiological and clinical research. The first is a predisposition to obesity. In one clinical series (Fairburn and Cooper, 1984b) 54 per cent had at some time weighed over 115 per cent of average for their age and height, as compared with 24.5 per cent amongst the general population. Similar findings were obtained in two community studies (Fairburn and Cooper, 1982; 1984a). Since the body weight of women with bulimia nervosa is no different from that of women in the general population, this observation suggests that they may need to exercise a particularly high degree of restraint over their food intake in order to attain an acceptable weight. The one study to measure the degree of dietary restraint in these patients found it to be significantly higher than amongst a sample of female undergraduates (Fairburn and Cooper, 1984b). It has been argued that dietary restraint is a crucial factor in the development of bulimia (Polivy *et al.*, 1984). Some tentative support for this hypothesis comes from laboratory research on non-patient samples (for example, Frost *et al.*, 1982). However, interpretation of the studies is complicated by the use of inadequate measures and the absence of any research on patient populations.

The second possible predisposing factor is a susceptibility to affective disorder. A systematic study of psychiatric disorder in the first-degree relatives of patients with anorexia nervosa or bulimia found the rate of major affective disorder to be the same as that found amongst the relatives of patients with bipolar affective disorder (Hudson *et al.*, 1983). It is interesting to note that a family history and personal history of an affective disturbance have been found to distinguish the bulimic sub-group of patients with anorexia nervosa from those who simply restrict their food intake (Casper *et al.*, 1980; Garfinkel *et al.*, 1980). These observations suggest that a predisposition to affective disturbance may be a vulnerability factor in the aetiology of bulimic episodes, although the nature of this association is obscure.

Treatment

Russell (1979), in his original description of bulimia nervosa, described the disorder as intractable, with a prognosis less favourable than 'uncomplicated anorexia nervosa'. He reported that inpatient management along the lines he proposes for anorexia nervosa (Russell, 1981) was largely inappropriate for these patients. Any benefits tended to be short-lived and relapse after discharge was highly likely. Nevertheless, it has been suggested that admission is indicated if there is severe depression and a high risk of suicide, or if the patient's eating habits remain grossly disturbed after a trial of outpatient care, or if the patient is in poor physical health (Fairburn, 1982).

The role of physical treatments is unclear. In the United States there has been particular interest in the use of anti-depressant drugs. Both tricyclic medication (Pope *et al.,* 1983a) and monoamine oxidase inhibitors (Walsh *et al.,* 1982) have been strongly advocated. However, there have been only two controlled treatment trials of anti-depressant medication and they have produced conflicting findings. An American study (Pope *et al.,* 1983b) found imipramine to be an effective short-term treatment for bulimia, 90 per cent of patients achieving a moderate or marked reduction in their frequency of binge-eating. In contrast, a British study (Sabine *et al.,* 1983) found the anti-depressant mianserin to have no specific effect on these patients' eating habits, attitudes or mental state. The issue therefore remains currently undecided and further trials are required. However, it seems likely that the minority of patients with bulimia nervosa who have a coexisting depressive disorder will require specific treatment of their mood disturbance, in addition to treatment for their eating disorder.

There have been a number of clinical reports concerned with the use of psychological forms of treatment (for example, Long and Cordle, 1982; Rosen and Leitenberg, 1982). However, one particular form of cognitive behaviour therapy has been described in detail (Fairburn, 1981, 1984b). This treatment, designed specifically to modify both the disturbed behaviour and attitudes characteristic of patients with bulimia nervosa, consists of a number of behavioural techniques derived from standard behavioural treatments of obesity, as well as a number of specific cognitive interventions. The treatment is problem-oriented, with definite goals being clearly specified throughout treatment. Responsibility for change resides explicitly with the patient, an approach which is welcomed by patients, since loss of self-control is perceived as the central problem.

A very detailed description has been provided of the various steps involved in this treatment (Fairburn, 1984b). In essence it is conducted in three phases. In the first, behavioural techniques are used to disrupt the habitual cycle of overeating and vomiting. The procedures used include self-monitoring, the prescription of a pattern of regular eating, and stimulus-control measures similar to those used in behavioural treatments of obesity. Patients are provided with information about body weight regulation, dieting, and the adverse consequences of using self-induced vomiting or purgatives as means of weight control. This stage of treatment generally lasts about four weeks and appointments are twice weekly. The second phase is more cognitively-oriented. It includes measures designed to reduce dietary restraint, training in problem-solving, and certain cognitive restructuring procedures. This stage lasts about two months and appointments are held at weekly intervals. The final phase is largely concerned with the maintenance of progress following discharge, and consists of three or four fortnightly appointments.

As yet there is no research evidence to support the use of this cognitive behavioural approach to the management of patients with bulimia nervosa, in preference to any other form of intervention. However, there is uncontrolled evidence that the treatment is effective. Fairburn (1981) reported a series of 11 patients with bulimia nervosa treated using this approach for an average of seven months. Although at presentation most patients were experiencing episodes of bulimia with self-induced vomiting many times a week (mean of 24 times a month; range 5 to 140), at the end of treatment nine patients were experiencing such episodes less than once a month. This behaviour change was accompanied by a reduction in the intensity of patients' abnormal attitudes to body shape and weight. A twelve-month follow-up of six of the patients indicated that the improvements were maintained. These findings have been supported by collective experience of this approach with over 50 patients; and a clinical trial comparing it with an alternative psychological treatment is nearing completion.

Another promising psychological treatment has been described (Lacey, 1983). It involves a combination of individual and group psychotherapy conducted over 10 weeks. Patients attend hospital for a full half-day each week. The individual sessions are partly behavioural in character and partly 'insight-oriented', whereas the group sessions are insight-oriented throughout. The specific techniques of the treatment have not yet been described in any detail. Although it has not been compared with any other approach, preliminary findings suggest that this treatment is effective in preventing binge-eating and self-induced vomiting, and that improvements are maintained (Lacey, 1983). However, it is not clear whether the treatment has any effect on these patients' dysfunctional attitudes to their shape and weight. Moreover, it seems that psychological disturbance often persists: thus, more than a third of the reported series considered or received further psychotherapy during the period of follow-up.

Clearly, controlled clinical trials are required to establish the efficiency of any form of treatment. However, if psychological treatments for bulimia nervosa are to be further developed and refined it is necessary to establish which particular aspects of the range of treatment techniques used act on which particular features of the disorder. There are two complementary approaches to this issue. First, the systematic introduction of therapeutic techniques with serial measurements of the full range of behavioural and cognitive disturbances would elucidate the process of change in treatment. This would provide some clarification of the relationship between individual treatment techniques and individual facets of the disorder. Second, laboratory research on the mechanisms of some of the pathological processes, such as dietary restraint, would clarify how the different aspects of the disorder relate to one another, and which are the central disturbances requiring treament and which might change incidentally. Both these lines of work require measures of far greater sensitivity than are currently available.

IMPLICATIONS FOR ANOREXIA NERVOSA

It has recently been suggested that a cognitive behavioural approach to the treatment of patients with anorexia nervosa may also be appropriate (Fairburn, 1984a; Garner and Bemis, 1982). Before examining the grounds for this assertion, it is worth briefly reviewing previous psychological approaches to the treatment of this disorder.

The literature on psychological treatment of anorexia nervosa is largely concerned with operant techniques for inducing weight gain. Although such techniques have been extensively investigated and refined (for example, Agras *et al.*, 1974), operant programmes are not only difficult to manage but may also be unnecessary. One recent study found no benefit of a 'strict' operant refeeding programme over a more 'lenient' one (Touyz *et al.*, 1984). Furthermore, one controlled study of weight restoration in anorexia nervosa found no difference in the rate or amount of weight gain between an operant programme and straightforward nursing care (Eckert *et al.*, 1979). This finding supports those of an earlier investigation in which patients treated with an operant conditioning programme were found to be no different at follow-up from those managed using various different forms of treatment (Garfinkel *et al.*, 1977). Indeed, there appears to be no special difficulty in inducing weight gain in patients with expert nursing care in the absence of any specific psychological techniques (Russell, 1977).

Certain other behavioural approaches to the management of anorexia nervosa have been proposed, based on various different formulations of the psychological processes underlying the disorder. For example, anxiety-reducing techniques have been advocated on the grounds that anorexia nervosa is essentially a phobia; that is, a phobic avoidance of normal weight (Crisp 1967; Schnurer *et al.*, 1973). Accordingly, systematic desensitization procedures have been used to reduce the anxiety associated with eating certain foods and gaining weight (Hallsten, 1965; Lang, 1965; Schnurer *et al.*, 1973). However, little can be concluded from these case reports, since in all cases treatments was conducted on an inpatient basis with many other influences operating. Furthermore, no systematic assessments were made and no follow-up data were reported. In any event, this approach is unlikely to prove an effective treatment for anorexia nervosa because the model of phobic avoidance on which it is based does not adequately account for the phenomenology of the disorder. Although these patients' avoidance of weight gain could be construed as a manifestation of a phobia, it is accompanied by (and perhaps secondary to) an active pursuit of thinness (Bemis, 1983). Moreover, unlike patients with phobias, those with anorexia nervosa generally do not recognize the irrationality of their fears and often have little desire to change. It is also worth noting that they do not display the psychophysiological responses indicative of anxiety when exposed to food or weight-related stimuli (Salkind *et al.*, 1980).

An alternative formulation is based upon certain similarities between anorexia nervosa and obsessive compulsive neurosis: for example, a ritualistic pattern of eating, and so-called 'compulsive eating' and 'compulsive exercising'. Support for this formulation comes from two psychometric studies which have shown that patients with anorexia nervosa have high scores on the Leyton Obsessional Scale (Smart *et al.,* 1976: Solyom *et al.,* 1982). Indeed, Solyom and colleagues reported that more than half their series of patients with anorexia nervosa fulfilled diagnostic criteria for obsessive compulsive neurosis. In accordance with this formulation, treatment using response prevention measures has been proposed by Mavissakalian (1978). However, the evidence in support of this approach is meagre, since only two cases were presented and they were concurrently on a ward programme designed to induce weight gain. In any event, three lines of argument run counter to the contention that anorexia nervosa is merely an unusual manifestation of an obsessive compulsive neurosis. First, many of the obsessional features in anorexia nervosa are personality traits which occur in many other patient and non-patient groups and are therefore of no diagnostic significance (Garfinkel and Garner, 1982). Indeed, the scores on the Leyton Obsessional scale of patients with anorexia nervosa are similar to those of patients with a diagnosis of depressive disorder (Kendell and DiScipio, 1970). Second, certain of the obsessional symptoms present in anorexia nervosa are found in all starvation states and they could therefore be a non-specific feature of starvation (Garfinkel and Garner, 1982). Third, the so-called 'compulsive eating' which is found in about half of those with anorexia nervosa (Casper *et al.,* 1980; Garfinkel *et al.,* 1980) is not strictly an obsessive compulsive ritual, since the behaviour is neither stereotyped nor truly repetitive, and neither is it associated with obsessional thoughts.

The theoretical grounds for believing that a cognitive behavioural approach may be suitable for patients with anorexia nervosa derive from the observation that most aspects of the disorder, as with bulimia nervosa, appear to be secondary to and maintained by dysfunctional beliefs and values concerning body shape and weight. For example, the extreme dieting, the frequent weighing or total avoidance of weighing, the preoccupation with food and eating as well as the compensatory behaviour of self-induced vomiting, laxative abuse and excessive exercising, can all be understood in terms of these patients' fear of becoming fat and their positive pursuit of thinness. Even the bulimic episodes seen in about half of these patients may be purely cognitively determined, since such episodes may represent a secondary response to extreme dietary restraint (Polivy *et al.,* 1984). It therefore seems likely that change in these central disturbances is necessary for full recovery. Indeed, perhaps the generally poor results of previous treatments may be explained by the fact that they did not attempt to produce cognitive change.

The principles of one possible cognitive behavioural approach to the treatment of anorexia nervosa have been outlined (Garner and Bemis, 1982). The treatment consists of a modification of the techniques proposed by Beck and colleagues (Beck *et al.,* 1979) for the treatment of depression. In addition, it includes specific strategies for increasing the motivation of these patients. The authors report that their results using this approach are encouraging, although no supporting clinical data have been provided.

Preliminary results using a modification of the cognitive behaviour therapy for bulimia nervosa have been mixed (Cooper and Fairburn, 1984). The major problem is that these patients are poorly motivated to change, since their behaviour is consonant with their beliefs and values. Indeed, as is well recognized, many of these patients see no need for treatment. However, it appears that it may be possible to overcome the difficulty over motivation with the 'bulimic' sub-group. Such patients are highly distressed by the sense of loss of control which accompanies bulimic episodes and they react positively to the self-control strategies used in the early stages of treatment. Once they have achieved an ordered pattern of eating, weight restoration can be presented as a necessary step in maintaining and enhancing control. In contrast, it appears to be more difficult to motivate the 'restricting' patients (that is those who do not binge-eat). These observations, although highly tentative, are of interest since the bulimic sub-group has previously been found to have a less favourable outcome than those who simply restrict their food intake (Garfinkel *et al.,* 1977).

It is generally agreed that once considerable weight loss has occurred, outpatient treatment for anorexia nervosa is rarely successful (Russell, 1977), perhaps because starvation itself perpetuates the disorder. Hospitalization for weight restoration is therefore necessary. A number of approaches to the inpatient management of patients with anorexia nervosa have been described, but none has been shown to produce superior results (Garfinkel and Garner, 1982). Nevertheless, many appear capable of inducing weight gain. Surprisingly, there has been little attention in the literature to the post-hospitalization management of these patients. This is a notable omission, given the high relapse and readmission rate (Hsu, 1980). It is here that cognitive behavioural treatments carry the most promise.

CONCLUSION

There is strong evidence that bulimia nervosa is a common disorder which causes much distress. Although this condition was thought to be intractable, it now seems clear that most cases respond to a specific form of cognitive behaviour therapy, and improvements appear to be maintained. In addition, there are reasons to think that this approach, with appropriate modification, may prove suitable for use with some patients with anorexia nervosa. These conclusions have important implications for practising clinical psychologists.

The cognitive behavioural approach to the treatment of bulimia nervosa employs techniques derived from behavioural treatments for obesity and habit disorders, and from various other cognitive treatments. However, considerable modification of standard therapeutic procedures is necessary in applying these techniques to the treatment of eating disorders. Some specialist training may therefore be necessary. In addition, some knowledge of the physiological processes which complicate these disorders and their treatment is required. For example, patients with bulimia nervosa have disturbed sensations of hunger and satiety; they sometimes experience dramatic rebound water retention on stopping vomiting or purgative use; and, as noted earlier, they are at risk of serious physical complications. Obviously, the therapist must inform patients of such dangers and, when necessary, arrange for them to be physically assessed and treated. In addition, these patients need to be provided with information concerning weight regulation mechanisms and dieting, since many harbour gross misconceptions about food and eating and about their shape and weight. Clearly, in order to educate these patients, therapists themselves have to be well-grounded in such matters.

The evaluation of depressive symptoms in patients with bulimia nervosa is particularly important. However, their assessment is complicated by the direct effects of the eating disorder on mood, appetite, weight, sleep, energy, interest, and concentration. As already noted, a small proportion of these patients appear to have a coexisting depressive disorder and, in addition to treatment for their eating problem, they may require treatment with anti-depressant medication. Such patients should be detected at an early stage, since they do not appear to respond to behavioural measures on their own. Clearly, the assessment of suicidal ideation is also of importance. Suicide is a common cause of death amongst patients with anorexia nervosa, and Russell (1979) has reported that the risk of suicide is even greater amongst those with bulimia nervosa.

It has been suggested that there would be considerable advantages if each NHS region had a specialist unit for the treatment of anorexia nervosa (Russell, 1981). It would seem resonable to propose that this notion be extended to include patients with bulimia nervosa. Such units could not only provide a specialist service for treating these patients, but could also create a system for training health professionals in their assessment and management.

Acknowledgements

I am grateful to Drs Christopher Fairburn and Zafra Cooper for their helpful comments on the original draft of this chapter, and to Tracy Kelly for her help in preparing the manuscript.

REFERENCES

ABRAHAMS, S.F. and BEUMONT, P.J.V. (1982) How patients describe bulimia or binge-eating. *Psychological Medicine, 12,* 625–635.
AGRAS, W.S., BARLOW, D.H., CHAPIN H.N., ABEL G.G., and LEITENBERG, H. (1974) Behaviour modification of anorexia nervosa. *Archives of General Psychiatry, 30,* 279–286.
AMERICAN PSYCHIATRIC ASSOCIATION (3rd edn, 1980) *Diagnostic and Statistical Manual of Mental Disorders.* Washington DC: American Psychiatric Association.

BECK, A.T., RUSH A.J., SHAW B.F., and EMERY, G. (1979) *Cognitive Therapy of Depression: A Treatment Manual.* New York: Guilford Press.

BEMIS, K.M. (1983) A comparison of functional relationships in anorexia nervosa and phobia. In: P.L. Darby, P.E. Garfinkel, D.M. Garner and D.V. Coscina (eds) *Anorexia Nervosa: Recent Developments in Research.* New York: Alan Liss.

CASPER, R.C., ECKERT, E.D., HALMI, K.A., GOLDBERG, S.C. and DAVIS J.M. (1980) Bulimia: its incidence and clinical importance in patients with anorexia nervosa. *Archives of General Psychiatry, 37,* 1030–1034.

COOPER, P.J. and FAIRBURN, C.G. (1983) Binge-eating and self-induced vomiting in the community. *British Journal of Psychiatry, 142,* 139–144.

COOPER, P.J. and FAIRBURN, C.G. (in press) The depressive symptoms of bulimia nervosa. *British Journal of Psychiatry.*

COOPER, P.J. and FAIRBURN, C.G. (1984) Cognitive behaviour therapy for anorexia nervosa: some preliminary findings. *Journal of Psychosomatic Research, 28,* 493–499.

COOPER, P.J., WATERMAN, G.C. and FAIRBURN, C.G. (1984) Women with eating problems: a community survey. *British Journal of Clinical Psychology, 23,* 45–52.

CRISP, A.H. (1967) The possible significance of some behavioural correlates of weight and carbohydrate intake. *Journal of Psychosomatic Research, 11,* 117–131.

ECKERT, E.D., GOLDBERG, S.C., HALMI K.A., CASPER, R.C. and DAVIS, J.M. (1979) Behaviour therapy in anorexia nervosa. *British Journal of Psychiatry, 134,* 55–59.

FAIRBURN, C.G. (1981) A cognitive behavioural approach to the management of bulimia. *Psychological Medicine, 11,* 707–711.

FAIRBURN, C.G. (1982) Binge-eating and its management. *British Journal of Psychiatry, 141,* 631–633.

FAIRBURN, C.G. (1983) Bulimia nervosa. *Hospital Medicine, 29,* 537–542.

FAIRBURN, C.G. (1984a) Bulimia: its epidemiology and management. In: A.J. Stunkard and E. Stellar (eds) *Eating and Its Disorders.* New York: Raven Press.

FAIRBURN, C.G. (1984b) A cognitive behavioural treatment for bulimia. In: D.M. Garner and P.E. Garfinkel (eds) *Handbook on Psychotherapy for Anorexia Nervosa and Bulimia.* New York: Guilford Press.

FAIRBURN, C.G. and COOPER, P.J. (1982) Self-induced vomiting and bulimia nervosa: an undetected problem. *British Medical Journal, 284,* 1153–1155.

FAIRBURN, C.G. and COOPER, P.J. (1984a) Binge-eating, self-induced vomiting and laxative abuse: a community study. *Psychological Medicine, 14,* 401–410.

FAIRBURN, C.G. and COOPER, P.J. (1984b) The clinical features of bulimia nervosa. *British Journal of Psychiatry, 144,* 238–246.

FROST, R.A., GOOLKASION, G.A., ELY, R. and BALNCHARD, F.A. (1982) Depression, restraint and eating behaviour. *Behaviour Research and Therapy, 20,* 113–121.

GARFINKEL, P.E. and GARNER, D.M. (1982) *Anorexia Nervosa: a Multidimensional Perspective.* New York: Brunner/Mazel.

GARFINKEL, P.E., MOLDOFSKY, H. and GARNER, D.M. (1977) The outcome of anorexia nervosa: significance of clinical features, body image and behaviour modification. In: R.A. Vigersky (ed.) *Anorexia Nervosa.* New York: Raven Press.

GARFINKEL, P.E., MOLDOFSKY, H. and GARNER, D.M. (1980) The heterogeneity of anorexia nervosa: bulimia as a distinct subgroup. *Archives of General Psychiatry, 37,* 1036–1040.

GARNER, D.M. and BEMIS, K.M. (1982) A cognitive-behavioural approach to anorexia nervosa. *Cognitive Therapy and Research, 6,* 123–150.

GARNER, D.M. and GARFINKEL, P.E. (1979) The Eating Attitudes Test: An index of the symptoms of anorexia nervosa. *Psychological Medicine, 9,* 273–279.

GARNER, D.M. and GARFINKEL, P.E. (1980) Socio-cultural factors in the development of anorexia nervosa. *Psychological Medicine, 10,* 647–656.

HALLSTEN, E.A. (1965) Adolescent anorexia treated by desensitization. *Behaviour Research and Therapy, 3,* 87–91.

HSU, L.K.G. (1980) Outcome of anorexia nervosa: a review of the literature. *Archives of General Psychiatry, 37,* 1041–1046.

HUDSON, J.I., POPE, H.G., JONAS, J.M., YURGELUN-TODD, D (1983) Family history study of anorexia nervosa and bulimia. *British Journal of Psychiatry, 142,* 428–429.

KENDELL, R.E. and DISCIPIO, W. (1970) Obsessional symptoms and obsessional personality traits in patients with depressive illness. *Psychological Medicine, 1,* 65–72.

LACEY, J.H. (1983) Bulimia nervosa, binge-eating, and psychogenic vomiting: a controlled treatment study and long term outcome. *British Medical Journal, 286,* 1609–1613.

LANG, P.J. (1965) Behaviour therapy with a case of nervous anorexia. In: L.P. Ullman and L. Krasner (eds) *Case Studies in Behaviour Modification.* New York: Holt, Rinehart and Winston.

LONG, C.G. and CORDLE, C.J. (1982) Psychological treatment of binge-eating and self-induced vomiting. *British Journal of Medical Psychology, 55,* 139–145.

MITCHELL, J.E., PYLE, R.L., ECKERT, E.D., HATSUHAMI, D. and LENTZ, R. (1983) Electrolyte and other physiological abormalities in patients with bulimia. *Psychological Medicine, 13,* 273–278.

MAVISSAKALIAN, M. (1982) Anorexia nervosa treated with response prevention and prolonged exposure. *Behaviour Research and Therapy, 20,* 27–31.

POLIVY, J., HERMAN, C.P., JAZWINSKI, C., OLMSTEAD, M.P. (1984) Restraint and binge-eating. In: R.C. Hawkins, W. Fremouw and P. Clement (eds) *Binge-Eating: Theory Research and Treatment.* New York: Springer.

POPE, H.G., HUDSON, J.I. and JONAS, J.M. (1983a) Anti-depressant treatment of bulimia: preliminary experience and practical recommendations. *Journal of Clinical Psychopharmacology, 3,* 274–281.

POPE, H.G., HUDSON, J.I., JONAS, J.M. and YURGELUNN-TODD, M.S. (1983b) Bulimia treated with imipramine: a placebo-controlled double-blind study. *American Journal of Psychiatry, 140,* 554–558.

PYLE, R.L., MITCHELL, J.E. and ECKERT, E.D. (1981) Bulimia: a report of 34 cases. *Journal of Clinical Psychiatry, 42,* 60–64.

PYLE, R.L., MITCHELL, J.E., ECKERT, E.D., HALVORSON, P.A., NEUMAN, P.A. and GOFF, G.M. (1983) The incidence of bulimia in freshman college students. *International Journal of Eating Disorders, 2,* 75–85.

ROSEN, J.C. and LEITENBERG, H. (1982) Bulimia nervosa: treatment with exposure and response prevention. *Behaviour Therapy, 13,* 117–124.

RUSSELL, G.F.M. (1977) General management of anorexia nervosa and difficulties in assessing the efficacy of treatments. In: R.A. Vigersky (ed.) *Anorexia Nervosa.* New York: Raven Press.

RUSSELL G. (1979) Bulimia nervosa: an ominous variant of anorexia nervosa. *Psychological Medicine, 9,* 429–448.

RUSSELL, G.F.M. (1981) The current treatment of anorexia nervosa *British Journal of Psychiatry, 138,* 164–166.

SABINE, E.J., YONACE, A., FARRINGTON, A.J., BARRATT, K.H., WAKE-LING, A. (1983) Bulimia nervosa: a placebo controlled double-blind therapeutic trial of mianserin. *British Journal of Clinical Pharmacology, 15,* 195S–202S.

SALKIND, M.R., FINCHAM, J. and SILVERSTONE T. (1980) Is anorexia nervosa a phobic disorder? A psychophysiological enquiry. *Biological Psychiatry, 15,* 803–808.

SCHNURER, A.T., RUBIN, R.R. and ROY, A. (1973) Systematic desensitization of anorexia nervosa seen as a weight phobia. *Journal of Behaviour Therapy and Experimental Psychiatry, 4,* 149– 153.

SMART, D.E., BEUMONT, P.J.V. and GEORGE, G.C.W. (1976) Some personality characteristics of patients with anorexia nervosa. *British Journal of Psychiatry, 128,* 57–60.

SOLYOM, L., FREEMAN, R.J. and MILES, J.E, (1982) A comparative psychometric study of anorexia nervosa and obsessive neurosis. *Canadian Journal of Psychiatry, 27,* 282–286.

STUNKARD, A.J. (1982) Obesity. In: A.S. Bellack, M. Herson and A.E. Kazdin (eds) *International Handbook of Behaviour Modification and Therapy.* New York: Plenum.

TOUYZ, S.W., BEUMONT, P.J.V., GLAUN, D., PHILLIPS, T. and COWIE, I. (1984) A comparison of lenient and strict operant conditioning programmes in refeeding patients with anorexia nervosa. *British Journal of Psychiatry, 144,* 517–520.

WALSH, B.T., STEWART, J.W., WRIGHT, L., HARRISON, W., ROOSE, S.P., GLASSMAN, A.H. (1982) Treatment of bulimia with monamine oxidase inhibitors. *American Journal of Psychiatry, 139,* 1629–1630.

WING, J.K., COOPER, J.E. and SARTORIUS, N. (1974) *The Measurement and Classification of Psychiatric Symptoms.* Cambridge: Cambridge University Press.

PAIN

Jane Wardle

Pain has traditionally been viewed as a symptom of disease or injury, and this is in accordance with common sense, where an unfamiliar pain is a signal for concern about the possible physical cause. Clinical experience however has never entirely supported this view, as disease can progress in the absence of pain (for example, cancer, heart disease), and conversely pain can be experienced in the absence of demonstrable pathology (for example, phantom limb pain, casualgia).

Pain also occupies a unique position in the sensory systems. This is firstly because the stimuli for pain are multimodal, and indeed the receptor mechanisms are still not fully understood. Secondly, pain is more than a sensory process, but has an inherent affective component, namely, it is unpleasant. This affective or motivational aspect of pain has in the past led to its being classified along with the emotional states, rather than the sensory systems (Marshall, 1895). This is not the prevailing view, but the drive properties of pain have been elaborated in two recent accounts of pain by Wall (1979) and Bolles and Fanselow (1980). They suggest that pain serves to organize behaviour in the interests of recuperation, thus motivating rest and the avoidance of taxing and effortful activity. When activity is called for, for example while excaping from danger, pain may be inhibited, only to reappear when fight or flight have been completed.

Psychological investigations of pain

Among the earliest contributions of psychological research to the study of pain was classical psychophysics, in which stimulus magnitude is related to the subject's discriminative ability. Hardy et al. (1952) attempted to apply these techniques to pain responses, using themselves as subjects. Their initial challenge was to develop instruments for the infliction of standard noxious stimuli and these included the application of heat to blackened skin, electrical stimulation of the tooth pulp and pressure applied to the forehead. Their

16

results indicated that consistent thresholds and scales of pain intensity could be obtained, but only with highly practised subjects and constant prevailing conditions. Pain reaction, they found, was susceptible to mood, fatigue, anxiety, concurrent sensory stimulation, suggestion, and numerous other psychological factors. Other workers, using larger groups of untrained subjects, were struck by the individual variability in threshold and tolerance for pain (Chapman and Jones, 1944).

These variables which obstructed the psychophysical researchers are the very ones which have subsequently provided the basis of the psychological study of pain. Initially, the focus was on individual differences in susceptibility to pain, and a series of experiments has related pain responses to personality characteristics. Introversion and neuroticism (Lynn and Eysenck, 1961), augmentation (Petrie, 1978) and sensitization (Davidson and Bobey, 1970) have all been associated with lower thresholds or lower tolerance for pain in laboratory settings. Unfortunately, these results have not stood up well to replication (Levine *et al.*, 1966), and have been complicated by disparate clinical findings. Bond and his colleagues (Bond and Pearson, 1969) found that extraversion predicted higher levels of pain report and more, rather than less, analgesic demand in women with cancer pain, while Eysenck (1961) found that extraversion was related to higher levels of childbirth pain. Individual difference research has often been based on the assumptions that differences in pain responses to a single modality of stimulation could be generalized across types of stimuli, and that laboratory responses could be generalized to clinical pain responses. The validity of these notions, however, has never been satisfactorily demonstrated, and given the complexity of pain stimuli and pain responses it seems inherently unlikely that individuals occupy a stable position.

Anthropological observations have long implicated social and cultural factors in the expression of pain, and particular emphasis has been placed on the contrast between the childbirth practices of Western society and less developed cultural groups. The extreme case is 'couvade' in which it is the father rather than the mother who retires in pain during and after the birth. Religious and maturity rites have also attracted attention, and the sight of young men suspended from hooks inserted through the muscles of their backs, with no discernible expression of pain, has attested to the potential variability of pain responses (Melzak and Wall, 1983). The drawback of anthropological research is the failure to acquire systematic data on subjective experience, which renders it impossible to differentiate analgesia from stoicism.

The influence of social factors has also been demonstrated in laboratory settings. Craig and Prkachin (1978) found that the pain ratings of subjects given electric shock were affected by prior observation of a model who gave either high or low pain ratings. This effect extended to psychophysiological measures, and to the sensitivity (d') and response criterion (β) components of a sensory decision theory analysis. In other words, observing a model who rates stimuli as relatively painless reduces many aspects of the pain responses to those same stimuli. The clinical extension of this work has been primarily in the area of preparation for noxious medical procedures, where viewing a coping model has been shown to have diverse beneficial effects (Melamed, 1977), but specific assessments of pain have not generally been included.

Transient mood states have also been thought to influence pain responses, and anxiety in particular has been given a central role. The interdependence of anxiety and pain has formed the basis of many approaches to pain relief, but surprisingly the evidence relating anxiety to pain is not substantial. Laboratory studies utilizing threat of shock as a means of inducing anxiety have typically failed to influence pain (Malow, 1981), and the problem has not yet been examined in many other settings. In the light of recent suggestions that drives for safety and drives for recuperation may be mutually inhibitory, and the pharmacological evidence that fear increases the release of naturally occurring opiates, the whole area should perhaps be reconsidered.

From the vantage point of more cognitively based theories of anxiety, there is a distinction to be drawn between anxiety about the pain situation itself, (for example, is it going to get worse, is there any treatment, is it fatal?) and unrelated anxiety (for example, of approaching examinations or escape from danger). It is possible that pain-irrelevant worries might have the power to distract the sufferer from pain, in addition to any direct psychological effects, while pain-relevant fears might exacerbate it. Certainly, in the case of surgical pain pre-operative anxiety has generally been found to be related to more pain or poorer recovery (Matthews and Ridgeway, 1981) and the mechanisms underlying this may well lie in the cognitive sphere.

Another line of research, which has yet to be satisfactorily resolved, has concerned the role of the predictability and controllability of pain. A considerable body of research indicates that these are associated with lower ratings of the unpleasantness of noxious stimuli. Initially this was thought to represent a change in the perceived intensity of sensation, but with increasing sophistication of experimental design it appears that it is the affective component of the pain response rather than the sensory component which is susceptible. In other words, a predictable pain is less unpleasant and better tolerated, but may be rated just as intense as an unpredictable pain (Thompson, 1981). The related clinical findings have generally concerned providing patients with information about the likely sensations involved in noxious medical procedures. Commonly, this improves their tolerance for the procedure, and may reduce global pain ratings, as well as specific ratings of distress or intensity (Auerbach, 1979). The mechanism of this effect is not yet resolved, for provision of information which is based at best on modal reports from previous patients gives predictability of the crudest kind and any beneficial effects cannot reasonably be attributed to a precise matching of expectation and experience.

The force of these observations on the wealth of psychological variables which can affect the expression or experience of pain lies their influence on prevailing views of pain. A simple sensory model, as expressed in many textbooks of physiology, simply cannot contain the variability of human pain.

Physiological theories of pain

Physiological theories have been divided between those following von Frey's 'specificity' approach and those following Goldscheider's 'pattern' approach (Dallenbach, 1939). The specificity theorists have emphasized the role of nerve fibres and pathways specialized for the transmission of information about noxious stimuli. The small myelinated (Aδ) fibres and the unmyelinated (c) fibres constitute the peripheral portion of the pain system, and transmit through specialized spinal pathways to the parts of the brain concerned with the perception of pain. Essentially, the experience of pain was held by the specificity theorists to be determined by the frequency of activity in these peripheral fibres. The pattern theorists proposed it was the amount and pattern of the total peripheral input, along with any central summation which, on reaching a critical level, resulted in pain.

Each of these theoretical approaches has successfully accounted for some of the anatomical, physiological and clinical observations on pain, but neither has been entirely satisfactory.

In 1965 Melzack and Wall published a new theory of pain, the Gate Control Theory, which contained aspects of both physiological theories, and, additionally, incorporated a psychological dimension. This model acknowledged the evidence for receptor/fibre specialization for stimulus input, along with the evidence for the importance of the total sensory inflow but also had scope for the infinitely complex relationship between stimulus intensity and pain experience.

In essence, the Gate Control Theory proposes that pain (in all its facets) is the result of a complex integration of the peripheral sensory input and the central input. The anatomical focus of this integrative focusing is in the dorsal horn of the spinal cord, within which, in an area known as the substantia gelatinosa, low threshold sensory fibres, high threshold sensory fibres, fibres from the brainstem reticular formation and from the cortex converge, both directly and via inter-neurones, on the spinal transmission (T) cells. It is the output of these T cells which, they propose, governs the perception of pain.

The high threshold sensory fibres will tend to increase activity in the T cells by direct stimulation and indirect facilitation. The low threshold sensory fibres can also increase T cell output under some circumstances (for example, gentle touch on sensitized hyperaesthetic skin can elicit pain), but commonly will inhibit T cell output via an inhibitory interneuron. Finally, the descending fibres from the brainstem can also inhibit T cell activity.

Neither the anatomical site of the gating mechanism, nor the neurophysiology of the synaptic connections is entirely agreed, but there is now little doubt that the input from the pain fibres is but one part of the pain-production system, and that non-noxious input from the skin, as well as descending inputs from the brain play an important part.

The psychological strength of the model lies in the emphasis placed on inputs from higher cortical processes, which gives anatomical and conceptual reality to the psychological variables that are crucial in the determination of pain. A wide range of factors, including attention, expectation, salience, mood, and past experiences are given the role of varying the level at which sensory stimulation triggers the pain action system.

At a clinical level the gate control theory contributes to the explanation of a number of puzzling pain syndromes, by suggesting mechanisms for triggering the pain action system in the absence of significant small fibre input. It also has implications for pain treatment. Implicit in the model is the rejection of simple surgical interventions such as nerve sections, as many unsuccessful operations have already demonstrated. On the positive side, the gating system contains numerous control mechanisms which are accessible physically, pharmacologically or psychologically and which promise to aid in pain control.

The concept of pain

The gate control theory contributed not only to the understanding of the mechanisms whereby pain is produced, but also to the conception of pain, emphasizing the multidimensional nature of the pain experience. Melzack and Casey (1968) proposed that the sensory and affective aspects of the pain experience are subserved by different parts of CNS, both of which receive projections from the T cells.

The existence of separate subjective affective and sensory dimensions of pain can be demonstrated in a number of ways. The language for pain includes both sensory and affective descriptors, for example, 'burning', 'torturing', 'pricking', 'distressing'; and these words formed the basis of the Melzack Pain Questionnaire (Melzack, 1975). Pain patients are also able to make independent ratings of the intensity and aversiveness of their pain, and these two parameters have come under independent experimental control (Johnson, 1973).

The cognitive evaluation of pain is presented by Melzack and Wall as a higher central process, activated by the entire stimulus setting, and acting upon the subjective experience of pain. This has a clear parallel with Meichenbaum and Turk's cognitive conceptualization of pain from which the cognitively-based pain treatment programmes are derived (Meichenbaum and Turk, 1976). The cognitive model proposes that pain in human subjects is accompanied by an elaborate appraisal, describable in terms of thought or images. Such thoughts are not objective or neutral appraisals, but are potentially subject to a variety of distortions, both positive and negative.

These appraisals in turn influence pain experience and pain behaviour. The influence of cognitions on pain has been demonstrated most spectacularly in the context of research on hypnosis. Hypnotized subjects are instructed to adopt a particular mental set; for example, a subject with her hand in iced water might be asked to imagine that she is walking in a hot dry desert, and comes across a blissfully cool pool. The evidence shows clearly that such instructions improve tolerance for pain, and may also reduce the subjective and physiological responses. The hypnotic state *per se* is not essential to the use of cognitive strategies for pain control (Barber and Hahn, 1962), as non-hypnotized subjects also are able to utilize cognitive approaches.

In the light of the rapid development of cognitive approaches to depression and anxiety, it is likely that the cognitive dimension of pain will in the future assume a more central role.

A behavioural view of pain

The discussion so far has centred upon the complexity of the experience of pain, and has not yet touched on pain behaviour. There are, however, a class of overt behaviours which tend to be linked with reports of pain and are called pain behaviour. These include grimacing, moaning, verbalizations of distress, limping, seeking medication, sitting or lying rather than standing, cessation of ongoing activity and many others. The relationship between pain experience and pain behaviour is necessarily inexact because all of these behaviours are responsive to countless other factors. Courage and stoicism, social demands and exediency all affect pain behaviour; mothers will restrain expression of pain in front of their children, and a hot cup is not dropped if it is Worcester porcelain. The consequences of pain behaviour therefore influence its expression, and when pain is prolonged there is ample opportunity for the associated behaviour to come under the control of environmental contingencies. The role of learning and conditioning effects on pain behaviour has been developed by Fordyce and colleagues (Fordyce, 1976, 1982) in an operant model of pain which provides a radical departure from the essentially respondent-based alternatives.

The main proposition of the operant model is that sustained pain behaviours are subject to a wide variety of positive and negative reinforcement. Family attention, medical attention, the prescription of powerful narcotic analgesic drugs to be 'taken as needed' and even direct financial compensation are all potential consequences of pain behaviour. Other behaviours are reinforced by pain reduction or avoidance: limping, guarding an injured limb, cessation of effortful activity and lying down may all reduce or avoid acute pain, and in so doing can be established as longstanding habits. The other side of the coin is the 'well' or 'active' behaviours which may be lost through the punishing effects of painful consequences, or the rewards from avoidance of disliked activities.

Fordyce draws a distinction between respondent pain, which results from the sensory input associated with injurious experiences, and operant pain, which results from reinforcement processes. Any sustained respondent pain is in principle susceptible to conversion to operant pain, though the factors which govern this transition are not yet established. The position of subjective experiences in this model is of course a dificult issue. A strictly behaviorist account does not profess to encompass the subjective domain, but it would be extraordinary, or even meaningless, to discuss pain without this. Most of the studies in the operant framework have acknowledged verbal report of pain as a relevant dimension, and provide data on pain ratings before and after treatment. These results suggest that major and significant behavioural changes can be produced in chronic pain patients, but in the context of persisting reports of pain (Roberts and Reinhardt, 1980).

Support for the operant model comes almost entirely from research with chronic pain patients, and is based on demonstrating that pain behaviour and related well behaviour can be brought under experimental control. Numerous individual cases show that exercise duration (often profoundly reduced in chronic pain) can be influenced by the prevailing contigencies including verbal reinforcement and substitution of an 'exercise quota' for an 'exercise to tolerance' regime (Fordyce, 1982). Essentially, behaviour patterns which have been attributed entirely to the subjective experience of pain have been shown to be consistently responsive to environmental contingencies.

Psychogenic pain

The real power of the behavioural model of pain lies in its contribution to our understanding of persisting pain problems in the absence of demonstrable tissue pathology, for it is with the problems of chronic pain that other theories and treatments have been revealed at their most inadequate.

With the increase in understanding of the neurophysiology of pain over the last century, the 'reality' of a pain had come to be synonymous with the extent to which tissue pathology was present, and the term 'psychogenic pain' was used to describe the pain in the absence of demonstrable tissue pathology. Psychoanalytic interpretations of psychogenic pain were elaborated, and research concentrated on contrasting the personality profiles of patients with 'organic' and 'psychogenic' pain (Pilowsky and Spence, 1976). Szasz (1974) has developed the idea of patients 'needing' their pain, 'or making a career of pain', which stemmed from the alleged reluctance of patients to get well.

The validity of these interpretations of chronic pain has not gone unchallenged on empirical or conceptual grounds. Several studies have indicated that the personal attributes of pain patients may be a consequence, not a cause, of chronic pain (Sternbach and Timmermans, 1975). Other studies have failed to discriminate organic from psychogenic pains in terms of the descriptive language used by patients themselves (Klein and Brown, 1967), or the response to analgesic drugs.

The operant model moved outside this framework by emphasizing the behaviour of pain patients, and once the focus of the explanation was moved from private to public behaviour, the world of possible cures and causes was expanded. It was, however, as Fordyce himself says, 'a behavioural model for pain behaviour', and not for pain *per se* . All who agree that pain and pain behaviour are not identical will recognize that the explanatory value of the model of depends on the relationship between 'pain' and pain behaviour. If subjective pain remains when pain behaviour is extinguished, then the behavioural model must be said to contribute more to the rehabilitation of chronic pain patients than to the aetiology of pain problem.

THE ASSESSMENT OF PAIN

Quantifying or measuring human pain raises all the difficulties inherent in attaching numbers to an unobservable experience. External reports, be they ratings, grimaces, or analgesic demands, undoubtedly reflect pain experience, but they are also sensitive to numerous other factors.

In laboratory settings the stimulus properties are directly measurable (duration of radiant heat, pressure exerted, etc.), and these have been related to pain threshold or tolerance point or the more sophisticated measures developed from the statistical decision theory. At a behavioural level, the psychophysiological responses have received most attention, although the relationship of psychophysiological change to pain experience is not a simple one (Davidson and Neufield, 1974).

In clinical pain there is usually no measurable stimulus, and so thresholds and tolerance points have no meaning. The simplest way to assess pain is with a rating scale, and visual analogue scales of some sort are commonly used (Ohnhaus and Adler, 1975; Keefe and Brown, 1982). Their principal disadvantage stems from the multidimensional nature of pain so that unidimensional represention cannot be entirely valid. Some attempts have been made to specify the dimensions, as in Johnson's studies, where 'intensity' and 'distress' are rated separately (Johnson, 1973). Even so, the problems of reliability and validity are enormous, and laboratory research has indicated that untrained subjects may assign wildly different values to the same stimulus. Although reliability can be improved by careful training, the implications are that patients rating clinical pain are highly unlikely to use rating scales in a consistent fashion, therapy limiting the potential for comparisons within and between individuals.

In an attempt to improve the precision of pain ratings, Melzack and Torgerson (1971) introduced the McGill Pain Questionnaire, which was based on a list of 75 pain descriptors. All the words described some qualitative aspect of pain, for example, 'pricking', 'stabbing', 'hot', 'burning', but they were also chosen according to their connotations of intensity. Research with medical staff, pain patients and normal subjects indicated that pain descriptors show stability in their intensity connotations, and as such, the patient's choice of words reveals not only qualitative but also quantitative aspects of pain. The words were then classified into three groups: sensory, affective and intensity. In the final questionnaire these are put together with questions about location and temporal variation, and the whole (lengthy) product gives a full and multidimensional representation of pain (Melzack, 1975).

The validity of this scale has been examined principally by comparisons between clinical groups, such as dental patients, obstetric patients, or cancer patients. The selection of different adjectives by these patients attests to the discriminative power of the questionnaire (Melzack and Wall, 1983).

The clustering of the adjectives used by Melzack and Torgerson was examined in a replication by Reading *et al.* (1982), who asked normal subjects to categorize and then rate the entire pool of adjectives. The categories obtained showed striking similarities to the originals, but the results from the ratings were less encouraging, as there were large individual differences in the ratings. To this extent, assumptions of quantitatively distinct categories each comprising a single intensity dimension are probably not appropriate.

This same objection is likely to apply to any adjective-based rating system, and suggests that in clinical use the meanings of the descriptors may have to be established for each subject individually. In that case the advantage of adjectival descriptors over simple rating scales becomes practical rather than psychometric.

Assessment of the behaviour of pain patients has not reached any degree of sophistication, and in many accounts of pain assessment it is not acknowledged at all (Wolff, 1978). Fordyce (1976) recommended a diary, in which patients (or observers) record activities. This permits an analysis in terms of activity and inactivity, or 'up-time' and 'down-time', as it has come to be known. This can be supplemented with more detailed specific measures of behaviours which are the focus of treatment, such as distance walked or number of repetitions of an exercise. On the basis of interviews or checklists (Philips and Hunter, 1981; Turk *et al.,* 1983; Richards *et al.,* 1982) the details of the behavioural adjustments which pain patients make, such as avoidance of a particular leisure activity, or requests of spouse to give massage, can also be identified.

PAIN TREATMENT

The advances in analgesia and anaesthesia over the past hundred years have dramatically changed the place of acute pain in medicine. Most patients need suffer little pain in acute illness or during noxious medical procedures, for pharmacological anaesthesia and analgesia will usually, although not always, give relief.

Chronic pain however, poses a different problem. By definition, no further medical procedures acting on the underlying physical pathology are possible, either because the underlying physical pathology is at present untreatable (rheumatoid arthritis, post-herpetic neuralgia, advanced malignancies) or because no treatable pathology can be identified (headache, low back pain, stump pain). In contrast to acute pain, analgesics are of limited use: the less potent ones are seen as insufficient, while the more potent narcotic analgesics have multiple side-effects and risks of dependence.

With the development of laboratory paradigms for clinical pain, research on psychological procedures for the control of pain have flourished, but the adequacy of the laboratory paradigm has been questioned, and especially in the case of chronic pain, where persistence and longevity is of the essence, extrapolation from laboratory to clinical settings must be done with the utmost caution.

What might otherwise appear to be a rather disparate collection of treatment techniques can best be organized around the point of intervention in a multidimensional scheme of pain. The three main targets have been sensory input, cognitions, and consequences, which have been modified respectively by biofeedback and relaxation, cognitive behaviour therapy, and operant conditioning. More recently, the multimodal pain package, drawing on all these techniques, has become popular, and theoretical differences are being eroded in the interests of helping these very distressed and disabled patients (Chapman *et al.*, 1981).

Biofeedback and relaxation

One of the earliest systematic approaches to pain relief was based on the notion that functional disturbances in bodily activities in the absence of pathological changes could generate pain. A prime example has been muscle tension, commonly believed to be the cause of tension headache. At a diagnostic level the psychophysiology of headache is more complex (Philips, 1978), but is has proved an excellent model of the reciprocal relationship between muscle tension and pain. Other clinical pain problems such as migraine, myofacial pain and dysmenorrhoea, have also been attributed to muscle tension, which has functioned both as a primary cause, and as a secondary manifestation which itself generates pain. The importance of the link between pain and tension is amplified when the role of anxiety is also included, for anxiety about pain can produce tension, which may further increase pain.

If muscle tension can cause or exacerbate pain, then relaxation training or EMG biofeedback would appear to be the appropriate methods of treatment. Unfortunately, the intuitively plausible pain/tension relationship has not been convincingly demonstrated; nevertheless, there are numerous reports on the efficacy of relaxation training and biofeedback. Both of these treatments have been found to be effective, immediately after treatment and at follow-up, in reducing headache frequency, intensity and medication use (Cox *et al.,* 1975; Chesney and Shelton, 1976). Contrary to expectation, however, EMG biofeedback has not proved superior to general relaxation, and economic considerations tend to the support the use of the simpler relaxation training, unless developments in biofeedback technology, such as ambulatory feedback, can improve its efficiency.

Biofeedback of other physiological systems, notably alpha EEG, skin temperature, and temporal artery pulse volume has also been used, typically for vascular-type headaches. Neither the alpha EEG enhancement nor handwarming have good empirical support, but temporal artery pulse volume reduction appears to have a more specific role in modifying migraine headache (Bild and Adams, 1980).

The value of relaxation training for patients with so-called tension headache is undoubted, and it appears to be more effective than medication placebo (Cox *et al.,* 1975) or no treatment (Blanchard *et al.,* 1979). Relaxation is also incorporated in almost all pain clinic behavioural programmes, and uncontrolled case reports support its use in diverse pain syndromes (Keefe *et al.,* 1981). Typically, the comparison groups have not included a fully credible placebo, and so the relative contributions of relaxation *per se* and the non-specific aspects of treatment remain to be assessed. On present evidence therefore, relaxation can confidently be included as a valuable component of treatment for pain patients, while we await a better understanding of the mechanism of the effect.

Cognitive treatment for pain

The roots of cognitive treatments for pain lie partly in the domain of hypnosis. Hypnotic analgesia and anaesthesia were reported in the early ninetennth century and were based on advising the highly suggestible subject to ignore or transform the sensory input from the injured part of the body. Clinical research has produced numerous case reports of the dramatic effects of hypnosis, but the move to better controlled outcome studies is yet to come. In laboratory settings, hypnotized subjects can be shown to tolerate noxious stimulation and to give lower pain ratings when hypnotized (Barber, 1963). Equally good results have been reported for what is termed 'waking analgesia' (Barber and Hahn, 1962), in which subjects told to behave 'as if' hypnotized, and, furthermore, encouraged to believe that this will produce analgesia, showed analgesic effects as strongly as the group who had undergone hypnotic induction.

This encouraged Barber and his colleagues to investigate the extent to which cognitive strategies, used spontaneously, or on the advice of an experimenter could contribute to pain reduction, and they showed that distraction, coping imagery, dissocation and imaginative transformation all reduced pain responses (Scott and Barber, 1977). Many other researchers, particularly from the area of self-control research (Kanfer and Goldfoot, 1966), have contributed to the development of cognitive methods for control of pain, for which there is now considerable empirical support, and these have formed the basis for exciting developments in the management of chronic pain.

In clinical settings cognitive approaches are commonly used as part f multifaceted treatment, usually in combination with preparatory or rehearsal approaches, and often in the wider context of stress inoculation training (Meichenbaum and Turk, 1976). Clinically, the unique contribution of the cognitive strategies themselves has yet to be estimated, but they form an integral part of these multimodal methods.

In stress inoculation training, patients are first introduced to a model of pain which emphasizes the influence of cognitive factors – the educative phase. Implicit in this is a change in the perceived controllability of the pain. The importance of detailed records is also emphasized. This is followed by a training phase in which the various diversionary and transforming cognitive tactics are taught, along with advice to the patient to reward him or herself for applying them. Attention is also given to the ongoing cognitions, and 'coping' as opposed to 'catastrophizing' self-statements are encouraged. In the final phase the skills are applied in response to induced or imagined pains.

Treatment regimes of this type have been applied to many clinical problems, as well as to the response to noxious medical procedures. These have included among others headache pain (Holroyd *et al.,* 1977), post-surgical pain (Langer *et al.,* 1975), and the pain of treatment for severe burns (Wernick *et al.,* 1981). The results have on the whole been positive, although in some cases (for example, Holroyd and Andrasik, 1978) the comparison groups have achieved equally good results.

For patients with chronic and persistent pain the stress inoculation training approach has been tested less thoroughly. Uncontrolled studies have shown that it can be useful (Hartman and Ainsworth, 1980) and a small number of controlled studies (Rybstein-Blinchik, 1979) have confirmed its value in diminishing reports of pain in patients with diverse diagnosis. Longer term follow-up (Turner, 1982) indicates that the patients in the cognitive-behavioural group showed continuing improvement.

Cognitive approaches emphasize coping as opposed to cure. Esentially, the patients learn to manage their pain more effectively. For the most part the efficacy has been tested with relatively acute or at least intermittent clinical pains, which makes sense. Preparation, rehearsal and practice imply pain-free times, and many patients comment on the tremendous mental effort involved in cognitive treatments. In principle, cognitive techniques could be so successful that pain is eliminated, but the more usual outcome is diminution in severity. Longer term pain problems are also likely to include significant behavioural change resulting from the pain experience, which constitutes a problem in its own right.

Operant treatment for pain

Cognitive treatment programmes may include procedures designed to modify behaviour directly. That is often on the basis that activity and excercise are in themselves beneficial (Turner, 1982; Turk *et al.*, 1982), but there are progressively closer links to the techniques derived from an operant analysis of pain, in which modification of behaviour is the central feature of treatment.

The procedures involved in pain treatment programmes are comparable to other operant behaviour modification procedures. With the patient's full co-operation the treatment targets are identified and specified precisely, along with the intervening sub-goals. Appropriate reinforcers are also identified, and then manipulated so that they are contingent upon the desired behaviour. Usually the behavioural problems are tackled simultaneously from many points of view: physiotherapists identify exercise and activity goals, and patients are encouraged to exercise to quota rather than to a tolerance point; medication is given on a fixed schedule and is systematically and gradually reduced; inpatient unit staff and family at home ignore pain complaints and sick behaviour, and reward well behaviour, and return to leisure and work activity is planned and rewarded.

The effect of these programmes is typically judged on the results from uncontrolled case series, which indicate consistent improvement in activity level and a reduction in medication (Fordyce *et al.*, 1973) that is generally maintained at follow-up. The only controlled study reported (Roberts and Reinhardt, 1980) compared the treated group with a control group comprising patients who were rejected from the treatment programme, or who were offered but refused treatment. On all measures (including subjective pain reports) the treated patients did better than the untreated ones, but the very unsatisfactory selection of the control groups detracts from the value of these results. In all, the operant regime must be viewed as promising, but awaiting further investigation. Anticipating positive results from controlled trials, many pain programmes are now combining relaxation/cognitive therapy and operant programmes in a multimodal package. The theoretical basis of such procedures therefore moves from the strictly operant, to an essentially pragmatic, atheoretical position.

Interpretation of the effects of cognitive behavioural programmes has also begun to change because of the desynchrony between behaviour and subjective report. Continuing, albeit decreased, pain reports combined with behavioural improvement are subsumed more readily in a rehabilitative as opposed to a curative model. Treatment results are therefore appropriately evaluated in terms of the patient's psychological adjustment in the face of some continuing pain, along with the extent of their return to an active and productive life-style.

OVERVIEW

Advances in physiological and psychological research over the past few decades have matured the simple sensory and psychogenic models of pain to a sophisticated psychobiological system. Basic undimensional representations of pain have given way to multi-dimensional models in which affective, cognitive, motivational and behavioural dimensions all play their part. This broader perspective on the problem of pain has opened correspondingly more avenues for treatment and rehabilitation, and an impressive array of therapeutic approaches is now available.

In the near future, psychological research must concentrate on refining and evaluating the wealth of new ideas which have emerged. In the longer term, the greatest benefits are likely to be reaped from interdisciplinary collaboration, drawing together the dramatic advances in the neurochemistry, physiology and psychology of pain.

REFERENCES

AUERBACH, S.M. (1979) Preoperative preparation for surgery. In: D.J. Osborne *et al.* (eds) *Research in Psychology and Medicine, Volume 2.* London: Academic Press.
BARBER, T.X. (1963) The effects of 'hypnosis' on pain. A critical review of experimental and clinical findings. *Psychosomatic Medicine, 25,* 303–333.
BARBER, T.X. and HAHN, K.W. (1962) Physiological and subjective responses to pain producing stimuli under hypnotically-suggested and waking imagined 'analgesia'. *Journal of Abnormal and Social Psychology, 65,* 411–418.
BILD, R. and ADAMS, H. (1980) Modifications of migraine headache by cephalic blood volume pulse and EMG biofeedback. *Journal of Consulting and Clinical Psychology, 48,* 51–57.
BLANCHARD, E.B., AHLES, T.A. and SHAW, E.R. (1979) Behavioural treatment of headaches. In: M. Hersen, R.M. Eisler and P.M. Miller (eds) *Progress in Behaviour Modification, Volume 8.* New York: Academic Press.
BOLLES, R.C. and FANSELOW, M.S. (1980) A perpetual-defensive-recuperative model of fear and pain. *The Behavioural and Brain Sciences, 3,* 291–323.
BOND, M.R. and PEARSON, I.B. (1969) Psychological aspects of pain in women with advanced cancer of the cervix. *Journal of Psychosomatic Research, 13,* 13–19.
CHAPMAN, S.L., BRENA, S.F. and BRADFORD, L.A. (1981) Treatment outcome in a chronic pain rehabilitation program. *Pain, 11,* 255– 268.
CHAPMAN, W.P. and JONES, C.M. (1944) Variation in cutaneous and visceral pain sensitivity in normal subjects. *Journal of Clinical Investigation, 23,* 81–91.
CHESNEY, M.A. and SHELTON, J.L. (1976) A comparison of muscle relaxation and electromyogram biofeedback treatments for muscle contraction headache. *Journal of Behaviour Therapy and Experimental Psychiatry, 7,* 221–225.
COX, D.J., FREUNDLICH, A. and MEYER, R.C. (1975) Differential effectiveness of electromyographic feedback, verbal relaxation instructions and medication placebo with tension headaches. *Journal of Consulting and Clinical Psychology, 43,* 892–898.

CRAIG, K.D and PRKACHIN, K.M. (1978) Social modelling influences on sensory decision theory and psychophysiological indexes of pain. *Journal of Personality and Social Psychology, 30,* 805–815.

DALLENBACH, K.M. (1939) Pain: history and present status. *American Journal of Psychology, 52,* 331–347.

DAVIDSON, P.O. and BOBEY, M.J. (1970) Repressor-sensitiser differences on repeated exposures to pain. *Perpetual and Motor Skills, 31,* 711–714.

DAVIDSON, P.O. and NEUFIELD, R.W.J. (1974) Response to pain and stress: a multivariate analysis. *Journal of Psychosomatic Research, 18,* 25.

EYSENCK, S.B.G. (1961) Personality and pain assessment in childbirth of married and unmarried mothers. *Journal of Mental Science, 107,* 417–430.

FORDYCE, W.E. (1976) *Behavioural Methods for Chronic Pain and Illness.* St. Louis: C.V. Mosby.

FORDYCE, W.E. (1982) A behavioural perspective on chronic pain. *British Journal of Clinical Psychology, 21,* 313–320.

FORDYCE, W.E., FOWLER, R., LEHMANN J., DELATEUR, B., SAND, P. and TREISCHMANN, R. (1973) Operant conditioning in the treatment of chronic pain. *Archives of Physiological Medical Rehabilitation, 54,* 399–408.

HARDY, J.D., WOLFF, H.G. and GOODELL, H. (1952) *Pain Sensations and Reactions.* Baltimore: Williams and Williams.

HARTMAN, L.M. and AINSWORTH, K.D. (1980) Self-regulation of chronic pain: preliminary empirical findings. *Canadian Journal of Psychiatry, 25,* 38–43.

HOLROYD, K.A. and ANDRASIK, F. (1978) Coping and the self control of chronic tension headache. *Journal of Consulting and Clinical Psychology, 46,* 1036–1045.

HOLROYD, K.A., ANDRASIK, F. and WESTBROOK, T. (1977) Cognitive control of tension headache. *Cognitive Therapy and Research, 1,* 121–133.

JOHNSON, J.E. (1973) Effect of accurate expectations on the sensory and distress components of pain. *Journal of Personality and Social Psychology, 27,* 261–275.

KANFER, F.H. and GOLDFOOT, D.A. (1966) Self-control and tolerance for noxious stimuli. *Psychological Reports, 18,* 79–85.

KEEFE, F.J., BLOCK, A.R., WILLIAMS, R.B. and SURWIT, R.S. (1981) Behaviural treatment of chronic low back pain – clinical outcome and individual differences in pain relief. *Pain, 11,* 221–231.

KEEFE, F.J. and BROWN, C.J. (1982) Behavioural assessment of chronic low back pain. In: F.J. Keefe and J. Blumenthal (eds) *Assessment Strategies in Behavioural Medicine.* New York: Grune and Stratton.

KLEIN, R.F. and BROWN, W. (1982) Pain descriptions in the medical setting. *Journal of Psychsomatic Research, 10,* 367–372.

LANGER, E.J., JANIS, I.L. and WOLFER, J.A. (1975) Reduction of psychological stress in surgical patients. *Journal of Experimental and Social Psychology, 1,* 155–165.

LEVINE, F.M., TURSKY, B. and NICHOLS, D.C. (1966) Tolerance of pain, extroversion and neuroticism; failure to replicate results. *Perceptual and Motor Skills, 23,* 847–850.

LYNN, R. and EYSENCK, H.J. (1961) Tolerance for pain; extraversion and neuroticism. *Perceptual and Motor Skills, 12,* 161–162.

MALOW, R.M. (1981) The effects of induced anxiety on pain perception: a signal detection analysis. *Pain, 11,* 397–405.

MARSHALL, H.R. (1895) Pleasure-pain and emotion. *Psychological Review, 2,* 57–64 and 166–168.

MATHEWS, A. and RIDGEWAY, V. (1981) Personality and surgical recovery: a review. *British Journal of Clinical Psychology, 20,* 243–260.

MEICHENBAUM, D.H. and TURK, D.C. (1976) The cognitive-behavioural management of anxiety, anger and pain. In: P.O. Davidson (ed) *The Behavioural Management of Anxiety, Depression and Pain.* New York: Brunner/Mazel.

MELAMED, B.G. (1977) Psychological preparation for hospitalization. In: S. Rachman (ed.) *Contributions to Medical Psychology, Volume 1.* Oxford: Pergamon Press.

MELZACK, R. (1975) The McGill Pain Questionaire: major properties and scoring methods. *Pain, 1,* 277–299.

MELZACK, R. and CASEY, K.L. (1968) Sensory, motivational and central control determinants. In: P.R. Kenshalo (ed.) *The Skin Senses.* Springfield, Ill.: C.C. Thomas.

MELZACK, R. and TORGERSON, W.S. (1971) On the language of pain. *Anaesthesiology, 34,* 50–59.

MELZACK, R. and WALL, P. (1965) Pain mechanisms – a new theory. *Science, 150,* 971–979.

MELZACK, R. and WALL, P. (1983) *The Challenge of Pain.* Harmondsworth: Penguin Books.

OHNHAUS, E.E. and ADLER, R. (1975) Methodological problems in the measurement of pain: a comparison between the verbal rating scale and the visual analogue scale. *Pain, 1,* 379–384.

PETRIE, A. (1978) *Individuality in Pain and Suffering.* Chicago: University of Chicago Press.

PILOWSKY, I. and SPENCE, N.D. (1976) Pain, anger and illness behaviour. *Journal of Psychosomatic Research, 20,* 411–416.

PHILIPS, C. (1978) Tension headache: theoretical problems. *Behaviour Research and Therapy, 10,* 249–261.

PHILIPS, C. and HUNTER, M. (1981) Pain behaviour in headache sufferers. *Behavioural Analysis and Modification, 4,* 257–266.

READING, A.E., EVERITT, B.S. and SLEDMERE, C.M. (1982) The McGill Pain Questionaire: a replication of its construction. *British Journal of Clinical Psychology, 21,* 339–349.

RICHARDS, J.S., NEPOMUCENO, C., RILES, M. and SVER, Z. (1982) Assessing pain behaviour. The UAB Pain Behaviour Scale. *Pain, 14,* 393–398.

ROBERTS, A.H. and REINHARDT, (1980) The behavioural management of chronic pain: long-term follow-up with comparison groups. *Pain, 8,* 151–162.

RYBSTEIN-BLINCKIK, E. (1979) Effects of different cognitive strategies on chronic pain experience. *Journal of Behavioural Medicine, 2,* 93–101.

SCOTT, D.S. and BARBER, T.X. (1977) Cognitive control of pain: effects of multiple cognitive strategies. *Psychological Record, 27,* 373–383.

STERNBACH, R.A. and TIMMERMANS, G. (1975) Personality changes associated with reduction of pain. *Pain, 1,* 177–181.

SZASZ, T. (1974) A psychiatric perspective on pain and its control. In: F.D. Hart (ed.) *The Treatment of Chronic Pain.* Lancaster: Medical and Technical Books.

THOMPSON, S.C. (1981) Will it hurt less if I can control it? A complex answer to a simple question. *Psychological Bulletin, 90,* 89–101.

TURK, D.C., MEICHENBAUM, D. and GENEST, M. (1983) *Pain and Behavioural Medicine.* New York: Guilford Press.

TURNER, J.A. (1982) Comparison of group progressive-relaxation training and cognitive-behavioural group therapy for chronic low back pain. *Journal of Consulting and Clinical Psychology, 50,* 757–765.

WALL, P. (1979) On the relation of injury to pain. *Pain, 6,* 253–267.

WERNICK, R.L., JAREMKO, M.E. and TAYLOR, P.W. (1981) Pain management in severley burned adults: a test of stress innoculation. *Journal of Behavioural Medicine, 4,* 103–109.

WOLFF, B.B. (1978) Behavioural measurement of human pain. In: R. Sternbach (ed.) *The Psychology of Pain.* New York: Raven Press.

CHRONIC ILLNESS IN CHILDREN

Dorothy Fielding

In recent years there has been an increasing interest in the application of psychological theory and principles to the assessment and treatment of child health problems. Terms such as 'pediatric psychology' (Christophersen and Rapoff, 1979) and 'behavioural pediatrics' (Varni, 1983) have been used to delineate this rapidly developing field of enquiry. Some of the developments in this field have simply involved a transfer of techniques and approaches found useful in a community or child psychiatric setting to similar emotional or behavioural problems in the paediatric clinic. In other cases an entirely new area of clinical practice and research has been opened up. The growing number of children who are now surviving with life threatening diseases as a result of advances in paediatric medicine have provided one such new area of work. Whilst the total prevalence of children with chronic illnesses is still fairly small at 10 per cent (Pless, 1968; Pless and Douglas, 1971), the impact of these disorders and even the ensuing treatment can have profound and disrupting effects on the psychological well-being of the family of the chronically sick child. Indeed, this has led some paediatricians to suggest that certain children from 'at risk' families should not be admitted to treatment programmes (Korsch *et al.,* 1971).

Increasing medical concern about the chronically ill child has given rise to a number of different avenues of research. The earliest of these examined the psychological adjustment of chronically ill children and their families. A second more recent line of enquiry has focused upon ways of communicating with the families of chronically sick children so that children might be better prepared for hospitalization and painful treatment procedures, as well as more able to carry out important aspects of treatment themselves. A third area of investigation has studied the effectiveness of psychological approaches in the management of the distressing consequences of the disease. For example, the management of acute and chronic pain, urinary incontinence, vomiting, nausea and epileptic seizures.

The following sections of this chapter will outline major developments in these three areas and comment on implications for the practice of clinical psychologists in paediatric settings.

PSYCHOLOGICAL EFFECTS OF CHRONIC ILLNESS IN CHILDREN AND ADOLESCENTS

Chronic illness refers to a disorder with a protracted course. The disease may be progressive and fatal, or the child may have a relatively normal life span despite impaired physical or cognitive functioning (Mattsson, 1972). The term encompasses a wide range of physical disabilities. Among the most common are asthma (about 2 per cent of the population under 18) epilepsy (1 per cent) cardiac conditions (0.5 per cent) cerebral palsy (0.5 per cent) and diabetes mellitus (0.1 per cent). *Table 1* gives a classification for these disorders and a number of other less commonly encountered illnesses. *Table 2* lists prevalence rates for a number of specific chronic conditions.

Table 1. Classification of long-term childhood disorders (amended from Mattsson, 1972)

---

1. *Disease due to chromosomal aberrations:* Down's syndrome, Klinefelter's syndrome, Turner's syndrome
2. *Diseases as results of abnormal hereditary traits:* Spherocytosis, sickle cell anaemia, haeophilia, cystic fibrosis, muscular dystrophy, osteogenesis imperfecta, diabetes mellitus, inborn errors of metabolism; certain forms of 'congenital malformations' such as microcephaly, club-foot, cleft palate, dislocation of the hip, blindness and deafness
3. *Diseases due to harmful intrauterine factors:* Infections such as, rubella, congenital syphillis, and toxoplasmosis with their attendant malformations; damage from massive radiation, various drugs, prenatal hypoxia, and blood type incompatibilites
4. *Disorders resulting from perinatal traumatic and infectious events* including permanent damage to central nervous system and motor apparatus
5. *Diseases due to serious postnatal and childhood infections, injuries, neoplasms and other factors:* Meningitis, encephalitis, tuberculosis, rheumatic fever, chronic renal disease; physical injuries with permanent handicaps; tumours and leukaemia; orthapaedic diseases; convulsive disorders; atopic conditions; mental illness and mental retardation of organic aetiology

---

Although these physical problems are biologically very diverse, they have in common a number of long-term and disabling consequences. For example, a child with chronic illness may have to face unpleasant and often painful symptoms of the disease and in addition cope with management procedures which may in themselves be painful. Drug treatments administered to control symptoms may have unpleasant side effects, such as loss of hair or the development of cushingoid features. Furthermore, treatment may necessitate frequent hospital admissions with consequent separation from families, and disruption in school attendance, academic achievement and peer relationships.

The changes in the total lifestyle of the family brought about when a child is chronically ill may give rise not only to personal costs but also great financial restraints. For example, parents may have to give up work to care for the sick child, and in addition there may be the extra expense of travelling long distances to hospital clinics. It may be necessary to obtain special equipment, or provide special diets and adaptations to the home. Given these extreme pressures it is not surprising that clinicians and research workers have turned their attention to an examination of the psychological adjustment of families with a chronically ill child.

Table 2. Prevalence rates for specific chronic disorders in childhood (amended from Pless and Douglas, 1981)

Data	N	National survey rate/1000
Asthma	90	21.0
Blindness	4	0.8
Bronchiectasis	6	1.2
Cerebral palsy	11	2.3
Cleft palate or lip	5	1.0
Club foot	6	1.2
Congenital heart	11	2.3
Deafness	24	4.9
Diabetes	1	0.2
Eczema	206	43.6
Legge-Perthes	3	0.6
Orthopaedic	14	29.6
Rheumatic heart	8	1.6
Speech	116	24.6
Spina bifida	3	0.6
Strabismus	229	48.5

N = 4,724

The early literature consistently suggested that amongst chronically ill children there were many who were socially maladjusted, and many who showed low self esteem and immaturity (Knowles, 1971; Mattsson, 1972; Gayton and Friedman, 1973; Steinhauer *et al.,* 1974; Korsch *et al.,* 1971). However, much of this work was anecdotal, based on clinical impressions, subjective evaluations and uncontrolled investigations. More recent investigations have challenged these early assertions, suggesting instead that groups of chronically ill children could not be easily differentiated from normal healthy children on standardized measures of psychological functioning (Tavormina *et al.,* 1976; Bedell *et al.,* 1977; Kellerman *et al.,* 1980). However, despite these less pessimistic findings, clinical practice suggests that in certain families many problems of adjustment still occur which warrant social and psychological investigation and treatment. It is clear that further research is necessary in this field.

Underlying the recent studies is the possibly erroneous assumption that chronic illness may be regarded as a unitary phenomenon which makes a similar impact in a group of children at a single point in time. There are two reasons why this assumption may be incorrect. In the first instance, it seems likely that different chronic illnesses of different levels of severity have quite different psychological effects. Secondly, in many chronic conditions both the illness and the reaction of the child and family follow a fluctuating course. Where a heterogeneous group of children are studied at a single point in time, some of these will have stable medical conditions while others may be 'deteriorating'. Thus, attempts to measure psychological factors may present a confused picture.

There is some evidence for both these contentions. For example, in one study examining the impact of chronic illness in adolescence, quite different impacts were experienced by adolescents with different illnesses. Children with cancer faced major disruptions in many areas of their life. In contrast, some youngsters with renal disease reported less disruption than a group of normal healthy adolescents (Zeltzer *et al.*, 1980). Severity of the illness may also affect levels of functioning. Paradoxically, it has been suggested that individuals with mild forms of an illness may show poorer coping strategies than individuals with a severe form of the disease (Seidel *et al.*, 1975; Markova, 1979).

Two additional problems beset these types of investigation. Firstly, many studies include children of wide age ranges in their 'ill sample'. It has therefore proved difficult to find assessment measures which are appropriate across the age range which will make group comparisons meaningful. Secondly, many parents and children respond to the situation of chronic illness in one family member by denying the existence of problems, or rather by an unwillingness to admit these difficulties in paper and pencil tests. To some extent this may be an adaptive mechanism. However, it undoubtedly provides problems for research in this area.

Clearly, the situation is more complex than initial impressions might suggest. Recent research suggests that children with chronic illnesses need to be assessed in longitudinal studies, in which their patterns of adjustment are monitored over time. Moreover, the analysis of results needs to take into account important variables such as devlopmental level, age, age on diagnosis, severity of illness, and treatment regime. Where these variables have been examined, interesting findings have emerged (Koocher *et al.*, 1980; Moore, 1983; Hudson, 1984). For example, in a follow-up study of youngsters who had childhood cancer, age of onset of the disease was related to later psychological adjustment. Those whose cancer was diagnosed and treated in early childhood were less likely to experience adjustment problems later in life than those diagnosed and treated in middle childhood and adolescence (Koocher *et al.*, 1980). Age was also an important factor in two further studies. Adolescents undergoing haemodialyis (Hudson, 1984) and haemophilic adolescents over 15 years of age (Klein and Nimorwicz, 1982) showed greater levels of depression and psychological distress than younger children with these diseases.

Such studies illustrate the importance of the developmental stage of the child. The impact of chronic illness may have quite different effects, depending upon the developmental tasks that a child has to face. Sudden enforced immobility during haemodialysis may be made more difficult to face for previously healthy adolescents than for youngsters who have grown up regarding themselves as sick and consequently restricted. Furthermore, it may only be in adolescence, when children are becoming more independent and achieving greater cognitive maturity, that these youngsters realize the full extent of their restrictions.

The preceding comments have concentrated upon the psychological reactions of the chronically ill child. However, it is clear from clinical and research accounts that other family members may also present with difficulties. For example, increased incidences of depression, anxiety, psychosomatic problems and marital conflict have been reported amongst the parents of chronically ill children (Steinhauer *et al.*, 1974; Wolters *et al.*, 1973; Moore, 1983; Sabbeth and Leventhal, 1984). In addition, frequent reference has been made to the occurrence of attention-seeking behaviour, psychosomatic problems and underachievement at school amongst siblings (Gayton *et al.*, 1977; Breslau *et al.*, 1981; Ferrari, 1984). Moreover it has been suggested that particular kinds of family interaction may arise in some families when one child is chronically ill (Lask, 1982; Walker, 1983), thus making it difficult for the family to deal with conflict and change. Unfortunately, to date there have been few systematic studies of these important aspects of family functioning.

Whilst the issue of psychological problems in the family of chronically ill children may appear academic in nature, there are many pressing and relevant clinical questions which could be answered by detailed and systematic study of the psychological reaction of parents and children to chronic illness in one of the children. It is clear from the accounts of paediatricians and nurses working with chronically ill children that many families fail to adapt to the changing medical conditions of the child and this can present major management problems. For example, it has been said that in poorly adjusted families children refuse to take medication, or fail to keep to special dietary measures, whilst parents may inadequately carry out a number of important monitoring procedures, such as testing samples of blood and urine. Obviously, failure to adhere to therapeutic regimes may result from a whole range of variables, including family reaction to illness, and family functioning, as well as the management procedure used in the hospital unit and the ability of medical and nursing staff to deal with distressed families. An important focus of future research could be to investigate the inter-relationship of the factors. Moreover, such investigations may suggest appropriate strategies to increase compliance in treatment, such as family therapy aimed at improving problem-solving skills (Steidl *et al.*, 1980) or staff training procedure (Varni 1983).

Table 3. Developmental stages of children's concepts of illness

Approximate age range	Study		Examples
	Bibace and Walsh, 1980	Perrin and Gerrity, 1981	
	0 Incomprehension	0 No answer or response unrelated to question	
	⎫	1 Don't know	
	1 Phenomenism ⎬ PRELOGICAL	2 Circular, magical or global response	'How do people get colds?' 'From the sun.' 'How does the sun give you a cold?' 'It just does.'
4–7 years	2 Contagion ⎫	3 Concrete rules: concrete rigid response with parrot-like quality – little comprehension by children	'How do people get colds?' 'By going out without a coat in cold weather.' 'By eating junk food'
	3 Contamination ⎬ CONCRETE ⎭ LOGICAL		
7–11 years	4 Internalization ⎬	4 Internalization and relativity: increased generalization with some indication of child's contribution to response – quality of invariant causation remains	'What is a cold?' 'You sneeze a lot, you talk funny and your nose gets clogged up.' 'How do people get colds?' 'In winter they breathe in too much air into their noses and it blocks up the nose.' 'How does this cause colds?' 'The bacteria gets in by breathing. Then the lungs get too soft (child exhales), and it goes to the nose.' 'How does it get better?' 'Hot fresh air, it gets in the nose and pushes the cold air back.'
		5 Generalized principles Beginning use of under-lying principles – greater delineation of causal agents or illnesses	
		6 Physiologic processes and mechanisms	
11 years and over	5 Physiologic ⎫ FORMAL ⎬ LOGICAL 6 Psychophysiologic ⎭		'What is a cold?' 'It's when you get all stuffed up inside, your sinuses get filled up with mucus. Sometimes your lungs do, too, and you get a cough.' 'How do people get colds?' 'They come from viruses, I guess. Other people have the virus and it gets into your bloodstream and it causes a cold.'

Further attention will be given to these strategies in the next section.

COMMUNICATING WITH CHRONICALLY ILL CHILDREN AND THEIR FAMILIES

Effective communication between health care professionals and patients is a difficult process even when two adults are the only participants. Research on doctor–patient communication has demonstrated that a wide range of factors influence patient satisfaction with such communications and patient compliance. These factors include patient expectations (Korsch *et al.,* 1968), medical knowledge and misconceptions about medical matters (Spelman and Ley, 1966; Ley and Spelman, 1967; Boyle, 1970), perceived importance of information (Ley, 1972), attitude of the physician (Korsch *et al.,* 1968; Francis *et al.,* 1969), and patient anxiety (Ley *et al.,* 1974; Ley, 1977).

When the patient is a child, effective communication may be further hampered by a clinician's inability to use language appropriate for the child's stage of development and the child's difficulty in conveying his or her needs to the clinician. Until recently there was little systematic information available concerning children's understanding of illness and its treatment. The following section considers some recent work which provides the beginnings of a useful framework for communicating with both acutely and chronically ill children. Further sections consider factors of importance in preparing children for hospitalization and painful treatment procedures.

Children's concepts of illness, treatment and prevention

Illness. Recent investigations of healthy children have demonstrated a clear progression with age in the development of concepts of illness (Bibace and Walsh, 1980; Perrin and Gerrity, 1981). Accordingly, young children tend to explain illness with recourse to a single factor, whilst an understanding of illness as a complex multifaceted process only emerges at approximately 12 years of age. The developmental stages of illness concepts delineated in two recent studies are illustrated in *Table 3* .

Whilst age level can broadly predict the level of explanation of illness given by children, much more important is the child's general level of cognitive ability, and wide variations in individual children's understanding of illness concepts have been reported within each age level. Level of cognitive ability has also proved to be a good predictor of a child's ability to discriminate between painful situations. Furthermore, cognitive ability was more important in this respect than the number of pain descriptors that a child was able to use (Bradley, 1984). Such findings underline the importance of determining a child's level of cognitive development as a first step towards effective communication with children in a hospital setting. Medical and nursing staff may be easily misled by a child's age or by his or her use of vocabulary, and assume greater levels of understanding than is in fact the case.

An additional block to effective communication may arise from a child's

Table 4. Preparation for medical treatment procedures in chronically ill children

Subjects	Educational programme	Given by
10 children (a)* on haemo-dialysis	Systematic training using 65 specific steps. Social reinforcement and corrective feedback.	Nurse instructors
6 children (b) with asthma (7–12 years)	Teaching programme for use of inhalation therapy equipment.Three behaviours (eye fixation, facial posturing, dia-phragmatic breathing) taught using token re-inforcement, prompting and feedback.	Psychologists and paediatric nurses
26 asthmatic children (c) (2–14 years) and families	Education about illness and treatment. Self-management skills, observation, discrimination, decision making, communication, self reliance. Parents instructed to create opportun-ities to practice skills and use positive reinforcement to maintain skills.	Nurse educators
28 diabetic (d) children (6–9 years) at summer camp	Peer modelling film of insulin injections and specific instructions	Instructor
5 families with (e) haemo-philic children	Instructional strategies and behavioural techniques for teaching factor replacement therapy to parents (modelling, behavioural rehearsal, corrective feedback, social reinforcement)	Paediatric nurse

Outcome measures	Comments
Days to criteria	Learnt faster than group taught by traditional methods (36 vs 47 days). Patients felt more confident
Number of inappropriate behaviours during training sessions and subsequent use of apparatus. Effectiveness of treatment score (multiple baseline design)	Mean effectiveness of treatment score 41% pre-intervention 82.3% post-intervention. Inappropriate behaviours decreased during treatment and at follow up. Nurses were able to carry out the treatment programme effectively.
Symptom diary, medication record, school attendance, no. of medical visits and hospital admissions. Family attitude and knowledge assessment	Comparison with control group receiving standard care. Study group had fewer asthma attacks, fewer absences from school, fewer hospitalizations. Greater adherence to medication. Cost of treatment less
State-Trait Anxiety Inventory. Palmar Sweat Index. Behaviour Profile Rating Scale. Co-operation Rating Scale. Anxiety Rating Scale. Behavioural Skills Test	No difference between 14 children in experimental group and 14 children in control group on anxiety measures, but these were at normal levels. Skills were improved in older girls – who showed fewer errors
Behavioural check list (single case design)	Performance increased 15% during baseline, 92% end of treatment, 97% at follow up. Comparison group of 7 parents trained by traditional method only 65% adherence to procedures

* (a) – (e) refer to the following studies: (a) Lira & Mlott, 1976; (b) Renne & Creer, 1976; (c) Fireman *et al.*, 1981; (d) Gilbert *et al.*, 1982; (e) Sergis-Davenport & Varni, 1982.

misconceptions about illness. For example, a number of studies have indicated that a common misconception of young sick children is that their illness was caused by their own misdemeanours (Nagera, 1978; Brewster, 1982).

Treatment and prevention. There is rather less information concerning the development of children's concepts concerning what must be done to cure illness and what must be done to prevent it. The information that is available suggests that these concepts follow the same developmental lines (with prevention being the most difficult concept to grasp). Accordingly, four to six-year-olds may say that they recover from illness either automatically or by following a set of rules like 'staying in bed' or 'drinking chicken soup'. On the other hand, nine and ten-year-olds may say that illness is prevented by avoiding sick people, whilst recovery is accelerated by 'taking care' and 'following the doctor's orders' (Perrin and Gerrity, 1981). It is not until the formal operation stage that children appear to develop more complex notions of cure and prevention, which include the body's own response as a critical ingredient in the recovery process.

Two further interesting points emerge from studies which investigate the development of chidren's beliefs concerning health and prevention of illness. Firstly, it has been found that with increasing age there is a decreasing variability in children's notions about how health is maintained. Older children (that is, those above 8 years of age) have a more fixed and consolidated view about prevention of illness than younger children (Dielman *et al.,* 1980). Secondly, as children grow older they begin to understand that there are things that they can do to improve and maintain their health, that is, the health locus of control becomes internal rather than external (Parcel and Meyer, 1978).

Implications. Taken together the findings above have a number of important implications for communicating with children about illness, treatment and prevention. Firstly, it would seem to be important for health professionals to take into account the developmental level of a child when talking to them about their illness and treatment. Fears expressed by a child may appear more understandable and therefore will be less likely to be dismissed if viewed within a developmental framework. For instance, the erroneous belief of hospitalized five and six-year-olds that they might catch a disease from particular room-mates may be considered as normal for the child in the 'contagion' stage of cognitive development (Bibace and Walsh, 1980).

Secondly, if a child's belief is causing distress, an attempt might be made to change it. Bibace and Walsh suggest that this might be done either by providing a somewhat different and less negative account of illness within the same developmental stage as the child's original explanation, or by offering an explanation characteristic of the next stage of cognitive development.

Thirdly, the ability to understand abstract conceptualization of internal processes like haemophilia or epilepsy will require attainment of formal operational thought. Explanation to the child at early stages should be at a concrete level, and include the use of metaphor, drawing, and play (Whitt *et al.,* 1979; Varni, 1983). Similarly, when preparing younger children pre-operatively, emphasis might be placed upon external observable events (for example, lights in the operating room, nurses' uniforms) and they may be given equipment to examine (for example, an anaesthetic mask). In contrast, pre-operative teaching for the 12-year-old might focus on details of anatomy and procedures during the operation.

Fourthly, management strategies should take account of the increasing development of a child's sense of personal control. For example, at early developmental levels, appeals to personal control, such as avoiding certain foods, will have little effect. At later levels, the child may be asked to assume greater levels of responsibility.

Finally, health education whether directed at ill or healthy children, should take into account the developmental stage of the child. For example, because young children cannot readily conceptualize internal body parts, health pamphlets for younger children should restrict descriptions to observable phenomena. Moreover, the research outlined above subjects that attempts to change health beliefs may be most influential between the ages of six and eight years, before the child's view on health are fully consolidated.

Preparation for hospitalization and surgery

The preparation of young children for hospitalization and surgery has received a considerable amount of attention in recent years, no doubt arising from the findings that young children may react adversely to such experiences even when hospitalized for quite short periods of time (Vernon *et al.,* 1966; Douglas, 1975; Quinton and Rutter, 1976). Where children are admitted for much longer periods of time or under emergency conditions and suffering serious and disabling symptoms, psychological reactions are likely to be much more severe (Hollenbeck *et al.,* 1980; Cataldo *et al.,* 1982). Much of the research on preparation for hospitalization and surgery has been carried out on children undergoing relatively minor surgery. Nevertheless, these findings may have considerable relevance for chronically ill children and their families. Hospital preparation programmes have sometimes been aimed at children alone and sometimes at parents and children. The involvement of parents in preparation would seem to be particularly important, given the high correlation between anxiety in mothers concerning hospitalization and anxiety in their children (Vardaro, 1978; Zabin and Melamed, 1980). Several methods of preparation have been examined. These include filmed modelling (Melamed and Siegel, 1975; Melamed *et al.,* 1976; Ferguson, 1979; Peterson and Shigetomi, 1981), information booklets (Wolfer and Visintainer, 1979), pre-admission home visits (Ferguson, 1979), cognitive strategies to relieve anxiety and pain (Peterson and Shigetomi, 1981), stress point nursing (Visintainer and Wolfer, 1975), and visual aids for simulating hospital procedures (Wolfer and Visintainer, 1979).

The studies reported above all employ different methodologies and different assessment measures of a child's response to hospitalization. Direct comparison is therefore difficult. However, all of these studies demonstrate the usefulness of the preparation procedures used when compared with routine hospital procedure or simple supportive care. Information is now needed on the relative advantages and disadvantages of each mode of preparation for different age groups of children, and for different types of hospital admissions. Evidence available to date suggests that younger children (6 to 7-year-olds) need to be prepared nearer to the date of hospitalization than older children (Melamed *et al.*, 1976), and that they respond more readily to visual rather than verbal material (Ferguson, 1979). Furthermore, it cannot necessarily be assumed that a combination of different methods of preparation will increase effectiveness. In some studies, groups of children who were prepared for hospitalization using a combination of preparation methods showed similar levels of anxiety to those receiving preparation by a single method (Ferguson, 1979; Peterson and Shigetomi, 1981).

Finally, some methods of preparation may be employed for their very specific effects. For example, one study showed that a pre-admission home visit by a paediatric nurse was more effective in reducing maternal anxiety and produced greater satisfaction with treatment than a peer modelling film (Ferguson, 1979). Further information is required to enable clinicians to select the appropriate methods of preparation for different groups of children. It is also important in this process to assess family-related and child-related variables which may predict which children are likely to respond poorly to hospitalization. For example, one recent investigation found that children of parents who used positive reinforcement modelling and persuasion as ways of encouraging their children to deal with fearful situations showed less anxiety when hospitalized than children whose parents used punishment force as reinforcement of dependency (Zabin and Melamed, 1980).

Preparation for complex or painful management procedures

Many chronic conditions require complex and sometimes painful management procedures to be carried out at home by the parents or the child. These may involve strict dietary regimes, frequent injections, monitoring of urine or blood samples or manipulation of medical equipment such as that employed in the home haemo- or peritoneal dialysis. A number of recent investigations have begun to systematically investigate different preparatory educational methods for introducing children and parents to these procedures. The prime aim of these investigations has not been to reduce psychological distress (few studies have measured child and parent anxiety levels) but to reduce errors and encourage adherence to these complex regimes. However, it may reasonably be assumed that procedures which encourage rapid learning are also those which keep anxiety at a moderate level. *Table 4* describes five such studies. In most cases nurses were employed as instructors and in all studies preparatory methods showed improvements on traditional teaching procedures.

PSYCHOLOGICAL APPROACHES IN THE MANAGEMENT OF CHRONIC ILLNESS

The introduction of psychological approaches in the management of chronic conditions in children is of fairly recent origin. Although procedures are obviously complimentary to important medical intervention, there has been a growing recognition that psychological factors may influence the expression of symptomatology and the effects of medical treatments in a number of ways. For example, a child may refuse to co-operate in treatment by eating

Table 5. Pain management procedures for chronically-ill children

	Procedure	Study
	Deep muscle relaxation	Varni, 1981; Elliott & Olsen, 1983
	Guided imagery	Varni, 1981; Elliott & Olsen, 1983
PAIN PERCEPTION REGULATION	Distraction	Zeltzer & Le Baron, 1982; Elliott & Olsen, 1983
	Meditative breathing	Varni, 1981; Elliott & Olsen, 1983
	Hypnosis	Zeltzer & Le Baron, 1982; Zeltzer *et al.*, 1979; Varni *et al.*, 1983
	Systematic desensitization	Katz, 1974
	Biofeedback	Varni *et al.*, 1983
PAIN BEHAVIOUR REGULATION	Socio-environmental modification (reinforcement of well-behaviours)	Varni *et al.*, 1980

inappropriately or by failing to take medication. Alternatively, stress or anxiety generated by environmental events may exaccerbate symptomatology (Rose *et al.*, 1983). In this final section attention will be given to recent studies which have focused upon teaching skills to parents and children to reduce pain and distress encourage adherence regimes, and modify some disabling consequences of the disease.

Pain

For children with chronic conditions, pain may derive from the disease process itself (for example, haemophilia, arthritis, sickle cell anaemia), or from medical procedures used in the management of the disorders (lumbar punctures, bone marrow aspiration, injections). Pain associated with the disease may be acute or chronic. For example, in a child with haemophilia acute pain may arise during a specific bleeding episode, whilst chronic pain experienced over an extended period of time may result from the chronic degenerative arthritis associated with repeated haemorrhages into joint areas.

In order to assess the effectiveness of any treatment procedure for pain modulation adequate outcome measures are necessary. In the studies reviewed in *Table 5* a variety of measures have been used, including self-ratings of pain (Zeltzer and Le Baron, 1982; Varni and Gilbert, 1982), behavioural rating scales (Katz *et al.*, 1980), number of hospitalizations or hospital visits (Zeltzer *et al.*, 1979), amount of medication (Varni and Gilbert, 1982), and days of pain (Varni, 1981).

However, measurement of pain in young children is a problematic and as yet under-researched area (Bradley, 1984; Wells, 1984). In particular, when assessing acute pain, especially that related to medical procedures, it has proved difficult to differentiate pain measures from anxiety measures. (Shacham and Daut, 1981) Recognizing this, one group of workers have adopted an observational measure of behavioural distress which incorporates behavioural aspects of both anxiety and pain (Katz *et al.*, 1980). Clearly, for advances to be made in this area, much more research is required in order to develop adequate assessment instruments for use with children of all age groups.

Although a considerable number of articles concerning the management of pain have appeared in the literature, very few have been concerned with paediatric pain (Elliott and Olson, 1983), and even fewer have been concerned with children suffering from chronic illnesses. Nevertheless, recent developments suggest that this may be a promising area for future research.

Table 5 lists a number of pain management procedures used with children suffering from chronic pain (Varni *et al.*, 1980; Varni, 1981; Varni and Gilbert, 1982), and acute pain caused by their illnesses (Zeltzer *et al.*, 1979; Varni *et al.*, 1983; Masek, 1983), or by medical procedures employed in the management of their condition (Zeltzer and Le Baron, 1982; Elliott and Olson, 1983; Varni *et al.*, 1983).

Most studies of pain perception regulation have employed a combination of techniques, though all have capitalized on the ability of children to use fantasy and imagery following progressive relaxation or hypnotic induction procedures. A variety of suggestions or instructions during guided imagery have been employed. For example, in some studies a series of pleasant scenes was conjured up (Varni, 1981; Zeltzer and Le Baron, 1982), whilst in ohters, suggestion of mastery and control of pain were introduced by 'magic potions' or 'dimmer switches' to control the pain (Varni *et al.*, 1983). Others have used suggestions which reinterpret the context of pain. For example, during hydrotherapy a child with severe burns imagines he is swimming to his friends to save them from drowning (Elliott and Olson, 1983).

Conclusions drawn from these investigations must be tentative. So far, few patients have been studied, pain measures are on the whole rudimentary, and follow-up data are frequently lacking. Moreover, one study has indicated that generalization to situations where the therapist was absent did not occur (Elliott and Olson, 1983). Nevertheless, the results must be viewed against the problems of medical management of pain in these children. It has been noted that children may fail to habituate to noxious medical interventions and that many children show substantial increases in anxiety and stress with repeated treatments, such as chemotherapy or bone marrow aspiration in the case of childhood cancers and hydrotherapy, or debridement and dressing changes in the case of severe burns (Katz *et al.*, 1980; Varni *et al.*, 1983; Elliott and Olson, 1983). Furthermore, youngsters may become increasingly dependent on large doses of analgesics to relieve pain (Varni *et al.*, 1981).

Obviously, further research is needed. Comparison between different pain management procedures should be carried out. Information is also required which would enable clinicians to tailor pain management procedures to the individual child.

Adherence to treatment regimes

Treatment regimes for chronically ill children such as those with diabetes or end stage renal failure are often complex. Moreover, they are carried out over long periods of time and require considerable alterations in the child's and the family's daily lifestyle. It is well known that compliance rates are poor under such circumstances (Litt and Cuskey, 1980; Shope, 1981). Nevertheless, the consequences of non-adherence may be serious. For example, children on haemodialysis who are non-compliant with dietary regimes are at risk for bone disease, congestive heart failure, hypertension, fluid overload uremia and excessive serum potassium. Several approaches have been suggested to increase compliance with medical procedures. These have been summarized by Varni (1983). Early discussion has alluded to the complex group of factors which may produce non-compliance. A functional analysis approach to non-compliance advocated by Varni may be particularly appropriate under these circumstances. Accordingly, identification of antecedents and consequences related to various health-related behaviours may be ascertained by self-monitoring or parental monitoring. This alone has proved beneficial in some cases (Eney and Goldstein, 1976; Hudson, 1984). Where non-compliance is related to the aversiveness of the therapeutic regime, the anxiety management and pain management procedures described earlier may be appropriate. Where misunderstanding, lack of comprehension or recall is the issue, then care should be taken to provide preparatory verbal and written information that is specific, categorized and dispensed carefully over time. Alternatively, if non-adherence results in major disruption in the child or family's lifestyle, then additional strategies may be adopted, such as self-reinforcement, parent reinforcement and contigency contracting. In studies where such methods have been adopted, there have been some promising results. Varni reports the beneficial effects of peer reinforcement in groups of boys with haemophilia undergoing therapeutic exercise (Varni *et al.,* 1983). Similar strategies have improved dietary adherence in youngsters on renal dialysis (Magrab and Papadoupoulou, 1977) and regulation of urine glucose levels in diabetic children (Epstein *et al.,* 1981).

Symptomatic control

Studies which have attempted to modify symptoms of chronic illness fall into three groups. Firstly, there are those studies which have attempted to teach children relaxation or anxiety management skills on the assumption that stress factors may exaccerbate symptomatology. Such approaches have been used with asthmatic (Alexander *et al.,* 1979; Miklich *et al.,* 1977) and diabetic (Rose *et al.,* 1983) youngsters. Whilst some benefits were found for patients in these studies, the results have to be interpreted with caution. In the case of asthmatic youngsters, no clinically significant changes in pulmonary functioning occurred when relaxation therapy was employed on its own (Alexander *et al.,* 1979), although where relaxation was used as part of a desensitization programme, statistically significant changes in pulmonary function did occur (Milklich *et al.,* 1977). It has been suggested that better use of psychological procedures for asthmatic children might be found in the self-management studies reported earlier (Renne and Creer, 1976; Creer *et al.,* 1982). In the case of diabetic youngsters, anxiety management training did appear to lower and stabilize urine glucose levels. However, methodological problems inherent in this study made it difficult to separate out non-specific effects of the programme. Urine glucose levels may have stabilized simply by greater efforts on the part of the child to adhere to the diabetic regime. This seems quite likely, as self-reported levels of anxiety did not change through treatment (Rose *et al.,* 1983).

A second group of treatment studies have attempted to train chronically ill youngsters in skills which were previously absent, perhaps as a result of organic damage. Accordingly, a number of recent investigations have attempted to reduce urinary and faecal incontinence in youngsters with spina bifida by biofeedback procedures (Whitehead *et al.*, 1981; Wald, 1981; Jeffries *et al*, 1982). Biofeedback procedures have also been developed for children with long-term diurnal incontinence (Maizels *et al.*, 1979; Sugar and Firlit, 1982), children with cerebral palsy (Cataldo *et al.*, 1978; Finley *et al.*, 1977), and children with epilepsy (Mostofsky and Balaschali, 1977).

Finally, a third group of studies have attempted to modify chronic symptomatology by rearranging environmental consequences. Such approaches appear to be most appropriate where self-help skills are being taught (Feldman *et al.*, 1982) or where symtoms are exaccerbated by 'secondary gain' mechanisms (for example, Varni *et al.*, 1980).

CONCLUDING COMMENTS

As survival rates for children with chronic illnesses increase, a growing number of paediatricians are asking for psychological help with pressing social and psychological problems in the management of chronically ill children. This chapter has attempted to review the beginnings of a useful literature which may help the practising clinical psychologist when faced with requests for help. At the present stage of development, child clinical psychologists are too few in number to offer a comprehensive service in this field. Moreover, it would be premature to make great claims for the efficacy of many of the procedures described above. Much painstaking and systematic research is still needed.

A review of this type has necessarily been brief. No mention has been made here of illness prevention programmes, the important area of counselling the terminally ill child and adolescent (Lansdown, 1983), or work with the nursing staff who care for chronically sick youngsters. Furthermore, discussion of the vexed ethical question of whether medical intervention should be made at all with some seriously ill children has been avoided (Korsch *et al.*, 1971). However, the present chapter is based on the philosophy that while some children are surviving with chronic and life threatening diseases, psychological knowledge and research might usefully be directed towards increasing the mastery and coping skills of these children and if possible improving their general quality of life.

REFERENCES

ALEXANDER, A.B., CROPP, G.J.A. and CHAI, H. (1979) Effects of relaxation training on pulmonary mechanics in children with asthma. *Journal of Applied Behaviour Analysis, 12,* 27–35.

BEDELL, J.R., GIORDANI, B., AMOUR, J.L., TAVORMINA, J. and BOLL, T. (1977) Life stress and the psychological and medical adjustments of chronically ill children. *Journal of Psychosomatic Research, 21,* 237–242.

BIBACE, R. and WALSH, M.E. (1980) Developments of children's concepts of illness. *Paediatrics, 66,* 912–917.

BOYLE, C.M. (1970) Differences between doctors' and patients' interpretation of some common medical terms. *British Medical Journal, 2,* 286–289.

BRADLEY, A. (1984) Acute pain in children with burns. Paper read to Pain Interest Group Conference, Liverpool, June.

BRESLAU, N., WEITZMAN, M. and MESSENGER, K. (1981) Psychological functioning of siblings of disabled children. *Paediatrics, 67,* 344–353.

BREWSTER, A. (1982) Chronically ill hospitalized children's concepts of their illness. *Paediatrics, 69,* 355–362.

CATALDO, M.F., BIRD, B.L. and CUNNINGHAM, C.E. (1978) Experimental analysis of EMG feedback in treating cerebral palsy. *Journal of Behavioural Medicine, 1,* 311–322.

CATALDO, M.F., JACOBS, H.E. and ROGERS, M.C. (1982) Behavioural/-environmental consideration in paediatric inpatient care. In: D.C. Russo and J.W. Varni (eds) *Behavioural Paediatrics Research and Practice.* New York: Penguin Press.

CHRISTOPHERSEN, E.R. and RAPOFF, M.A. (1979) Behavioural pediatrics. In: O.F. Pomerleau and J.P. Brady (eds) *Behavioural Medicine: Theory and Practice.* Baltimore: Williams and Wilkins.

CREER, T.L., RENNE, C.M. and CHAI, H. (1982) The application of behavioural techniques to childhood asthma. In: D.C. Russo and J.W. Varni (eds) *Behavioural Pediatrics: Research and Practice.* New York: Plenum Press.

DIELMAN, T.E., LEECH, S.L., BECKER, M.H., ROSENSTOCK I.M. and HOVARTH, W.J. (1980) Dimensions of chidren's health beliefs. *Health Education Quarterly, 7,* 219–238.

DOUGLAS, J.W.B. (1975) Early hospital admissions and later disturbances of behaviour and learning. *Developmental Medicine and Child Neurology, 17,* 456.

ELLIOTT, C.H. and OLSON, R.A. (1983) The management of children's distress in response to painful medical treatment for burn injuries. *Behaviour Research and Therapy, 21(6),* 675–683.

ENEY, R.D. and GOLDSTEIN, E.D. (1976) Compliance of chronic asthmatics with oral administration of theophylline as measured by serum and salivary levels. *Pediatrics, 57,* 513–517.

EPSTEIN, L.H., BECK, S., FIGUEROA, J., FARKAS, G., KAZDEN, A.E., DANEMAN, D. and BECKER, D. (1981) The effects of targeting improvements in urine glucose on metabolic control in children with insulin dependent diabetes. *Journal of Applied Behavioural Analysis, 14,* 365–375.

FELDMAN, W.S., MANELLA, K.J., APODACA, L. and VARNI, J.W. (1982) Behavioural group parent training in spina bifida. *Journal of Clinical Child Psychology, 11,* 144–150.

FERGUSON, B.F. (1979) Preparing young children for hospitalization. A comparison of two methods. *Pediatrics, 64,* 656–664.

FERRARI, M. (1984) Chronic Illnesses. Psychological effects on siblings – I Chronically ill boys. *Journal of Child Psychology and Psychiatry, 25,* 459–476.

FINLEY, W.W., NIMAN, C.A., STANDLEY, J. and WANSLEY, R.A. (1977) Electrophysiologic behaviour modification of frontal EMG in cerebral palsied children. *Biofeedback and Self Regulation, 2,* 59–79.

FIREMAN, P., FRIDAY, G.A., GIRA, C., VIERTHALER, W.A. and MICHAELS, L. (1981) Teaching self-management skills to asthmatic children and their parents in an ambulatory care setting. *Pediatrics, 68,* 341–348.

FRANCIS, V., KORSCH, B.M. and MORRIS, M.J. (1969) Gaps in doctor patient communication patients response to medical advice. *New England Journal of Medicine, 280,* 535–540.

GAYTON, W.F. and FRIEDMAN, S.B. (1973) A review of the psychological aspects of cystic fibrosis. *American Journal of Diseases in Childhood, 126,* 856–859.

GAYTON, W.F., FRIEDMAN, S.B., TAVORMINA, J.F. and TUCKER, F. (1977) Children with cystic fibrosis – I Psychological test findings, siblings and parents. *Pediatrics, 59,* 888–894.

GILBERT B.O., JOHNSON, S.B., SPILLO, R., MCCALLUM, M., SILVERSTEIN, J.H. and ROSENBLOOM, A. (1982) The effects of a peer modelling film on children learning to self inject insulin. *Behaviour Therapy, 13,* 186–190.

HOLLENBECK, A.R., SUSMAN, E.J., NANNIS, E.D., STROPE, B.E., HERSH, S.P., LEVINE, A.S. and PIZZO, P.A. (1980) Children with serious illness: behavioural correlation of separation and isolation. *Child Psychiatry and Human Development, 11,* 3–11.

HUDSON, J. (1984) Psychological factors relating to adherence to medical regimes in children undergoing haemodialysis and CAPD. M.Clin.Psych. dissertation, University of Liverpool.

JEFFRIES, J.S., KILLAM, P.E. and VARNI, J.W. (1982) Behavioural management of fecal incontinence in a child with myelomeningocele. *Pediatric Nursing, 8,* 267–270.

KATZ, E.R., KELLERMAN, J. and SIEGAL, D.E. (1980) Distress behaviour in children with cancer undergoing medical procedures: Developmental considerations. *Journal of Consulting and Clinical Psychology, 48,* 356–365.

KELLERMAN, J., ZELTZER, L., ELLENBERG, L., DASH, J. and RIGLER, D. (1980) Psychological effects of illness in adolescents. I. Anxiety, self esteem and perception of control. *Journal of Pediatrics, 97,* 126–131.

KLEIN, R.H. and NIMORWICZ, P. (1982) The relationship between psychological distress and knowledge of disease among haemophilia patients and their families: a pilot study. *Journal of Psychosomatic Research, 26,* 387–391.

KNOWLES, H.C. (1971) Diabetes mellitus in childhood and adolescence. *Medical Clinics of North America, 55,* 1007.

KOOCHER, G.P., O'MALLEY, J.E., GOGAN, J.L. and FOSTER, D.J. (1980) Psychological adjustment among pediatric cancer survivors. *Journal of Child Psychology and Psychiatry, 21,* 163–173.

KORSCH, B.M., GOZZI, E.K. and FRANCIS, V. (1968) Gaps in doctor–patient communication I doctor patient interaction and patient satisfaction. *Pediatrics, 42,* 855–871.

KORSCH, B.M., FINE, R.N., GRUSHKIN, C.M. and NEGRETE, V.F. (1971) Experiences with children and their families during extended haemodialysis and kidney transplantation. *Pediatric Clinics of North America, 18,* 623–637.

LANSDOWN, R. (1983) The development of the concept of death and its relationship to communicating with dying children. Paper presented at the Annual Merseyside Course in Clinical Psychology, September.

LASK, B. (1982) Physical illness and the family. In: A. Bentovim, Gorell Barnes, and A. Cooklin (eds) *Family Therapy. Volume 1 of Theory and Practice.* London: Academic Press.

LEY, P. (1972) Primacy, rated importance and recall of medical information. *Journal of Health and Social Behaviour, 13,* 311–317.

LEY, P. (1977) Psychological studies of doctor patient communication. In: S. Rachman (ed) *Contributions to Medical Psychology, Volume 1.* Oxford: Pergamon.

LEY, P., BRADSHAW, P.W., KINCEY, J. COUPER-SMARTT, J. and WILSON, M. (1974) Psychological variables in weight control. In: W.L. Burland, P.D. Samuel and J. Yudkin (eds) *Obesity.* London: Churchill Livingstone.

LIRA, F.T. and MLOTT, S.R. (1976) A behavioural approach to hemodialysis training. *Journal of American Association of Nephrology Nurses and Technicians, 3,* 180–188.

LITT, I.F. and CUSKEY, W.R. (1980) Cpmpliance with medical regimes during adolescence. *Pediatric Clinics of North America, 27,* 3–15.

MAGRAB, P.R. and PAPADOUPOULOU, Z.L. (1977) The effect of a token economy on dietary compliance for children on hemodialysis. *Journal of Applied Behaviour Analysis, 10,* 573–578.

MAIZELS, M., KING, L.R., and FIRLITT, C.F. (1979) Urodynamic biofeedback: A new approach to treat vesical sphincter dyssynergia. *Journal of Urology, 122,* 205–209.

MARKOVA, I. (1979) Rearing a child with haemophilia. *Developmental Medicine and Child Neurology, 21,* 812–814.

MATTSSON, A. (1972). Long-term physical illness in childhood: a challenge to psychological adaptation. *Pediatrics, 50,* 801–811.

MELAMED, B.E., MEYER, R., GEE, C. and SOULE, L. (1976) The influence of time and type of preparation on children's adjustment to hospitalization. *Journal of Pediatric Psychology, 1,* 31–37.

MELAMED, B.E. and SEIGEL, L.J. (1975) Reduction of anxiety in children facing hospitalization and surgery by the use of filmed modeling. *Journal of Consulting and Clinical Psychology, 43,* 511– 521.

MIKLICH, D.R., RENNE, C.M., CREER, T.L., ALEXANDER, A.B., CHAI, H., DAVIS, M.H., HOFFMAN, A. and DANKER-BROWN, P. (1977) The clinical utility of behaviour therapy as an adjunctive treatment for asthma. *Journal of Allergy and Clinical Immunology, 60,* 285–294.

MOORE, B. (1983) The effects on the family of end stage renal failure in children. M.Clin.Psych. disseration, University of Liverpool.

MOSTOFSKY, D.I. and BALASCHAK, B.A. (1977) Psychological control of seizures. *Psychological Bulletin, 84,* 723–750.

NAGERA, H. (1978) Children's reactions to hospitalization and illness. *Child Psychiatry and Human Development, 9,* 3–19.

PARCEL, G.S. and MEYER, M.P. (1978) Development of an instrument to measure children's health locus of control. *Health Education Monographs, 6,* 149–159.

PERRIN, E.C. and GERRITY, P.S. (1981) There's a demon in your belly: Children's understanding of illness. *Pediatrics, 67,* 841– 849.

PETERSON, L. and SHIGETOMI, C. (1981) The use of coping techniques to minimise anxiety in hospitalized children. *Behaviour Therapy, 12,* 1–14.

PLESS, I.B. (1968) Epidemiology of chronic disease. In: M. Green and R.J. Haggerty (eds) *Ambulatory Pediatrics.* Philadelphia: W.B. Saunders.

PLESS, I.B. and DOUGLAS, S.W.B. (1971) Chronic illness in childhood: Part 1. Epidemiological and clinical characteristics. *Pediatrics, 47,* 405–414.

QUINTON, D. and RUTTER, M. (1976) Early hospital admissions and later disturbances of behaviour: An attempted replication of Douglas' findings. *Developmental Medicine and Child Neurology, 18,* 447.

RENNE, C.M. and CREER, T.L. (1976) Training children with asthma to use inhalation therapy equipment. *Journal of Applied Behaviour Analysis, 9,* 1–11.

ROSE, M.I., FIRESTONE, P., HEICK, H.M.C, and FRAUGHT, A.K. (1983) The effects of anxiety on the control of juvenile diabetes mellitus. *Journal of Behavioural Medicine, 6,* 382–395.

SABBETH, B.F. and LEVANTHAL, J.M. (1984) Marital adjustment to chronic childhood illness: a critique of the literature. *Pediatrics, 73,* 762–768.

SEIDEL, U.P., CHADWICK, O.F.D., RUTTER, M. (1975) Psychological disorders in crippled children a comparative study of children with and without brain damage. *Developmental Medicine and Child Neurology, 17,* 563–573.

SERGIS-DAVENPORT, E. and VARNI, J. (1982) Behavioural techniques in teaching hemophilia factor replacement procedures to families. *Pediatric Nursing, 8,* 416–419.

SHACHAM, M. and DAUT, R. (1981) Anxiety or pain: What does the scale measure? *Journal of Consulting and Clinical Psychology, 49,* 468–469.

SHOPE, J.T. (1981) Medication compliance. *Pediatric Clinics of North America, 28,* 5–21.

SPELMAN, M.S. and LEY, P. (1966) Knowledge of lung cancer and smoking habits. *British Jounral of Social and Clinical Psychology, 5,* 207–210.

STEIDL, J.H., FINKELSTEIN, F.O., WEXLER, J.P., FEIGENBAUM, R.N., KITSEN., J., KLIGER, A.S. and QUINLAN, D.M. (1980) Medical condition, adherence to treatment regimes and family functioning. *Archives of General Psychiatry, 37,* 1025–1027.

STEINHAUER, P.D., MUSHIN, D.N. and RAE-GRANT, Q. (1974) Psychological aspects of chronic illness. *Pediatric Clinics of North America, 21(4),* 825–840.

SUGAR, E.C. and FIRLIT, C.F. (1982) Urodynamic biofeedback: a new therapeutic approach for childhood incontinence/infection (vesical voluntary sphincter dyssynergia). *Journal of Urology, 128,* 1253–1258.

TAVORMINA, J.B., KASTNER, L.S., SLATER, P.M. and WATT, S.L. (1976) Chronically ill children: A psychologically and emotionally deviant population? *Journal of Abnormal Child Psychology, 4,* 99–110.

VARDARO, J.A. (1978) Preadmission anxiety and mother–child relationships. *Journal of the Association for the Care of Children in Hospitals, 7,* 8–15.

VARNI, J.W. (1981) Self-regulation techniques in the management of chronic arthritic pain in haemophilia. *Behaviour Therapy, 12,* 185–194.

VARNI, J.W. (1983) *Clinical Behaviour Pediatrics.* Pergamon Press: New York.

VARNI, J.W. and GILBERT, A. (1982) Self regulation of chronic arthritic pain and long-term analgesic dependence in a hemophiliac. *Rheumatology and Rehabilitation, 22,* 171–174.

VARNI, J.W., GILBERT, A. and DIETRICH, S.L. Behavioural medicine in pain and analgesic management for the haemophilic child with factor VIII inhibition. *Pain, 11,* 121–126.

VARNI, J.W., MASEK, B. and KATZ, E.R. (1983) Behavioural Pediatrics: Biobehavioural assessment and management strategies. Workshop presented to World Congress of Behaviour Therapy, Washington, 1983.

VARNI, J.W., BESSMAN, C.A., RUSSO, D.C. and CATALDO, M.F. (1980) Behavioural management of chronic pain in children: Case study. *Archives of Physical Medicine and Rehabilitation, 61,* 375– 379.

VERNON, D.T.A., SCHULMAN, J.L. and FOLEY, J.M. (1966) Changes in children's behaviour after hospitalization: some dimensions of response and their correlates. *American Journal of Diseases of Children, 111,* 581–593.

VISINTAINER, M.A. and WOLFER, J.A. (1975) Psychological preparation for surgical pediatric patients. The effect on children's and parents' stress responses and adjustment. *Pediatrics, 56,* 187–202.

WALD, A. (1981) Use of biofeedback in treatment of fecal incontinence in patients with myelomeningocele. *Pediatrics, 68,* 45–49.

WALKER, M.S.W. (1983) The pact: The caretaker-parent/ill-child coalition in families with chronic illness. *Family Systems Medicine, 1,* 6–29.

WELLS, C. (1984) Post operative pain in children. Paper read to Pain Interest Group Conference, Liverpool, June.

WHITT, J.K., DYKSTRA, W. and TAYLOR, C.A. (1979) Children's conceptions of illness and cognitive developments. *Clinical Pediatrics, 18,* 327–339.

WHITEHEAD, W.E., PARKER, L.H., MASEK, B.J., CATALDO, M.F. and FREEMAN, J.M. (1981) Biofeedback treatment of fecal incontinence in patients with myelomeningocele. *Developmental Medicine and Child Neurology, 23,* 313–322.

WOLFER, J.A. and VISINTAINER , M.A. (1979) Prehospital psychological preparation for tonsillectomy patients: Effects on children's and parents' adjustments. *Pediatrics, 64,* 646–655.

WOLTERS, W.H.G., BONEKAMP, A.L.M. and DONKERWOLCHE, R. (1973) Experiences in the development of a haemodialysis centre for children. *Journal of Psychosomatic Research, 17,* 271–276.

ZABIN, M.A. and MELAMED, B.G. (1980) Relationship between parental discipline and children's ability to cope with stress. *Journal of Behavioural Assessment, 2,* 17–38.

ZELTZER, L.K., DASH, J. and HOLLAND, J.P. (1979) Hypnotically induced pain control in sickle cell anaemia. *Pediatrics, 64,* 533–536.

ZELTZER, L., KELLERMAN, J., ELLENBERG, L., DASH, J. and RIGLER, D. (1980) Psychological effects of illness in adolescents. II Impact of illness in adolescents – crucial issues and coping styles *Journal of Pediatrics, 97,* 132–138.

ZELTZER, L. and LE BARON, S. (1982) Hypnosis and non-hypnotic techniques for reduction of pain and anxiety during painful procedures in children and adolescents with cancer. *Journal of Pediatrics, 101,* 1032–1035.

TRIADIC WORK WITH CHILDREN

Martin Herbert

One of the most interesting – perhaps significant – developments in the last fifteen years or so, in the field of child treatment, has involved psychologists in the altruistic task of 'giving away' their skills to others. The triadic model has built into it the objective of making the therapist redundant as soon as possible in the life of a particular case or client. Hopefully, such an approach is not subversive to the profession; far from making the psychologist's role surplus to requirement, it provides a new and powerful focus for his or her expertise.

The use of the triadic model of intervention for treatment, training or remedial work began from an assumption that parents, surrogate parents, teachers and other caregivers have a profound effect on children's development and mental health. Because they exert such a significant foundational influence during the impressionable years of childhood, they are usually in a strong position to facilitate prosocial learning, and moderate the genesis of behaviour disorder.

Rationale

The behavioural approach, based as it is upon social learning theory, has crucial implications not only for the way in which the psychologist works, but also for the location of that work. The child's natural environment (be it home, classroom or playground) becomes the setting for the therapeutic endeavour (Herbert, 1980 a,b). The parents – to take one category – are drawn into the therapeutic alliance, but on the basis of a very *active* partnership. Help is directed, then, to the modification of the child and his or her environment; parents and siblings, as significant aspects of that environment, may be asked to change their actions and attitudes as well.

Natural environment interventions take advantage of the on-going intensive social influence of those in closest contact with the 'client' (we shall return to this term) in attempting to modify deviant behaviour and teach new skills and behavioural repertoires (*see* Herbert, 1981). The triadic model by-passes the problem of generalizing improvements from the consulting room to the outside world. Parents (and teachers) – as primary mediators of change – are *in situ* most of the time, and are in a position to instruct, model and apply contingencies in a variety of situations. This, at least, is the theory!

Whatever the *apparent* theoretical advantages of this orientation there are many practical difficulties associated with its application. In addition, natural setting work means, in effect, 'unnatural' experimental investigations, as it is so difficult to specify and control pre- and post-treatment conditions with precision. Nevertheless, as Repucci and Saunders (1974) were at pains to point out at an early stage in the development of triadic work (and their comments remain apposite), the boundaries of behaviour modification are expanding, and the crucial issues to be resolved include the *social* application of behavioural methods. They foresaw that the actual environment can also be at times a somewhat unnatural, thorny therapeutic environment in which to work. The behaviour therapist (modifier) encounters a wide range of problems that do not relate directly to theoretical issues in behaviour modification, and which are absent or minimal in the laboratory or clinical research situation. They can be a nightmare for the clinician who wishes to conduct rigorous evaluative research. The domestic 'hurly-burly' is a stranger to neat research designs.

However, let us look, for a moment at that 'traditional' clinical situation. By contrast with the developments described above, the traditional (often eclectic) treatment of problematic behaviour in children takes place in a clinic or a hospital. Parents bring the child to the professional (a psychiatrist, psychologist or social worker), who works primarily with the child as the target patient, with problems to be modified or worked through in the consulting room or playroom.

This is a situation far removed from the child's experience of life and occupies a miniscule proportion of it. Frequently, therapists are unable to see parent–child (or teacher–child) interactions in their natural settings, and indeed they may not even observe directly the behaviours or 'symptoms' for which the child was referred. What are these problems?

Behaviour problems

The generic term 'behaviour problems' refers to a large and heterogenous collection of disorders ranging from depression, anxiety, inhibition, and shyness to non-compliance, destructiveness, stealing and aggression. In essence, these problems represent exaggerations, deficits or disabling combinations of feelings, attitudes and behaviours common to all children (Herbert, 1974). There is a consensus among clinical and statistical studies for a meaningful distinction between those disorders which primarily lead to emotional disturbance for the child himself (for example, anxiety, shyness, depression, feelings of inferiority and timidity), and those which involve mainly the kinds of antisocial behaviour (for example, destructiveness, aggression, lying, stealing and disobedience), which disrupt the well-being of others, notably those in frequent contact with the child (Achenbach and Edelbrock, 1978).

The high 'spontaneous remission' rate of many childhood disorders must be taken into account in evaluating the success of different treatment methods. We know as a result of longitudinal studies that for the most part, children who suffer from 'emotional disorders' (the first of the above categories) become reasonably well-adjusted adults; they are almost as likely to grow up 'normal' as children drawn at random for the general population. Although these problems tend to be transitory, they do sometimes persist or reach levels of intensity which cause everybody concerned with the youngster, and not least the child, great distress. Behaviour therapy applied on a one-to-one (dyadic) basis – and conducted at the clinic – has produced very encouraging results in a wide range of child problems, such as specific phobias, school refusal, social inhibition and elective mutism (Herbert, 1981; Kazdin, 1979).

The second category of problems, involving extremes of physical and verbal aggressiveness, disruptiveness, irresponsibility, non-compliance and poor personal relationships, is far more resistant to traditional clinical-based therapies, be they behavioural or any other. This behaviour syndrome has been referred to as conduct disorder. Youngsters with conduct and delinquent disorders demonstrate a fundamental inability or unwillingness to adhere to the rules and codes of conduct prescribed by society at its various levels. Such failures may be related to the temporary lapse of poorly established learned controls, to the failure to learn these controls in the first place, or to the fact that the behavioural standards a child has absorbed do not coincide with the norms of that section of society which enacts and enforces the rules.

Social learning theorists suggest that children with such serious problems are maladjusted because their early social conditioning has been ineffective. As a consequence, they have failed to negotiate adequately the first stage in the internalization of an adequate conscience. There is an absence of a strong emotional aversion to antisocial acts, a diminished capacity to resist temptation, and a lack of feeling of remorse when harm has been inflicted. The long-term implications of persistent and intense non-compliant, and therefore antisocial, behaviour in children are serious (Herbert, 1978).

Time-span

These matters are mentioned because it is sometimes forgotten by psychologists, when they are being therapists rather than parents in their own right, that training (or re-training) children can be potentially a long-term endeavour. Slowly evolving, complex psychological attributes have to be fostered (for example, learning rules, developing a conscience, resistance to temptation, empathy and self-control). Some of these are internalized quickly (depending on self rather than external reinforcement); with others, parents will have to go on prompting and cajoling, month in and month out, and sometimes year in and year out. Some will remain forever situationally determined. Time scales vary, depending on the age and maturity of the child and the nature of the behavioural task, but parents – going about their business of rearing their offspring – should not (and usually do not) expect the child to acquire and maintain certain lessons without setbacks and repetitions. (This, by the way, has implications for the availability of frequent brief 'booster' sessions.)

The client

If it is accepted that problematic behaviours of childhood occur, in large part, as a function of faulty learning processes, then there is a case for the proposition that problems can most effectively be modified where they occur – by making good the deficits, or by changing the social training of the child and the contingencies supplied by social agents. It must be stressed that behaviour modification is not only about changing the undesirable behaviour of the nominated client – the problem child. It is about altering the behaviour of the persons – parents, teachers and others – who form a significant part of the child's social world. Diagnostic thinking has been influenced greatly by interactional frames of reference, explicit in systems thinking. Thus the unit of attention, particularly in relation to the family, is far more broadly conceived, and the focus of help not prejudged as the neurotic or antisocial child.

The behaviour assessment is based on the concept of a functional relationship with the environment, in which changes in individual behaviour produce change in the environment, and vice-versa. The contemporary causes of problem behaviour may exist in the client's environment or in his or her own thoughts, feelings or bodily processes (organismic variables) and they may exert their influence in several ways. Since abnormal behaviour is learned and maintained in the same way as normal behaviour, it can be treated directly, through the application of social learning principles.

PARENTS AS BEHAVIOUR MODIFIERS

At this point I would like to digress to reflect briefly on child development and the process of learning to become a social being. It is instructive to observe parents and their children at the seaside. There are so many opportunities for disruptive (not to mention deviant) actions on the part of the innovative youngster. There is sand to throw in the faces of brothers and sisters, buckets and spades to fight over, ice-creams to pester for. Then there are the exciting adventures which bring potential danger: floating the rubber boat out to sea, wandering away and getting lost. There are so many rules to learn and obey! Watching mothers (and fathers) at their work as child-rearers, caregivers, trainers, one is impressed by the enormous input, the seemingly endless 'lessons' whereby parents remind, instruct and modify their offsprings' actions. It is clear that the behaviour therapist is likely to suffer from the 'Ooh, I've tried that!' rejoinder every time a strategy for change is suggested. This is the price of using concepts and methods that are on a continuum with their day-to-day child training practices: 'Time out? Ooh, I've tried that'. 'Response-cost? I've tried that; that didn't work', and so on. Of course, parents may not be aware of the small print of learning principles: matters of timing, the need for careful specification, and contingency analysis. It is important for psychologists to remember that most parents, with little or no training – and parenting is in large part a skill – rear their children (with the help of other socializing agents) into socially acceptable and broadly norm-abiding adults; and normality is defined in terms of the social criteria, that is, social standards, that children learn. There seems to be a fair amount of latitude in learning conditions for those children with intact central nervous systems, healthy bodies and relatively unvolcanic temperaments. They acquire an understanding of, and willingness to abide by, society's conventions, despite parental inconsistency, double-binds and ambiguous rules. For them, parental inexperience or poor judgement seem no more than a minor hindrance in the business of growing up.

Available evidence suggests that what is important in childrearing is the general social climate in the home – the attitudes and feelings of the parents, which form a background to the application of specific methods and interactions of child-rearing. For example, the mother does best who does what she and the community to which she belongs believe is right for the child. Feeding and toileting and the like are important elements of the child's daily activities; but it is the social interactions they mediate – the manner in which parents undertake these tasks – that give them significance. It is how the young child is looked after that is crucial; and it is the social and psychological context of the care which matters, rather than its chronology and mechanics (Herbert, 1980a).

Transactional perspective

This raises a further child-rearing issue: the child's response to the world is thought to be more than a simple reaction to the environment; the child is actively engaged in attempts to organize and structure the world. The transactional model stresses the changing character of the environment and of the organism as an active participant in its own development. There are situations in which children are predisposed to problem formation by *handicaps* – temperamental lability, physical and/or mental impairments. A much more predictable and persistent learning environment then becomes essential. The demand characteristics of such children – the high rate, high intensity behaviour of a coercive kind so often associated with handicap – interact with parents' sensitivities and other attributes to produce an environment which is often fraught, unpredictable, and unpersevering.

Parents in circumstances like these may be 'knocked off their tracks' of self-confidence and intuitive spontaneity; because they feel ineffectual they may become thoroughly demoralized and more tentative and inconsistent (*see* case history, Herbert, 1981).

The normal developmental psychology literature is an important (but often neglected) source of useful information for developmental counselling, which should be part of the clinical psychologists' therapeutic armamentarium. The findings on child development, for example, suggest that simplistic 'either–or' schemes aimed at changing the child (for example, at the intra-psychic level) *or* the child's environment (in a stark operant sense) are likely to have limited success. Thomas *et al.* (1968) were repeatedly impressed by their inability to make a direct correlation between environmental influences, such as specific parental attitudes and practices, and the child's psychological development. It would seem that the complex interactions of person and social context make nonsense of the simple classical linear causality which is so pervasive in the literature on child treatment, parent education and preventive work. The high hopes of preventive education have been dashed because of its focus on content rather than on process, on finding techniques and formulae designed to satisfy an abstract principle of good adjustment in the child, rather than providing parents with a broad theoretical framework within which to analyse, and act upon, unique personal and familial dispositions.

There is a particular dilemma for many of the parents of conduct disordered children. The youngsters, in many cases, seem to be arrested at a demanding (egocentric) stage of development – whatever their age. The period between approximately one and three years of age is often a 'sensitive period' with regard to the development (and therefore prevention) of many conduct disorders (Herbert, 1978). They take root because of the inability of parents (for a variety of reasons, emotional or social) to confront their child's coercive behaviour (in some chidren of an extreme nature) in a manner that will launch him into the vital later stages of moral development, and those processes of socialization which have to do with empathy and impulse control.

Internalization

Now, one of the child's major acquisitions on the road to becoming a social being is the development of internal controls over behaviour – the 'internalization' of standards of conduct and morality implied by the term conscience. Put in behavioural terms, a series of actions might be considered to be internalized to the extent that their maintenance has become independent of external outcomes – that is, to the extent that their reinforcing consequences are internally generated, without the support of external events such as rewards and punishments. Norm-abiding behaviour ultimately depends not merely on avoidance of externally imposed consequences, but, more importantly, on the avoidance of noxious stimulation (anxiety/guilt) which has its source within the individual.

The developmental literature provides clear guidelines to supplement our behavioural theory in such cases. There is substantial agreement (Herbert, 1978) about conditions conducive to the acquisition of internalized rule (norm) formation: firm moral demands made by parents upon their offspring; the consistent use of sanctions; techniques of punishment that are psychological rather than physical (that is, methods which signify or threaten withdrawal of love/approval); and an intensive use of induction methods (reasoning and explanations). Aronfreed (1968) demonstrated in a series of developmental studies how parents may have a choice as to whether, and how much, they bring out one or other of the attributes of guilt and resistance to temptation in their children. This will depend primarily on two things: the timing of the sanctions they administer for misconduct and the nature of the explanation they provide when they do so. There is evidence that suggests that punishment which immediately precedes a forbidden act maximizes resistence to temptation and minimzes guilt.

Aronfreed extended his investigations in order to demonstrate the power of 'cognitive structure' in internalizing inhibition. The role played by the child's ability to recall behaviour in representational and symbolic form is of crucial importance. Under natural conditions, punishment is frequently far removed in time from the transgression. A reliable difference appeared between the situation in which the child received the verbal cognitive structure at the same time as punishment and the situation in which the cognitive structure was presented between trials. The latter produced less stable internalization. It would seem that punishment results in anxiety attaching to cognitive representations according to the same temporal gradient in regard to the behaviour itself. A verbalized cognitive structure focusing on the child's intention to transgress produced even stronger suppression than that which made no reference to intention.

There seems to be a subtle interaction between the child's cognitive structuring of situations, his ability to represent to himself punishment contingencies, and the extent of emotional arousal which is associated with his cognitions during the socialization process; his intellectual level, his verbal ability, and his ability to make a cognitive structure of the learning situation are important sources of control. They facilitate control by representing the potential outcomes of his behaviour and by enhancing the internalization of the social rules. Aronfreed has demonstrated that punishment that is above a certain optimal level of intensity produces a state of 'emotionality' in the child which appears to interfere with learning. If discrimination of the punished choice is difficult, intense punishment is actually more likely, subsequently, to lead to transgression.

This finding has clear implications for designers of treatment programmes and for disciplinary practices. A child unable to distinguish what aspect of behaviour is being punished will be unable to exercise control over the outcomes of behaviour. The child is therefore subject to periods of prolonged anxiety and frustration, and will also fail to experience the anxiety reduction associated with non-punished behavioural alternatives and so will not learn them.

THE CHILD TREATMENT RESEARCH UNIT

The Child Treatment Research Unit, at the University of Leicester, adopted the triadic approach in the late sixties in children's residential homes in Birmingham and later in children's natural homes in Leicester. For what, at that time, were thought to be compelling theoretical and practical reasons, but were still largely a matter of conjecture, we set out to evaluate the effectiveness of taking care-staff and parents into a therapeutic alliance, in which they were seen as the main mediators of change. The approach, based upon developmental and social learning theory, has provided encouraging evidence of the ability of parents to help themselves and their problematic children over a wide range of problems, ranging from conduct disorders (Herbert, 1978; Holmes, 1979); developmental disorders such as enuresis and encopresis (Herbert and Iwaniec, 1981); child abuse and failure-to-thrive (Iwaniec, 1983; Iwaniec and Herbert, in press); to maternal rejection (Herbert and Iwaniec, 1977) and mental handicap (Dean *et al.,* 1976).

Methods

The goal of behavioural work in home settings is to develop in the parents an awareness of their own importance in producing and maintaining desirable and undesirable behaviours in their children. Parents are taught to rehearse new strategies of child management, coping with stress and so on. This entails a multifaceted package which depends for its final shape on the behavioural assessment. It might include: differential reinforcement or positive reinforcement (social and sometimes material) of prosocial actions together with removal of reinforcement or application of punishment contingent on antisocial behaviours, timeout from positive reinforcement, response-cost and overcorrection procedures. Incentive systems (token economies) are negotiated and contracted between parents and children, and some are linked to behaviour at school. With the older children and parents (if relevant), we tend to use more cognitively-oriented methods, including self-control training (assertion and relaxation training, desensitization of anger, role-play, behaviour rehearsal), or problem-solving skill training (*see* Herbert, 1981). How do parents cope with these methods? The answer is: 'surprisingly well!'. All parents are informal learning theorists and all are in the business of behaviour modification (that is, changing behaviour). They use various techniques to train, influence and change the child in their care. Among those used are material and psychological rewards, praise and encouragement, giving or withholding love, reproof, corporal and psychological punishment, approval and disapproval, as well as direct instruction, setting an example and providing explanations of rules. Behavioural methods and rationale – if explained simply but in an unpatronizing manner – tend to have face validity for parents.

THE INTERVENTION: PRELIMINARY SCREENING

During the initial interview with the child and both parents (a crucial therapeutic configuration, we have found, in families where there are two parents), we explain some of the major issues generated by a triadic behavioural approach. In all there are 20 assessment and treatment steps (Herbert, 1981). *Table 1* shows the first six steps concerned with the preliminary screening.

Table 1. Preliminary screening

Step 1	Explain yourself and how you work
Step 2	Identify the problems
Step 3a	Construct a problem profile
Step 3b	Define and refine specific target behaviours
Step 4	Discover the desired outcomes
Step 5	Identify the child's assets
Step 6	Establish problem priorities
Step 7	Specify situations

It is demonstrated with in situ demonstrations or role-play how problems are not encapsulated within the child but are contingent upon things he has learned within a social context, including his own actions, and reactions to him. We warn parents that we will require them to do a good deal of 'homework', monitoring the child's (and their own) behaviours along lines that we will teach them.

The baseline phase

Table 2 contains steps 7 to 15, which are worked through with the parents and child – the baseline phase.

Table 2. Baseline phase

Step 8	Assess the extent and severity of the problem
Step 9	Provide client with appropriate recording material
Step 10a	Find out more about the behaviour
Step 10b	Find out how intense the behaviour is
Step 10c	How many problems are being manifested by the child?
Step 10d	Find out the duration of the problem
Step 10e	What sense or meaning is there in the problem behaviour?
Step 11	Assess the contingencies
Step 12	Identify reinforcers
Step 13	Assess organismic variables
Step 14a	Arrive at a diagnostic decision
Step 14b	Formulate objectives
Step 14c	Draw up a verbal agreement or written contract
Step 15	Formulate clinical hypotheses

The analysis is very much (but not exclusively) focused on what is called the 'ABC' sequence. An analysis is made (by ourselves and the parents) of environmental conditions and physical factors leading up to, and immediately preceding the occurrence of the problem behaviour, and those that follow the performance of such behaviour (antecedents/consequences).

Some parents report that the act of recording tense situations provides a cooling-off interlude, time to think. One problem for the experimentalist is that it is difficult to hold some parents to a baseline period. The parents 'get the idea' and wish to initiate their new-found understanding in practical child-management strategies. Parents frequently tell us at the debriefing interviews that the information and the 'insights' they gain from a more rigorous definition (and monitoring) of antisocial and prosocial behaviour mark the beginning of change in their interactions with their child and (for some) a growing sense of competence.

The intervention

After the baseline work we discuss with parents our formulation of the problem; next, a detailed plan is made with the parents for the intervention, which they initiate. It is vital to warn them, if one is not to lose them, that the child is likely to get worse before getting better – the post-extinction burst. The 'machiavellian' child is expert at producing target-behaviour criterion confusion, or slippage. A fairly intensive input at the beginning of a programme providing prompts, cues, moral support, modelling, etc., has proved invaluable in facilitating the work.

Not infrequently we have had to work at several levels, providing *practical* social support, for example, arranging day care or baby-sitting, giving marital counselling, carrying out an individualized programme for a depressed or anxious mother. Imaginative consideration of the meaning of the programme

Table 3. Intervention and termination

Step 16a	Plan your treatment programme
Step 16b	Take into account non-specific therapeutic factors
Step 17	Work out the practicalities of the treatment programme
Step 18	Evaluate the programme
Step 19	Initiate the programme
Step 20	Phase out and terminate treatment

for siblings is essential. Some have become difficult. We explain the programme to them and sometimes involve them in the pay-offs. Criterion slippage is the great danger, as tired mothers adopt the line of least resistance with a child and put him back on an intermittently reinforced schedule for deviant behaviour.

Fading out a programme requires careful planning. It is vital to have selected areas of change which are functional for the child. If the behaviours chosen have no natural reinforcing value for the child, and thus have no adaptive reward and survival functions, we are wasting everybody's time. It is our common experience that successful results have effects that ripple out well beyond the target interactions, in a way that makes for happier family life.

Effectiveness

There is little doubt that parents can be taught to use behavioural methods effectively with their children, and that for many disorders they work (Herbert, 1981). As with the history of systematic desensitization, the main thrust of research is to refine the triadic approach so as to discover the active therapeutic ingredients in what are usually multi-element treatment packages (*see* Horton, 1982). It is necessary to find out the most economical and effective techniques for changing maladaptive behaviours, and to elucidate a coherent theory of practice. The question of why some families fail to respond needs answering. The maintenance of change (temporal generalization) remains a formidable technical problem; so does the difficulty of working in single-parent homes and with parents who enjoy (or suffer) powerful theories/ideologies about child-rearing (Holmes, 1979). We still need to know what range of problems can be tackled by this approach. It is safe to say that it is particularly promising for parents with chronically handicapped children who are likely to need a strategy for coping with novel problems, or at least a succession of teaching tasks, in the future.

An unresolved issue that remains is how best to train parents (*see* O'Dell, 1974). Walder *et al.* (1969) describe three broad approaches to parent training. In the *individual consultation* approach, the parent complaining of specific problems is instructed in how to behave towards the child under various contingencies. Individual instructions can range from enabling parents to carry out simple instructions in contingency management to a full involvement as co-therapists in all aspects of observation, recording, programme planning, and implementation. The level of skill to which parents need to be trained in order to cope effectively with their child's problem is still a matter of debate. Another means of training parents is within *educational groups.* Courses vary in duration, intensity, and structure. Various aids to learning such as lectures, guides, manuals, role-playing, videotape feedback, modelling, discussion, and home exercises have been used. The *controlled learning* environment, another variant of parent training, involves highly structured individual instruction, with the consultant directly shaping or modelling parent-child interactions. Sophisticated signalling and feedback devices are used while the parents work with the child. Some workers have used techniques with each of these three approaches to training, simultaneously or in sequence.

It is imposible to do justice to the many issues involved in one chapter. Fortunately there are reviews and accounts available: for example, Alexander and Parsons (1973), (families of delinquents); Berkowitz and Graziano (1972), (review of parent training); Gambrill (1983), (review of child abuse studies); Griest and Wells (1983), (behavioural family therapy with conduct disorders in children); Glogower and Sloop (1976), (knowledge of general principles versus ad hoc-ery issue): Hemsley *et al.* (1978), (parents of autistic children); Herbert (1981), (a 'how-to-do-it' manual); Johnson and Katz (1973), (agressive behaviours); McAuley (1982), (review); McAuley and McAuley (1977), (a guide to practice); O'Dell (1974), (review); O'Leary and O'Leary (1977), (classroom management); Patterson (1973), (group and individual training); Sajwaj (1973), (difficulties and resistances); Tavormina (1974), (review of parent counselling); Yule and Carr (1980), (work with families of handicapped children).

CONCLUSION

There remain many questions to be answered in an approach which has produced promising results. At present, the Unit, renamed the 'Centre for Behavioural Work with Families' to reflect the 'centre of gravity' of our approach, is researching – *inter alia* – into the use of group and individual parent training and the use of correspondence courses for parents (an elaboration of bibliotherapy); also the effectiveness of self-help parent groups, as vehicles for staying in touch with the ex-clients, providing further input aimed at maintaining the consistency necessary for temporal generalization, and providing booster programmes. Also being examined is the use of home-based interventions out of different agencies, for example, local authority settings, hospitals, schools, etc.

In 1968, Wagner stated that 'if we are to use our manpower in the mental health field with maximum effectiveness, it is necessary for us to put the therapy where the problem is – in the home' (p.454). Children spend some 15,000 hours of their lives at secondary school and the same could be said of many of their problems there. Are they really most effectively dealt with by withdrawing them from the arena in which disruptive actions occur?

By providing non-psychologists with methods and skills to cope with (or prevent) future problems, behavioural work has shifted the focus of therapy toward a preventive model of mental health.

There is strong evidence available that should dispel any tendency to be apprehensive or patronizing about the 'therapeutic' or 'helping' potential of non-professionals – the essential requirement of the triadic approach. For example, Durlak (1979) reviewed 42 studies comparing the effectiveness of professional and paraprofessional therapist/helpers and found that paraprofessionals, overall, achieve clinical outcomes equal to or significantly better than those obtained by professionals.

Such provocative findings have to be treated seriously. Undoubtedly, parents and other non-professionals can be used as effective therapeutic agents. But it must be said from our experience in both natural and residential homes that a behavioural intervention has some very definite limitations which are not apparent in many of the published studies. First, implementation of treatment programmes may require very lengthy casework just to ensure that children *are* reinforced appropriately, records kept and the treatment regime applied consistently. Secondly, the collection of the careful records, which are crucial in behavioural analysis and treatment, may pose real difficulties if parents and child care staff are exhausted, overworked, or if they just do not see any reason for diary keeping. Third, like any therapy, behavioural interventions in individual cases may be of limited value if the wider social system is disruptive (poor housing, poverty, deviant peer group with influence), or if community homes are understaffed. Under these circumstances, the parents or staff may welcome the outside intervention of Child Treatment Research Unit Therapists but there is little that they can do to maximize the programme once the therapists withdraw from so active an involvement in treatment. The assumption that naturally occurring reinforcement for prosocial behaviour will take over is then unlikely to materialize.

This emphasis on the limitations of behavioural intervention is meant to sound a cautionary note, rather than appear pessimistic. Many practitioners may well assume that these well-tried methods can be applied in all settings. The evidence of our cases suggests that there are several significant limitations to such an assertion.

REFERENCES

ACHENBACH, T.M. and EDELBROCK, C.S. (1978) The classification of child psychopathology: A review and analysis of empirical efforts. *Psychological Bulletin,* *85,* 1275–1301.

ALEXANDER, J.F. and PARSONS, N.V. (1973) Short-term behavioural intervention with delinquent families: impact on family process and recidivism. *Journal of Abnormal Psychology, 81,* 219–225.

BERKOWITZ, B.P. and GRAZIANO, A.M. (1972) Parents as behaviour therapists: A review. *Behaviour Research and Therapy, 10,* 297–318.

BURLAND, J.R. and BURLAND, P.M. (1981) S.P.O.T. special programme of training for parents and children. *International Journal of Behavioural Social Work and Abstracts, 1,* 87–108.

DEAN, G., GANNOWAY, K., JAGGER, D., JEHU, D., MORGAN, R.T.T. and TURNER, R.K. (1976) Teaching self-care skills to the mentally handicapped in children's homes. Child Treatment Research Unit Paper No.6. Psychology Department, University of Leicester.

DURLAK, J.A. (1979). Comparative effectiveness of paraprofessional and professional helpers. *Psychological Bulletin, 86,* 80–92.

GAMBRILL, E. (1983). Behavioural intervention with child abuse and neglect. *Progress in Behaviour Modification, Volume 15.* New York: Academic Press.

GRIEST, D.L. and WELLS, K.C. (1983). Behavioural family therapy with conduct disorders in children. *Behaviour Therapy, 14,* 37–53.

GLOWGOWER, F. and SLOOP, E.W. (1976). Two strategies of group training of parents as effective behaviour modifiers. *Behaviour Therapy, 7,* 177–184.

HEMSLEY, R., HOWLIN, P., BERGER, M., HERSOV, L., HOLBROOK, D., RUTTER, M. and YULE, W. (1978) Treating autistic children in a family context. In: M. Rutter and E. Schopler (eds) *Autism: Reappraisal of Concepts and Treatment.* New York: Plenum.

HERBERT, M. (1974) *Emotional Problems of Development in Children.* London: Academic Press.

HERBERT, M. (1978) *Conduct Disorders of Childhood and Adolescence: A Behavioural Approach to Assessment and Treatment.* Chichester: Wiley (*see* Appendix C).

HERBERT, M. (1980a). Socialization for problem resistance. In: P. Feldman and J. Orford (eds) *Psychological Problems: The Social Context.* Chichester: Wiley.

HERBERT, M. Hyperactivity in the clasroom. *Special Education: Forward Trends, 7(2),* 8–11(b).

HERBERT, M. (1981) *Behavioural Treatment of Problem Children: A Practice Manual.* New York: Grune and Stratton/Academic Press.

HERBERT, M. and IWANIEC, D., (1977). Children who are hard to love. *New Society, 40,* 21 April, 109–111.

HERBERT, M. and IWANIEC, D. (1981). Behavioural psychotherapy in natural home settings: An empirical study applied to conduct disordered and incontinent children. *Behavioural Psychotherapy, 9,* 55–76.

HOLMES, A. (1979). The development and evaluation of hyperactive and conduct disordered children. Unpublished PhD thesis, University of Leicester.

HORTON, L. (1982). Comparison of instructional components in behavioural parent training: a review. *Behavioural Counselling Quarterly, 2,* 131–147.

IWANIEC, D. (1983). Social and psychological investigation of the aetiology and management of children who fail to thrive. Unpublished PhD thesis, University of Leicester.

IWANIEC, D. and HERBERT, M. (in press) Social work with failure-to-thrive children and their families. Part 1: Psychological factors; Part 2: Behavioural social work intervention. *The British Journal of Social Work .*

JOHNSON, C.A. and KATZ, C. (1973) Using parents as change agents for children: a review. *Journal of Child Psychology and psychiatry, 14,* 181–200.

KAZDIN, A.E. (1979) Advances in child behaviour therapy: Applications and implications. *American Psychologist, 34(10),* 981–987 (special issue).

McAULEY, R. (1982) Training parents to modify conduct problems in their children. *Journal of Child Psychology and Psychiatry, 23,* 335–342.

McAULEY, R. and McAULEY, P. (1977) *Child Behaviour Problems: An Empirical Approach to Management.* New York: Macmillan.

MORELAND, J,R., SCHWEBEL, A.I., BECK, S., and WELLS, R. (1982) Parents as therapists: A review of the behaviour therapy parent training literature – 1954 to 1981. *Behaviour Modification, 6,* 250–276.

O'DELL, S. (1974) Training parents in behaviour modification: a review. *Psychological Bulletin, 81,* 7, 418–433.

O'LEARY, K.D. and O'LEARY, S.G. (1972) *Classroom Management: The Successful Use of Behaviour Modification.* Oxford: Pergamon.

PATTERSON, G.R. (1973) Reprogramming the families of aggressive boys. In: C. Thoresen (ed.) *Behaviour Modification in Education.* 72nd Yearbook, National Society for the Study of Education.

PATTERSON, G.R. (1975) The coercive child: architect or victim of a coercive system? In: L. Hamerlynck, L.C. Handy and J. Mash (eds) *Behaviour Modification and Families: I: Theory and Research, II: Applications and Developments.* New York: Brunner/Mazel.

REPUCCI, N.D. and SAUNDERS, J.T. (1974) Social psychology of behaviour modification: problems of implementation in natural settings. *American Psychologist, 29,* 649–660.

SAJWAJ, T. (1973) Difficulties in the use of behavioural techniques by parents in changing child behaviour: guides to success. *Journal of Nervous and Mental Disease, 156,* 395–403.

TAVORMINA, J.B. (1974) Basic models of parent counselling: a critical review. *Psychological Bulletin, 81,* 827–835.

THOMAS, A., CHESS, S. and BIRCH, H.G. (1968) *Temperament and Behaviour Disorders in Children.* London: University of London Press.

WAGNER, M.K. (1968). Parent therapists: An operant conditioning method. *Mental Hygiene, 52,* 452–455.

WALDER, L.O., COHEN, S.I., BREISTER, D.E., DARTON, P., HIRSCH, I., and LEIBOWITZ, J. Teaching behavioural principles to parents of disturbed children. In: B. Guerney Jr (ed.) *Psychotherapeutic Agents: New Roles for Non-Professionals, Parents and Teachers.* New York: Holt, Rinehart and Winston.

YULE, W. and CARR, J. (1980) *Behaviour Modification for the Mentally Handicapped.* London: Croom Helm.

QUALITY OF CARE AND STAFF PRACTICES IN LONG-STAY SETTINGS

Anthony Lavender

In recent years there has been a trend towards providing long-term care in small community-based units rather than in large institutions (Bennett and Morris, 1983). There is, however, a growing body of evidence which suggests that the staff practices that were characteristic of the large institution can be either simply transplanted to the new location, or re-emerge later, to the detriment of the quality of care provided (Apte, 1968; Lamb, 1982). There is thus a growing need for clinicians to intervene to improve the quality of care offered in long-stay settings not only in hospital, but in the community as well. This chapter intends to provide a method of embarking on this task of improving the quality of care.

As there is a good deal of confusion about the concept of 'quality of care' (Shepherd, 1984) it is important to begin by offering some explanation for this confusion with regard to staff practices. The difficulty with quality of care is that different clinicians base their judgements about what constitutes 'quality care' on different theoretical models. (Why clinicians adopt a particular theoretical model or models is not the subject of this chapter, but is likely to be the result of such factors as training, personality and perceived effectiveness of particular practices.) For example, from a purely behavioural perspective the most crucial component in quality of care is likely to be the reinforcement contingencies operating in the environment (Whatmore *et al.,* 1975). From a psychoanalytic perspective it might be the level of understanding and depth of the emotional relationships between staff and patients (Altschul, 1972). From a normalization perspective, the extent to which the relationships and practices resemble those observed in 'normal' life (Wolfensberger, 1982) would be crucial, whilst from a humanistic perspective it would perhaps be the extent to which staff show empathy, warmth and genuineness (Rogers, 1951). This clearly is not an exhaustive list of theoretical models (for example, the social learning and organic have been omitted), but serves to demonstrate why 'quality of care' can mean different things to different clinicians, and thus why the concept remains somewhat confused.

70

The purpose of this chapter is not, however, to consider the numerous staff practices from differing theoretical positions. Rather, the purpose is to identify the staff practices which from a number of theoretical positions appear characteristic of high quality settings, and to propose a practical method by which clinicians might attempt to improve the quality of care in long-stay settings. This method has parellels with individual therapy in that it can be divided into a number of phases. Firstly, the assessment phase, where the clinician assesses the quality of the setting; secondly, an intervention phase, where attempts are made to change the staff practices in the setting; and thirdly, an evaluation phase, where the effectiveness of that intervention is evaluated in terms of both the effect on practice and residents' behaviour. It is important to consider each of these phases in more detail.

ASSESSMENT PHASE

In describing this phase it is important to identify the various categories of staff practice. These include:
1. Treatment practices, which can broadly be divided into somatic and psychological practices.
2. Community contact practices; that is, the extent to which clients have contact with people within the community and use community facilities.
3. Client management practices.
4. The nature (quantity and quality) of the interactions between staff and clients.

Within this brief chapter it is not possible to focus on all categories of practice, so an attempt will be made to focus on the first three categories. To some extent, the nature of the interactions will be considered within the client management category, but a fuller description can be found in Altschul (1972) and Durward and Whatmore (1976). Additionally, any assessment should consider the resources – human and physical environment – component, although it will not be examined here.

1. Treatment practices

Treatment practices in long-stay settings can be divided into two broad categories, somatic practices (where the interventions are aimed directly at the individual physiological state and include chemotherapy, electrotherapy and psychosurgery), and psychological practices (where the intervention is aimed at the individual psychological condition without directly altering physiology). Such interventions include inidividual and group psychotherapy, various forms of behaviour therapy, reality orientation, and the vast majority of practices that Watts and Bennett (1983a) have recently called rehabilitation practice. This distinction, unfortunately, rests on the mind–body distinction and it is undoubtedly true that a number of practices, such as physiotherapy, fall between the two, although here the division is useful on pragmatic grounds.

Few researchers have developed methods of assessing treatment practices in long-stay settings. Wing and Brown (1970) developed a measure of somatic practices, in terms of the quantity of medication used, in their comparative study of the practices in three psychiatric hospitals. Attempts to measure psychological practice have been less concerned with objective assessments than with attitudes of staff to practices based on particular therapeutic ideologies (Strauss *et al.*, 1964; Caine and Smail, 1966). An important task for the clinical psychologist working in a long-stay setting is to assess psychological practices, and it is helpful in doing this to break them down into a number of sub-categories. The following categorization system is not based on a particlar therapeutic ideology, but on the skills and knowledge necessary for the client to function in the community:

Self-care training. Activities designed to improve clients' ability to wash, dress, eat, use the toilet, etc.
Domestic skills training. Activities designed to improve client's ability to cook, clean, launder, budget etc.
Socialization training. Activities designed to improve or maintain clients' interpersonal relationships.
Occupation/constructive leisure training. Activities designed to improve or maintain occupational or constructure leisure time skills.
Community facility training. Activities designed to improve or maintain clients' ability to use community facilities, such as public transport, public entertainment and financial, health and social services.
Cognitive skills training. Activities designed to teach or maintain a client's literacy and numeracy skills, and knowledge of certain basic personal and situational information.

This system can be used as the basis for an assessment procedure which enables the clinician to identify the assets and deficits in the setting's psychological practices. Such an approach has been employed by Lavender (1984), using a questionnaire measure, and indicated, within a hospital setting, a tendency to concentrate on self-care training to the detriment of other areas of training, such as community facility and cognitive skills training.

2. Community contact practices

Long-stay settings, particularly for the psychiatrically disturbed, provide a place of asylum away from the community and family pressures. In the short term, this can have beneficial effects, but as time passes the client becomes increasingly estranged from the community. Numerous writers have pointed to the importance of lack of community contact in the process of institutionalization (Barton, 1956; Goffman, 1961; Sommer and Osmond, 1973). The lack of community contact can result in the loss of relatives and friends in the community, and of the knowledge and skills necessary for social interaction or for the use of community facilities.

A number of researchers have attempted to measure community contact: Morris (1969) and Raynes *et al.,* (1979), in settings for the mentally handicapped, and Wing and Brown (1970), Palmer and McGuire (1973), Wykes *et al.,* (1982) and Lavender (1984), in psychiatric settings. From this work it is possible to identify the following sub-categories of community contact:

CONTACTS TO THE COMMUNITY. Contacts by the client from the setting to the community:
   Indirect contacts. Letters, telephone calls, telegrams.
   Direct contacts. Visits to friends, relatives, volunteers, other professionals and use of public amenities (shops, public transport, cafes, pubs, church, banks, cinema, health services, social services, DHSS, etc).
CONTACTS FROM THE COMMUNITY. Contacts by the client from the setting to the community:
   Indirect contacts (as above).
   Direct contacts. From relatives, friends, volunteers, and the professionals.

Using this system it is possible to assess the extent to which the setting is helping its clients to become involved with the community, and thereby identify the unit's assets and deficits.

3. Client management practices

The client management practices observed in large institutions have developed over many years, about which Scull (1979) and Bennett (1983) have provided valuable historical accounts. The importance of these management practices have been recognized since the times of Tuke (1813) and Connolly (1856). More recently, Barton (1956) cites the loss of personal possessions and events in the creation of 'Institutional Neurosis'. Goffman (1961) in his rich description of the 'Underlife of a Public Institution' documents the practices which appeared to shape the behaviour of inmates (institutionalize them) and noted that of particular importance was the removal of autonomy, whereby actions previously under the control of inmates came under the control of staff.

More attempts have been made to assess client management practices than either of the two previous categories of practice. These have used one of three approaches:

1. An attitudinal approach which assumes that the management practices adopted are related to the attitudes of staff and that by assessing staff attitudes it is possible to assess the 'social environment' (Cohen and Streuning, 1962 , 1963; Stanton and Schwartz, 1954).
2. An ecological approach which attempts to assess the 'social environment' by assessing staff perceptions about particular aspects of ward life (Jackson, 1969; Moos, 1974).
3. An objective measurement approach which attempts to assess ward practices by direct observation or by asking staff specific detailed questions about those practices.

The most scientifically rigorous and clinically useful assessment methods have used the objective assessment approach. An example of this is the work of Wing and Brown (1970) who, in comparing the social environments of three British psychiatric hospitals, developed measures of Patients' Personal Possessions and Ward Restrictiveness and found important differences between the hospitals. Wykes *et al.* (1982) further developed these measures to produce a Hostel-Hospital Practice Profile which measured the following aspects of the social environment: restrictions on activity, residents' possessions, involvement of residents in meals, health and hygiene, and restrictions on use of and activity in the resident's own room. Similarly, in the field of mental handicap King *et al.* (1971) in their study of 26 institutions for mentally handicapped children developed a Child Management Scale. This measured four aspects of the social environment: rigid routines, block treatment, depersonalization, and social distance. These scales were later revised by Raynes *et al.* (1979), essentially covering the same areas, only in a single scale, who found considerable variation in the patterns of care in the living units of three institutions for the mentally handicapped in America. Shepherd and Richardson (1979a) adapted these scales for use in psychiatric day centres and again found the measures sensitive to differences in the social environments of a number of day centres.

In order to draw this work together and provide the clinician with a framework with which to assess the client management practices, it is useful to identify three dimensions of practice:

Autonomy–restrictiveness. The extent to which clients have real choice about their activities, such as when they rise, go to bed, wash, bath, engage in leisure activities, leave the setting, have meals and receive visitors.
Personalization–depersonalization. The extent to which clients have their own possessions (such as clothing, toiletries, writing paper, pens, scissors, purse, money and other leisure possessions), privacy (bath and toilet

alone, dress and undress in private, personalize their bed and work space), and participate in personal events such as birthdays and 'family' celebrations.

Staff/client integration–segregation. The extent to which the worlds of staff and client are separated as, for example, in the wearing of uniforms, the separation of staff and clients at meals, the distinction between staff and patient cutlery and crockery and the differential use of space within the setting (Ittelson *et al.,* 1970; Polsky and Chance, 1979) during activities such as games, watching TV and listening to the radio. Perhaps less easily observable is the tendency for staff to explain clients' behaviour in ways different from those they would use to explain their own actions. For example, 'he has aggressive outbursts' rather than 'he got angry because ...'.

The identification of these dimensions of practice is intended to clarify what particular aspects of practice to assess in long-stay units, and thus to enable the clinician to identify the specific assets and deficits in the settings management practices. For example, it has been found in the wards of some psychiatric hospitals that although the majority of patients have their own clothes, very few have leisure possessions of their own.

Summary

Much has been written about the difficulty of generalizing changes in clients' behaviour from particluar treatment situations to everyday settings (Shepherd 1977). It is now evident that the clinician, in order to encourage generalization, needs not only to introduce treatment practices but also to create social contexts which allow clients to practice and develop new behaviour. Thus, it often becomes crucial to introduce changes in community contact and client management practices to create such a context in which residents' functioning can be maximized. As Bennett (1978) clearly puts it, rehabilitation is helping 'the disabled person to make best use of his residual abilities in order to function at an optimum level in as normal a social context as possible.'

INTERVENTION PHASE

Following the assessment procedure outlined above, it will become clear that the introduction or change of certain practices would improve the quality of care provided. It is at this point, when attempting to introduce change, that many clinicians have come to grief. Georgiades and Phillimore (1975) have described how institutions have a tendency 'to eat hero innovators for breakfast' and Broome (1979) provides documentary evidence for their case. Milne (in press) similarly demonstrates how nurses who attended a behavioural training course showed good acquisition of knowledge and skills during and after the course, but a poor outcome in terms of the proportion of nurses able to put those skills into practice on returning to the ward. Thus, the major purpose of this chapter is not solely to recommend the adoption of particular forms of practice but to provide the clinician with some understanding and help with the intervention process. Again, it is perhaps useful to draw the parallel with individual therapy, with the intervention process paralleling the therapeutic process. In therapy, it is necessary to establish a therapeutic alliance and develop an intervention strategy which includes choosing appropriate intervention and identifying and resolving the sources of resistance to that intervention. Each of these components in the intervention process will be examined with special reference to the role of the clinical psychologist in long-term care settings.

1. The therapeutic/intervention alliance

The importance of establishing a therapeutic alliance has been described by others in terms of the creation of a cohesive staff group (Georgiades and Phillimore, 1975), and the management of the staff team (Watts and Bennett, 1983b). For clinical psychologists to achieve this, it is important to recognize that they have no clear position in the unit's professional hierarchy and as a result have little institutionalized authority. As Georgiades and Phillimore point out, their major way to gain credibilty and influence is through knowledge and expertise. It should, however, be added that it is also important to know where your knowledge and expertise ends and where the knowledge of others in the staff team begins. Admitting that you 'don't know' can be as useful as demonstrating your knowledge in staff meetings. (Fountains of knowledge have a tendency to make everybody else dry up.) Thus, acknowledging the contribution of others and, as Shepherd (1984) stresses, the ability to compromise and carefully assess the feasibility of suggested changes are important in the establishment and maintenance of a therapeutic alliance, and a staff group with a vested interest in change.

The creation of this therapeutic alliance is not something that can be completed and then forgotten. Rather, its maintenance is a continual part of the intervention process. It is suggested that the clinician approach the staff team bearing in mind the following guidelines, and that these will help in the establishment and maintenance of the therapeutic alliance.

1. Recognize your own level of authority and the nature of your influence on staff.
2. Remember that changes are slow and likely to occur after months or rather years rather than weeks (Towell and Dartington, 1976). This is particularly true when the change involves a fundamental reorganization of the setting's practices, such as the introduction of a key worker system as suggested by Watts and Bennett (1983b).

3. Allow a role in the decision making regarding a change to those who will be involved in its implementation (Shepherd, 1984).
4. Facilitate the development of more than one innovator in the team.

2. Choice of intervention

A clinician's choice of which practices to introduce or change is often dependent on the particular theoretical model they favour, as was outlined at the beginning of the chapter. It is not possible to examine how different practices relate to each theoretical model and, indeed, it would perhaps be better to develop a separate body of knowledge concerned with the theory and practice of rehabilitation, as attempted by Watts and Bennett (1983a). However, when deciding which practices to introduce it is important to consider the emprical evidence evaluating the effects of practices on residents' functioning. Here it is possible to review only briefly the major studies relating to each area of staff practice included in this chapter.

The most extensively and rigorously researched treatment practices in long-stay settings are those associated with the social learning/token economy approach. The most impressive comparative evaluations include those of Hall *et al.* (1977) and Paul and Lentz (1977). The latter study was the most comprehensive, and indicated that the social learning approach was more effective than either a therapeutic milieu or a traditional ward in improving patients' functioning. The problem with such large scale studies is that they often fail to indicate which particular practices are crucial. This may be revealed better by smaller-scale investigations of individual staff practices. The work on the effectiveness of social skills training (Shepherd, 1977) illustrates this point, where it was found that although patients change within sessions, this does not generalize to everyday settings unless special measures are taken to ensure that this occurs (Shepherd and Richardson, 1979b). For a more comprehensive review of the effects of psychological treatment practices, readers are referred to Watts and Bennett's (1983a,b) recent book.

The empirical evidence concerning the effects of community contact and client management practices comes from correlational studies (Wing and Brown, 1970; Raynes *et al.,* 1979; Segal and Moyles, 1981), rather than longitudinal studies. Some longitudinal studies have been carried out evaluating the effects of particular practices, such as nurses wearing everyday clothes, (Newnes, 1981; Lavender, 1984) but these are rare. At present, the clinician can only by guided by the correlational work as to what practices appear worthy of change and further evaluation.

In summary, the lack of empirical work in all aspects of practice demonstrates that it is still far from clear which are the best practices to adopt. As Watts and Bennett (1983a) write, there is no area of rehabilitation in which a substantial development of research is not needed.

3. Resistance to change

Georgiades and Phillimore (1975) in their series of guidelines to innovators recommend following the path of 'least resistance' when introducing change. This involves choosing a 'healthy' part of the system, where the majority of staff involved in implementing and authorizing the change are in favour of it (Towell and Dartington, 1976). This easy path to change is, unfortunately, rarely found, and the literature abounds with reports of fallen innovators (Georgiades and Phillimore, 1975; Broome, 1979). Thus, in introducing changes in staff practices, resistance to change usually occurs, and it is therefore crucial to develop a strategy for dealing with resistance. The strategy described is based on an understanding of the more important sources of resistance.

Within the institutional change literature, Davis and Salasin (1975) and Shepherd (1984) recommend the adoption of a problem-solving model when trying to implement changes. This is particularly useful when dealing with the resistance to change in long-stay settings. The model involves four stages:
1. Identifying the problems (by generating a list of reasons why a particular practice cannot be adopted with staff);
2. Developing strategies to overcome them;
3. Implementing the strategies;
4. Evaluating these strategies in terms of whether change occurs.

The effects of adopting this model are to make the nature of the resistance (problem) clear, and thus enable staff to make a proper evaluation about whether it can be overcome. Not all resistance can be overcome, and indeed, it is an important 'clinical skill' to be able to judge when an identified but apparently unresolvable problem hides a resolvable but painful source of resistance. For example, after abandoning the distinction between staff and patient crockery on a ward and resolving a number of problems, a number of staff persisted in the segregated practice. At a staff meeting numerous objections were raised until apparently the 'real' reason emerged, namely two patients were drinking urine from cups. Once the problem was identified the patient's key workers were able to devise programmes which resolved this problem, and after a somewhat prolonged period when no urine drinking was observed the distinction was finally abandoned. At this stage, rather than citing more examples, it is helpful to consider briefly the major problems (sources of resistance) that emerge when introducing change, and how they might be overcome.

Staffing levels. Low staffing levels are probably the most frequently cited reason for not adopting a change. It is important for the staff team to become clear *exactly* why low staffing levels prevent the adoption of a particular practice and to see whether more effective use of staff would make the change possible. There is some evidence that low staffing prohibits the development of active rehabilitation programmes and community contact (Sutton, 1981; Lavender, 1984), although it does not effect the nature of management practices (King *et al.,* 1971; Lavender 1984).

Lack of staff knowledge and skills. Deficiencies in staff knowledge about why certain practices provide a better quality of care, and lack of the skills needed to carry out new practices are factors that underlie much resistance. They are accentuated by the fact that many long-stay settings are closed systems (Bridger, 1980), receiving little information from outside. An important task for psychologists can be to open the system, and this is best achieved by helping staff to arrange attendance on outside courses, to visit settings known to provide a high quality of care, and to introduce and teach new skills (Milne, in press).

Lack of patient change. The relative lack of slowness of patient change amongst long-term disabled clients has frequently been noted (Woods and Cullen, 1983; Bennett and Morris, 1983), and this can result in staff considering that it is unimportant which practices are adopted because 'nothing works'. Woods and Cullen (1983) have pointed out how lack of observable success results in staff behaviour not being effectively reinforced, even though client improvement may be occurring at a slow rate. The challenge is to devise sensitive measures of behaviour change and develop systems of monitoring and feedback to provide staff with the necessary reward. Sometimes, maintaining the clients' present level of functioning and preventing deterioration deserves to be regarded as a 'success'. Providing staff with encouragement and feedback after adopting new practices has been shown to maintain those practices by Stoffelmeyer *et al.* (1979).

Relative ease of providing custodial care. Fowlkes (1975) points out that it is easier for hospital staff to provide custodial than any other form of care. Individual programmes, community contact, and client oriented management practices designed to encourage patients' independence involve staff in a more varied and active role (Ramsden, 1980). Staff are not always willing to take on a more active role, and if this is the case it can lead to great difficulty in identifying the source of resistance. Clements (1979) resolved this problem by imposing new practices via the hospital management hierarchy. Occasionally, it may be possible for change to occur only if new staff are introduced. It should be stressed that this is also the easiest reason for the innovator to leap to in explaining the failure of change, but in the author's experience this is rarely the case.

Nature of staff–client relationships. Changing staff practices in the ways outlined results in a change in the nature of staff's relationships with clients.

Quite simply, staff become more personally involved than under custodial regimes, and this often introduces a series of previously avoided conflicts. For example, as direct care staff take more responsibility for individual patient programmes, they can become angry and frustrated with the patient if there is no improvement. If staff are not helped to cope with these feelings they may try to avoid such conflict-laden situations. Other emotional conflicts concerned with dependence and sexuality are also likely to emerge and are discussed in more detail by Menzies (1959) and Rosenberg (1970). Staff groups, if skilfully handled, are one way of dealing with these issues.

In summary, it is clearly not possible to test general hypotheses about all sources of resistance to change, or, indeed, all solutions to them, as these to a large extent will be dependent on the particular setting. However, the problem-solving model provides an approach to dealing with resistance to change and tackling the difficulties when old practices re-emerge.

EVALUATION PHASE

It is perhaps a mistake to have the evaluation phase at the end of the chapter as it needs to be considered from the start of the intervention. Indeed, the need for further evaluation has been continually stressed, and often the clinical psychologist is the person in the staff team most able to carry this out. Long-stay settings provide particularly good places in which to carry out research, in that they offer stable environments in terms of patient and staff populations and physical and social conditions. This makes them ideal settings in which to evaluate changes in the effects of practices, as demonstrated by Lavender (1984) in a study of the effects of nurses adopting everyday clothes in preference to uniforms. Given this, it is somewhat surprising that research is so rarely carried out in such settings (Watts and Bennett, 1983a).

In recent years there has been a greater demand from government for psychiatric services to monitor their standards of treatment and care (for example, DHSS, 1979). Lavender (1984) in following up these recommendations devised a series of questionnaires (four model standard questionnaires) to monitor the standards of treatment and care in the long-stay wards of a psychiatric hospital. The information collected was fed back to the wards, using a controlled design, in the form of a series of specific recommendations. The re-assessment of practices nine months later revealed a significant overall improvement in practices. For one questionnaire this was clearly the result of feedback, whilst for the remaining questionnaires it provided the most likely explanation of the improvement. A number of writers have suggested using feedback from surveys to generate change (Davis and Salasin, 1975; Prue *et al.*, 1980), but few appear to have attempted such investigations.

Three potential kinds of evaluative research have been suggested by this chapter:

1. The evaluation of the effects of practices on clients' behaviour using longitudinal designs;

2. The investigation of the process of change within long-stay settings;

3. The evaluation of particular strategies of change in modifying or introducing new practices.

Distinguishing these approaches may stimulate further research in an important and neglected area.

REFERENCES

ALTSCHUL, A.T. (1972) *Patient–Nurse Interaction: A Study of Interaction Patterns in Acute Psychiatric Wards.* London: Churchill Livingstone.
APTE, R.G. (1968) *Halfway Houses* (Occasional papers on social administration, No. 27). London: Bell.
BARTON, R. (1956) *Institutional Neurosis.* Bristol: Wright.
BENNETT, D.H. (1978) Social forms of psychiatric treatment. In: J.K. Wing (ed.) *Schizophrenia: Towards a New Synthesis.* London: Academic Press.
BENNETT, D.H. (1983) The historical development of rehabilitation services. In: F.N. Watts and D.H. Bennett (eds) *Theory and Practice of Psychiatric Rehabilitation.* Chichester: Wiley.
BENNETT, D.H. and MORRIS I. (1983) Deinstitutionalization in the United Kingdom. *British Journal of Mental Health, 11,* 5–23.
BRIDGER, H. (1980) *The implication of ecological change on groups, institution and communities* – reviewing a therapeutic community experience with open-system thinking. Proceedings of the VII International Congress of Group Psychotherapy, Copenhagen.
BROOME. A.K. (1979) Setting targets for institutional care. Paper given at 1979 Annual Conference of The British Psychological Society, Nottingham University.
CAINE, T.M. and SMAIL, D.J. (1966) Attitudes to treatment of medical staff in therapeutic communities. *British Journal of Medical Psychology, 39,* 329–334.
CLEMENTS, J. (1979) Behaviour analysis and social problems in mental handicap. *Behavioural Analysis and Modification, 3,* 21–31.
COHEN, J. and STREUNING, E.L. (1962) Opinions about mental illness in the personnel of two large mental hospitals. *Journal of Abnormal and Social Psychology, 64(5),* 349–360.
COHEN, J. and STREUNING, E.L. (1963) Opinions about mental illness: mental illness occupational profiles and profile clusters. *Psychological Reports, 12,* 111–124.
CONNOLLY, J. (1856) *The Treatment of the Insane without Mechanical Restraints.* London.
DAVIS, H.R. and SELASIN, S.E. (1975) The utilisation of evaluation. In: E.L. Streuning and M. Guttentag (eds.) *Handbook of Evaluation Research, Volume 1.* Beverley Hills, Ca.: Sage.

DEPARTMENT OF HEALTH AND SOCIAL SECURITY (1979) *Organisation and Management Problems of Mental Illness Hospitals: Report of a Working Group* (Nodder Report). London: DHSS.

DURWARD, L. and WHATMORE, R. (1976) Testing measures of the quality of residential care: A pilot study. *Behaviour Research and Therapy, 14,* 149–157.

FOWLKES, M.R. (1975) Business as usual at the state mental hospital. *Psychiatry, 38,* 55–64.

GEORGIADES, N.J. and PHILLIMORE, L. (1975) The myth of the hero innovator and alternative strategies for organisational change. In: C.C. Kiernan and F.D. Woodford (eds) *Behaviour Modification with the Severely Retarded.* Amsterdam: Associated Scientific Publishers.

GOFFMAN, E. (1961) *Asylum: Essays on the Social Situation of Mental Patients and Other Inmates.* London: Penguin.

HALL, J.N., BAKER, R.D. and HUTCHINSON, K. (1977) A controlled evaluation of token economy procedures with chronic schizophrenia patients. *Behaviour Research and Therapy, 15,* 261– 283.

ITTELSON, W.H., RIVLIN, L.G. and PROHANSKY, H.M. (1970) The environmental psychology of a psychiatric ward. In: H.M. Prohansky, W.H. Ittelson and L.G. Rivlin (eds) *Environmental Psychology: Man and His Physical Setting.* New York: Holt, Reinhart and Winston.

JACKSON, J.M. (1969) Factors of the treatment environment. *Archives of General Psychiatry, 21,* 39–45.

KING, R.D., RAYNES, N.V. and TIZARD, J. (1971) *Patterns of Residential Care.* London: Routledge, Keegan and Paul.

LAMB, H.R. (1982) *Treating the Long Term Mentally Ill.* New York: Jossey Bass.

LAVENDER, A. (1984) Evaluation and change in settings for the long term psychologically handicapped. PhD Thesis submitted for examination, University of London, King's College Hospital Medical School.

MENZIES, I.E. (1959) Case study in the functioning of a social system as a defence against anxiety. *Human Relations, 12,* 95–121.

MILNE, D.L. (in press) The development and evaluation of a structured format introduction to behaviour therapy for psychiatric nurses. *British Journal of Clinical Psychology, 23 .*

MORRIS, P. (1969) *Put Away: A Sociological Study of Institutions for the Mentally Retarded.* London: Routledge, Keegan and Paul.

MOOS, R.H. (1974) *Evaluating Treatment Environment: A Social Ecological Approach.* New York: John Wiley.

NEWNES, L. (1981) Black stockings and frilly caps? *Nursing Mirror,* October, 28–30.

PALMER, J. and MCGUIRE, F.L. (1973) The use of unobstructive measures in mental health research. *Journal of Consulting and Clinical Psychology, 40,* 431–436.

PAUL, G.L. and LENTZ, R. (1977) *Psychological Treatment of Chronic Mental Patients.* Cambridge, Mass.: Harvard University Press.

POLSKY, R.H. and CHANCE, M.R.A. (1979) An ethological perspective on social behaviour in long stay hospitalised psychiatric patients. *Journal of Nervous and Mental Diseases, 167,* 658–668.

PRUE, D.M., KRAPEL. J.E., NOAH, J.C., CANNON, S. and MALEY, R.F. (1980) Managing the treatment activities of state mental hospital staff. *Journal of Organisational Behavioural Management, 2,* 165–181.

RAMSDEN, A. (1980) The role of the nurse: a hospital rehabilitation unit. In: J.K. Wing and B. Morris (eds) *Handbook of Psychiatric Rehabilitation Practice.* Oxford: Oxford Medical Publications.

RAYNES, N.V., PRATT, M.W. and ROSES, S. (1979) *Organisational Structure and the Care of the Mentally Retarded.* London: Croom Helm.

ROGERS, C.R. (1951) *Client Centred Therapy: its Current Practice, Implications and Theory.* Boston: Houghton Mifflin.

ROSENBERG, S.D. (1970) The hospital culture as a collective defense. *Psychiatry, 33,* 21–38.

SCULL, A.T. (1979) *Museums of Madness: The Social Organisation of Insanity in Nineteenth Century England.* Harmondsworth: Penguin Books.

SEGAL, S.P. and MOYLES, E.W. (1981) Management style and insititutional dependency in sheltered care. *Social Psychiatry, 14,* 159–165.

SHEPHERD, G.W. (1977) Social skills training and the generalisation problem. *Behaviour Therapy, 8,* 100–109.

SHEPHERD, G.W. (1984) *Institutional Care and Rehabilitation.* London: Longman.

SHEPHERD, G.W. and RICHARDSON, A. (1979a) Organisation and interaction in psychiatric day centres. *Psychological Medicine, 9,* 573–579.

SHEPHERD, G.W. and RICHARDSON, A. (1979b) Social skills and beyond environment for the care of chronic problems. *Behavioural Psychotherapy, 7,* 31–38.

SOMMER, R. and OSMOND, H. (1973) Symptoms of institutional care. *Social Problems, 8,* 254–263.

STANTON, A.H. and SCHWARTZ, M.S. (1954) *The Mental Hospital.* New York: Basic Books.

STOFFELMAYR, B.E., LINDSAY, W. and TAYLOR, V. (1979) Maintenance of staff behaviour. *Behaviour Research and Therapy, 17,* 271– 273.

STRAUSS, A.M., SCHATZMAN, L., BUCHER, R., EHRLICH, D. and SAB-ASKIN, M. (1964) *Psychiatric Ideologies and Institutions.* New York: Free Press, Glencoe.

SUTTON, G. (1981) The role of the nurse. The organisation and administration of nursing services for long stay patients. In: J.K. Wing and B. Morris (eds) *Handbook of Psychiatric Rehabilitation Practice.* Oxford: Oxford University Press.

TOWELL, D. and DARTINGTON, T. (1976) Encouraging innovations in hospital care. *Journal of Advanced Nursing, 1,* 391–398.

TUKE, S. (1813) *A Description of the York Retreat.* York.

WATTS, F.N. and BENNETT, D.H. (1983a) Introduction: The concept of rehabilitation. In: F.N. Watts and D.H. Bennett (eds) *Handbook of Psychiatric Rehabilitation Practice.* Chichester: Wiley.

WATTS, F.N. and BENNETT, D.H. (1983b) Management of the staff team. In: F.N. Watts and D.H. Bennett (eds) *Handbook of Psychiatric Rehabilitation Practice.* Chichester: Wiley.

WHATMORE, R., DURWARD, L. and KUSHLICK, A. (1975) Measuring the quality of residential care. *Behaviour Research and Therapy, 13,* 227–236.

WING, J.K. and BROWN, G.W. (1970) *Institutionalism and Schizophrenia.* Cambridge: Cambridge University Press.

WOLFENSBERGER, W. (1982) *The Principles of Normalisation in Human Services.* Toronto: National Institute of Mental Retardation/ Leonard-Crawford.

WOODS, P.A. and CULLEN, C. (1983) Determinants of staff behaviour in long term care. *Behavioural Psychotherapy, 11,* 4–17.

WYKES, T., STURT, E. and GREER, C. (1982) Practices of day and residential units in relation to social behaviour of residents. In: J.K. Wing (ed.) *Long Term Community Care Experience in a London Borough* (Psychological Medicine, Mongraph Supplement 2). Cambridge: Cambridge University Press.

WORKING WITH GROUPS OF MENTALLY HANDICAPPED ADULTS

Chris Cullen

It is often claimed that teaching individually, on a one-to-one basis, is more effective than teaching in groups. This view also holds for most other aspects of the care of mentally handicapped people, so that a general maxim has become 'small is beautiful'. While it may be generally true that there are advantages in dealing with people on an individual basis, and disadvantages to having them in groups, there are dangers in adopting a simple slogan or maxim as the major determinant of service delivery. In particular, there are complexities in social situations which make it highly unlikely that one arrangement will be the best for all desirable outcomes. It could be, for example, that a group of mentally handicapped people would make more progress if taught as a group rather than as individuals if the group teacher had a good grasp of the technology of teaching, and teachers in a 'one-to-one' setting were singularly inefficient.

Unfortunately, though, it is not usually the effectiveness of procedures which determines which system of service delivery will be used (Stolz, 1981). Other factors tend to be more powerful, and among these are economic and practical considerations. There are not enough staff to help mentally handicapped people on a one-to-one basis, nor enough resources to recruit and train extra staff. Attention has turned in recent years, therefore, to ways of helping groups of handicapped people with relatively few staff. The purpose of this chapter is to review some of these methods and to identify issues which may be relevant to that successful implementation. This will not be a comprehensive review. Instead, I want to choose a few examples which allow consideration of important variables of general interest. Much of the work described here is still in progress, and full results will be available in the near future, but the state of the field is such that there is relatively little already published which addresses the issues raised here.

An important initial consideration when working with a group of people is to ask what the group is for. Is the intention that people will be functioning *in* a group or *as* a group? The distinction is crucial, since it determines what

84

procedures and outcomes should occur. In the former (by far the most common), one is usually aiming to help an individual to achieve particular individual goals whilst in a setting where there are other people. In the latter, it is the group which is to achieve, with the achievement of an individual being closely related to the presence of other people (for example, learning how to co-operate on a task).

MENTALLY HANDICAPPED PEOPLE IN A GROUP

Room mangement and activity period procedures

In the early 1970s the Living Environments Group of the University of Kansas, under the direction of Todd R. Risley, were conducting research into ways of encouraging groups of people, such as the elderly residents of nursing homes, to participate in activities. In 1976, Jan Porterfield, who had worked with Todd Risley in Kansas, came to Britain to join Roger Blunden at the Mental Handicap in Wales Applied Research Unit, based in Cardiff. She initiated a series of studies, based on the Kansas approach, atempting to increase the amount of 'engagement' during specified activity hours. The approach involves the designation of one person as a room manager, and it has since become known as the 'room management procedure'. The dramatic and immediate improvements in levels of engagement she was able to demonstrate, vividly and articulately described at conferences and workshops throughout the country, resulted in a spate of replications and refinements. Several dissertations were produced by trainee clinical psychologists, demonstration projects by educational and clinical psychologists, and PhDs embarked upon. Many hospitals, special schools and Adult Training Centres set up Room Management Units, and there was, for a five-year period from the original publication (Porterfield and Blunden, 1978), a quite remarkable 'growth industry'. One of the surprising aspects of all this was that it was essentially a British phenomenon. Virtually no studies describing the procedure emanated from the United States, despite its American lineage, and the rare examples of American work which seemed closely related – for example, Spangler and Marshall (1983), on a procedure describing the role of a play manager in facilitating purposeful activities with mentally handicapped boys – make no reference to the British work.

Although there have been some changes and minor additions to the original procedure, it involves three elements, basically. It is his/her job to move around the group, praising trainees who are using the available material or who are otherwise engaged, ensuring that everyone has access to enough materials, briefly prompting trainees who are not busy, and changing activities for those who have finished. The *individual helper* spends a predetermined time, dependent mainly on the staff–client ratio, but usually around 10 minutes, with each trainee in turn. During this time individual training takes place. The individual helper is also the person who answers the telephone, takes people to the toilet, deals with emergencies, and so on. In many settings it has been found necessary to designate a third person for this role, since it has been found that, due to the frequency of such events, very little individual training could take place. Since both the room manager and the individual helper roles involve similar levels of expertise, it is usual for staff to alternate between them.

A third element was soon added to the package, that of *supervisor*. This person is responsible for seeing that the activity period takes place as planned, and that the room manager and individual helper are doing these jobs properly. S/he does this by positive monitoring, that is, by commenting on how well the other staff are doing their jobs. More on this aspect of the procedure later.

Each of these elements of the activity period package is sufficiently precise to allow detailed checklists of functions to be produced. These can be useful not only in training staff in their roles, but also for monitoring their effectiveness.

An impressive amount of data has now been collected to show that the procedure does alter the level of engagement of mentally handicapped trainees. Changes from around 30 per cent of trainees engaged during baseline to 80 per cent of trainees engaged during the activity period are common, with the effect being clearly a result of the implementation of the procedure rather than of some artefact. Furthermore, at a follow-up of 84 days, engagement levels remained high, suggesting that it is a very powerful procedure indeed. Although some methodological inadequacies have been noted in the original study (Sturmey and Crisp, 1982) and the exact effects of the individual components have yet to be eluciated, the procedure was quickly adopted in many settings for mentally handicapped clients.

The story sounds almost too good to be true, and unfortunately this is so. Although widely adopted, the procedure very rarely lasts more than a short time. Even the follow-up data in the original study were collected within three months. Woods and Cullen (1983) report changes from around 10 per cent of residents engaged during baselines to around 65 per cent during the activity period. Follow-up data were obtained at monthly intervals with high levels of engagement up to four months. At 15 months, however, even though the activity period was supposedly still in effect, the engagement level had dropped to 20 per cent. This is the only study to *demonstrate* the long-term failure of the procedure, but the 'disappearance' of many of the other projects around the country tells the same message. At one point, when Jan Porterfield telephoned the site of the original study to arrange a visit, they asked if she wanted them to put on the activity period for her when she came! They have also made a video recording of the activity period which they can show to visitors, rather than have to implement the procedure for the day.

The failure of the activity hour procedure to endure was, of course, apparent to the original researchers. In a replication study on a hospital ward they found that, after the end of the researcher's involvement, what thereafter was referred to as the activity period bore litle resemblance to the original procedure. Coles and Blunden (1979) then devised a procedure for maintaining the activity hour procedure. The concepts of the *supervisor* and *positive monitoring* were introduced. Basically, in order for the activity hour to be maintained it must be made to occur as part of an organization's routine, very much as mealtimes, giving out medication, and bathing are routines. By agreement with the hospital management, a system was set up whereby the ward charge nurses were trained to monitor the behaviour of ward staff as room managers and individual helpers, and to record this. Ward staff received feedback from the charge nurses on how well they were doing. In addition, graphed summaries of changes in the trainee's behaviour were sent to the Nursing Officer, who then gave positive monitoring to ward staff. He in turn reported the outcomes to the Senior Nursing Officer, who gave a written report to the Sector/Health Care Team. He informed the Nursing Officer of the outcome of these proceedings.

With this new 'chain' established, the activity period was sustained, and is reputed to be ongoing as late as March 1984. Unfortunately, one of the original reasons for implementing the activity period procedure – that of increasing the skill levels of mentally handicapped people – has been forgotten. At a symposium on organizing environments for mentallly handicapped people held at the University of Manchester in March 1984, Roger Blunden had to report that although the activity hour is still operated on that ward, the residents are still using the same table-top tasks, not having progressed at all!

The activity hour package is a complex set of environmental events, involving a number of factors, some of which might be effective, some of which might not. Further, the effects on mentally handicapped trainees are complex, with various reports of concomitant reductions in undesirable behaviour, interactions between the initial level of behavioural skill and changes in engagement, and so on. At the time of writing (April 1984) there are research projects investigating the effects of these factors.

J.A. Beswick is pursuing a research programme, the results of which will be submitted to the University of Manchester as a PhD thesis. Rather than simply implement the whole room management 'package', he is investigating the effects of a gradual introduction of the individual components. After collecting baseline data on a ward for severely and profoundly mentally handicapped, behaviour disordered women, he introduced the first experimental condition, which was to move the staff and residents off the ward and into a recreation hall for one hour each day. Data were here collected as they had been during baseline on the resident's behaviour – which was coded as engaged, neutral or inappropriate, in a manner similar to that reported by

Coles and Blunden (1979). In addition, whether or not a member of staff was in contact with a resident was also recorded.

The next experimental phase was to provide the new toys and activities that are traditionally used in activity hour procedures, but not, at this stage, to provide any specific staff training. Again, data were collected. Formal training in the room management procedure then followed, with psychologists acting as the supervisors who monitored staff behaviour. The next phase was to train a Nursing Officer in positive monitoring, the psychologists serving now only to collect data on residents' behaviour and staff contact.

A reversal followed, with the Nursing Officer ceasing to visit the recreation hall to provide positive monitoring. Two weeks later, positive monitoring was re-introduced and the situation was followed up for 11 months. It is not possible here to summarize all the results of this complex study, but the main result was that there was a significant increase in engagement as each change was made, up to and including full implementation of the activity hour period. Monitoring by Nursing Officers as opposed to psychologists did not increase the engagement level, but removing the monitoring component led to a decrease in engagement back to the level that obtained when toys and activities were provided but no activity hour was in operation. Reinstating the monitoring increased the engagement levels, and these were maintained at eleven months follow-up. Clearly, then, although each component of the procedure improves engagement, monitoring seems to be critical in maintaining the highest levels.

There were also corresponding reductions in neutral and inappropriate behaviour as the components were added, although the changes in inappropriate behaviour were not so striking as the changes in engagement and neutral behaviour. The relationship between staff contact and changes in residents' behaviour was not a simple one and requires a more careful analysis of the *type* of contact (that is, whether positive or negative).

One other noteworthy aspect of this study is that the levels of engagement obtained (around 50 per cent compared to 5 per cent at baseline) were less than the high figures reported by Porterfield and Blunden (1978). In a further study, Beswick has determined that there is a relationship between the levels of engagement obtained with an activity hour period and the level of adaptive functioning of the group of residents. If residents have a high level of adaptive behaviour, then they are likely to achieve higher levels of engagement. It is not possible to make a meaningful comparison between Beswick's subjects and Porterfield's, so we cannot say whether this is the decisive factor in understanding the different engagement levels obtained. There are, though, many other potentially important differences between the settings.

As Beswick's studies show, though room management can be a powerful procedure it is also a complex one, and until we have a more thorough understanding of the contributions of, and relationships between, its different aspects, there will be a high degree of unpredictablility about its effects. Another researcher, Peter Sturmey, has been investigating other relevant variables for a PhD thesis submitted to the University of Liverpool. He started from the premis that room management was only one way of structuring the environment of a group of mentally handicapped people and should be compared with other ways.

His first comparison was of room management with small groups, wherein each member of staff was allocated four or five students, then had to provide them with appropriate materials, prompt and reinforce their use and provide individual training on a goal-planning base. His results show that room management was generally superior with regard to the amount of individual training received and the proportion of goals completed, but group engagement levels were higher during small groups. Various other measures, such as the time students spent on task, were not different between the two conditions. A second study compared room management with individual training, where staff worked with a particular student on an activity for a specified period, other students being occupied with a 'holding' activity. In this study, the individual training arrangement resulted in more students being trained, students receiving a greater proportion of time being trained, staff spending a greater proportion of time training and a slightly greater (though non-significant) proportion of successful goals. Other measures taken, such as the proportion of time with materials available and the amount of time spent on task, favoured the room management procedure. Clearly, one cannot argue that one method of organization is always 'better' than another – it depends on which part of the student's behavioural repertoire one is trying to change.

Since previous research had indicated that room management procedures might have a benficial effect on undesirable behaviour, Sturmey investigated the effects in his studies on stereotyped and self-injurious behaviour. Behaviours such as picking skin, rocking, inappropriate speech, and slapping people were monitored in six people. Room management may be viewed as the differential reinforcement of other behaviour (DRO – not necessarily incompatible behaviour) and Sturmey's research seems to indicate the same mixed success at reducing stereotyped and self-injurious behaviour as other DRO studies. For some people, difficult behaviour reduced in frequency, while for others there was no effect. This somewhat inconclusive result is similar to that obtained by Beswick.

In all the studies of room management and related procedures, there have arisen a number of conceptual issues which must be addressed. The most pressing of these is concerned with the nature of the tasks which trainees are expected to engage in. As reported above, the mentally handicapped residents of one ward where room management has been ongoing for around five years are apparently still occupied with the *same* tasks as they were given when the study commenced! If the ultimate goal of room management (as with most other procedures) is to establish new and adaptive skills, then clearly this is not happening. All that is going on is a rigid routine which may 'engage' the handicapped person, but provides no particular benefit.

Room management seems to be a better way of organizing environments than the most usual systems under which handicapped people find themselves spending their time, but it puts a spotlight immediately on to the common deficiency of our not being able to provide useful and meaningful activities for mentally handicapped adults. Doing jigsaws and form-boards, threading beads, and playing with Lego are activities difficult to justify other than as 'offering something to do'. A challenge for the future is to introduce into room management appropriate activities which are changed as the client achieves success in steps towards a clearly defined goal.

I have already remarked upon the wide variance in final engagement figures reported in varying studies. Relevant to this, and related to the last point about the nature of the task, is the lack of data on the social validity of room management procedures. This refers to the acceptibility by the wider community of the goals achieved by a programme and the methods of achieving them. If we confine ourselves to the first point, what does the level of engagement have to be before an unbiased observer can come into the room and agree that everyone is busy? It might be relatively easy to change a very low level of engagement into a higher one, and for that difference to be statistically significant, thereby satisfying the requirements of journal editors and conference organizers. But is it enough to have achieved a *clinically* significant change for the trainees? J.A. Beswick is currently investigating whether unbiased observers can reliably differentiate between levels of engagement, and he is seeking to find out what levels are describe as 'busy' and which are not.

A third issue which should be considered in future studies is that of the dependent and independent variables. The number of possible environmental operations which combine together to form the room management 'package' is large, and there is rarely enough descriptive information to allow a comparison of studies. What is called 'room mangement' in one place might be quite different in another. Regarding the dependent variables, there are obviously a lot of potential behavioural changes when a huge environmental change takes place. Measuring only the proportion of people in the group who are engaged obscures many other potentially interesting effects, and the number of reports of detailed changes for individual trainees should increase.

Token economies

Since the publication in 1968 of Ayllon and Azrin's now classic book on the token economy, there have been many hundereds of reports in the literature of token economies with varied client populations, and comparing the token economy with other therapeutic methods. The general procedure and rationale are too well known to need elaboration here, so I will confine myself to drawing attention to some general issues.

Self-care behaviours have been a major focus of attention in token economy programmes with the mentally handicapped, as with other client groups. There have been a large number of studies showing that residents in institutions can improve the performances of various self-care behaviours when a token economy is in force on the ward. With children there have been several reports of token economies based in classrooms, where the focus has been on behaviour such as following instructions and 'academic' activities such as reading and writing. In sheltered workshop settings, tokens have been used to increase the work-rate of handicapped adults. An example of this latter type of study will serve to give a 'flavour' of the approach.

McNally *et al.* (1983) worked with a group of 10 handicapped adults, ranging in age from 23 to 56 years (mean age 32 years) and IQ from 30 to 41 (mean IQ 37). They were expected to assemble eight different items together and to place them into a plastic bag as one unit. In order to assemble the eight items, a cardboard template was used, each item covering its own shape on the template. Each plastic bag was placed in a rack capable of holding only 10 packages.

White tokens placed in a pile upon red tokens were situated next to each trainee. S/he was instructed to take a white token each time a rack with 10 packages had been filled. The goal was to work down to the red tokens, the number of white tokens being determined separately for each trainee from observations of their baseline performances. Once the red tokens were reached, the trainee was exceeding her/his baseline level of performance. Trainees earning at least one red token were allowed 30 minutes of extra leisure time at the end of the four hours' work. Those failing to earn any red tokens continued to work for an extra 30 minutes. To encourage trainees to continue working after reaching their first red token, a degree of competition was introduced. Red tokens were displayed on a board and the person earning most red tokens earned a meal at a local restaurant.

In a later phase of the study, the group was divided into two teams and a group contingency came into operation. All members of the team with most red tokens now earned the extra 30 minutes' leisure time, regardless of individual team members failing to earn red tokens. The running total of red tokens was posted throughout the day to inform everyone which team was winning.

As in many other successful token economy studies, the tokens achieved the desired effect of increasing behaviour, in this case trainees' work rate. (The effect of the group contingency will be discussed in the next section.) However, even after more than 15 years, there are several issues which the token economy must address if it is to become a widespread system of managing the behaviour of groups of people. These have been clearly described in reviews by Kazdin and Bootzin (1972) and Kazdin (1982).

1. What procedures must be devised to ensure that the newly acquired behaviours become functional for the client and generalize to a more natural environment? There is no doubt that a token economy is a prosthetic environment, and the literature is replete with examples of the loss of skills once the client is moved or the token economy is no longer in force. Solutions such as the introduction of half-way houses or the gradual withdrawal of tokens have been tried, sometimes with success and sometimes without. What is more rarely considered as a possibility, but perhaps deserves to be, is that if a prosthetic environment such as a token economy is successful in maintaining high levels of adaptive behaviour, then why not, for some clients at least, keep it going in perpetuity *if* the only available alternative is a loss of skills and a consequently poorer quality of life?

2. Sometimes clients do not succeed in a token economy, either because the contingencies make no contact with their behaviour (they are unresponsive), they resist the system and refuse to co-operate or they circumvent the contingencies (for example, by stealing tokens). The data show that a small percentage of clients in most token economies do not succeed for one of these reasons. To anyone who understands anything of the nature of behaviour–environment relationships it would be surprising if this were not so, since the token economy, like any procedure designed to deal with a group of people, will find it hard to deal with the individual variations in behaviour which are so important. Successful token economies can be differentiated from unsuccessful ones by the degree to which they have built-in procedures to allow for individual contingencies, such as not everyone earning the same number of tokens for the same behaviour, clients being able to participate in the decision about how to earn tokens, some people earning tokens for different specific behaviours, and the token exchange rate being different for different clients. This sort of adaptability must be built-in for the system to survive.

3. Token economies depend for their success on adaptive behaviour having a contingent and regular effect on the environment. This effect is the token-giving of staff, so the onus on staff to be consistent, reliable, and sensitive to the behaviour of the handicapped person is clear. However, in mental handicap settings, at least in Britain and probably elsewhere also, direct care staff receive very little formal training which could equip them to perform this function. This has always been a problem in token economies, and has resulted in a substantial amount of relevant research, which space precludes discussion of here. However, it is now known that formal lectures and workshops have very little lasting impact on the daily care practices of staff and that for staff training to result in changes in the behaviour of staff it must be not only *linked to,* but actually *part of* a more general alteration in the organization or ecology of which the token economy is a part. This is closely related to a fourth problem which has been endemic in token economies.

4. Most token systems (probably the vast majority) last no more than a few months before they cease functioning. This is usually not because they have failed to have an impact on residents' behaviour but is for various reasons to do with the organizational structure. A failure to train staff appropriately has already been referred to, but this is only one of the problems. By its nature, the token economy is a system quite unlike the usual structure of an institution or a school. It requires special procedures, such as the allocation of extra finances to purchase back-up reinforcers and a high degree of consistency in staffing, which do not usually pertain in the rest of the setting. While most programmes can be maintained for a short time, the 'novelty' effect playing an important role, eventually the rest of the system will, directly or indirectly, subvert the token economy. In order to avoid this, the token system has to become 'self-supporting' and effectively independent of the surrounding structures. Moreover, within the token economy there must be special monitoring systems to ensure that staff behaviour is maintained appropriately and does not 'drift', thereby destroying the important relationships between resident behaviour and staff behaviour (the giving of tokens). Again, this is not the place to discuss the research on organizational change, but it must be pointed out that we have so far progressed only a short way along the road to understanding how to implement and maintain system changes, and a lot of further research is necessary (Stolz, 1981).

Both token economies and room management procedures share similar problems in the maintenance of staff behaviour (*cf.* Woods and Cullen, 1983). Both also have complex effects on the client's behaviour. These are important considerations which deserve further systematic research, and which undoubtedly must be taken into account by anyone setting up a formal system to manage a group of mentally handicapped people.

MENTALLY HANDICAPPED PEOPLE AS A GROUP

Group-oriented contingencies have been less well researched than individual contingencies, even though there are obvious advantages to establishing the co-operative behaviour necessary to work as a member of a group. The largest body of research is concerned with classrooms, but the emphasis is usually on children of normal intellectual abilites. The focus of this chapter is on mentally handicapped adults, and here there is very little which has been done, making this a priority area for future work. A useful distinction may be drawn between two possible ways of arranging group contingencies (*cf.* Hayes, 1976).

1. *Dependent* – where the same contingencies are in effect for all members of the group, but the performance of only one person (or a small number of

people) is used as the criterion. This might be a useful procedure for dealing with a target individual who is thought to be susceptible to peer pressure. For example, if a person is disruptive and refusing to co-operate in the work of a group, outcomes for the whole group can be made dependent on the co-operative behaviour of the troublesome individual.

2. *Interdependent* – where the same contingencies are in effect for each member of the group but are applied to a level of group performance. The study by McNally *et al.* (1983), described in the section on token economies, had a phase with this arrangement. All members of a team earned extra leisure time when the team gained more red tokens than the other team. The effect of this procedure was to increase even further the productivity when compared with the self-delivered tokens contingency.

For many mentally handicapped people, group-oriented contingencies may not be effective, since a relatively advanced susceptibility to delayed consequences and to social consequences (such as peer pressure and competition) is needed. However, the McNally *et al.* study is one of a small number which have demonstrated that some mentally handicapped adults can benefit from this type of approach. A number of research questions pose themselves:

1. What prerequisite repertoires do handicapped people need before they can benefit from group contingencies?
2. Under what circumstances are dependent or interdependent contingencies favoured?
3. What positive side-effects (for example, increased social behaviour away from the training situation) can be identified as a result of group contingencies, and are there negative side-effects?
4. When are group learning situations more effective and less effective than individual learning situations?
5. Are there optimum group sizes?

The use of group contingencies is very common in some countries, notably in Russian-influenced countries, and in the People's Republic of China. In China I have several times seen groups of mentally and physically handicapped children, in institutions, being treated *as* a group, learning to sing and dance, to write Chinese characters, to read simple signs, and so on, but, unfortunately, there is no published research available. In Hungary, the system of conductive education devised by Professor Andras Peto has had quite remarkable effects with groups of physically handicapped children (although again there is relatively little available research literature), but when the method has been evaluated in Britain with profoundly mentally and physically handicapped children it has been shown to have no better effect than the usual school procedures (Rooke *et al.,* in press).

CONCLUSION

As in so many aspects of the field of mentally handicap, the important variables in group work will still have to be identified. Such research is a severe test of methodology, because people interacting with people is an exceedingly complex area. It is an important enterprise though, because for mentally handicapped people to be a real part of the community we must be able to help them to co-operate with others, not only with other mentally handicapped people, but with all people. We still have a long way to go.

Acknowledgements

I am immeasurably grateful to Joe Beswick and Peter Sturmey for allowing me to describe some of their unpublished research. Such generosity is unusual and I hope I have not misrepresented their work in any way. I also wish to thank Diane Irwin for her patience whilst typing the manuscript.

REFERENCES

COLES, E. and BLUNDEN, R (1979) The establishment and maintenance of a ward-based activity period within a mental handicap hospital. *Report Number 8.* Cardiff: Mental Handicap in Wales Applied Research Unit.

HAYES, L.A. (1976) The use of group contingencies for behavioural control: a review. *Psychological Bulletin, 83,* 628–648.

KAZDIN, A.E. (1982) The token economy: a decade later. *Journal of Applied Behaviour Analysis, 15,* 431–445.

KAZDIN, A.E. and BOOTZIN, R.R. (1972) The token economy: an evaluative review. *Journal of Applied Behaviour Analysis, 5,* 343– 372.

McNALLY, R.J. NORUSIS, P.L., GENTZ, S.A., and McCONATHY, L.C. (1983) Use of self-delivered reinforcement and group contingency management to increase productivity of severely retarded workers. *Psychological Reports, 52,* 499–503.

PORTERFIELD, J. and BLUNDEN, R. (1978) Establishing an activity period and individual skill training within a day setting for profoundly mentally handicapped adults. *Journal of Practical Approaches to Developmental Handicap, 2,* 10–15.

ROOKE, P.J., McCARTNEY, E., and CULLEN, C. (in press) A study of the effectiveness of an educational approach based on conductive education pronciples for profoundly retarded multiply handicapped children. *British Journal of Disorders of Communication* .

SPANGLER, P.F., and MARSHALL, A.M. (1983) The unit play manager as facilitator of purposeful activities among institutionalized profoundly and severely retarded boys. *Journal of Applied Behaviour Analysis, 16,* 345–349.

STOLZ, S. B. (1981) Adoption of innovations from applied behavioural research: 'Does anybody care?' *Journal of Applied Behaviour Analysis, 14,* 491–505.

STURMEY, P. and CRISP, A.G. (1982) Improving environments for the mentally handicapped: A methodological note. *British Journal of Clinical Psychology, 21,* 191–198.

WOODS, P.A. and CULLEN, C. (1983) Determinants of staff behaviour in long-term care. *Behavioural Psychotherapy, 11,* 4–17.

ALTERNATIVES TO SPEECH FOR THE MENTALLY HANDICAPPED

Alastair Ager

Difficulties of speech are a characterisitc feature of mental handicap. Despite notable exceptions, the incidence of speech disorders (including the total absence of speech) typically varies directly with degree of intellectual impairment (Fawcus and Fawcus, 1978). It has consistently been observed that such speech difficulties are generally more extreme than would be predicted in relation to the rest of an individual's abilities (Mittler, 1978). In addition, in most cases not only is speech production affected in this manner, but also its comprehension.

With regard to all this – and recognizing the importance for an individual of establishing functional communication – many early behavioural interventions with the mentally handicapped sought to improve individuals' verbal abilities. Although some programmes reported promising results (for example, Bricker and Bricker, 1970), the overall impact of such work was disappointing. Historically, this lack of success with verbally-oriented programmes appears to have played an important part in the development of an interest in communication involving alternatives to speech. Through the 1970s attention to this area steadily grew both in Britain (Kiernan, 1977) and the United States (Fristoe and Lloyd, 1978) with the result that in the 1980s non-vocal communication is one of the major topics of interest in the field of mental handicap, from both a clinical and research perspective.

Psychological input to discussions relating to the use of alternatives to speech for mentally handicapped individuals is highly relevant. An efficient means of communication should be a central component of an individual's behavioural repertoire and, where this is lacking, represents an important potential focus for an intervention programme. In many cases such work would appropriately be within the context of a multidisciplinary team, which might include not only speech therapists but also nurses, occupational therapists, and so on. Within such a team the clinical psychologist has many relevant skills to offer but, in particular, may have an important role to play in communicating recent research findings concerning learning processes in the mentally handicapped, many of which are directly pertinent to the use of non-vocal communication.

The work of O'Connor and Hermelin (1978), for example, may be seen to offer some form of empirical basis for the use of alternatives to speech. These workers showed that mentally handicapped individuals, when presented with an appropriate choice, exhibited a preference for coding information in visuo-spatial, as opposed to auditory-sequential terms. The possibility then arises that mentally handicapped people may tend to process visual information more efficiently than verbal information. This hypothesis has subsequently won some experimental support (*see* Kiernan, 1983; Ager, 1983a), although there remains considerable variation in the extent of such a coding bias between individuals.

A suggested tendency to handle visual information better than verbal information clearly has major implications for the normal adoption of visually-based, non-vocal communication systems in work with the mentally handicapped. It is less frequently realized, however, that it also calls into question some of our teaching methods, many of which are still heavily speech-oriented. Although, theoretically, these two issues are closely related, clinically it may frequently be necessary to separate them on pragmatic grounds. It will subsequently be argued, for instance, that in many circumstances where it would be inappropriate to introduce the use of a formal non-vocal communication system, encouraging bias towards general non-vocal teaching procedures (using pictorial stimuli, gesture, etc.) may still be a sensible course of action. In the light of this, our subsequent discussion will address separately the use of formal non-vocal communication systems and the more general question of the adoption of non-vocal teaching strategies.

NON-VOCAL COMMUNICATION SYSTEMS

General use

As Kiernan (1983) has noted, development in the field of non-vocal communication systems for the mentally handicapped has essentially been practitioner led. Whereas growth in the use of behavioural training approaches during the sixties and seventies may be seen to have involved the application of earlier, academically well established research findings, no such comprehensive research base can be defined for the use of communication based on media other than speech (Poulton and Algozzine, 1980). Whilst efforts have been made in this direction, many research questions fundamental to work in this area remain unanswered (Remington and Light, 1983).

Given this theoretical uncertainty, the rapid rise over recent years in the use of non-vocal communication systems with the mentally handicapped is somewhat remarkable. Clearly, such systems have met a widely perceived need across a range of services. In a series of surveys of special schools in Great Britain, for example, researchers at the Thomas Coram Research Unit have shown the usage of non-vocal systems within the ESN(S) sector rising from 53 per cent in 1978 to over 96 per cent in 1982 (Reid *et al.,* 1983).

Such broad figures obviously hide considerable differences in the nature of use in various settings. A non-vocal communication system may be introduced to fulfil one of at least three distinct roles, for example. With some individuals – especially those with no speech and for whom the prognosis for linguistic development is poor – a system may potentially offer the only viable means of communication with those in their environment. For others it may act as an adjunct to speech which is unclear and often misinterpreted, serving to establish more reliable communication. In a third role – generally with younger and more able individuals – a non-vocal system can be adopted in the hope of facilitating the development of normal speech. Although a specific non-vocal communication programme within a service may often attempt to fulfil at least two of these roles simultaneously (with different individuals), it remains worthwhile distinguishing these distinct functions to the extent that some systems may be more appropriate than others to a given role.

Specific systems

It is appropriate at this point, therefore, to consider some of the many non-vocal communication systems that have been used with mentally handicapped people. In describing such applications, a distinction is commonly made between sign systems and symbol systems – the former involving communication via manual gesture and the latter via pictographic or logographic means (Fristoe and Lloyd, 1978). Whilst we will adopt the widely accepted 'sign' and 'symbol' nomenclature here, Remington and Light (1983) have offered the alternative terms 'formed sign' and 'preformed sign' to describe these two categories of system. The advantage of this latter formulation is that it serves to highlight factors particularly pertinent in deciding which type of system is appropriate in a given circumstance. To produce 'formed signs' (that is, manual signs), for example, often requires a complex motor response, prompting of which may be difficult. In comparison, to produce a communication using 'preformed signs' (that is, symbols) generally requires a much simpler motor response (for example, pointing), prompting of which is relatively simple. The latter approach may be favoured, therefore, in circumstances where an individual has particular difficulty in making appropriate hand gestures, due either to physical handicap or gross attentional/learning difficulties.

Within the range of manual sign systems, Kiernan (1977) has distinguished between naturally occurring sign languages (typically of the deaf), such as British Sign Language (BSL) and American Sign Language (ASL), and derivatives or developments of these languages, such as Signed English and the Paget Gorman Sign System (PGSS). The major significance of this distinction becomes apparent when we consider the prospective use of a non-vocal communication system in the third role previously identified, that is for the purposes of facilitating the development of speech. As a 'living language', BSL, for example, does not preserve spoken English word order, and simultaneous speaking–signing thus disrupts either natural word orders or word–sign correspondence. The PGSS, on the other hand, was devised specifically to retain spoken English word order and generally conforms to English grammar in a manner not found in BSL. It has correspondingly been argued that PGSS is a preferable system to adopt if normal spoken English is the eventual goal.

This logic only holds, of course, with relatively advanced speech. With the many signing programmes with the mentally handicapped which aim initially to involve only very restricted language concepts, for instance, the above argument is largely redundant. In such circumstances decisions between systems can tend to be made on less technical grounds. In this regard, the 'image' of PGSS as a complex system suitable only for the more able individual – which remains despite much successful work with severely mentally and physically handicapped individuals (*see* Rowe, 1978) – appears to have been one of the major factors leading to its decreasing popularity within mental handicap (*see* Kiernan, 1983). Its usage in ESN(S) schools in Britain, for example, has declined from nearly 28 per cent of those schools adopting a system in 1978 to below 4 per cent in 1982 (Reid *et al.,* 1983).

The same period has seen BSL – notably in the form of the Makaton Vocabulary – assume increasing dominance as a signing system with the mentally handicapped. In 1982, of those schools in Britain with a signing programme, 95 per cent reported use of the Makaton Vocabulary (Reid *et al.,* 1983). In fact, whilst no equivalently comprehensive data have been collected outside the educational system, it is now clearly apparent that Makaton has won broader acceptance than any other signing system throughout services for the mentally handicapped in Britain.

The Makaton Vocabulary is a programme that was designed specifically for use by mentally handicapped individuals. It is a sub-set of standard BSL signs grouped into stages – with each stage generally involving more complex linguistic concepts (*see* Walker, 1978). It should be noted that there has been little research evidence to support rigid conformity to the stage structure recommended. However, it appears likely that – allied to the organizational support of the Makaton Vocabulary Development Project – such structure, in providing explicit guidance for those implementing a signing programme, has contributed significantly to the successful dissemination of the system.

Of those symbol-based systems adopted for use with mentally handicapped people, Blissymbolics (frequently termed simply 'Bliss') is generally the most frequently employed. Again, use in Britain is most thoroughly researched within the field of special education, due to the surveys of the Thomas Coram

Research Unit. These have shown that, although Bliss's widest use is within schools for the physically handicapped, over 20 per cent of ESN(S) schools surveyed in 1982 also reported using the system. This compares with just below 14 per cent using Rebus or Rebus-type programmes, Rebus being the other major symbol-based system used in this field (Reid *et al.*, 1983).

Both Bliss and Rebus involve visual designs representing words. The former adopts a convention of combining visual elements – each representing a basic concept – to form symbols conveying more complex meanings. The symbol for mother, for example, combines elements representing 'woman' and 'protection'. This logical structure clearly serves the more able user in the extension of vocabulary. However, it does also mean that related words share visually similar symbols, which can lead to discrimination problems with some individuals – particularly the less able. Nonetheless, with a comparatively restricted lexicon not requiring too many fine discriminations, Bliss may provide a successful mode of communication even for those with the most severe mental handicaps (Bailey and Hammond, 1978). Finally, an important feature of the system is that a symbol is always accompanied by the word it represents, which allows communication with people who are themselves unfamiliar with Bliss.

Any symbol or picture which represents a word may be termed a 'rebus'. Rebus systems – such as the Peabody Rebus Scheme – were initially designed as early reading programmes, but over recent years their more general potential for aiding communication of the mentally handicapped has been recognized (Kiernan, 1983). When a number of rebuses are mounted on a board for an individual to select via pointing (or, with physically handicapped individuals, perhaps via some form of electronic device), the clear relationship with 'picture boards' is readily apparent. This form of system may be so primitive as to allow an individual to signal only one or two items – a cup may be shown signifying 'drink' and a flannel signifying 'wash', for instance. The value to an individual of being able to communicate such needs, however, should not be underestimated. Despite their lack of sophistication, simple Rebus schemes and 'picture boards' may be an important first step in allowing a mentally handicapped person to express choice within the environment.

The above comprises of necessity, only the briefest of reviews of non-vocal communication systems presently adopted for use with the mentally handicapped. For a more detailed consideration of particular systems, the reader is referred to the sources indicated at the close. It must be emphasized that no attempt has been made here to present arguments for the adoption of particular systems within specified circumstances. The fact is that we do not, at present, have the data which would enable us to make such judgements with any reliability. Recently, however, there have been moves towards addressing issues, understanding of which would bring us closer to identifying the factors which influence the general success of a non-vocal communication programme. Given that these issues have considerable psychological significance it is to these that we now turn.

Psychological issues

Remington and Light (1983) identify several key issues which arise in relation to the introduction of a formal system of non-vocal communication within a setting. We may distinguish four of these as being of particular relevance to the interests of a clinical psychologist. These are issues relating to:

1. The role of iconicity in sign or symbol use;
2. The facilitation of speech through non-vocal communication;
3. Appropriate methods for teaching signs or symbols;
4. Maintenance and generalization of system use.

Iconicity. Iconicity refers to the relationship which may exist between a sign or symbol and its referent (that is, the word it 'stands for'). Whilst visual resemblance is an important form of iconicity, in research in this area a sign/symbol has been termed iconic if it provides virtually any type of clue to its meaning (*see* Kiernan, 1983). Obviously enough, the notion has been presented that highly iconic signs and symbols will be learned more easily than those which involve no such clue to their referent. This proposition has met with rather limited support, however. An important factor in accounting for this may be, as Kiernan (1983) notes, that handicapped learners frequently do not perceive the relationships which exist between sign or symbol and referent, many of which involve complex and/or tenuous associations. Evidence suggests, however, that the mentally handicapped will often perceive a relationship based on a clear visual resemblance, and that this can benefit initial learning of signs or symbols (Remington and Light, 1983). On the other hand, dependence on this form of similarity can ultimately restrict the development of more complex communication.

A concept related to that of iconicity, and of relevance in both the learning and use of a non-vocal communication system, is that of transparency. This refers to the extent to which those unfamiliar with a system can guess the meaning of a sign or symbol. Studies of the Amerind system – developed from American Indian Hand Talk – have indicated that over 80 per cent of its signs may be successfully guessed by naive (non-handicapped) subjects (Kiernan, 1983). For most other systems, however, this figure would be much lower. Despite a lack of hard data on the subject, high transparency clearly stands to benefit initial sign learning. Moreover, it means that difficulties in communicating with non-users of the system will be minimized.

Speech facilitation. Proponents of non-vocal communication systems frequently assert that their use facilitates the development of speech in mentally handicapped individuals. Poulton and Algozzine (1980) conclude that the literature broadly supports this position, although Kiernan (1983) points out that we are unable to quantify the phenomenon in any meaningful way with respect to survey and case report data on the subject. There is certainly no empirical basis for the counter argument that using alternatives to speech is likely to inhibit normal spoken language.

The manner in which use of signs or symbols may come to facilitate speech is of particular interest from a psychological perspective. One possiblity is that establishing – for the first time – an effective mode of communication for an individual may exert a general facilitatory effect on language development. Demonstrating that control over their environment is possible may – in this analysis – serve as a prompt for a range of communicative behaviours, including speech.

Another mechanism by which signs or symbols may facilitate speech is through functional equivalence (Sidman, 1971). An individual using a sign system, for example, will not only learn relationships between signs and objects but, with many teaching approaches (*see* next section), will also be exposed to sign–word correspondence. An individual speaking the name of an object may, in these terms, then be evidence of the establishment of functional equivalence between an object and a word, mediated by their common relationship with a sign. Kiernan (1983) presents a detailed review of work in this area, and concludes that with further research we may be able to specify the skills (such as vocal imitation) prerequisite for the facilitation of speech by a non-vocal communication programme.

Teaching methods. Non-vocal communication programmes adopt a variety of strategies in teaching individuals the use of signs and symbols. This range is reflected in the literature, but, unfortunately, few studies are reported in sufficient procedural detail to allow a valid judgement to be made on the benefits of a particular approach (Remington and Light, 1983). At the broadest level, teaching can involve either general 'immersion' in a sign or symbol-based milieu or structured training in the acquisition of specified signs/symbols. In practice, however, these two approaches are likely to be used in conjunction with each other rather than as alternatives.

Structured training can merely involve repeated presentation of a sign or symbol and its referent, but there have been more imaginative strategies adopted. Smeets and Striefel (1976) report use of a transfer of stimulus control procedure, for example, whereby sign–object equivalence was established by – beginning with simultaneous presentation – gradually increasing the delay between presenting the sign and its referent object. Using a related technology, stimulus shaping procedures based on the work of Schilmoeller and Etzel (1977) have successfully been used to establish discriminations between perceptually similar Blissymbols.

Perhaps the major issue to be faced when deciding upon a teaching strategy, however, which arises with either a milieu or structured approach, is whether or not to accompany presentation of signs or symbols with speech. This is of particular concern in the case of sign systems, where a technique involving simultaneous signing and speech – commonly referred to as Total Communication – has frequently been commended. It was noted in the previous section that this approach may be useful in encouraging the development of speech. However, there is a counter-argument, summarized by Kiernan (1983), which suggests that due to the overselectivity of many mentally handicapped individuals (that is, their predisposition towards attending to a restricted number of environmental cues), the addition of speech to sign may be irrelevant, or even disruptive. An approach recommended by Walker (1978), whereby a sentence is fully spoken but only key words are signed, is the strategy apparently adopted by most ESN(S) schools (Kiernan *et al.,* 1983). Whilst this appears to be something of a compromise position with respect to the above alternatives, it results in a disruption of sign–word correspondence which one might expect to reduce – rather than enhance – speech facilitation effects. As yet, however, despite a growing number of relevant experimental studies, few firm conclusions can be drawn with respect to the appropriate role for speech in signing programmes.

Maintenance and generalization. Whilst most of the issues focused upon so far can rightly be said to have been under-researched, this is particularly true of the maintenance and generalization of system use. The introduction of a non-vocal communication programme within a service setting is a major environmental manipulation, affecting both staff and clients of that service. Two major factors contributing to the success, or otherwise, of a programme will be the extent to which mechanisms have been devised:

1. To maintain the behaviours of staff prerequisite to facilitating non-vocal communication by clients, and
2. To generalize the use of non-vocal communication by clients from structured training environments to the setting as a whole.

The detailed study of a signing programme by Schepis *et al.,* (1982) is, however, a rare report of an attempt to identify such mechanisms. These workers showed the efficacy of an 'incidental teaching strategy' on both maintenance and generalization of sign use. The strategy involved rearranging the service environment to prompt signing, altering routine staff–client interactions to prompt, manually guide and/or reinforce signing, and arranging 'mini-training sessions' at intervals throughout the day.

In the absence of studies evaluating other procedures it is impossible to judge the relative value of these particular methods. Nevertheless, it is clear that programmes that make no attempt to integrate, in the fashion described, the use of signs or symbols into the other activities of a service setting are far less likely to be able to report such consistent use across both time and situation. A key notion here is that of functionality. Maintenance and generalization of system use will be considerably fostered by the system proving genuinely functional for individuals – that is, they are able to influence the environment effectively through its use. The selection of an appropriate lexicon of signs and symbols is clearly one important factor in this (Fristoe and Lloyd, 1980). Others include selection of a system appropriate to the 'communication community' of an individual. A system that is to prove functional for a mentally handicapped person mixing with a wide range of non-handicapped non-system users, for example, would clearly need to be highly transparent. Transparency would be less of a concern, however, for individuals restricted in their social contacts to users of the same system.

From the above discussions it should be clear that we are still some way off from a working understanding of several key features of non-vocal communication programmes. Recent research has succeeded, however, in suggesting some important questions that should be answered before such a programme is introduced within a setting. These questions have implications not only for the system introduced but also for the manner in which it is taught and its use encouraged. Within the constraints of this present review it has not been possible to address many other issues of relevance here. The whole area of user assessment (*see* Ferrier and Shane, 1983) has not been considered, for instance. The issues that have been focused on here, however, should serve to demonstrate the wide range of concerns that introducing a non-vocal communication programme naturally raises. Because it has so rarely been examined in the past, it is probably appropriate in this regard to stress consideration of mechanisms for the maintenance and generalization of system use. At present, few programmes appear to produce genuinely functional communication by users, and only if failure to do so is squarely addressed is this level of achievement likely to be bettered. It appears that considerably more effort will have to be invested in restructuring staff behaviour and physical environments if progress is to be made. Where resources to create such changes in structure are not available, it may be appropriate to conclude that a formal non-vocal communication programme is not viable in that setting. In such circumstances, however, reverting to a reliance on verbally-based interaction with individuals should not be seen as the only option. Particularly in environments emphasizing education and training – which within mental handicap services should include most settings – nurturing the general use of non-vocal teaching strategies may be an important alternative focus for development.

NON-VOCAL TEACHING STRATEGIES

There are many situations where the introduction of a formal non-vocal communication system would be inappropriate. This includes not only settings as just discussed, where implementing such a programme would not be feasible, but also those where it would be superfluous. Despite the high incidence of speech disorders with mentally handicapped individuals, many attain a high level of functional communication with speech and/or other idiosyncratic methods. In such circumstances the productive communication of individuals may not be the focus for concern. If we conceive of learning difficulties as an inability to efficiently receive instruction, however, improving the receptive communication of mentally handicapped individuals is always likely to be a relevant task. The work on information processing by the mentally handicapped reviewed earlier (O'Connor and Hermelin, 1978; Ager, 1983a) suggests that an improvement may be brought about simply by biasing our teaching strategies away from the auditory, and towards the visual modality.

Retrospectively we may conceive of many of the major innovations in teaching the mentally handicapped as resulting from the rejection of traditional speech-oriented methods of the sort which permeate most other fields of education. Much of the work in the 1950s of Tizard, Clarke and their colleagues – which did so much to change our understanding of the capabilities of severely mentally handicapped individuals – was, for example, based upon training in spatially-oriented assembly tasks (*see* Clarke and Clarke, 1978). In addition, the continued success of behavioural approaches may be attributed, in part at least, to the clear communication of task requirements via applied antecedent and consequent contingencies (which are essentially non-verbal).

Present instructional methods remain heavily speech-oriented, however. The use of verbal prompts is still frequently recommended, for instance. Whilst this may be appropriate in tasks where a verbal command is always to act as a discriminative stimulus for the behaviour being taught, in other circumstances the use of the auditory modality may be disruptive to learning. In some cases a verbal prompt arbitrarily interjected within a stream of behaviour can be most difficult to fade out (*see* Tennant *et al.,* 1981).

The technology of fading and shaping procedures which has developed over recent years allows the possibility of totally avoiding the use of speech whenever it does not form an inherent part of a task. In such circumstances the transition in stimulus control required in learning the new behaviour can be achieved by physical manipulations of the learning environment, these manipulations most commonly being within the visual modality. The pragmatics of this approach can best be summarized as follows. First, those features of a task salient for its correct completion are identified. Second, these features are emphasized or enhanced, so that a handicapped individual begins to behave appropriately with respect to them. Third, emphasis or enhancement is then removed by increments sufficiently small that the individual's appropriate behaviour is not disrupted. To illustrate this, consider the simple example of a task where an individual is required to select the larger of two squares. The relative size of the squares is clearly the salient feature of the task. Consequently a teaching programme might begin by presenting a very, very large square alongside a very small one. With this level of enhancement appropriate responding should be readily established, whereupon the difference in the size of the squares can be gradually returned to 'target' limits. Something of the concept of size has been taught here, without tortuous and confusing use of spoken language. This broad approach has now been adopted for teaching a variety of skills (*see* Schilmoeller and Etzel, 1977; Tennant *et al.*, 1981; Ager, 1983b), generally with most favourable results.

Identifying the central elements of teaching a new skill in this manner has been an important factor in opening up the possibility of using microcomputers in the education and training of mentally handicapped individuals. Given a suitably simple method of registering a response, even the most severely mentally handicapped individual may have access to microcomputer-based teaching programmes. An important feature of such programmes is that they may be written to monitor an individual's performance and adjust the difficulty of a presented task accordingly (Ager, 1984). Such flexibility is of particular value in controlling the visual display from the microcomputer, with incremental emphasis or enhancement of relevant task features – frequently a problem in normal task presentation – being easily achieved.

The development of speech synthesis on microcomputers may consequently prove something of a 'mixed blessing' in this field. Whilst it will allow a greater variety of tasks to be presented on the computer, the prior absence of speech output has encouraged the development of teaching programmes using an imaginative range of non-verbal cues. There is no comparative literature in this area as yet, but it is probable that these programmes would prove considerably more effective than those involving speech. Synthesized speech – presented, as it is, divorced from any form of non-verbal context such as lip movement or facial expression – is likely to be, for the mentally handicapped, a particularly difficult medium from which to extract information.

With or without the aid of microcomputers, there are thus many alternatives to speech as a mode of instruction for staff working with the mentally handicapped. Further exploitation of these alternatives would appear to be an important focus for future development in mental handicap services, and the role of the clinical pychologist is clearly a potentially significant one in such moves.

SUMMARY

Interest in the use of non-vocal communication with the mentally handicapped appears to have grown in response to the generally disappointing impact of speech training programmes with this population, and work which indicates a preference of mentally handicapped individuals to code information in visuo-spatial, as opposed to auditory-sequential, terms. Although work in the area is theoretically integrated, a distinction can be drawn – either on purely pragmatic grounds or on the basis of relative emphasis on productive or receptive concerns – between the introduction of formal non-vocal communication programmes, and a more general bias towards the use of non-vocal teaching strategies.

Development in the field of non-vocal communication systems has been largely practitioner led. Thus, whilst system use is widespread, a number of fundamental research questions remain unanswered. Non-vocal systems have variously been adopted as a genuine alternative to speech, as an adjunct to speech and as a facilitator of speech. Several sign systems (including the Paget Gorman Sign System and the Makaton Vocabulary of the British Sign Language) and symbol systems (including Blissymbolics and Rebus) are currently in use in Britain with mentally handicapped people.

Issues relating to the use of non-vocal communication systems which are of particular relevance to the interests of a clinical psychologist include:

1. The role of iconicity in sign or symbol use;
2. The facilitation of speech through non-vocal communication;
3. Appropriate methods for teaching signs or symbols;
4. Maintenance and generalization of system use.

Further research is required in each of these areas, but an increased awareness of factors likely to contribute to the establishment of functional communication seems particularly called for.

Non-vocal teaching strategies comprise a variety of approaches united by their common rejection of traditional speech-oriented methods in work with the mentally handicapped. The success, for example, of many behavioural interventions may, in part at least, be attributed to their non-verbal bias. The technology of fading and shaping procedures offers a particularly useful non-vocal teaching approach. Whilst appropriate for structuring tasks presented in a standard fashion, this also lends itself to microcomputer-based teaching. This is likely to become an increasingly important area because of the unique opportunities it provides for presenting tasks in a flexible manner, tailored to the abilities of the individual.

Further information

For further information on certain of the non-vocal communication systems briefly reviewed the reader is referred to the following addresses:

Blissymbolics Communication Resource Centre, South Glamorgan Institute of Higher Education, Llandaff, Cardiff CF5 2YB.

Makaton Vocabulary Development Project, 31 Firwood Drive, Camberley, Surrey GU15 3QD.

Paget Gorman Society, 3 Gypsy Lane, Headington, Oxford OX3 7PT.

REFERENCES

AGER, A.K. (1983a) An analysis of learning and attentional processes in mentally handicapped individuals. *International Journal of Rehabilitation Research, 6(3),* 369–370.

AGER, A.K. (1983b) An analysis of learning and attentional processes in mentally handicapped individuals. Unpublished doctoral dissertation, University of Wales.

AGER, A.K. (1984) MICROMATE: A microcomputer-based system for mentally handicapped individuals. In: E. Hudson (ed.) *The Computer as an Aid for Those with Special Needs: International Conference Proceedings.* Sheffield: Sheffield City Polytechnic.

BAILEY, P.A. and HAMMOND, J.M. (1978) The Bliss Symbol System. In: T. Tebbs (ed.) *Ways and Means.* Basingstoke: Globe Education.

BRICKER, W.A. and BRICKER, D.D. (1970) A program of language training for the severely language handicapped child. *Exceptional Children, 37,* 101–111.

CLARKE, A.M. and CLARKE, A.D.B. (1978) Severe subnormality: capacity and performance. In: A.M. Clarke and A.D.B. Clarke (eds) *Readings from Mental Deficiency: The Changing Outlook.* London: Methuen.

FAWCUS, M. and FAWCUS, R. (1978) Disorders of communication. In: A.M. Clarke and A.D.B. Clarke (eds) *Readings from Mental Deficiency: The Changing Outlook.* London: Methuen.

FERRIER, L.J. and SHANE, H.C. (1983) A description of non-speaking population under consideration for augmentative communication systems. In: J. Hogg and P.J. Mittler (eds) *Advances in Mental Handicap Research, Volume 2: Aspects of Competence in Mentally Handicapped People.* Chichester: Wiley.

FRISTOE, M. and LLOYD, L.L. (1978) A survey of the use of non-speech systems with the severely communication impaired. *Mental Retardation, 16,* 99–103.

FRISTOE, M. and LLOYD, L.L. (1980) Planning an initial expressive sign lexicon for persons with severe communication impairment. *Journal of Speech and Hearing Disorders, 45,* 170–180.

KIERNAN,C.C. (1977) Alternatives to speech: a review of research on manual and other forms of communication with mentally handicapped and other non-communicating populations. *British Journal of Mental Subnormality, 23,* 6–28.

KIERNAN, C.C. (1983) The exploration of sign and symbol effects. In: J. Hogg and P.J. Mittler (eds) *Advances in Mental Handicap Research, Volume 2: Aspects of Competence in Mentally Handicapped People.* Chichester: Wiley.

KIERNAN, C.C., REID, B.D. and JONES, L.M. (1983) *Signs and Symbols: A Review of Literature and Survey of the Use of Non-Vocal Communication Systems.* London: London University Insititute of Education/Heinemann.

MITTLER, P.J. (1978) Language and communication. In: A.M. Clarke and A.D.B. Clarke (eds) *Readings from Mental Deficiency: The Changing Outlook.* London: Methuen.

O'CONNOR, N. and HERMELIN, B. (1978) *Seeing and Hearing and Space and Time.* London: Academic Press.

POULTON, K.T. and ALGOZZINE, B. (1980) Manual communication and mental retardation: a review of research and implications. *American Journal of Mental Deficiency, 85,* 145–152.

REID, B.D., JONES, L.M. and KIERNAN, C.C. (1983) Signs and Symbols: the 1982 survey of use. *Special Education: Forward Trends, 10(1),* 27–28.

REMINGTON, B. and LIGHT, P. (1983) Some problems in the evaluation of research on non-oral communication systems. In: J. Hoggard and P.J. Mittler (eds) *Advances in Mental Handicap Research, Volume 2: Aspects of Competence in Mentally Handicapped People.* Chichester: Wiley.

ROWE, J. (1978) The Paget Gorman Sign System: manual communication as an alternative method. In: T. Tebbs (ed.) *Ways and Means.* Basingstoke: Globe Education.

SCHEPIS, M.M., REID, D.H., FITZGERALD, J.R., FAW, G.D., VAN DEN POL, R.A. and WELTY, P.A. (1982) A program for increasing manual signing by autisitc and profoundly retarded youth within the daily environment. *Journal of Applied Behaviour Analysis, 15,* 363–379.

SCHILMOELLER, K.L. and ETZEL, B.C. (1977) An experimental analysis of criterion-related and non-criterion-related cues in errorless stimulus control procedures. In: B.C. Etzel, J.M. le Blanc and D.M. Baer (eds) *New Developments in Behavioural Research: Theory, Methods and Application.* Hillsdale, NJ: Lawrence Erlbaum Associates.

SIDMAN, M. (1971) Reading and auditory-visual equivalences. *Journal of Speech and Hearing Research, 14,* 5–13.

SMEETS, P.M. and STREIFEL, S. (1976) Acquisition of sign reading by transfer of stimulus control in a retarded deaf girl. *Journal of Mental Deficiency Research, 20(3),* 197–205.

TENNANT, L., CULLEN, C. and HATTERSLEY, J. (1981) Applied behavioural analysis: intervention with retarded people. In: G.C.L. Davey (ed.) *Applications of Conditioning Theory.* London: Methuen.

WALKER, M. (1978) The Makaton vocabulary. In: T. Tebbs (ed.) *Ways and Means.* Basingstoke: Globe Education.

COGNITIVE RETRAINING OF NEUROLOGICAL PATIENTS

Edgar Miller

Whilst clinical psychology in general is now largely concerned with questions of management and treatment, psychologists working in neurological settings have tended to maintain the clinical psychologist's more traditional role of diagnostic assessment. It is only relatively recently that it has been realized that psychologists might have something to contribute to the management and rehabilitation of people with neuropsychological impairments. This realization has been fuelled by two things. One is an appeciation of the fact that many who suffer disease or damage of the central nervous system retain significant handicaps for the rest of their lives and therefore need some form of rehabilitation. The other is the development of increasingly sophisiticated radiological techniques, such as computerized tomography and the more recent nuclear magnetic resonance scanners, which undermine the importance of neuropsychological assessment in diagnosis. In theory, psychology ought to be able to contribute to the rehabilitation of neuropsychological impairments. Since most of these are fundamentally disorders of cognitive functioning, the term 'cognitive retraining' probably describes the field as well as any other. Nevertheless, the extent to which cognitive skills and abilities are actually being trained or retrained is rather limited.

What follows in this chapter is a necessarily brief and selective review of some of the basic issues underlying 'cognitive retraining', as well as the description of a few examples of the kinds of technique that are being developed and put into practice. In a short presentation of a complex field, the writer is forced to make assumptions or put forward arguments without full justification for them. A more detailed and extensive account of the material presented here can be found in Miller (1984).

THE NATURE OF THE PROBLEM

It is well recognized that those who suffer some form of 'brain damage' (by strokes, head injury, the consequences of encephalitis, etc.) can be left with significant impairments in one or more aspects of cognitive functioning, such as memory, language or the judgement of visuopatial relationships. What is known about the nature of these impairments is set out in some of the standard texts on neuropsychology, such as Heilman and Valenstein (1979). What is not so widely considered is the fact that typically there is some recovery from the initial level of impairment. This recovery may be influenced by a number of factors, such as the subject's age, the degree of overlearning of the skill that has been affected and the subject's experience since the onset of the deficit (Miller, 1984). Any attempt to further enhance recovery needs to take into account the natural recovery processes and also needs to set suitable goals.

Knowledge of the processes underlying natural recovery is sketchy at best, but three different types of mechanism have been suggested, one of which can loosely be described as 'artifact theories'. In essence these assume that some permanent loss of function occurs but that other functions may be temporarily supressed because of the action of certain changes which accompany the primary neural damage. Several such processes, of which oedema is probably the best-known example, are known to occur (Schoenfeld and Hamilton, 1977) but are generally too short lived to explain recovery over anything longer than a few days. The most frequently cited theory in this group is von Monakow's (1914) principle of diaschisis. This assumes that tissue linked in some way with the area of primary damage, either because it is adjacent or because it is linked by pathways to this area, will be likely to suffer a form of 'shock'. This is rather speculative physiological process and is referred to as diaschisis. Diaschisis will impair the functioning of tissue that it affects, but it will usually pass away slowly, thus allowing the affected area to resume its normal functioning. The specific nature of diaschisis is not described, but von Monakow was clear that it was not the same process as oedema and that its effects would last much longer.

Such artifact theories present an attractive model for recovery. The trouble is that the secondary processes of established validity, like oedema, are short lasting and cannot explain recovery extending over weeks or months. Diaschisis could explain longer-term recovery but the only well-conducted experimental test of the notion of diaschisis has given negative results (West *et al.*, 1976).

Another popular general model of recovery is that of 'anatomical reorganization' or substitution. Here the assumption is that if one part of the brain is damaged, then another part may take over the function originally subserved by the damaged part. It is often claimed that recovery from aphasia occurs in this way, with the right hemisphere taking over some of the language functions originally carried out by the damaged left hemisphere.

Evaluating this kind of model is a complex business (Miller, 1984). Briefly, in order to show that substitution has occurred it is necessary to prove certain things. These are that a part of the brain not previously involved in the affected function has now become involved. Secondly, that the part of the brain that is newly involved did not originally possess the function that has recovered. Finally, the individual should not just be using a different set of strategies to achieve the same goal. With regard to the latter point, a brain-damaged person who loses the ability to appreciate visuopatial relationships and then recovers the ability to find his way around may not have actually re-acquired the lost ability. He may have merely learned to find his way from on place to another by an entirely different mechanism, such as by learning a sequence of verbal cues that he can relate to key points on his route.

In general, the various studies that have been claimed as demonstrating anatomical reorganization or substitution have not managed to control for all these points. In particular, in studies of recovery from aphasia there is some evidence indicating greater involvement of the right hemisphere in speech. The research on split brain subjects has also shown that even strongly right-handed and left speech-dominant people have some ability to possess speech in the right hemisphere. Where the right hemisphere becomes more involved in speech after aphasia it becomes pertinent to ask whether this is because the individual is now falling back on language capabilites that were already present in the right hemisphere, rather than devloping new right hemisphere speech abilities. This complication is typically not taken into account.

This is not to claim that anatomical reorganization cannot and does not play any part in recovery. The fact that very young children who survive massive left hemisphere lesions that would be expected to result in severe and permanent aphasia in adults often grow up with near normal speech suggests that the right hemisphere can indeed taken over speech in the young and that brain plasticity of this type is possible. That it can occur in adults has yet to be proven.

The final recovery mechanism can be described as functional adaptation or compensation. Given the complexity of much behaviour it is always possible that a particular goal can be achieved by alternative strategies once the original mechanism has been disrupted. There are many instances where compensatory strategies have been observed in brain-damaged individuals. Gazzaniga (1978) describes how split brain subjects can develop sophisticated cross-cueing strategies, as when the left (verbal) hemisphere appears to be able to answer questions about information presented to the left visual field and relayed to the separated right hemisphere. Landis *et al.* (1982) describe how a patient with acquired dyslexia extended his reading ability by tracing the outline of letters with his finger and thereby introducing additional kinaesthetic feedback. It seems quite likely that this kind of mechanism accounts for a considerable part of longer-term recovery in adults (Miller, 1984).

If this analysis of the natural processes of recovery is correct and if cognitive training is to build on natural recovery, then it follows that cognitive retraining will generally involve assisting the impaired individual to achieve desired goals by means of the capabilities left to him. It will therefore not involve retraining the lost or impaired function *per se* but will involve using other functions to achieve desired goals or trying to train the person to use his remaining capability in the most efficient way.

This same conclusion arises from another line of reasoning. Research into both normal and disturbed cognitive functioning has revealed models which are useful in understanding disorders like amnesia or aphasia. Such models do not readily lead to suggestions as to how, say, lost memory capacity might be restored to normal. If a memory problem can be seen in terms of a reduced short-term or working memory, or an impaired ability to encode material at deeper levels, then it is difficult to derive psychological techniques that might be useful in correcting these faults. What psychological models or theories do suggest are ways in which alternative strategies might be developed or means by which remaining powers of memory might be used to the best advantege. In effect what psychological interventions might do is assist recovery in terms of functional adaptation, or, in other words, contribute to the amelioration of handicaps produced by neuropsychological impairments, rather than their direct removal.

METHODS OF INTERVENTION

In this section three examples of cognitive retraining procedures will be outlined, relating to three different types of cognitive impairment. The particular examples have been selected to show three relatively substantial areas of work within the emerging field of cognitive retraining and to show applications to rather different types of problem. This section certainly cannot give anything like a comprehensive overview, and a much more extensive account of the literature can be found in Miller (1984) or Powell (1981).

Memory

Disorders of memory are common after many forms of cerebral pathology and can be extremely handicapping to those who suffer them. In this context the concern is more with the milder or more moderate memory disorders that typically result from head injury, various types of cerebro-vascular disease, etc., rather than the severe amnesic syndromes associated with such rarer conditions as the alcoholic Korsakoff syndrome, which dominate the more theoretical neuropsychological research into amnesia.

One well-known finding in work on normal memory is that the use of imagery can enhance the learning or retention of experimental material, such as paired associates in the laboratory (for example, Paivio, 1969). Further experimental studies, by Jones (1974) amongst others, have demonstrated that many patients with memory problems can similarly benefit from using imagery in laboratory-type memory situations, although there is some indication that this may not be the case for those with the severest amnesias. Where imagery helps, it does not bring their performance up to normal levels but it does appear to enhance retention to a similar degree to that of normal subjects.

The next stage was of course to try to get patients to use imagery in order to lessen the impact of their memory impairments in real-life situations. One common complaint is a difficulty in remembering people's names. Music Hall performers with what appear to be quite phenomenal memories have described how to use imagery to remember names, and claim that this is the technique that they use in their acts (for example, Lorayne and Lucas, 1974). Imagery is used to link certain features of the individual's face or body with his name. For example, Mr Hook is imagined as having a large and exaggerated hooked nose or Mr MacDonald as wearing a kilt (for a Scottish name) and holding a large yellow Donald Duck.

A group working in Oregon, and associated with Lewinsohn, have looked at the possibility of using this particular technique in clinical settings. In a preliminary experiment, Lewinsohn *et al.* (1977) showed that imagery assisted subjects with memory problems in recalling names linked to photographs. This benefit, which was demonstrated at recall testing 30 minutes after learning, was unfortunately lost at follow-up a week later. Nevertheless, the same group used the technique in trying to improve recall of names in a single patient who actually presented with the problem of being unable to remember the names of people that he encountered regularly (Glasgow *et al.*, 1977). The subject was asked to keep a record of how many times each day this occurred. After a baseline period, training in the use of imagery was introduced. The data gave little indication that imagery was helpful, which was disappointing. Recall of names in the real-life setting was improved by a much simpler procedure. The subject was simply asked to write down names that he felt he should have been able to remember on a card. He was then encouraged to go over this card for a short period three times a day and just try to envisage the person who corresponded to each name. Many other accounts of the use of imagery in dealing with memory disorders can be found in the literature (*see* Miller, 1984) but true clinical effectiveness has yet to be proven.

Where imagery is effective in laboratory-type studies using subjects with memory disorders it is not clear why this is so. Crovitz (1979) points out that rate of presentation can affect learning and later retention. Experiments on imagery with memory-disordered subjects have typically not controlled for rate of presentation. It could be that any effect of imagery is derived from the fact that it forces the subject to attend more carefully to the to-be-remembered stimuli, and for much longer. Further studies of imagery are obviously required both from the point of view of its use as a clinical technique and in terms of its mode of action. It is also the case that there are alternative ways of trying to tackle memory problems (Miller, 1984) and these may prove to be useful even if it turns out that imagery is of little value. The more practical aspects of dealing with memory disorders are well described by Wilson and Moffatt (1984).

Language

It is easy to understand that aphasia, especially if it is severe, can have a drastic effect on a person's life. Conventional speech therapy is often used, but its effectiveness remains to be demonstrated. One controlled trial has yielded positive results (Basso *et al.,* 1979), but there are reasons for treating this with a little suspicion, and the remaining trials are unconvincing. Approaches to aphasia therapy based on operant conditioning have also been tried, but again, evidence of efficacy is lacking (Miller, 1984).

One area of aphasia therapy that has produced interesting developments is in relation to global aphasia. Global aphasia is fortunately not as common as the milder forms of dysphasia and refers to a state where the patient's speech is, at best, confined to a few words or noises. Some single words may be used, or even one or two standard phrases, but the patient is unable to string sequences of words together in order to communicate. Recovery from global asphasia is generally very poor.

Given such severe handicaps the question arises as to whether such patients can be taught alternative means of communication. Those with very severe asphasia are likely to have difficulty in coping with any complex form of communication and so the aim is to try to teach them an alterantive from of communication that will enable them to express such things as basic needs in a more effective way than would otherwise be possible. The level of sophistication involved is well short of that involved in normal speech.

One source of inspiration for this kind of work comes from studies of artificial language in chimpanzees (for example, Premack, 1971). In this series of experiments, Premack taught a chimpanzee to communicate using plastic tokens to refer to objects and relationships between them. This was extended for use with asphasics by Glass *et al.* (1973). Gardner *et al.* (1976) have developed a visual communication system known as VIC. This consists of a set of cards containing ideographic symbols for nouns, verbs, etc. The system has a number of basic symbols that all subjects will need to learn, but it can be readily extended by adding extra symbols to cope with the particular needs of individual patients.

Although there have been no properly controlled trials of the use of these systems, it does appear that globally asphasic subjects with almost no worthwhile oral speech can learn to use the elements of such systems and often to a degree that exceeds their capacity to communicate orally in conventional speech. What remains to be seen is whether such subjects can generalize what has been learned to outside the hospital setting in which it took place, and actually manage to use these systems to enhance communication in everyday life. There are potential limitations to their practical value, in that other people in the patient's environment also have to be able to use the system and it is not always practicable to push around cards or plastic tokens in order to communicate.

A different non-vocal communication system is provided by 'Amerind'. This is a manual system based on the sign language used by the North American plains Indians (Skelly, 1979). Skelly is herself from an American Indian background. As a potential means of communication for those with very severe asphasia, it does have a number of useful features. It is based on a relatively small repertoire of signs that are used in telegraphic style. The signs can all be performed with one hand, and this is important since there is a strong association between global asphasia and hemiplegia (that is, paralysis down one side of the body). Finally, the meanings of most of the signs are fairly obvious and it is claimed that normal subjects can guess the meanings of about 80 per cent of the signs with no prior instruction. This is still a useful feature, even if the asphasic patient is less competent at initial recognition of the signs, since people in the patient's environment also have to be capable of detecting the meaning of the signs if communication is to take place.

Amerind is now being taught quite widely to those who deal with aphasic patients, especially speech therapists. Although it is a system with considerable potential for use, with the small number of very severely aphasic patients it does need careful evaluation, lest the enthusiasm should turn out to be unwarranted. As with other alternative communication systems, the crucial question is not so much whether such patients can learn to use it in the hospital setting, but its practical value in everyday life.

Neglect

Neglect is a common phenomenon in those who have suffered lesions (for example, as a result of a stroke) in the posterior portions of the right hemisphere. Subjects with neglect show a complete or partial tendency to ignore stimuli arising to one side of the body midline (usually stimuli from the left after a right-sided lesion). The most severe visual neglect, where the subject fails to respond to any visual stimulus to the left of centre, is typically associated with a visual field defect (left homonymous hemianopia). Milder degrees of visual neglect are necessarily asociated with field defects and the experimental evidence suggests that neglect is not just the consequence of a loss of sensory input from the afflicted side (Bisiach *et al.,* 1979). Neglect may also be an important factor in the rehabilitation of those who have become hemiplegic as a result of a stroke. In general, those with paralysis of the right side of the body (as a result of left hemisphere stroke) are more successfully rehabilitated than those with left-sided paralysis, despite the fact that the former are likely to suffer aphasia as well. Denes *et al.* (1982) have suggested that spatial neglect may be an important factor in holding back the recovery of hemiplegics.

A group at the New York Institute of Rehabilitation Medicine has attempted to study neglect in a systematic way, and a general account of their work can be found in Diller and Gordon (1981). As part of its work, this group has tried to devise means to overcome the problem of neglect. In this respect, two experiments are of particular interest (Weinberg *et al.,* 1977, 1979). In both, the subjects were patients who had suffered right hemisphere strokes with consequent visual neglect. The general strategy was to have control subjects undergo the unit's standard occupational therapy programme whilst the experimental group had 20 hours' special training in addition to the occupational therapy package.

```
 1 -  Early in life Mr. Harding had found himself  -  1
 2 -  located at Barchester. A fine voice and a    -  2
 3 -  taste for sacred music had decided the       -  3
 4 -  position in which he was to exercise his      -  4
 5 -  calling, and for many years he performed      -  5
 6 -  the easy but not highly paid duties of a      -  6
 7 -  minor canon. At the age of forty a small      -  7
 8 -  living in the close vicinity of the town      -  8
 9 -  increased both his work and his income and    -  9
10 -  at the age of fifty he became the            - 10
```

Figure 1. Example of the kind of material used by Weinberg *et al.* (1977) in training patients with visual neglect to read again.

The special training procedures varied slightly between the two experiments but included such things as facing a board on which stimuli could appear in different positions. They then practised such things as identifying stimuli which moved in sequence from the unaffected side, across the subject's midline and into the other side of the board. Subjects also had to search for lights in different parts of the board. Practice was also given on cancellation tasks where, for example, the subject had to cross out all the eights on a page with numbers distributed all over it. (Typically, subjects tend to miss those on the left.)

Subjects with neglect can also have problems in reading. They tend to miss out the first few syllables or words on the left-hand side of each line of text. Subjects were therefore given practice in reading text like that set out in *Figure 1*. The subject can use the thick black line on the left as an anchor point to be identified before commencing to read each line. The numbers at the beginnings and ends of the lines can be used to ensure that the individual lines of text are read in the right order. As practice proceeds, these cues can be faded and withdrawn in sequence. The numbers on the right are removed first, then those on the left, and finally the anchoring line.

A further training used by this group was intended to enhance sensory awareness. Subjects sat facing the back of a manikin to represent the upper half of the human torso. They were repeatedly touched on their backs and then had to indicate where they had been touched by pointing to the corresponding part of the manikin.

In these experiments, not only did the experimental group receiving the special training procedures show improvement as compared to subjects who only received conventional occupational therapy, but this improvement showed some generalization to tasks not used in the special training procedures. It is probably not all that surprising that even severely brain-damaged patients should show some improvement on specific tasks subject to extensive training or practice. It is particularly encouraging when this seems to reduce the impact of a problem like neglect, even in situations not used in training.

FINAL COMMENT

As already indicated, the work described above is merely a small sample of the range of activity that is now going on in the field of cognitive rehabilitation. Considered as a whole, this work is encouraging and it is highly likely that psychologists will play an increasingly important role in the management and rehabilitation of patients with neurological disease. Nevertheless, it would be sensible to bear in mind a number of limitations.

As a general rule those working in the field of cognitive retraining have tended to concentrate on the development of techniques, followed by some sort of demonstration that their techniques are feasible, in the sense that they can be used with real patients. There have been few well-designed trials to test effectiveness. Where such trials have been carried out the results have not always been positive. Those positive results that have been obtained often reflect relatively small improvements when viewed in the light of the considerable therapeutic efforts that have been put in.

Evaluation also needs to be taken further than this. To demonstrate that techniques are of real clinical value it has to be shown that the teaching of signing systems to the globally aphasic or training procedures to counteract neglect go beyond just enabling the aphasic to sign more effectively than he can speak or improving performance on certain experimental tasks known to be affected by neglect. Real clinical usefulness means going beyond this to show that these procedures work to such a degree that they have a definite effect on the individual's daily life and enable him to go about his daily affairs with greater facility. So far, evaluation in this wider sense has not been attempted.

Another possible limitation for cognitive retraining is that many of the 'brain-damaged' populations for whom cognitive retraining might be appropriate can also exhibit marked personality changes and alterations in social functioning. Brooks (1984) has provided a useful review of these with regard to head injury, but similar problems can arise after strokes and other forms of pathology of the brain. Characteristics like disinhibition, lack of insight, and other so-called 'frontal' changes make the amelioration of cognitive impairments, as well as overall rehabilitation, that much more difficult.

Cognitive retraining is in the early stages of development, and the point of drawing attention to the limitations and complications is not in any way to suggest that the whole exercise will ultimately prove to be of doubtful value. In fact, the writer's own view is relatively optimistic in the long run. The issue to be grasped is that this fascinating and exciting area of development has yet to surmount some difficult obstacles. New techniques need to be developed and some older ones refined and extended before psychology can make a major impact on the rehabilitation and adjustment of those who have suffered neuropsychological impairments. This impact should be achieved eventually, but we are just at the start of the long haul that will be necessary before the goal of widespread clinical effectiveness is achieved.

REFERENCES

BASSO, A., CAPITANI, E. and VIGNOLO, L.A. (1979) Influence of rehabilitation on language skills in aphasic patients: a controlled study. *Archives of Neurology, 36,* 190–196.

BISIACH, E., LUSATTI, C. and PERANI, D. (1979) Unilateral neglect, representational scheme and consciousness. *Brain, 102,* 609–618.

BROOKS, D.N. (1984) *Closed Head Injury: Psychological, Social, and Family Consequences.* Oxford: Oxford University Press.

CROVITZ, H.F. (1979) Presentation limits on memory retrieval. *Cortex, 15,* 37–42.

DENES, G., SEMENZA, C., STOPPA, E. and LIS, A. (1982) Unilateral spatial neglect and recovery from hemiplegia: a follow-up study. *Brain, 105,* 543–552.

DILLER, L. and GORDON, W.A. (1981) Rehabilitation and clinical neuropsyhology. In: S.B. Filskov and T.J. Bell (eds) *Handbook of Clinical Neuropsychology.* New York: Wiley.

GARDNER, H., ZURIF, E.B., BERRY, T. and BAKER, E. (1976) Visual communication in aphasia. *Neuropsychologia, 14,* 275–292.

GAZZANIGA, M.S. (1978) Is seeing believing: notes on clinical recovery. In: S. Finger (ed.) *Recovery from Brain Damage.* New York: Plenum Press.

GLASGOW, R.E., ZEISS, R.A., BARRERA, M. and LEWINSOHN, P.M. (1977) Case studies on remediating memory deficits in brain-damaged individuals. *Journal of Clinical Psychology, 33,* 1049–1054.

GLASS, A.V., GAZZANIGA, M.S. and PREMACK, D. (1973) Artificial language training in global aphasics. *Neuropsychologia, 11,* 95–103.

HEILMAN, K.M. and VALENSTEIN, E. (1979) *Clinical Neuro-psychology.* Oxford: Oxford University Press.

JONES, M.K. (1974) Imagery as a memonic aid after left temporal lobectomy: contrast between material specific and generalized memory disorders. *Neuropsychologia, 12,* 21–30.

LANDIS, T., GRAVES, R., BENSON, D.F. and HEBBEN, N. (1982) Visual recognition through kinaesthetic mediation. *Psychological Medicine, 12,* 515–531.

LEWINSOHN, P.M., DANAHER, C.B. and KIKEL, S. (1977) Visual imagery as a mnemonic aid for brain-injured persons. *Journal of Consulting and Clinical Psychology, 5,* 717–723.

LORAYNE, H. and LUCAS, J. (1974) *The Memory Book.* Briarcliff, NY: Stein & Day.

MILLER, E. (1984) *Recovery and Management of Neuropsychological Impairments.* Chichester: Wiley.

PAIVIO, A. (1969) Mental imagery in learning and memory. *Psychological Review, 76,* 241–263.

POWELL, G.E. (1981) *Brain Function Therapy.* Aldershot: Gower.

PREMACK, D. (1971) Language in chimpanzee. *Science, 172,* 808– 822.

SCHOENFELD, T.A. and HAMILTON, L.W. (1977) Secondary brain changes following lesions: a new paradigm for lesion experimentation. *Physiology and Behaviour, 18,* 951–967.

SKELLY, M. (1979) *Amer-Ind Gestural Code Based on Universal American Indian Hand Talk.* New York: Elsevier.

VON MONOKOW, C. (1914) *Die Lokalisation im Grosshirn und der Abbau der Function durch Kortikale Herde.* Wiesbaden: J.F. Bergmann.

WEINBERG, J., DILLER, L., GOTDON, W.A., GERSTMAN, L.J., LIEBERMAN, A., LAKIN, P., HODGES, G. and ESRACHI, C. (1977) Visual scanning training effect on reading-related tasks in acquired brain damage. *Archives of Physical Medicine and Rehabilitation, 58,* 479–486.

WEINBERG, J., DILLER, L., GOTDON, W.A., GERSTAMN, L.J., LIEBERMAN, A., LAKIN, P., HODGES, G. and EXRACHI, C. (1979) Training sensory awareness and spatial organization in people with right brain damage. *Archives of Physical Medicine and Rehabilitation, 60,* 491–496.

WEST, D.R., DEADWYLER, S.A., COTMAN, C.W. and LYNCH, G.S. (1976) An experimental test of diaschisis. *Behavioural Biology, 22,* 419–425.

WILSON, B.A. and MOFFATT, N. (1984) *Clinical Management of Memory Problems.* London: Croom Helm.

AUTOMATED CLINICAL ASSESSMENT

Robin G. Morris

The aim of this chapter is to show how recent developments in computing technology have made it possible to automate many psychological assessment procedures in clinical psychology. The possibility has been recognized for a long while, and powerful arguments have been developed for moving in this direction (Miller, 1968). However, it is only recently that technological developments have advanced sufficiently for the standard use of automated testing in clinical practice to be more than just a prediction for the future.

Arguably, the most significant technological advance in recent years has been the development of the microprocessor. The effect of this latest development has been a rapid decrease in the cost of computing technology and a corresponding increase in range of application. The microprocessing revolution has allowed the development of microcomputers which have the same facilities as minicomputers and the same amount of storage – but which are a fraction of the price. In the last 10 years the cost of a mainframe computer has decreased approximately 10-fold and they now store approximately 30 times the amount of information.

A further development is that computer facilities are no longer confined to computing laboratories or outlying terminal stations. Firstly, there has been the development of computer network technology. It is now possible to access information from a computer which is literally thousands of miles away by using a device called the 'modem', combined with telecommunication lines. This means that information and data available to a computer user are not confined to one particular computer. Secondly, the last few years have witnessed the advent of low cost microcomputers with applications in business, education and in the home. There is a huge market for micro-computer systems, ranging from recreational to serious commercial use. The microcomputer boom has done much to remove the mystique of computing for the layman. More importantly, microcomputers can be acquired, operated and programmed by people with little or no training and background in computing. Also, the operating costs of microcomputers are minimal in

121

comparison with minicomputers or mainframe computers.

One aspect of these developments is that computers are being used in domains of work which involve interpersonal interaction. Thus, such tasks as interviewing, disseminating information, instruction and transactions can be performed by a computer. Since much of the work in clinical psychology falls within these categories, it is not surprising that computer applications in clinical psychology appear to have a promising future. At present, computers are used in the profession specifically for:

1. Psychological testing – either for automated administration of exisiting psychometric tests or for development of novel ones (Thompson and Wilson, 1982);
2. Interviewing and questionnaire administration (Carr *et al.,* 1983);
3. Providing psychological treatment, such as behavioural therapy or psycho-therapy (Colby, 1980);
4. Administering biofeedback (Lang, 1980);
5. Collecting, organizing and analysing data, and constructing reports.

Computers have been used to fulfil the functions listed above for about two decades but mostly on an experimental basis. It is only recently that the result of such research has begun to penetrate into standard clinical practice, mainly because of the development of microcomputers.

RECENT DEVELOPMENTS IN TECHNOLOGY

Perhaps the most popular microcomputers in clinical use are the *Apple* and *Pet* systems. Complete with peripheral devices such as printers and disc-drives they cost in the order of £2,500. Cheaper versions such as the BBC Micro are also in wide use, realistically reducing the cost of a system which has general application in clinical psychology to around £1,000 (Simpson and Linney, 1983). This figure is often well within the budget of most district Clinical Psychology Departments. Typically, the microcomputers consist of a monitor, a keyboard, the microprocessor and a disc-drive for permanent storage of programs and data. The requirements for a system adapted for clinical use have been comprehensively reviewed by Beaumont (1982); despite the rapid advance in computing technology, his description is still applicable. Most microcomputers are designed to be run using the ubiquitous BASIC programming language, mainly because this is one of the easiest to learn. However, for more sophisticated purposes many people use PASCAL. To convert the computer to use this language it is necessary to use a PASCAL language compiler. For psychological testing, precise timing is often a requirement and the system has to be supplemented with a clock mechanism. In the case of the *Apple II*, clocks such as the Mountain Hardware Clock are commercially available. Another consideration is the choice of response media; that is, the hardware which enables the subject to interact with the computer. The psychologist can obviously use the QWERTY keyboard but this is not always suitable for patients, particularly if they are mentally or physically impaired. The standard array of typewriter keys can be too confusing for some patients. One solution is to programme the computer so that only a restricted set is in operation. With some systems, the irrelevent keys are covered over. More usually, the system is supplemented by a separate keyboard (keypads), many of which are commercially available. Alternative response media are currently being explored, some of which enable the subject to respond directly on to the monitor. For example, the light pen is designed so that the subject makes a response by placing the tip of the pen at an appropriate position on the screen. Illuminated portions of the screen serve as targets. Another response system is the touch-sensitive screen, in which the subject responds by touching the surface of the screen with a finger. Recently, relatively reliable systems have become available at realistic prices. Their applicability for automated clinical testing is currently being researched in Great Britain by French and Beaumont (1984) in Leicester, and Bob Woods at the Institute of Psychiatry in London.

Finally, the graphics capabilities of a system are a major consideration. Most recent microcomputers have 'high resolution' systems which allow quite complex graphical representations to be presented on the monitor. The current trend is for improvement in this area, partly because of the development of computer games. High quality computer graphics are an obvious asset, both in making human interaction with a computer more interesting and also for designing certain psychological tests. Recently, relatively cheap camera systems have become commercially available, which can convert images into computer code for storage and subsequent use.

The microcomputer can, in principle, carry out *all* of the functions listed in the introduction. To illustrate: French and Beaumont (1984) have recently programmed the Apple II computer to administer psychometric tests such as the Wisconsin Card Sorting Task and Ravens Progressive Matrices; Carr and his colleagues at the Institute of Psychiatry have developed sophisticated software for microcomputers which will take a psychiatric case history, administer questionnaires such as the Fear Questionnaire and elicit the characteristics of patient's phobias (Carr *et al.,* 1983). At the moment, however, the profession has been relatively slow (for example, compared to education) to embrace and develop the new technology. Some of the reasons for this, and the practical problems of automating psychological procedures will become apparent later.

One of the main arguments for using computers in clinical psychology is to save the psychologist time. Routine functions can be performed by the computer, leaving the clinical psychologist with more time to concentrate on the treatment and management of patients. This argument has been applied to the automation of what used to be considered the bread and butter of a psychologist's work, namely psychological testing.

AUTOMATED PSYCHOLOGICAL TESTING

One of the reasons why psychological testing is in disfavour is that it is repetitive and mechanical (Denner, 1977). However, these very features make it easier to automate. The most straightforward tests to automate are those in questionnaire form, particularly if they require multiple-choice answers. However, it could be argued that automation offers little advantage, with the exception of saving the test administrator from the task of scoring (Acker, 1983). Tests of mental ability tend to be more difficult to automate partly because the stimulus material is often more complex, especially if objects or pictorial stimuli are used in the standard version. Also, the types of response can be more varied and sometimes do not lend themselves to computer analysis. Much of the work involved in developing automated tests has been devoted to solving these problems.

It has long been argued that automated psychometric testing is potentially more accurate and objective, since it minimizes human error and more closely controls how a test is administered. Even quite rigorously defined procedures, such as those described in the Wechsler Adult Intelligence Scale (WAIS) manual, are subject to individual differences in administration and inter- pretation. In contrast, a computer can be programmed to perform *exactly* the same procedure with each subject.

There is currently a debate concerning whether the emphasis should be on automating existing psychometric tests or developing new ones. The advan- tage of converting existing tests is that they are familiar and well tried. Many of them were constructed during the height of interest in psychometry and were carefully designed. Furthermore, they are more likely to be familiar to clinical psychologists; it might be thought easier to adapt an automated version of an old test than learn to use a completely new one. One view is that the first stage of development will be the conversion of existing tests (Thompson and Wilson, 1982). This will give way to the development of novel tests which will use the features of the new technology to their full advantage.

TESTS OF MENTAL ABILITIES

Automating existing tests

In most of the early automated versions of tests of mental ability, stimulus material was presented on slide-projectors, and subjects responded by pressing response keys. The system was either computer-based, or controlled by minicomputers or mainframe computers. An early example was Elwood's (1969) automation of the WAIS. Elwood and Griffin (1972) report high test–retest correlations on a sample of outpatients, suggesting that the automated version was as reliable as the standard version. For verbal IQ these correlations were 0.92 and 0.95 respectively. For performance IQ they were 0.93 and 0.88 and for full-scale IQ they were 0.95 and 0.96. However, it was found that performance on the automated version tended to be lower; much of this difference can be accounted for by difficulties that subjects had in using response keys for the Digit Symbol subtest.

The majority of studies have concentrated on single tests or selected items from tests batteries. These have been briefly reviewed by Thompson and Wilson (1982) and include, for example, the automated Hidden Figures Tests (Brinton and Rouleau, 1969), the Peabody Picture Vocabulary Tests (Overton and Scott, 1972; Knights *et al.,* 1973; Klinge and Rodziewicz, 1976), the Reitan Category Test (Beaumont, 1975), the WAIS Digit Symbol Subtest (Gilberstat *et al.,* 1976), the Mill Hill Vocabulary Test (Watts *et al.,* 1982) and the Ravens Progressive Matrices (Gilberstat *et al.,* 1976; Calvert and Waterfall, 1982). Typically, these have only been validated on a small, select sample of subjects. The largest sample in the studies listed above was the 40 subjects tested by Watts *et al.* (1982). Frequently the equipment has been purpose-built and none of the automated versions have been properly standardized. What these studies show is that it is possible to automate traditional psychometric tests successfully and use them as relatively reliable measures of mental functioning.

Most recent studies employ microcomputers, since these are much more flexible in their application. Microcomputers can be used to run a fully automated system with the data recorded, scored and processed automatically. The two studies described below illustrate some of the most recent developments in automating tests of mental ability using microcomputers.

At the Royal Hospital and Home for Incurables, in London, Sarah Wilson and her colleagues have produced automated versions of the Mill Hill Vocabulary Scale (synonyms section), the AH4 (Part I) and the Digit Span Test (Wilson *et al.,* 1982) for use with the severely physically handicapped. These tests have been automated on the Apple II computer, with the patients producing their responses on a row of seven touch-sensitive keypads. Six of the keys were used for making responses in each trial, with an additional 'pass' key used by the patients to indicate that they did not want to respond. These standard and automated versions have been validated on 30 severely handicapped patients. For the Mill Hill Vocabulary Scale the correlation between the scores for the two techniques was significant (0.87) and there was no difference in overall performance. For the AH4 test there was also a significant correlation (0.81), but the overall score was higher for the automated version. This is accounted for by the fact that all the questions were multiple-choice in the automated test, increasing the probability of correct answers. Only forward Digit Span was automated and, with six response keys, the set was confined to digits 1 to 6. The correlation with the standard version was poor but significant (0.62) and performance was substantially lower. Wilson *et al.* (1983) are currently improving the automated version using digits 1 to 9 and including reverse digit span.

One of the most significant recent contributions to computerized psychometric assessment is the DHSS/Leicester project co-ordinated by Graham Beaumont (Beaumont, 1982; French and Beaumont, 1984; Beaumont, 1984). He has developed a battery of automated psychometric tests on the Apple II computer. The stimulus material is presented on a monitor and the subjects respond using specified keys on the QWERTY keyboard, or with some versions, via a touch-sensitive screen or light pen. Using this system, Beaumont has automated the Ravens Standard Progressive Matrices, the Mill Hill Vocabulary Test, Digit Span, the DAT language and spelling usage tests, the Money Road Map Tests and Wisconsin Card Sorting Test. The automated versions have been developed and elegantly refined since about 1980. For example, in the automated version of the Ravens Progressive Matrices, the subject is presented with a visual array of response alternatives which correspond to the stimulus item. The subject can respond by either touching one of the response alternatives on the screen manually or by using a light pen.

The automated versions have recently been validated (French and Beaumont, 1984) on 275 psychiatric patients from five hospitals in Great Britain. The sample mainly included patients diagnosed as psychotics, mental retardates, organics and personality disorders. Some subjects were tested on the automated version first, followed by the standard version; others were tested on the standard version followed by the automated version. The correlations between automated and standard versions tended to be high both between subjects and within subjects. This can be taken as strong evidence that as a whole the automated versions have a high validity.

An exception to this trend was performance of the patients on the Ravens Progressive Matrices. With this test, patients tended to perform worse on the automated version when it was administered first, thus accounting for the low correlations. Beaumont and French suggest that this is due to the relatively low resolution of the automated presentation of stimulus material. The patients had difficulty in recognizing the shapes of the figures unless they have previously seen them printed in high resolution in the standard version.

French and Beaumont also report that the patients consistently score lower with the automated version of the Digit Span Test – both with the keyboard response and the touch-sensitive screen. Wilson *et al.* (1983) found this as well. One explanation of this is that with the automated version the digits are presented visually, whilst in the standard version they are presented auditorily. It is commonly accepted that auditorily presented verbal material is more easily remembered. Beaumont (1984) has replicated and studied this phenomenon in greater depth using a range of response media. Firstly, he compared the performance of subjects using the standard keyboard, a keypad or a light pen to make their responses. Digit span performance with the standard keyboard is superior to that with the key pad. He suggests that this is because the subjects are more familiar with the standard keyboard. Performance is worse with the light pen, which probably relates to the fact that subjects report the device to be clumsy and uncomfortable to use for extended periods.It also introduces a delay between the subjects responding and the computer acknowledging the response, which could interfere with the memory for the digits. In a subsequent experiment, he found that the digit span of the subjects using the touch sensitive screen was similarly reduced.

Clearly, much more work is needed to automate existing tests of mental abilities using microcomputers. The studies described above highlight some of the problems involved in this field. Firstly, in producing the automated version, it is often necessary to change the form of presentation and response media. Such factors are bound to alter the performance of subjects, and even what aspects of mental functioning are being measured. For example, in the automated Digit Span Test developed by Wilson *et al.* (1983) and Beaumont (1984) the digits are presented visually rather than auditorily and the response is manual rather than verbal. With some tests, this type of modification might be trivial but, as Beaumont has shown, this is not always the case.

A second problem is that, for most patients, automated assessment will be a novel experience. It has been shown that training subjects to interact with a computer can substantially affect their performance (Johnson and White, 1980). This may be critical in tests of mental ability, particularly where the subjects have to perform under time pressure. The French and Beaumont (1984) study revealed practice effects on some of the automated versions which would obviously pose problems if they were to be used as clinical instruments.

These problems need to be considered in relation to each individual test. The tests then have to be validated to see whether they will work with clinical populations. Given that the automated version changes the nature of the test, it would also have to be re-standardized. This is a substantial undertaking, beyond the resources of a single investigator. For these reasons, the cost of implementing automated versions of existing tests of mental abilities will have to be carefully balanced against their clinical usefulness.

Modifying existing tests and creating new tests

The main argument for developing new automated tests is that they can be designed to incorporate many of the positive features of computing technology. For example, computers can be used to generate stimulus material for each individual subject, and control the level of complexity of a test. They can also be used to monitor the level of performance of the subject and adjust the level of difficulty of a test accordingly. Precise timing of presentation and response speed can be easily achieved. An important, and sometimes overlooked feature is that tests can be made more interesting, exciting and friendly for the subject.

One of the earliest automated clinical tests was the Picture Matching Test (PMT) developed by Gedye and others (*cf.* Gedye and Miller, 1969). There are various versions: the one marketed in 1976 by Questel Ltd consisted of a back-projection screen system and two response keys. The system was linked to a PDP8 minicomputer using a GPO line and modem device. A main feature of the system is to test the ability of patients to match to sample; subjects are presented with a central stimulus and two peripheral stimuli (the stimuli are pictures of common objects). The object is to see whether the subjects are able to judge which peripheral stimulus matches the central stimulus. The PMT was developed for psychogeriatric patients and had a limited use in evaluating the effects of psychotropic drugs on mental performance (Exton-Smith, 1980). An important design feature is that the test is tailored to suit the level of functioning of the patients. This is done by using a branching program which switches to different subtests according to the performance of the patients. The problem with this feature is that the gradation of difficulty levels is inconsistent (Volans and Levy, 1982), and improvement in this sphere would be needed if it were to become a standard clinical instrument. However, the PMT is not being developed further because it is relatively expensive to use and it has only one particular application.

The branching feature of the PMT has yet to be fully exploited in other clinical tests of mental abilities. Another test which illustrates how computing technology can be specially adapted to form part of the test structure is the automated version of the Perceptual Maze Test (Weinman, 1982; Elithorn *et al.*, 1982). Originally the test was automated using minicomputers but it has since become microprocessor-based. The subject is presented with a lattice structure of routes which has a number of dots superimposed over the intersections. The object is to move along the lattice passing through as many dots as possible. The subject is constrained to move forward to the left or the right.

The maze is presented on a monitor, and the subject is required to denote a move to the left or right by pressing appropriate response keys. A computer can be programmed to generate mazes of different complexities and solve each maze almost instantaneously. Computer automation makes it possible to segment the overall response time into the component parts and derive indices for component aspects of the subject's performance. For example, the computer measures the time that subjects take to search the maze before initiating their first response, the time taken to move along the maze, and the time that subjects pause at the end to check their responses. Elithorn *et al.* (1982) maintain that the automated version can be used to differentiate the effects of psychotropic drugs on mental functioning. However, this test has yet to be validated on a substantial clinical population and is not commercially available.

A notable British development is the combination of the Bexley-Maudsley Automated Psychological Screening (BMAPS) and Bexley-Maudsley Card Sorting Test (BMCST). These were developed by Acker and Acker (1982a,b) at the Institute of Psychiatry to screen patients for brain damage associated with non-specific dementias. They are now commercially available from NFER-Nelson for use on Commodore Pet and Apple II microcomputers. Stimulus material is presented on the monitor of the microcomputer and the subjects make their response on nine response keys, which are mounted over the standard key board.

The BMAPS consists of five tests derived from existing pyschometric procedures or experimental psychology:

1. *The 'little man test':* the patients are presented with a picture of a manikin which is holding an object in one hand. The manikin may be upright, upside down, facing backwards or forwards and the patients are required to judge which hand holds the object (left or right);
2. *Symbol Digit:* this is a modified version of the WAIS Digit Symbol subtest;
3. *Visual Perceptual Analysis:* three designs are presented on the monitor and the patient is required to determine which is the odd one out. The designs are generated by the computer and consist of a square shape divided up into an eight-by-eight matrix of smaller squares, filled or unfilled. There are two levels of difference between the matching and non-matching designs;
4. *Verbal Memory:* the patients are presented with a sequential list of words which they are required to remember. They are then presented with each word and two distractor items and required to judge which item had been seen before;
5. *Visual Spatial Memory:* the stimulus material is similar to that used in the Visual Perceptual Analysis test. Patients are shown a single matrix and then, after a variable retention interval, the same matrix with two alternative matrices. They have to judge which one had been shown before.

The BMCST is a modified form of the Wisconsin Card Sorting Task in which a series of patterns have to be sorted according to a set of rules which govern the patterns. The rules have to be abstracted by the patients and thus the test is a measure of non-verbal abstract thinking. In the automated version the sorting rules are defined by four 'category cards' which are presented at the top of the monitor. Further cards are presented at the bottom of the screen which have to be matched with one of the 'category cards'.

The BMAPS and BMCST have been validated on 103 alcoholic patients attending an alcoholic treatment unit and matched controls (Acker *et al.,* 1982). The publishers claim that the tests can be administered by support staff supervised by a clinical psychologist or psychiatrist, and that they can be completed in approximately one hour. Using a computer to automate these tests has a number of advantages. The computer is programmed to generate the shapes used in the Visual Perceptual Analysis and Visual Spatial Memory tests using a pseudorandom generator. Thus the patterns are different each time the tests are used. With the BMCST, the computer can analyse the patient's errors in detail, a task which is too time-consuming to be done by hand for standard clinical practice. Finally, despite the fact that the tests are relatively complex, they can be administered with relatively little practice by non-psychologists.

The BMAPS and BMCST are probably the most sophisticated recent projects in developing novel tests of mental ability on computers for clinical use. There are other projects in progress, which include, for example, production of an automated memory test (Colbourn *et al.*, 1983), a digit recall test with a telephone dial as the response mode and a test of semantic memory (Simpson and Linney, 1983). There are currently two projects headed by Ogden *et al.* (1984) and by Bob Woods at the Institute of Psychiatry in which new tests of mental functioning are being developed for use with the elderly. It is likely that the number of projects will increase as more departments obtain microcomputers and their clinical use becomes more sophisticated. However, there is clearly a long way to go before there is a good choice of novel clinical computerized tests which have been properly validated and standardized.

PERSONALITY AND PSYCHIATRIC ASSESSMENT

Automating paper and pencil questionnaires

Many tests of personality are in questionnaire form. They are constructed so that responses can be coded and scored, and usually the questionnaires are in multiple-choice format. It is a relatively easy matter to program a computer to administer such a test: the questions are presented as text on the monitor and response keys are used for the patients to indicate their choices. The computer then automatically scores the tests and files the results. Questions can be repeated if they are not answered immediately, so that there is no chance of items being omitted unintentionally.

Recent examples of 'straight' computerised automation of paper-and-pencil tests include the Hamilton Depression Rating Scale (Carr *et al.*, 1981), the Minnisota Multiphasic Personality Inventory (MMPI) (Johnson *et al.*, 1978), the Eysenck Personality Inventory (EPI) (Ridgeway *et al.*, 1982), the Eysenck Personality Questionnaire (EPQ) (French and Beaumont, 1984). Recently, Sinclair marketed an automated version of the Cattel 16 PF, making it available to the general public. As part of more complex assessment schedules the Beck Depression Inventory (BDI) (Selmi *et al.*, 1981), the Fear Questionnaire and the Hopkins Symptoms Checklist (Carr and Ghosh, 1983 a,b) have been automated. There are many other examples, reflecting the ease of automation of this type of test.

On the whole, the automated versions do not alter substantially the nature of the tests and where such tests have been validated the results appear promising. For example, Ridgeway *et al.* (1982) report that the construct validity of the EPI remains unchanged, as assessed by the intercorrelations between the paper-and-pencil and computer versions. In the case of the automated Hamilton Rating Scale (Carr *et al.*, 1981), 97 per cent of normal and depressed patients were classified correctly; the severity of depression as assessed by the patient's scores on the automated scale correlated significantly with assessments of severity by psychiatrists. Furthermore, the computer administration is usually acceptable to patients; French and Beaumont (1984) found that the EPQ was enjoyed more when presented initially on the computer and that patients were more willing to take another test following the computerized version.

More sophisticated testing procedures

However, it has been argued that it is not worth dedicating the power of a computer to simple paper-and-pencil tests (Acker, 1983). Even if resources are freely available, the computerized version limits the location of testing and introduces the problems inherent in person–machine interaction. It is easier to justify using a computer in administering a personality test when the scoring is lengthy and complex computation is involved – thus saving the effort and time of the tester.

Tests can also be made much more sophisticated: the computer can be used to establish a friendly dialogue with the patient, creating a personal atmosphere which might be missing when filling in a form. By programming the computer to branch (*cf.* Vale, 1981) after each response, the computer can exclude irrelevant questions and focus in on particular aspects of the patient's personality traits or states which need following up in detail. Thus, the patient is never confronted with a long string of questions, some of which are irrelevant. The computer can also be programmed to generate questions which are tailored to a particular individual. Computerized interviewing has been developed in this fashion in psychiatry and has been shown to assess symptoms accurately and in a way that is acceptable to patients (Lucas *et al.*, 1977). The computer can also be programmed to be more active in eliciting and making sense of incoming information.

An obvious example of the latter is the development of Repertory Grid computer programs (Slater, 1977) to analyse the personal constructs of an individual. In the past, these programs were mainly for experimental purposes and confined to mainframe computers. However, recently they have been transferred to microcomputers and modified so that they can be used to elicit a grid from a person directly. For example, the PLANET suite has been modified by Shaw (1982) and contains a program called PEGASUS which is used to elicit a single grid and at the same time provide a person with comment and feedback.

Another example in clinical psychology is the semi-automated Personal

Relations Index (PRI) (Mulhall, 1977). The aim of this instrument is to assess how people perceive the nature of their interaction with other people, representing their perceptions in graphical form. In a free discussion the tester elicits descriptions of attitudes, feelings or behavioural states, termed elements. These are then fed into a computer and used to construct a questionnaire which is unique to a particular person. The questions concern how the person would respond in terms of their elements to the elements of a significant other, and vice versa. The computer uses the answers to construct the graphical representation of the interaction. The PRI was developed in a psychiatric setting and has been used mainly in counselling to modify the impact imposed on relationships by physical handicap or mental illnesses.

BEHAVIOURAL ASSESSMENT

In recent years there have been a number of projects in computerized behavioural assessment. The assessment consists of a dialogue with the patient in which problem behaviours, moods and cognitions are elicited. Angle *et al.* (1977) have computerized a comprehensive behavioural assessment which takes from 4 to 10 hours but which, they report, is preferable, for many patients, to the standard interview. Lucas *et al.* developed a system for the screening of alcohol related problems, finding that people told the computer that they drank 30 per cent more alcohol than they had told a human interviewer. Selmi *et al.* (1981) are currently developing a computerized system for assessment and cognitive behavioural therapy in depression. The computer elicits dysfunctional automatic thoughts which cause depression.

A computerized system for the assessment and treatment of phobias is under development at the Institute of Psychiatry in London (Carr and Ghosh, 1983a,b) on a SWTPC 6800 microprocessor. The computer communicates with the patient by displaying text on a monitor, and the patient is required to respond by typing onto a standard QWERTY keyboard. The computer is programmed so that the patient is taught how to respond using the keyboard before the assessment begins. The patient is then screened for other psychiatric disorders, such as depression and generalized anxiety, with a series of questions. If the patients are unsuitable for behavioural treatment (the computer is programmed to make this decision), they are referred to the clinician and the interview is terminated. Otherwise, the computer starts questioning the patient concerning the nature of his or her phobias and ascertains the contexts in which phobic behaviour occurs. The branching facility of the computer is used to ensure that the questions are relevant to the particular problems of the patient. The prinicples of behavioural assessment are also explained to the patient.

A key feature of the system is that at this point the patient is given a description of his or her problems based on the assessment. The patient then has the option of redefining the problems so that particular points are specified more accurately. This is an interactive process which continues until the problems are sufficiently well specified to be used to determine target behaviours which form the basis for treatment. The computer also administers the Fear Questionnaire, the Hamilton Rating Scale and the depression, anxiety and phobia sections of the Hopkins Symptom Checklist 90 (SCL 90).

The accuracy of this sytem has been investigated by Carr and Ghosh (1983a) on 26 randomly selected patients who were referred for treatment of phobic disorders. The patients received a general psychiatric assessment from the experimenters, the computerized behavioural assessment, and a standard behavioural assessment from independent blind assessors. In general, the ratings of the severity and intensity of different types of phobias using the computerized questionnaire assessment accorded well with global ratings by the independent assessors. Of most interest was the fact that in terms of practicability, precision and appropriateness for treatment the blind assessors rated the target behaviours elicited by the computer as highly as those recommended independently by psychiatrists.

In a separate study using the same procedure, Carr and Ghosh (1983b) reported that phobic patients found the computerized assessment at least as acceptable as a standard interview. Half of the 53 patients who completed the interview in their study claimed that it was more acceptable than that with a clinician: the computer interview was easier than a clinical interview, and made them less anxious. They liked the leisurely style of interacting with the computer, and did not feel the same pressure of time which can occur in an interview with a busy clinician.

FUTURE DEVELOPMENTS

The research presented above is in some sense fragmentary, but the underlying trends are clear. Automated psychological assessment is nearing the end of an experimental phase, in which it has been established that many existing psychometric tests can be automated. It has also been shown that there is a great potential for using the new technology to create new assessment procedures. It is not unreasonable to predict that there will be a preliminary period of parallel conversion of existing psychometric tests and the development of novel assessment procedures (Thompson and Wilson, 1982). The latter will take over as existing tests become outmoded. Until this stage is reached, there will be continuing debate concerning whether it is worth the expense of validating and re-standardizing conventional psychometric tests – particularly if they are becoming dated. At the moment, the marketing of many psychometric tests is closely controlled by copyright, and some test publishers have been cautious about allowing automated versions of existing tests to be produced (Cornford, 1983). However, with the increasing availablity of computing technology to the clinician, there is likely to be much greater demand in this area. This demand should be consolidated when the availability of technology becomes more stable.

Developing new psychometric tests which are marketable is a large project; it is noticeable that, despite the wide availability of low cost microcomputers, NFER-Nelson only market one automated test battery (the BMAPS and BMCST). Thus, in the immediate future the clinician cannot realistically rely on purchasing computer software for the purposes of psychological assessment. Until this situation changes clinicians will tend to use automated assessment on an experimental basis, developing their own software or sharing it with others. The result is likely to be a proliferation of small scale projects with some duplication of effort. Various schemes could be used to help clinical psychologists to share software and avoid wasting resources. With this in mind Sarah Wilson, at the Royal Hospital and Home for Incurables in London, has instituted the Directory in Research in Automated Testing (DRAT). The directory lists psychologists who are currently developing software and gives a short description of the material. It is available to computer users, provided that they send in details of the software or systems that they are developing. A possible future development is the establishment of a library system housing software which can be used or copied by members.

One problem with using other people's experimental software is that it inevitably needs refining. Unless the user is familiar with the program it is very difficult to alter. To cope with this problem, some have advocated the development of a 'tool box' approach, in which the program is written so that the function of the different sections are clearly specified. Key features of the program are also specified, so that a computer user who is not familiar with the program can easily change the parameters of the test (Simpson and Linney, 1984). The advantage of this approach is that experimental software can be more easily developed for other people without having to offer backup support.

In the long term, future development of automated assessment is bound to be influenced by the continued increase in the speed and storage facilities of computers. An important development is likely to be in the use of computer speech synthesis and speech recognition. This could vastly improve the human–computer interface, and mean that automated assessment could be used with a wider range of patients. Already, computerized assessment procedures have been developed which employ speech recognition. For example Scott Richards *et al.* (1982) have developed a version of the MMPI with a voice response unit for use with motor-impaired patients; their system includes the Apple II microcomputer and a Heuristics Speechlink H2000. However, the system only works with patients who can produce a consistent speech pattern. Speech synthesis systems do not appear to have been used in clinical psychology. Part of the problem is that it is only very recently that speech production systems have become available with a large enough vocabulary combined with acceptable quality.

Another new direction is likely to be how the computer makes sense of the information elicited from the client or patient. The behavioural assessment procedure developed by Carr and his colleagues (Carr and Ghosh, 1983a) shows how the computer can be programmed to interact with patients to construct a relatively high-level behavioural analysis of phobias. There are also quite sophisticated interpretative programs which give a clinical interpretation to the response to personality tests. Labeck *et al.* (1983) are currently developing an interpretative program for the MMPI for use on a microcomputer. One aspect of this project is that clinicians are being employed to evaluate and improve the interpretation rules. Thus the test can be continuously validated and refined. With the advent of the fifth generation computers and the growth of artificial intelligence, a long-term goal could be to develop automated assessment systems which are able to update and refine themselves.

Finally, the development of automated testing procedures inevitably raises a host of questions about their use. Should they replace the work of a clinical psychologist, or should they be seen as a useful aid? How will automated psychological assessment affect the relationship between the clinical psychologist and patient? Will automation have a detrimental effect on the quality of service? Or will it be embraced as a means of saving the clinician's time and thus increasing the number of people who can benefit from psychological treatment? These questions will continue to preoccupy the minds of clinical psychologists as the computer becomes as familiar to the profession as the WAIS box.

REFERENCES

ACKER, B. (1983) What can we sensibly computerise? Microprocessing in diagnosis and treaments: Learning and relearning. Paper presented at The British Psychological Society Annual Conference, York.

ACKER, W. and ACKER, C.F. (1982a) *Bexley-Maudsley Automated Psychological Screening.* London: NFER-Nelson.

ACKER, W. and ACKER, C.F. (1982b) *Bexley-Maudsley Category Sorting Test.* London: NFER-Nelson.

ACKER, W., ACKER, C.F. and SHAW, G.K. (1982) Microcomputer assessment of intellectual functioning in detoxified chronic alcoholics. Paper presented to The British Psychological Society Scientific Meeting, York.

ANGLE, H.B., HAY, L.R., HAY, W.M., and ELLINWOOD, E.H. (1977) Computeraided interviewing in comprehensive behavioural assessment. *Behaviour Therapy, 8,* 747–754.

BEAUMONT, J.G. (1975) The validity of the category test administered by on-line computer. *Journal of Clinical Psychology, 31* 458–462.

BEAUMONT, J.G. (1982) System requirement for interactive testing. *International Journal of Man–Machine Studies, 17,* 311–320.

BEAUMONT, J.G. (in press) The effects of microcomputer presentation and response medium on digit span performance. *International Journal of Man–Machine Interaction* .

BRINTON, G.and ROULEAU, R.A. (1969) Automating the hidden and embedded Figures Tests. *Perceptual and Motor Skills, 29,* 401–402.

CALVERT, E.J., and WATERFALL, R.C. (1982) A comparison of conentional and automated administration of Raven's Standard Progressive Matrices. *International Journal of Man–Machine Studies, 17,* 305–310.

CARR, A.C., ANCILL, R.J. and MARGO, A. (1981) Direct assessment of depression by microcomputer: A feasibility study. *Acta Psychiatrica Scandinavia, 64,* 414–422.

CARR, A.C. and GHOSH, A. (1983a) Accuracy of behavioural assessment by computer. *British Journal of Psychiatry, 142,* 66–70.

CARR, A.C. and GHOSH, A.A. (1983b) Response of phobic patients to direct computer assessment. *British Journal of Psychiatry, 142,* 60–65.

CARR, A.C. and GHOSH, A. and ANCILL, R.J. (1983) Can a computer take a psychiatric history? *Psychological Medicine, 13,* 151–158.

COLBY, K.M. (1980).Computer psychotherapists. In: J.B. Sidowski, J.B.Johnson and T.W. Williams (eds) *Technology in Mental Health Care Delivery Systems.* Norwood, N. J.: Ablex.

COLBOURN, C.J., KAPUR, N., TOTI, M., WERSEN, M., and SMITH, D. (1983) Automated memory testing using a microcomputer-based portable projection system. Paper presented at Symposium on Automated Testing, Royal Hospital and Home for the Incurables, London, 21 June 1983.

CORNFORD, T. (1983) The publishers' view of Automated Testing. Paper presented at the Annual Conference of The British Psychological Society. *Bulletin of The British Psychological Society, 36,* A51.

DENNER, S. (1977) Automated psychological testing: A review. *British Journal of Social and Clinical Psychology, 16,* 175–179.

ELITHORN, A., MORNINGTON, S. and STARRON, A. (1982) Automated psychological testing: some principles and practice. *International Journal of Man–Machine Studies, 17,* 247– 263.

ELWOOD, D.L. (1969) Automation of psychological testing. *American Psychologist, 24,* 287–289.

ELWOOD, D.I. and GRIFFIN, H.R. (1972) Individual intelligence testing without the examiner: Reliability of an automated method. *Journal of Consulting and Clinical Psychology, 28,* 9–14.

EXTON-SMITH, A.N. (1980) A psychometric test battery for evaluating the action of psychotropic drugs. In: B.G. Barbagallo-Sengiorgi and A.N. Exton-Smith (eds) *The Ageing Brain: Neurological and Mental Disturbances.* New York: Plenum Press.

FRENCH, C.C. and BEAUMONT, J.G. (1984) The Leicester–DHSS project on microcomputer aided assessment. Paper presented at Symposium on Automated Testing, Royal Hospital and Home for the Incurables, London.

GEDYE, J.L. and MILLER, E. (1969) The automation of psychological assessment. *International Journal of Man–Machine Studies, 1,* 237–262.

GILBERSTADT, H., LUSHENE, R. and BUEGEL, B. (1976) Automated assessment of intelligence: The TAPAC test battery and computerised report writing. *Perceptual and Motor Skills, 43,* 627–635.

JOHNSON, J.H., GIANETTI, R.A. and WILLIAMS, T.A. (1978) A self-contained microcomputer system for psychological testing. *Behaviour Research Methods and Instrumentation, 10,* 579–581.

JOHNSON, D.F. and WHITE, C.B. (1980) Effects of training on computerised test performance in the elderly. *Journal of Applied Psychology, 65,* 133–150.

KLINGE, B. and RODZIEWICZ, T. (1976) Automated and manual intelligence testing of the Peabody Picture Vocabulary Test on a psychiatric adolescent population. *International Journal of Man–Machine Studies, 8,* 243–246.

KNIGHTS, R.M., RICHARDSON, D.H. and McNARRY. L.R. (1973) Automated versus clinical administration of the Peabody Picture Vocabulary Test and Coloured Progressive Matrices. *American Journal Mental Deficiency, 78,* 223–225.

LABECK, L.J., JOHNSON, J.H. and HARRIS, W.G. (1983) Validity of a computerized on-line MMPI interpretive system. *Journal of Clinical Psychology, 39,* 412–416.

LANG, P.J. (1980) Behavioural treatment and biobehavioural assessment: Computer applications. In: J.B. Sidowski, J.H. Johnson and T.A. Williams (eds) *Technology in Mental Health Care Delivery Systems.* Norwood, N.J.: Ablex.

LUCAS, R.W., MULLIN, P.J., LUNA, C.B.X. and MCINROY, D.C. (1977) Psychiatrists and a compute as interrogators of patients with alcohol related illnesses: A comparison. *British Journal of Psychiatry, 132,* 160–167.

MILLER, E. (1968) A case study of automated clinical testing. *Bulletin of The British Psychological Society, 21,* 75.

MULHALL, D.J. (1977) The representation of personal relationships: An automated system. *International Journal of Man–Machine Studies, 9,* 315–335.

OGEN, M., KELLETT, J.M., MERRYFIELD, P., and MILLARD, P.H. (1984) Practical aspects of automated testing of the elderly. *Bulletin of The British Psychological Society, 37,* 148–149.

OVERTON, W.G. and SCOTT, K.G. (1972) Automated and manual intelligence testing: data on parallel form of the Peabody Picture Vocabulary Test. *American Journal of Mental Deficiency, 76,* 639– 643.

RIDGEWAY, J., MacCULLOCH, M.J. and MILLS, H. (1982) Some experiments in administering a psychometric test with a light pen and microcomputer. *International Journal of Man–Machine Studies, 17,* 265–278.

SCOTT RICHARDS, J., WILSON, T.L., FINE, P.R. and ROGER (1982) A voice operated response unit for use in the psychological assessment of motor impaired subjects. *Journal of Medical Engineering and Technology, 6,* 65–67.

SELMI, P.M., KLEIN, M.H., GREIST, J.H., JOHNSON, J.H., and HARRIS, W.G. (1981) An investigation of computer-assisted cognitive-behaviour therapy in the treatment of depression. *Behaviour Research and Instrumentation, 14,* 181–185.

SHAW, M.L.G. (1982) PLANET: Some experience in creating an integrated system for repertory grid applications on a microcomputer. *International Journal of Man–Machine Studies, 17,* 345–360.

SIMPSON, J.M. and LINNEY, A. (1983) Computer controlled assessment of cognitive change in organically mentally-impaired old people. Paper presented at Symposium on Automated Testing, Royal Hospital and Home for the Incurables, London.

SIMPSON, J. and LINNEY, A. (1984) The end-user psychologist and the elusive programmer: A possible compromise strategy. Paper presented at Symposium on Automated Testing, Royal Hospital and Home for the Incurables, London.

SLATER, P. (ed.) (1977) *The Measurement of Interpersonal Space by Grid Technique. Volume 2, Dimensions of Interpersonal Space.* Chichester: Wiley.

THOMPSON, J.A. and WILSON, S.L. (1982) Automated psychological testing. *International Journal of Man–Machine Studies, 17,* 279– 289.

VALE, C.D. (1981) Design and implementation of a microcomputer-based adaptive testing system. *Behaviour Research Methods and Instrumentation, 13,* 399–406.

VOLANS, P.J., and LEVY, R. (1982) A re-evaluation of an automated tailored test of concept learning with elderly psychiatric patients. *British Journal of Clinical Psychology, 21,* 93–101.

WATTS, K., BADDELEY, A.D. and WILLIAMS, M. (1982) Automated tailored testing using Raven's Matrices and Mill Hill Vocabulary Tests: A comparison with manual administration. *International Journal of Man–Machine Studies, 17,* 331–344.

WEINMAN, J.A. (1982) Computer analysis of test performance. *International Journal of Man–Machine Studies, 17,* 321–330.

WILSON, S.L., THOMPSON, J.A. and WYLIE, G. (1982) Automated psychological testing for the severely physically handicapped. *International Journal of Man–Machine Studies, 17,* 291-296.

WILSON, S.L., THOMPSON, J.A. and WYLIE, G. (1983) A new digit span test and its assessment on a sample of physically handicapped adults. Paper presented at Symposium on Automated Testing, Royal Hospital and Home for the Incurables, London.

SMALL N EXPERIMENTAL DESIGNS IN CLINICAL RESEARCH

David F. Peck

It is often claimed that the unique contribution of clinical psychologists to the National Health Service is their extensive training in research design and statistics. However, a cursory survey of the activities of clinical psychologists would reveal that research is not a major activity. There are many reasons for this. Research is a very cumbersome procedure which can consume a great deal of time and resources, can often produce unusable results, and can generate so much data (for which complex statistical analysis may be required) that it is difficult to pinpoint clinical relevance. Research is therefore seen as incompatible with clinical realities and procedures. These reservations are often justified in the case of large scale group or factorial experimental designs (Kazdin, 1976). However, this is only one kind of research, and there are many others which are more suitable for clinical settings. Research is not synonymous with large numbers of subjects. One methodology that seems to be particularly suitable for clinical research has been called, amongst other things, intensive, single case investigations; single subject research; repeated measures designs; and small N experimental designs. The last term will be used in this chapter.

Much of the work of a clinical psychologist is concerned with analysing the behaviour of individual clients; a similar focus on individual subjects in clinical research is essential if we are to bridge the gap between research and practice. Gentile (1982) has described the unique value of a small N approach. Discussing the comparative evaluation of two treatments, he claimed that for all subjects to experience two treatments is a very different situation from having half of the subjects experience one treatment, and the other half a second treatment. Experiencing both treatments, together or sequentially, provides a context or contrast for evaluating each treatment in a way not possible in a traditional experimental design, where subjects would be allocated to one treatment or the other. He further suggested that obtaining differences between two treatments may be more likely when subjects have experienced both.

139

If small N designs are useful in clinical research, why are they not used more often? This is partly because they receive little attention at both undergraduate and postgraduate level, despite the fact that small N designs have a very respectable, even pre-eminent, position in the history of experimental and clinical psychology. If psychologists were asked to name the most influential figures since the turn of the century, total unanimity would be unlikely; but four names would probably appear on the majority of lists: Pavlov, Freud, Skinner and Piaget. At first glance these four may seem to have little in common, since they used different experimental technologies, employed different subject groups, and worked from different experimental traditions. However they have in common a basic methodology: they obtained their data from systematic, intensive observations of single cases (or of a small number of cases). They did not use statistical manipulations to counteract the effects of uncontrolled variables.

A second reason for the lack of attention given to small N designs is that it has often been assumed that they are useful only within a behavioural framework, and clinical psychologists who espouse other approaches have been loath to use an allegedly behavioural method. This is unfortunate. A main aim of this chapter is to demonstrate that small N designs are applicable across the whole spectrum of clinical problems and approaches. There is little which is new in advocating small N designs, the case having been eloquently argued a quarter of a century ago (Sidman, 1960; Shapiro, 1961). What is new is the more widespread appreciation of the value of these designs, and their increasing use in diverse areas of clinical research, including individual psychotherapy (Warnock *et al.,* 1979), psychoanalysis (Donnellan, 1978), psychopharmacology (Conners and Wells, 1982), and forensic psychology (Schnelle *et al.,* 1977). This diversity is reflected in the examples selected to illustrate the designs in this chapter.

There are two main kinds of small N experimental designs: single case designs and multiple baseline designs. These will be discussed separately. However, before doing so it should be pointed out that small N does not necessarily refer to a small number of individuals. The term may refer, for example, to all the subjects on a single ward, all the employees in a building, or all the residents of an old people's home. The term 'small N' simply refers to the number of target populations being treated, which can comprise any number of individuals.

SINGLE CASE EXPERIMENTAL DESIGNS

It should be emphasized that the methodology of single case investigation involves not a standard procedure, but a collection of experimental ploys or elements intended to demonstrate a systematic relationship between clinical intervention and a change in clinical outcome. The investigator may construct a design from whichever ploys he feels are appropriate. The following examples are not intended as an exhaustive catalogue, but to illustrate general principles, and to indicate the range of possible designs. The designs have the following characteristics in common:

1. Continuous (or very frequent) measurement; that is, patients' problems are assessed on numerous occasions before, during, and after treatment.
2. Information from an extensive baseline or pre-intervention period is gathered; at least two measures, preferably many more, are obtained.
3. Once a stable baseline has been observed, the intervention is introduced and the effects are measured on at least four occasions.
4. The intervention is withdrawn for a short period, and the outcome is still measured. The intervention is then reinstated and the effects are again observed.

The logic of this is clear: if there is a systematic relationship between, for example, the treatment applied and a clinical problem, the clinical problem should remain unaltered during baseline measurements, and during treatment withdrawal, but should show improvement during the treatment phase. When the intervention is not applied, this is referred to as the 'A' phase; when it is applied, this is referred to as the 'B' phase. Although this is how the term 'AB' is often used, the 'A' phase could comprise any form of intervention (including no formal intervention, as is conventional) without compromising the underlying rationale, as Birnbrauer (1981) has recently pointed out. The 'A' phase is also sometimes referred to as the 'reversal' phase, but the term 'withdrawal' is more generally inclusive, and will be used here.

The A B design

This is the simplest and least satisfactory of all the single case designs, because it omits step (4). It consists only of comparing baseline with the intervention phase. Because a relationship between intervention and outcome is indicated on only one occasion, this is not a powerful design. There are many other reasons apart from the intervention which could account for any change. (The patient's life conditions may have improved, there may have been a change in ward regime, there may have been an improvement in marital relationships, and so on.) One cannot therefore unequivocally conclude that the treatment *per se* was responsible for the change in outcome. This design is not recommended unless there are pressing reasons why it would be undesirable to institute a withdrawal phase, such as with patients whose condition is life-threatening, or where the change is unlikely to be reversed. It can provide useful information when there is more than one outcome variable and where a clinical problem is of long duration, having proved resistant to previous treatments. A long follow-up would also strengthen the conclusion that the intervention produced the change.

Clinical example: Peck (1977). This study was concerned with the treatment of chronic blepharospasm (spasmodic winking) in a female patient who had received extensive prior treatment from a variety of health professionals with little effect on spasm severity. After two baseline and two placebo sessions, she was given EMG biofeedback from the muscles around the eyes, and spasm frequency and EMG levels were monitored. A marked decrease in both outcome measures was obtained over 17 sessions, and improvement was maintained at a four-month follow-up.

B A B design

In this design, ongoing treatment is interrupted or changed and then reinstituted. Meanwhile, the outcome is continuously monitored. If treatment is responsible for the change, there should be a deterioration when it is removed. Because baseline information is not systematically obtained, and there is only one treatment interruption phase, the design is not recommended, but it can be usefully employed when treatment is already in progress, for whatever reason.

Clinical example: (Truax and Carkhuff, 1965). The authors examined the effects of high and low levels of empathic understanding and warmth on three patients during one hour of psychotherapy. The hour was divided into three 20-minute phases: during the first 20 minutes the therapist displayed high levels of such therapeutic conditions, in the second 20 minutes he displayed low levels and in the final 20 minutes he again displayed high levels. The sessions were recorded and rated by 'blind' observers, the outcome variable being 'depth of intrapersonal exploration'. Over all three patients, it was found that there was less intrapersonal exploration under low therapeutic conditions.

The A B A B design

In this design, baseline data are recorded, there is an intervention phase, a withdrawal phase, and a second intervention phase. This design is approaching the level at which unequivocal interpretations of a causal relationship between intervention and outcome are possible. Because one has demonstrated a functional relationship between intervention and outcome on two occasions, alternative explanations of the change are less plausible.

Clinical example: (Brownell et al., 1980). This study was concerned with promoting an increase in exercise in daily working lives. A record was kept of how many people walked upstairs, rather than took the lift, for several days at a range of public locations. A poster was placed by the lift door for two weeks advocating the benefits of an increase in physical fitness, and suggesting that people should walk up the stairs rather than take the lifts. Again, they recorded how many took the lifts and how many walked upstairs. The poster was taken away (the withdrawal phase) fo two weeks and later replaced. It was found that the use of the stairs virtually doubled when the poster was present but returned to approximately baseline levels when it was removed.

Variations and extensions of the basic AB design

The AB design is a basic 'building block' for a number of other complex designs which follow the same logic. One could for example have an A-B-A-C-A-B or C, in which two interventions (B and C) are compared, the most effective of which is reinstituted after the second withdrawal phase; or one could examine the effects of isolating different components of a treatment 'package' in an A-BC-B-BC design. Furthermore it is not necessary for the intervention and withdrawal phases to alternate in this regular fashion.

Clinical examples: 1. Stabenau et al. (1970). Stabenau *et al.* were interested in the alleged presence of 'pink spot' in the urine of schizophrenics. A number of studies had implicated a dietary source, in particular tea, but previous work had not fully controlled for drug or other dietary factors. Three normal volunteers had a free diet (including tea), followed by a dextrose diet with no tea, a dextrose diet including tea, dextrose diet alone, and finally free diet plus tea was resumed. It was found that pink spot was found in urine when tea had been recently included in the diet, but was absent when tea was exluded.

2. Blackman et al. (1976). This exemplary study was concerned with increasing the amount of social interaction in the institutionalized elderly. Coffee and orange juice were made available to those elderly residents who were present on the ward solarium, thereby facilitating social interaction, in the morning. After baseline measures, the drinks were made available for several weeks, then were not given for several days; later the drinks were again made available. In addition to this ABAB control procedure, there were also some days during the overall reinforcement periods in which drinks were not made available. It was possible therefore to compare the amount of social activity on designated 'drink days' when drinks were and were not actually made available, as well as to compare 'drink days' with 'non-drink days'. It was found that the amount of social activity increased only on 'drink' days when the coffee and orange juice were available. This study is impressive in the elegance of its experimental design and in the thoroughness of its description.

From these examples it will be clear that there is a wide range of possible extensions of the basic ABAB design, and it would be tedious to list them all. It is up to the individual clinician to arrange the design which is most appropriate to the particular clinical problem. However, in doing so the logic behind the design should be maintained. With the increasing complexity of AB designs, it may become more difficult to interpret the results clearly.

Limitations and problems in AB designs

1. Extreme variablility. The logic behind AB designs involves a comparison of baseline data with data obtained during treatment intervention. The validity of any conclusions depends on how clear the effects of treatment intervention are, and one factor which can obscure the effects is baseline variability. Ideally, one should take baseline measures until the pattern of the data is stable and clearcut. In clinical situations, however, this may be impossible and alternative methods may have to be employed. If the intervention is a powerful one, the effects should still be clear. If not, one strategy is to analyse systematically the factors related to the variability; for example a child who is injuring himself may do so at a different rate, according to whether there are other children or staff present. Teasing out such factors may enable a stable baseline to be obtained, as well as providing additional clinical information. As a last resort, it may be possible to obtain data from elsewhere, such as nursing reports; this is not very satisfactory however, since the data will be in a different form from those obtained during the treatment phases.

2. Reversibility. The logic of AB designs requires that the behaviour be reversed when the treatment or intervention is removed. However, some effects of intervention may not be easily reversed. There are many examples of this, such as experimental instructions, patient expectancies, or the gaining of muscular control through biofeedback. A related problem is that the treatment must not be so powerful or intensive to produce enduring change, which would be resistant to reversal: the treatment should, however, be powerful enough to produce noticeable effects. This would suggest that AB designs may be appropriate only for weak treatments, detracting from one of the main arguments upon which the use of AB designs is advocated. One solution is to extend the AB phases indefinitely, anticipating that at each reversal phase the behaviour will not revert fully to baseline levels, but that there will be a cumulative increase in treatment effects. It is unlikely, however, that clinical outcome would covary with treatment intervention so neatly, and even a weak treatment may build up a cumulative effect so rapidly that reversal could be demonstrated in only a few phases.

3. Enduring effects. With many treatment methods, the effects can continue for long periods after treatment has stopped. There may therefore be a lag between stopping the treatment and the subsequent reversal. If the duration of this lag is known, an AB design could still be used. However, with many treatments, particularly drug treatments, the lag may vary considerably between and within individuals.

4. Ethical considerations. Although AB designs do not require a control group, there will be many clinical circumstances when it would be unethical to withdraw what is an apparently effective treatment. This is particularly so for life-threatening or severely damaging behaviour. In such circumstances a reversal phase would not be justified.

5. Generalizability. The fact that one has unequivocally demonstrated a relationship between treatment and behaviour change in one patient, does not of course mean that the same method would be useful in other patients. With group designs one can allegedly obtain an estimate of how many patients may benefit from the particular form of treatment, but this is impossible with single cases. The solution is to apply systematically the method on other patients with similar problems. If one can build up a series of patients, demonstrating the efficacy of the same methods for the same problems, this would be very convincing evidence in favour of the treatment. If, however, some patients do not demonstrate the same improvement, a small N design would permit the formulation of a number of hypotheses as to the factors responsible for the varying effectiveness. This is not a simple task, and if a large number of interacting variables which appear to have a bearing on outcome are found, more complex group designs may be required. In addition, treatment failures must be reported more systematically to enable a clear picture of effectiveness to emerge.

6. Comparing global treatments. The final limitation of AB designs arises when comparing the effectiveness of two global or composite interventions; for example, comparing client-centred therapy and social skills training in the treatment of socially withdrawn adolescents. Because each method is time-consuming and complex and requires numerous sessions comprising different activities, it would be invalid to use an AB design.

Although some tentative solutions have been suggested to these problems and limitations, it will be evident that there are many circumstances in which AB designs cannot be used. There are, however, a number of recently devised alternatives, still using small numbers or single cases, which to some degree are less affected by these limitations. However, the issues of variability and generalizability remain problematic. These alternatives include the multiple baseline designs.

MULTIPLE BASELINE DESIGNS

There are three types of multiple baseline designs: across subjects, across problems, and across settings. They have the following in common: the outcome variable is measured in several domains for an extended baseline period; intervention is applied to one domain, but measurement continues over all the others; after a set period of time, the intervention is applied to a second domain and then to a third and so on for all the rest, continuing to measure in all the domains throughout the exercise. If the intervention is responsible for any change, the change should only occur in the particular domain when the intervention is applied and not before. If generalization across domains does occur, this will reduce the persuasive power of the design, and an additional component (for example, instituting a withdrawal phase) may have to be considered. On the other hand, knowledge of the circumstances under which generalization does occur is itself very valuable clinical information; the occurrence of generalization in multiple baseline designs is not so much a disaster as a pointer to how to proceed.

Multiple baseline across subjects

In this design at least four patients with the same kind of clinical problem are investigated. Extensive baselines, preferably over several weeks, are obtained for all patients. The treatment is applied to one patient, but data continue to be obtained for them all. After a further period, comparable in duration to the baseline, treatment is applied to a second patient and again data are obtained across all patients. Treatment is sequentially applied to each patient in this manner, until all patients have received the treatment. If the treatment is the effective factor in bringing about any change, the change should only occur soon after the onset of the treatment. A major advantage of this method is that the behaviour is not required to be reversible, but there may be some ethical problems related to the delay in treatment for the later patients.

Clinical example: Jones et al. (1981). This study was concerned with training five children to implement emergency fire drill skills; that is, training in escaping from a bedroom in a house on fire. All the children had previously been through a similar programme of training and the study was concerned with the effectiveness of booster sessions. Each child was trained, starting at different times, to deal with nine different fire drill situations, and performance was assessed over 15 weeks. It was found that each child improved when training was applied, and not before. It was concluded that the brief reinstatement of training was effective in restoring fire emergency drill peformance to high levels.

Although not strictly a small N design, similar reasoning lay behind the study by Freeman *et al.* (1978) in the evaluation of electroconvulsive therapy (ECT). Two groups of depressed patients were given ECT, but one group received 'simulated ECT' for two sessions before genuine ECT was given. It was found that the recovery amongst the patients given simulated ECT lagged behind that of the genuine ECT patients, but that they had caught up by the final sessions.

Multiple baseline across problems

In this design a number of separate but related outcomes are specified. The baseline frequency of all of them is assessed and the intervention is applied to one of them; the remaining ones continue to be measured. Subsequently, the treatment is applied to the second, and then the third, and so on. If the problem outcome changes only when the intervention is applied, this is strong evidence that the intervention produced the change.

Clinical example: Barton et al. (1970). This study was concerned with improving behaviour during meals in a ward of mentally handicapped males. The problems included stealing food, eating with the fingers, eating spilled food and eating straight off the plate. The treatment comprised removing the patient from the dining room if any of these were exhibited. This 'time out' method was applied first to one problem and when that had been reduced, it was applied to the rest sequentially. The particular mealtime problem improved only when the removal was contingent upon it. It was therefore concluded that the treatment was responsible for the improvement in eating.

Multiple baseline across settings

In this method the treatment is applied to a single subject for a single problem, but sequentially across different settings.

Clinical example: Carr and Wilson (1983). This single case study was of a young male paraplegic who was reluctant to ease himself out of his wheelchair in order to reduce pressure. The patient had already developed pressure sores and did not perform the requisite number of 'push-ups'. There were four settings where the patient was seated continuously over long periods: workshop, during lunch, during tea and coffee breaks, and on the ward. Baselines were taken in each setting and a pressure-sensitive pad was put in the wheelchair, which counted push-ups that lasted for at least the minimum time considered effective in reducing the sores. The patient was informed of how many push-ups he had done, and social reinforcement was given if he had performed the specified number. The procedure was introduced sequentially across the four settings over a period of seven weeks. It was found that generally the rate of push-ups increased only when the treatment started in each setting. The increased rate of push-ups was accompanied by improvement in skin condition.

SOME OTHER SMALL N DESIGNS

As already noted, there are numerous variations to the more commonly used small N designs. Two of these will be discussed here; an extended discussion may be found in Berryman and Cooper (1982).

The changing criterion design

This design has been used in situations where the outcome can be precisely quantified, permitting clear-cut targets to be set. Criteria are set which gradually decrease from session to session. If the behaviour change closely follows the criterion change, it is assumed that the treatment has been effective. For this conclusion to be valid, the fit between the criterion and the change must be close. Also, the time interval between sessions should be variable, to rule out the influence of spontaneous temporal variations. An interpretative difficulty with this technique is that the change may occur more rapidly than the set criteria (that is, the patient may improve more quickly than agreed in the goal-setting) which would reduce the closeness of the fit, and hence the credibility of the effectiveness of the intervention.

Clinical example: Bernard et al. (1981). This study was concerned with excessive coffee and tea drinking in a 40-year-old female, using self-monitoring, response cost and social reinforcement. She was instructed to drink one less cup of tea or coffee than during the previous treatment phase. Coffee and tea drinking were virtually halved over a period of approximately six weeks.

Periodic treatment design

In much clinical work it is difficult to state precisely where a particular phase or treatment session ends. For example, in cognitive therapy clients are often instructed to practise in their daily lives those skills which they have learned during sessions. Accordingly one might find that clients continue to show improvement even when there have been no further treatment sessions. The periodic treatment design is one way of proceeding in this kind of situation.

The problem behaviour is recorded very frequently, perhaps by self-monitoring and treatment sessions are held periodically. The intervention is said to be effective if there is an acceleration in the level of improvement immediately after it. It is preferable if the treatment sessions are held at varying intervals and the outcome variable should be capable of fine, precise measurement over a wide range. If there are five or six treatment sessions, the outcome variable must have a sufficiently wide range to permit an accelerated change to show itself after each session. Psychophysiological methods might usefully be employed as outcome measures in this design.

Clinical example. A published example of this design does not seem to be available, but a good description appears in Hayes (1981).

ARE STATISTICAL INFERENCE METHODS NECESSARY?

This issue has been adequately discussed in Kazdin (1976) and some of the issues will be only briefly discussed here. Opponents of statistical analysis argue that if the outcome effects are so subtle that their demonstration requires statistical analysis, they are unlikely to be of sufficient magnitude to be useful in clinical practice. It has also been suggested that researchers may be tempted to use statistical techniques as a control procedure, rather than make rigorous efforts to gain control experimentally. On the other hand, the data from small N experimental designs are often quite complex and ambiguous, and simply analysing the data by visual inspection may lead to errors in interpretation.

Assuming, however, that statistical analysis is useful, are conventional techniques such as *t* and *F* tests appropriate? Unfortunately, they are not. The reason is as follows: essentially, statistical inference is concerned with determining the total amount of variation in sets of scores, and estimating how much of that variation can be explained by the independent variables. The variation which cannot be explained is referred to as 'error variance', and it is the ratio of explained variance over error variance which determines whether the result is statistically significant. Any factor which reduces the amount of error variance will increase the proportion of explained variance, and thereby increase the likelihood of a particular result being statistically significant. In small N designs, because the data are obtained from the same subject or subjects, a certain amount of the variation will be due simply to that fact. This is called 'serial dependency', and is a very common property of the data from small N designs. Accordingly, the total error variance may be spuriously reduced, and the null hypothesis may be rejected when it is in fact true (the well known 'type 1' error). In other words, one may conclude that an intervention has been effective when any changes could be due to chance. A second problem with conventional statistics is that such techniques are mainly used only to compare means; it is, however, quite feasible that in the baseline data there is an upward trend which becomes a downward trend after the intervention. The mean of these two phases may be identical, but the intervention would have produced a clear effect. Conventional statistical techniques may fail to take into account the slope of the data.

Fortunately, there are some relatively recent statistical advances, which may be appropriate for small N methodology. For both the AB and multiple baseline designs, 'time series analysis' has been suggested. Time series analysis determines the significance of changes in level and trend and can be particularly useful when the baseline data are not stable. However, many data points per phase are required. Recently Ward *et al.* (1983) in a study of biochemical response to stress, applied traditional statistical techniques (for example, ANOVA) to the data from their research subjects as a whole (N = 8), but further analysed data from the individual subjects using time series analysis. The latter procedure contributed much additional valuable information (particularly in highlighting intersubject variation), some of which entailed modifying the conclusions based on ANOVA alone. Horne *et al.* (1982) have discussed the value of time series analysis for small N designs.

For multiple baseline designs, another useful procedure is the Rn test, described in Kazdin (1976). For this, a minimum of four subjects, settings, or problems is required, and the order in which treatment is applied must be randomly determined. This test may not be appropriate if a series of patients has been treated successively, for example, as they were referred, since the requirement of random ordering of treatment would not have been met.

Does it make any practical difference whether one uses statistical inference or not? It is of course a very difficult question to answer since there is no final external criterion by which to assess whether a particular effect has occurred. If one comes to different conclusions from visual inspection or from statistical analysis, there is no way to determine unequivocally which is correct. It may, however, be useful to see how far these two approaches agree. Jones *et al.* (1978), on examining a number of published studies, reported that with high serial dependency, there is relatively poor agreement. With low serial dependency, and if the visual inspection suggests that there is no treatment effect, there is relatively good agreement. With statistical analysis, some significant trends were observed which had not been noted by the original authors using visual inspection alone.

Whether to use formal statistical techniques is still a matter of debate. The careful clinical researcher will probably find that using both statistical inference and visual inspection will serve his or her purposes best; certainly, there is little to be lost by using statistics. Computer programmes which include time series analysis are available for both large computers and microcomputers.

GENERAL ISSUES

Outcome variables in small N research

Because most small N research has been conducted from a behavioural standpoint, the dependent variables reported have typically comprised frequency counts of the occurrence of target behaviours. Many clinical psychologists will prefer to use other measures, such as the personal questionnaire, the repertory grid, the Q Sort, the semantic differential and psychophysiological measures, amongst others. These are all quite suitable for use in small N designs.

Some problems with small N designs

It has been claimed that small N designs avoid many of the problems associated with group experimental designs. Nevertheless, as intimated frequently in this chapter, they do have problems of their own. It is not intended to document all such problems here, but readers are referred to the excellent articles by Cuvo (1979) and Birnbrauer (1981) for illuminating discussions of the problems of measurement and generalization.

Conclusions

Small N experimental designs can be relatively simple to devise, be economical to carry out, provide meaningful answers to important clinical problems, and assist in building up a body of scientific knowledge about human problems. The use of these designs has stimulated the development of new research methods, and fostered the application of advances in statistical inference. Several problem areas remain, particularly in interpretation and generalization of findings. The more widespread use of these designs as part of routine clinical work, and across a wider theoretical spectrum, will help to bridge the unfortunate but enduring gap between the scientist and practitioner functions of clinical psychologists.

REFERENCES

BARTON, E.S., GUESS, D., GARCIA, E. and BAER, D.M. (1970) Improvement of retardates' mealtime behaviors by time-out procedures using multiple baseline techniques. *Journal of Applied Behavior Analysis 3,* 77–84.

BERNARD, M.E., DENNEHY, S. and KEEFAUVER, L.W. (1981) Behavioral treatment of excessive coffee and tea drinking: a case study and partial replication. *Behavior Therapy, 12,* 543–548.

BERRYMAN, D. and COOPER, D. (1982) The use of single subject research methodology in special education. *Educational Psychology, 2,* 197–213.

BIRNBRAUER, J.S. (1981) External validity and experimental investigation of individual behavior. *Analysis and Intervention in Developmental Disabilities, 1(2),* 117–132.

BLACKMAN, D.K., HOWE, M. and PINKSTON, E.M. (1976) Increasing participation in social interaction of the institutionalised elderly. *The Gerontologist, 16,* 69–76.

BROWNELL, K.D., STUNKARD, A.J. and ALBAUN, J.N. (1980) Evaluation and modification of exercise patterns in the natural environment. *American Journal of Psychiatry, 137,* 1540–1545.

CARR, S. and WILSON, B. (1983) Promotion of pressure relief exercising in a spinal injury patient: a multiple baseline across settings design. *Behavioural Psychotherapy, 11,* 329–336.

CONNERS, C.K. and WELLS, K.C. (1982) Single case designs in psychopharmacology. In: A.E. Kazdin and A.H. Tuma (eds) *Single Case Research Designs.* (New Directions for Methdology of Social and Behavioral Science, No. 13.) San Fransisco: Jossey-Bass.

CUVO, A.J. (1979) Multiple baseline design in instructional research: pitfalls of measurement and procedural advantages. *American Journal of Mental Deficiency, 84,* 219–228.

DONNELLAN, G.J. (1978) Single subject research and psychoanalytic theory. *Bulletin of the Menninger Clinic, 42,* 352–357.

FREEMAN, C.P.L., BASSON, J.V. and CRIGHTON, A. (1978) Double-blind controlled trial of electroconvulsive therapy (ECT) and simulated ECT in depressive illness. *The Lancet, i,* 738–740.

GENTILE, J.R. (1982) Significance of single subject studies (and repeated measures designs). *Educational Psychologist, 17,* 54–60.

HAYES, S.C. (1981) Single case experimental design and empirical clinical practice. *Journal of Consulting and Clinical Psychology, 49,* 193–211.

HERSEN, M. and BARLOW, D. (1976) *Single Case Experimental Designs: Strategies for Studying Behavior Change.* New York: Pergamon.

HORNE, G.P., YANG, M.C.K. and WARE, W.B. (1982) Time series analysis for single subject designs. *Psychological Bulletin, 91,* 178–189.

JONES, R.R., WEINROTT, M.R. and VAUGHT, R.S. (1978) Effects of serial dependency on the agreement between visual and statistical inference. *Journal of Applied Behavior Analysis, 11,* 277–283.

JONES, R.T., KAZDIN, A.E. and HANEY, J.I. (1981) A follow-up to training emergency skills. *Behavior Therapy, 12,* 716–722.

KAZDIN, A.E. (1976) Statistical analyses for single-case experimental designs. In: M. Hersen and D. Barlow (eds) *Single Case Experimental Designs: Strategies for Studying Behavior Change.* New York: Pergamon.

PECK, D.F. (1977) The use of EMG feedback in the treatment of a severe case of blepharospasm. *Biofeedback and Self Regulation, 2,* 273–277.

SCHNELLE, J.F., KIRCHNER, R.E., CASEY, J.D., USELTON, P.H. and McNEES, M.P. (1977) Patrol evaluation research: a multiple baseline analysis of saturation police patrolling during day and night hours. *Journal of Applied Behavior Analysis, 10,* 33– 40.

SHAPIRO, M.B. (1961) The single case in clinical psychological research. *Journal of General Psychology, 74,* 3–23.

SIDMAN, M. (1960) *Tactics of Scientific Research: Evaluating Experimental Data in Psychology.* New York: Basic Books.

STABENAU, J.R., CREVELING, C.R. and DALEY, J. (1970) The 'pink spot', 3,4-Dimethoxyphenylethylamine, common tea, and schizophrenia. *American Journal of Psychiatry, 127,* 611–616.

TRUAX, C.B. and CARKHUFF, R.R. (1965) Experimental manipulation of therapeutic conditions. *Journal of Consulting Psychology, 29,* 119–124.

WARD, M.M., MEFFORD, I.N., PARKER, S.D., CHESNEY, M.A., TAYLOR, C.B., KEGAN, D.L. and BARCHAS, J.D. (1983) Epinephrine and norepinephrine responses in continuously collected human plasma to a series of stressors. *Psychosomatic Medicine, 45,* 471–486.

WARNOCK, J.K., MINTZ, S.T. and TWEMLOW, S.W. (1979) Single case documentation of psychiatric treatment effectiveness. *Bulletin of the Menninger Clinic, 43,* 137–144.

Suggestions for further reading

CAMPBELL, D.T. and STANLEY, J.C. (1966) *Experimental and Quasi-Experimental Designs for Research.* Chicago: Rand-McNally.

HERSEN, M. and BARLOW, D.H. (1976) *Single Case Experimental Designs: Strategies for Studying Behavior Change.* New York: Pergamon.

KAZDIN, A.E. (1982) *Single Case Research Designs: Methods for Clinical and Applied Settings.* New York: Oxford University Press.

KAZDIN, A.E. and TUMA, A.H. (1982) *Single Case Research Designs.* (New Directions for Methodology of Social and Behavioral Science, No. 13.) San Fransisco: Jossey-Bass.

KRATOCHWILL, T.R. (1978) *Single Subject Research.* New York: Academic Press.

INTERPERSONAL PROCESS RECALL IN CLINICAL TRAINING AND RESEARCH

Chris Barker

> Oh wad some Power the giftie gie us
> To see oursels as others see us!
> It wad frae monie a blunder free us,
> An' foolish notion:
>
> *(Burns: To a Louse)*

Interpersonal Process Recall (IPR) is a simple yet powerful idea. It uses a tape recording of a conversation – between client and therapist, student and teacher, doctor and patient, husband and wife – to stimulate the participants' recall of their experiences during the conversation. These recalled experiences provide a valuable and unique perspective on the interaction, which can be used in a variety of applications.

The basic procedure is as follows. The target interaction is recorded, usually on videotape. Then, as soon as possible afterwards, one or more of the participants independently reviews the tape with the aid of a trained 'inquirer'. The tape is stopped at frequent intervals in order to stimulate the participant's recall of his or her moment-by-moment thoughts and feelings. The inquirer uses a series of non-directive questions and probes, so as to facilitate accurate recall while minimizing sources of inaccuracy, such as distortion and fabrication.

In clinical supervision and training, these recalled experiences may be used either as material for personal exploration, to examine the intention behind or the impact of various therapist statements, or to assist in the consideration of alternative courses of action (Kagan, 1980). In research applications, the participants' comments are recorded by the inquirer, partly with the help of structured questionnaires or rating scales, and used as one perspective of data on the interaction (Elliott, in press). Although developed within a humanistic counselling tradition, IPR is compatible with any orientation that accepts the utility of examining inner experience.

Most workers using IPR for the first time are impressed with the wealth of material it evokes. Accompanying even apparently trivial dialogue seems to be an enormous breadth and depth of thoughts, feelings and fantasies – often of a surprisingly primitive nature – that are often quickly forgotten or suppressed. IPR is the best way available of recapturing this internal stream of consciousness.

IPR is widely used in the United States, where it is closely associated with Norman Kagan and his group at Michigan State University, who pioneered the method over 20 years ago and have continued to refine and expand it since (Kagan, 1980, 1984a). Its main applications are in the training of clinical and counselling psychologists, and of medical students, and also as a tool for therapy process research. However, as yet only a handful of British workers are using it, and most of these are in fields other than clinical psychology, so that it qualifies as a 'New Development' in the sense used in this volume.

Historical overview

It is strange to reflect how recently the use of the audiotape recorder has become available to psychologists. Early attempts to record actual psychotherapeutic interactions, for example by Carl Rogers and his team in the 1940s, were widely regarded as a very daring and potentially hazardous enterprise (Kirschenbaum, 1979). Hitherto, such records as existed had been made by trained stenographers listening in from another room. The development of audiotape and later videotape technology opened new doors for psychologists, sociologists, linguists, and others interested in the study of interpersonal communication. It allowed them to examine objectively the process of interpersonal interactions, to produce minutely detailed transcripts, and to investigate the paralinguistic and non-verbal aspects of behaviour.

Surprisingly, given the phenomenological emphasis of many of the pioneer therapy process researchers, early research concentrated on third party accounts of interactions, rather than those of the participants themselves. The paradigm was to use trained judges to rate portions of a tape for the level of certain process variables, for example, empathy. In the educational context, Bloom (1954) had reported using audiotape recall methods to study teacher–student interactions, but it was some time before psychologists started to use these methods in the clinical context. The first systematic attempts to use videotape recall to examine clients' and therapists' accounts of psychotherapeutic process were reported by Walz and Johnson (1963) and by Kagan and his co-workers (Kagan *et al.*, 1963). Kagan coined the phrase 'Interpersonal Process Recall' to describe the procedure.

Kagan (1984a) describes how in the early 1960s Michigan State University was one of the first institutions to acquire videotaping facilities. He was put in charge of recording the presentations of a series of eminent visiting lecturers. Since videotape was such a rarity then, the lecturers frequently requested to review their own tapes. With little prompting, they would often launch into a critical commentary on their own performance:

> It was amazing to observe the extent to which the videotapes stimulated detailed recall of the experiences. Lecturers reported having forgotten passages and momentarily panicked; yet, the only unusual behavior on the videotape was a very slight hesitation...Most startling was the potential of the immediate playback for recognizing and labeling covert processes associated with uncomfortable behavior. These eminent visitors made such comments as 'I really seemed to look down at my audience – I look haughty – but really I was feeling a bit defensive', or...'I may not look it, but I was frightened to death – concerned that I'm not as good as my reputation'. (Kagan, 1984a, p.236)

This experience led Kagan and his colleagues to explore the possibility of using the IPR method as a way of enhancing the client's rate of progress in psychotherapy. Kagan *et al.* (1963) describe a case study in which client and therapist underwent simultaneous separate recall of segments of their interaction. Kagan *et al.* claim that the client's experience of viewing herself interacting with the therapist enabled her to see the transparency of her defences, and led to her being more open in the subsequent therapy. However, later studies of IPR as a clinical tool (Kingdon, 1975; Van Noord and Kagan, 1976) have been much more cautious in their claims for IPR's benefits in this area.

The major refinement of the IPR method has been the addition of affect simulation to the model (Kagan and Schauble, 1969). Affect simulation involves making video vignettes of actors talking directly to the viewer. The actor portrays feelings that commonly arouse anxiety in the recipient, such as hostility, rejection or attempted seduction. Initial work focused on using affect simulation to assist client growth in psychotherapy and counselling, but the method's potential for training helping professionals was quickly realized (Jason *et al.*, 1971).

The combined affect simulation/recall package has been used in training a variety of populations, such as medical students, clinical and counselling psychologists, and even US Army sergeants (Kagan, 1984a,b). Films and training materials are marketed by Mason Media (undated).

The other important application of IPR is as a tool in therapy process research. Starting in the mid-1970s, it has been used by a number of investigators interested in examining the process of psychotherapy. In the United States, Elliott and his associates are the most active workers (Elliott, in press); in the UK, the only known research application is by Barkham (1983). Both of these researchers are interested in the immediate impact on the client of various types of therapist response modes.

Having briefly summarized the historical development of IPR, I will now examine the current state of the art. This chapter consists of two major sections. The first examines the use of IPR in clinical training and supervision, the second its use as a research tool. My aim is to acquaint the reader who knows little about IPR with the range of possibilities it offers.

TRAINING AND SUPERVISION

Considering that the ability to communicate with clients is central to one's effectiveness as a clinical psychologist, the lack of systematic interpersonal skills training for clinical psychology students is remarkable. Formal courses in interpersonal skills are rarely given: such training as does exist usually occurs within the vagaries of the supervisory relationship.

Traditional clinical psychology training programmes, both in the UK and the US, have a number of major deficiences in their methods of teaching interpersonal skills (Shiffman, 1981). Firstly, the trainees are typically thrown in at the deep end. They are given little opportunity to practise their helping skills in a safe setting where they can make mistakes without adverse consequences; rather, they are given academic lectures on psychopathology, models of psychotherapy, and so forth, and then set to work on actual clients. Secondly, clinical supervision usually relies on the trainees' unassisted recall of their sessions; yet trainees, because of their anxiety and lack of experience, make very poor observers of their own performance. Their retrospective reports are frequently biased by such factors as selective attention, poor recall, and the need to appear competent in the eyes of their supervisor. Furthermore, much energy in supervision is often spent on speculating about what the client was thinking and feeling during the session, yet it is rare for the clients to be given an opportunity to comment directly on their own feelings about the process of the session or the performance of their therapist. This kind of consumer satisfaction data would be an important additional source of learning for most clinical psychology trainees.

In order to clarify the contribution of the IPR model, I will first outline a general helping skills training framework that attempts to meet some of the above deficiencies. The basic requirements of a training programme would appear to be:

1. Instruction on how to conceptualize therapeutic communication. Specifically, trainees should be taught a response mode system, that is, a set of categories for therapist reponses, such as Question or Interpretation (see review by Russell and Stiles, 1979). As yet, there is no agreed system: the choice of which to adopt is to some extent arbitrary. The point is simply that trainees should have a way of conceptualizing the possible alternative responses a therapist might make and know something about the expected impact of each one. However, it is important that the system is reasonably simple, comprehensive and pan-theoretical, that is, not tied to any one orientation of therapy (Goodman and Dooley, 1976).

2. Development of specific skills. Lambert succinctly outlines the sequence of this aspect of training:

> (a) focus on specific skills such as empathic responding, (b) the presentation of a rationale for this skill, (c) audiotape and videotape examples of the presence and absence of the skill in actual therapeutic interactions, (d) practice at the skill, with (e) feedback about performance. (Lambert, 1980, p.426)

3. Graded practice in helping communication – a kind of *in vivo* desensitization to therapeutic communication. The first step is for trainees to practise responding to videotaped, audiotaped, or sometimes written vignettes of client statements. Responses can then be evaluated by the trainer, and alternatives examined. The second step is to practise in co-counselling dyads with fellow trainees, who may either role-play a client or discuss a genuine personal concern. This has the merit of allowing the trainee to experience what it is like to be in the client role. The co-counselling interactions are taped and may include a structured recall from both therapist and 'client'.

4. Actual clinical experience. If possible this also should be done by graded practice, starting with clients without severe problems and progressing to more challenging ones, whilst gradually decreasing the intensity of super-vision. Trainees should routinely be encouraged to audiotape their own sessions. This has several advantages:

- It encourages the practice of self-supervision. Trainees (and practising professionals) can gain much from listening to tapes of their own practice: they rapidly appreciate the shortcomings of their perceptions and respon-ses. Also, repeated listening (say, five or six times) to short segments of tape is occasionally useful in revealing important microscopic aspects of therapy that usually pass by unnoticed. (For a fascinating analysis of psychotherapy on this level, *see* Labov and Fanshel, 1977.)
- The supervisor has an accurate record of what went on in the session, so he or she can point out important aspects that the therapist may not have perceived or remembered.
- The quality of the responses made by the trainee can be evaluated and possible alternatives discussed.
- The tape can be used to stimulate the trainee's recall of his or her experiences during the interaction and to explore common interpersonal blocks or difficulties, such as fear of intimacy or extreme liking or dislike of the client.
- Finally, an inquirer can also conduct recall sessions with the client, in order to obtain his or her perspective on what was helpful or hindering during the interaction.

Having laid out this somewhat idealized model of training and supervision, I will now examine how the IPR procedure fits into each of its stages.

Conceptualizing therapeutic communication

Kagan's response mode system is one of the least satisfactory aspects of the IPR model. Kagan (1984a) describes how it was developed as a result of contrasting videotapes of successful versus unsuccessful counsellors, though details of this study are not supplied. The system consists of four modes (Kagan, 1984a):

1. *Exploratory* – encouraging the client to explore further, for example by using open-ended questions;

2. *Listening* – listening and communicating attempts to understand the client;

3. *Affect* – focusing on the client's feelings;

4. *Honest labelling* – giving frank and honest feedback to the client.

The drawbacks of this system are that the categories are rather loosely defined, that they omit some important therapist activities (for example, advisement) and that they are overly restricted to a humanistic/dynamic model of psychotherapy – they are much less relevant to behavioural or cognitive approaches, for example.

Fortunately, the core parts of the IPR package are largely independent of Kagan's response mode system, so that other systems could be used with it. More satisfactory for training purposes are the systems of Egan (1982) or Goodman (1984).

Development of specific skills

A training film (Mason Media, undated) is available giving examples of therapist responses using and not using each of the Kagan response modes. The modes are presented as responses to be added to, rather than to replace the student's existing repertoire. Trainees are given an opportunity to practise each of them in response to a variety of filmed vignettes.

Graded practice

Kagan argues that skills instruction is insufficient by itself: trainees also have to deal with their basic fears about close relationships (including psychotherapy). Kagan (1974a) describes four core fears:

1. 'The other person will hurt me'...These fears were often expressed as 'I don't know why, but I almost feel as if I'm going to be picked up and hurt. Or somehow the other person will walk out, abandon me, and I won't be able to survive on my own, I'll die.'
2. 'I will hurt the other person.' This second concern was often expressed during recall as 'If I let myself go, if I don't cover up, my angry thoughts might somehow magically hurt you.'
3. 'The other person will engulf me.' This third concern was in the general area of intimacy, sexuality, affectionate stickiness. 'If you get too close, you'll engulf me. I'll lose my identity, my separateness.'
4. 'I will engulf the other person.' The fourth concern was that 'my dependency, my sexual curiosity, my intimacy, might be acted out on you,' (Kagan, 1984a, p.231).

The first step in the graded practice procedure consists of *affect simulation.* Trainees are exposed to a series of filmed vignettes in which actors talk directly to the camera, giving the viewer the sensation of being directly addressed. The vignettes are designed to capture each of the above four themes. They are used to enable trainees to confront some of their feelings associated with close relationships and also to help them to explore ways of responding to these kinds of situations during the actual therapeutic interaction.

The second stage of the graded practice, co-counselling with fellow trainees, is rarely mentioned by Kagan. However, it can easily and usefully be incorporated into the procedure. I use a format in which trainees are grouped into triads. One is the counsellor, one the client, and one an observer. The counsellor and client talk for 20 minutes and their interaction is audiotaped. Then 10 to 15 minutes are used for discussion of important incidents in the interaction, including review of the audiotapes and informal recall. The procedure is then repeated twice, rotating roles so that each person is in each role once.

Actual clinical work

The final step in the IPR model is to conduct recall with trainees seeing actual clients. The recall is initially conducted by a trained inquirer, with the trainee only. Control is in the hands of the trainee, who may stop the tape whenever he or she wishes. The inquirer encourages exploration of thoughts and feelings using such open questions as 'What are you feeling?', 'What pictures went through your mind?', and 'Were you satisfied with your own behaviour?' (Kagan, 1984a).

The rationale for this is twofold. Firstly, it enables the trainee to develop his or her observational powers. Kagan describes two common limitations of beginning therapists. One is 'tuning out' during the interaction, which arises from preoccupation with their discomfort in the therapist role:

This usually occurred when students were especially concerned about the impression they hoped to make on the client. For instance, during IPR sessions, medical students often heard their patients for the first time say things of importance that they had not heard during the interview! The most frequent explanation by the medical students was 'I kept worrying about how to say things in such a way that I would appear older and more experienced than I am. I kept thinking about how I should look and how I should phrase my statements at those times. Even though I look like I'm listening I haven't heard a thing the patient said.' (Kagan, 1980, p.264)

The other is a phenomenon Kagan calls 'feigning of clinical *naïveté*,' that is, when a trainee observes something clinically significant, but feels unable to act upon it. As one trainee expressed it in recall:

'I know she (the client) was very unhappy underneath that put-on smile but – and I know this is stupid – I was afraid she might cry if I told her I knew she was 'hurting', and then I would feel that I had made her cry.' (Kagan, 1980, p.264)

The second major reason for using recall procedure is to help trainees become more self-aware. It is especially useful for them to explore avoidance responses – for example, when something that the client says makes them feel uncomfortable and they consciously or unconsciously withdraw, or when their own problems or defences are touched off by some aspect of the client's material. Furthermore, IPR helps them gain a sense of their own interpersonal impact. They begin to understand how they are coming across to others; for example, when they are being too indirect or too wordy or too overbearing.

An elaboration of the procedure, still in the experimental stage, is to monitor physiological measures of the therapist's emotional responsiveness, and include these in the video playback using a split screen method (Archer *et al.*, 1972). Thus, trainees can see concrete evidence of their responsiveness as the session progresses. However, this aspect of the model is still rather expensive and elaborate and needs further development before it can be easily implemented.

After undergoing IPRs conducted by trained inquirers, trainees then learn inquirer skills themselves, partly as a way of using a 'pyramid therapy' approach, and thus saving time for the instructor, and partly in order to expand the trainees' own communication skills. The skills needed to be a competent IPR inquirer have considerable overlap with those needed to conduct exploratory psychotherapy.

When they have mastered the inquirer skills, trainees start conducting recalls with each other's clients. Clients' recall sessions follow the same procedure as therapists', going through the tape with the aid of the inquirer, stopping to comment on significant moments. The therapists are given the opportunity to hear their clients' tapes (with their clients' permission), thereby learning how their clients view their efforts to help. This is frequently an important learning experience. Therapists are often amazed by how aware their clients are of the subtleties of interpersonal process, even though they may not acknowledge it (or may even flatly deny it) during the interaction. Of course, it is wrong to regard the client's viewpoint as representing the 'truth' about an interaction. The client's perceptions may be distorted by transference feelings, or by a desire to impress the therapist, or simply because the client is an inexpert observer of psychotherapeutic process. But even taking these factors into account, there is usually much in client recall that can be of value to the therapist.

In the full IPR procedure, client and therapist also participate in mutual recall. That is, they review the tape together, with an inquirer, and discuss their mutual therapeutic process. I have not yet used this aspect of the IPR model, but it seems a powerful procedure that in skilled hands could greatly enhance the quality of the therapeutic alliance.

Evaluation of the IPR training model

A major problem with reviewing the research on IPR training is that the bulk of it is unpublished, being in the form of Michigan State University theses and dissertations. Thus, it is not readily available to the reader, especially the British reader. Furthermore, the fact that so little of the research has found its way into refereed journals does little to inspire confidence in its quality. Here, I will confine my attention to published research: more comprehensive reviews can be found in Kagan (1980, 1984a) and McQuellan (1982).

Archer and Kagan (1973) evaluated a community-oriented IPR programme to increase the interpersonal skills of American undergraduate volunteers. IPR groups led by paraprofessionals were found to be superior to an encounter-developmental comparison group and a no-treatment control on pencil-and-paper measures of empathy and actualization.

Spivack (1972), using a cross-over design to compare IPR and traditional training methods on an American postgraduate counselling course, found the IPR method led to greater gains in empathy than the traditional one. However, Kingdon (1975), making a similar comparison on the same population, found differential effects for only one of five variables studied: clients of IPR group trainees showed greater self-exploration than clients of traditionally supervised trainees.

Finally, Robbins *et al.* (1979) examined IPR's utility for enhancing the interpersonal skills of American medical residents. At least 68 per cent of US medical schools offer some form of organized interpersonal skills instruction (Kahn *et al.*, 1979). Robbins *et al.* compared an IPR with a didactic approach and found that the IPR group showed a greater level of empathy. A more general review of IPR in medical training, and some preliminary research findings, are given by Kagan (1984b).

Overall, the emprical evidence for the utility of IPR in training is at this point merely suggestive. Further work is clearly needed, preferably by investigators outside Kagan's research group. Two separate questions need to be addressed (Lambert, 1982): what changes in interpersonal skills (if any) does IPR produce, and to what extent do these changes in the therapist enhance the therapeutic progress of the client?

Summary

There is a plausible case for including some form of systematic interpersonal skills training in clinical psychology courses. IPR provides one possible way to do this. In essence, the training method consists of (a) affect simulation – the use of short video vignettes as an aid to exploring one's feelings about therapeutic relationships, and (b) tape-assisted recall – the use of videotape playback to help trainees understand their own thoughts and feelings during therapeutic interactions. Its unique feature is that it is a discovery-oriented approach: the learning comes from within the trainee rather than being provided from without. Furthermore, the addition of client feedback provides a perspective on the trainee's helping activities that is absent in other training methods.

The IPR model can be implemented in a cost-effective way if trainees are taught to serve as each other's inquirers, and the instructor then acts as a consultant for the group as a whole. IPR has the flexibility to be adapted to the needs of the particular training course. It can easily be combined with other types of instruction and supervision. I use it in conjunction with a structured helping skills training programme, such as Egan's (1982) or Goodman's (1979). The skills programme provides a conceptual knowledge base and IPR provides the experiential learning.

THERAPY PROCESS RESEARCH

Process research examines what actually happens between the client and therapist during therapy (as opposed to outcome research, which asks how much the therapy helped the client). Process researchers ask such questions as what are the immediate impacts of various therapist interventions, are there common factors between different schools of therapy, and what distinguishes therapy from other types of conversation?

As I mentioned in the introductory section, a common paradigm in process research is to audiotape segments of client–therapist interaction, to use trained raters to make judgements about those segments, and then to correlate these judgements with external criteria on the client, the therapist, or their relationship. The body of research on Rogers' (1957) necessary and sufficient conditions hypothesis provides a good example. Segments of tape are rated for the three conditions of empathy, warmth, and genuineness, and then the judges' ratings are correlated with measures of therapeutic efficacy (*see* review by Lambert *et al.,* 1978).

It is still relatively rare for researchers to seek the client's view about what is happening in therapy. On the one hand, this is understandable, since the variables being studied are complex and often abstruse, and expert raters are needed to identify them. Furthermore, some would argue that psychotherapy clients, by definition, suffer from disturbed perceptions and attitudes, and thus may not give an accurate representation of what has occurred during the interaction. On the other hand, the client is the ultimate target of the therapeutic intervention, and all change is mediated by his or her experience (Elliott, 1979). Thus, omitting the client's perceptions is omitting the most important variable in the equation.

One way of examining the client's perceptions is by questionnaires administered after the therapy session. For example, considerable research has been done on the Rogerian hypothesis using Barrett-Lennard's Relationship Inventory. However, this method can only summarize the client's feelings about the session: it cannot examine the fine detail of the process. What IPR provides is a way to study the client's and therapist's moment-by-moment experience, which makes it a uniquely valuable research tool.

The use of IPR in therapy process research is comprehensively reviewed by Elliott (in press). My debt to his work will be clear. Here I will give a brief, non-technical exposition aimed at a reader having little acquaintaince with process research. I will examine two illustrative research programmes, that of Elliott and his colleagues (of whom I was one), and that of Barkham.

IPR in process research

I will use a simple micro-process model to conceptualize the phenomena of interest (*see* Caskey *et al.,* 1984, for details). This model analyses therapy process at the level of the individual verbal response or 'talking turn'. It assumes that associated with each therapist response are one or more therapist intentions, and that each response has a certain impact on the client. For example, if a client is talking about feeling extremely depressed and the therapist asks 'How long have you been feeling like that?', the therapists's intention could be, say, to gather information, to explore with the client what situations elicit her depression, or to steer her away from talking about strong feelings, because the therapist feels uncomfortable with them. Possible impacts on the client could be feeling gratified by the therapist's attention, feeling distracted by the therapist's question, or being reminded of some event in her past.

Elliott and his colleagues (Caskey *et al.,* 1984; Elliott 1979; Elliott *et al.,* 1982) examined associations between therapist intentions, therapist response modes, and impact on the client. In each therapy session studied, they sampled four responses from each of three segments at 10, 25 and 40 minutes into the session. After each session, the client and therapist were given separate IPRs. This use of IPR was more structured than Kagan's: the tape was stopped after each therapist response in the sample, and, in addition to using open-ended probes, inquirers also asked several structured questions. For example, to assess therapist intentions, therapists and clients were asked 'What were you (or what was your therapist) trying to do in saying that?', and to assess impacts they were asked to rate each response on various scales such as helpfulness and empathy.

Three major questions were addressed, using data drawn from an analogue sample and an actual therapy sample. Elliott (1979) examined how clients perceive the intentions behind each of the Goodman-Dooley (1976) therapist response modes. For example, when the therapist is using a response that trained raters code as a reflection, does the client experience the therapist as trying to communicate empathy? The results generally supported the assumption behind the response mode framework, although correlations were only moderate. There were also some clinically interesting departures from the predictions: for example, clients tended to see advisement behind almost anything that their therapist tried to do.

Elliott *et al.* (1982) examined the impact of each response mode on the client, in order to test the assumptions contained in several interpersonal skills training programmes which teach therapists to reduce advisement and questions, and to increase reflections. In particular, they wanted to see to what extent each response mode was experienced as helpful by the client. The helpfulness measure was taken from the client recall; the response mode measures were taken from client and therapist perceived intentions and the raters' coding of the responses. The results generally did not support the assumptions behind the skills training programmes. The most helpful response modes were interpretation and advisement, and questions were experienced as being the least helpful.

Caskey *et al.* (1984), using the same sample, examined the 'Rashomon effect', named after the Kurosawa film in which a single event is seen by different observers in crucially different ways. In psychotherapy, the issue is how similarly do the client and therapist see the process. Results showed that while overlap between viewpoints could be demonstrated, it was generally small, leaving substantial proportions of variance specific to each perspective, thus supporting the existence of a 'Rashomon effect' at the micro-process level.

In his current work, Elliott is concentrating on using IPR to illuminate the nature of 'significant events' in therapy, that is, responses that stand out in recall as being especially positive or negative for the client. Elliott (1983b) has constructed a taxonomy of such events, arriving at a set of eight helpful event types and six hindering ones.

The only known British use of IPR in clinical psychological research is by

Barkham (1983), who was interested in the immediate impact of certain therapist response modes on the client's experience of feeling understood. In an ingenious and technologically sophisticated study, he used a variant of IPR to monitor the client's and the therapist's perceptions of when the client was feeling understood or misunderstood. In addition to the IPR procedure, he also measured the client's experience of being understood in real-time during the session using a cue button method. However, since this real-time procedure produced few significant results, possibly due to several measurement problems inherent in this method, I will concentrate here on the IPR aspect of the study.

Each session in the sample was separately reviewed by clients and therapists on videotape. They were instructed to press switches at any time they felt that the therapist was either understanding or misunderstanding the client. The signals from these switches were written directly on to a microcomputer disc for subsequent analysis.

The major research question concerned which response modes preceded client and therapist perceptions of empathy in both initial and later sessions. The findings were complex. In brief, responses constructed from a frame of reference shared by both client and therapist (a response mode labelled Exploration: see Shapiro *et al.,* 1984) were more likely to lead to experiences of empathy in both initial and later sessions than other response modes.

Methodological issues with IPR

The sceptical reader is probably aware that nothing so far has been said about the psychometric properties of IPR. It has been tacitly assumed that data obtained during recall sessions are an accurate representation of the person's experiences during the interaction. While it is true that workers using IPR are usually powerfully struck by the ability of the method to stimulate half-remembered experiences, it is also true that IPR is subject to a number of potential validity threats, such as forgetting, lack of expressive skills, social desirability, and fabrication (Elliott, in press). Some of these problems raise complex philosophical questions about the nature of personal experiences. Studies examining correlations between *in vivo* and recalled ratings of emotional state have generally revealed modest to good rate-rerate reliabilities (Hill *et al.,* 1981; Katz and Resnikoff, 1977), thus providing some evidence for the validity of IPR for assessing these variables. However, more work needs to be done on the basic psychometric properties of IPR before its use can be justified on firmer grounds than clinical plausibility.

Summary

IPR provides the process researcher with a unique way of examining participants' reactions to the flow of conversation in therapy. It is capable of being used in a structured way, examining categories of behaviour defined by the researcher, or in an unstructured, more phenomenological way, examining the participants' own ways of construing the therapeutic process.

Most studies have used a more or less structured method, being concerned with the immediate impact of various therapist verbal response modes. While these studies have yielded clinically useful findings, they are constricted by the content-free nature of their variables. Response mode systems only look at the form of the communication - the how rather than the what. They do not, for example, distinguish good from bad uses of each response mode, which places a ceiling on the effect sizes that can be obtained using them as sole variables (Barker, 1983). Future studies need to include evaluative as well as descriptive measures. More interesting uses of IPR, truer to its original spirit, lie in discovery-oriented research, in which the researcher allows the participants to define the phenomena of interest (*see* Elliott, 1983a).

Findings from existing research demonstrate both the utility and the complexity of examining therapy at a micro-process level. Clients appear to maintain an internal running commentary on their therapist's activity to a much greater extent that most therapists probably realize. This commentary also shows certain law-like properties. That is, given that the therapist makes a certain type of intervention, it is possible to predict, though not with great confidence, the client's likely reaction. This kind of data is a first step in building an empirically-based pan-theoretical science of psychotherapy process.

SUMMARY AND CONCLUSION

This chapter has described the applications of IPR to clinical psychological training and research. The IPR method of tape-assisted recall has two major advantages for both research and training: its ability to (1) recover important experiences that would otherwise be irretrievably lost, and (2) provide learning by discovery, working within the frame of reference of the student or research participant rather than the instructor or researcher.

I hope I have provided enough background to acquaint the interested reader with IPR's potential. I have tried to focus on its psychological aspects; practical details such as what kind of equipment to use and how to train IPR instructors are covered in many of the references, especially Elliott (in press) and Kagan (1984a).

Finally, as with most new developments in the field, practice has preceded research. There is ample case-study evidence for the utility of IPR, but published evidence from well-designed studies is still weak. There is much scope for psychologists to combine both research and practical applications of its use.

REFERENCES

ARCHER, J., FIESTER, T., KAGAN, N., RATE, L., SPIERLING, T. and VAN NOORD, R. (1972) New method for education, treatment and research in human interaction. *Journal of Counseling Psychology, 19,* 275–281.

ARCHER, J. and KAGAN, N. (1973) Teaching interpersonal skills on campus: A pyramid approach. *Journal of Counseling Psychology, 20,* 535–540.

BARKER, C. (1983) The psychotherapist. In: W.T. Singleton (ed.) *The Study of Real Skills: Volume 4, Social Skills.* Lancaster: MTP Press.

BARKHAM, M. (1983) Helper verbal response modes and perceived empathy. Unpublished PhD thesis, Brighton Polytechnic.

BLOOM, B.S. (1954) The thought process of students in discussion. In: S.J. French (ed.) *Accent on Teaching: Experiments in General Education.* New York: Harper and Brothers.

CASKEY, N., BARKER, C., and ELLIOTT, R. (1984) Dual perspectives: Clients' and therapists' perceptions of therapist responses. *British Journal of Clinical Psychology, 23,* 281–290.

EGAN, G. (rev. edn, 1982) *The Skilled Helper.* Monterey, Ca.: Brooks/Cole.

ELLIOTT, R. (1979) How clients perceive helper behaviors. *Journal of Counseling Psychology, 26,* 285–294.

ELLIOTT, R. (1983a) A discovery-oriented approach to significant change events in psychotherapy: Interpersonal Process Recall and comprehensive process analysis. In: L.N. Rice and L.S. Greenberg (eds) *Patterns of Change: Intensive Analysis of Psychotherapy Process.* New York: Guilford.

ELLIOTT, R. (1983b) Interpersonal Process Recall in the analysis of significant psychotherapy events. Paper presented at the Society for Psychotherapy Research annual meeting, Sheffield.

ELLIOTT, R. (in press) Interpersonal Process Recall (IPR): A psychotherapy process research method. In: L.S. Greenberg and W. Pinsoff (eds) *The Pyschotherapeutic Process: A Research Handbook.* New York: Guilford.

ELLIOTT, R., BARKER, C.B., CASKEY, N. and PISTRANG, N. (1982) Differential helpfulness of counselor verbal reponse modes. *Journal of Counseling Psychology, 29,* 354–361.

GOODMAN, G. (1979) *SASHAtapes: Self-led Automated Series on Helping Alternatives.* Los Angeles: UCLA Extension.

GOODMAN, G. (1984) SASHAtapes: Expanding options for help-intended communication. In: D. Larsen (ed.) *Teaching Psychological Skills.* Monterey, Ca.: Brooks/Cole.

GOODMAN, G., and DOOLEY, D. (1976) A framework for help-intended communication. *Psychotherapy: Theory, Research, and Practice, 13,* 106–117.

HILL, C.E., SIEGELMAN, L., GRONSKY, B.R., STURNIOLO, F., and FRETZ, B.R. (1981) Nonverbal communication and counseling outcome. *Journal of Counseling Psychology, 28,* 203–212.

JASON, H., KAGAN, N., WERNER, A., ELSTEIN, A.S., and THOMAS, J.B. (1971) New approaches to teaching basic interview skills to medical students. *American Journal of Psychiatry, 127,* 1404–1407.

KAGAN, N. (1980) Influencing human interaction: Eighteen years with IPR. In: A.K. Hess (ed.) *Psychotherapy Supervision: Theory, Research and Practice.* Chichester: Wiley.

KAGAN, N. (1984a) Interpersonal process recall: Basic methods and recent research. In: D. Larsen (ed.) *Teaching Psychological Skills.* Monterey, Ca.: Brooks/Cole.

KAGAN, N. (1984b) The physician as therapeutic agent: Innovations in training. In: L. Temoshok, L. Zegans and C. Van Dyke (eds) *Emotions in Health and Illness: Applications to Clinical Practice.* New York: Grune and Statton.

KAGAN, N., KRATHWOHL, D.R. and MILLER, R. (1963) Simulated recall in therapy using videotape – a case study. *Journal of Counseling Psychology, 10,* 237–243.

KAHN, G.S., COHEN, B., and JASON, H. (1979) The teaching of interpersonal skills in US medical schools. *Journal of Medical Education, 54,* 29–35.

KATZ, D., and RESNIKOFF, A., (1977) Televised self-confrontation and recalled affect: A new look at videotaped recall. *Journal of Counseling Psychology, 24,* 150–152.

KINGDON, M.A. (1975) A cost-benefit analysis of the Interpersonal Process Recall technique. *Journal of Counseling Psychology, 22,* 353–357.

KIRSCHENBAUM, H. (1979) *On Becoming Carl Rogers.* New York: Dell.

LABOV, W., and FANSHEL, D. (1977) *Therapeutic Discourse.* New York: Academic Press.

LAMBERT, M.J. (1980) Research and the supervisory process. In: A.K.Hess (ed.) *Psychotherapy Supervision: Theory, Research, and Practice.* Chichester: Wiley.

LAMBERT, M.J. (1982) Relation of helping skills to treatment outcome. In: E.K. Marshall and P.D. Kurtz (eds) *Interpersonal Helping Skills.* London: Jossey-Bass.

LAMBERT, M.J., DE JULIO, S.S., and STEIN, D.M. (1978) Therapist interpersonal skills: Process, outcome, methodological considerations and recommendations for future research. *Psychological Bulletin, 85,* 467–489.

MASON MEDIA (undated) Influencing Human Interaction. Mason Media, 1265 Lakeside Drive, East Lansing, Michigan 48823.

McQUELLAN, R.P. (1982) Interpersonal Process Recall. In: E.K. Marshall and P.D. Kurtz (eds) *Interpersonal Helping Skills.* London: Jossey-Bass.

ROBBINS, A.S., KAUS, D.R., HEINRICH, R., ABRASS, I., DREYER, J., and CLYMAN, B. (1979) Interpersonal skills: Evaluation in an internal medicine residency. *Journal of Medical Education, 54,* 885–894.

ROGERS, C.R. (1957) Necessary and sufficient conditions for therapeutic personality change. *Journal of Consulting Psychology, 22,* 95–103.

RUSSELL, R.L., and STILES, W.B. (1979) Categories for classifying language in psychotherapy. *Psychological Bulletin, 86,* 404–419.

SHAPIRO, D.A., BARKHAM, M., and IRVING, D.L. (1984) The reliability of a modified Helper Behaviour Rating System. *British Journal of Medical Psychology, 57,* 45–48.

SHIFFMAN, S.M. (1981) The effects of graduate training in clinical psychology on performance in a psychotherapy analog. (Doctoral dissertation, University of California, Los Angeles, 1981.) *Dissertation Abstracts International, 42,* 2084B– 2085B (University Microfilms No. 81-22837).

SPIVACK, J.D. (1972) Laboratory to classroom: The practical application of IPR in a Master's level prepracticum counselor education program. *Counselor Education and Supervision, 12,* 3–16.

VAN NOORD, R.W., and KAGAN, N. (1976) Stimulated recall and affect simulation in counseling: client Growth re-examined. *Journal of Counseling Psychology, 23,* 28–33.

WALZ, G.R., and JOHNSON, J.A. (1963) Counselors look at themselves on videotape. *Journal of Counseling Psychology, 10,* 232–236.

FAMILY APPROACHES TO SCHIZOPHRENIA: RECENT DEVELOPMENTS

Angus M. Strachan

Recent studies of the efficacy of family therapy and drug therapy in the treatment of schizophrenia have been promising (Anderson et al., 1981; Falloon et al., 1982; Goldstein et al., 1978; Leff et al., 1982). These programmes have differed from earlier 'intensive' family therapy with schizophrenia in that they assume a diathesis-stress rather than a psychoanalytic model of schizophrenia and are oriented to improving the course of the disorder once a psychotic breakdown has occurred rather than 'curing' schizophrenia.

There have been three major forces contributing to the renewed interest in family factors associated with schizophrenia. First, moves to put psychiatric inpatients back into the community to combat the negative effects of institutionalization have had mixed success (Lamb, 1981), This has been partly because of a lack of funding of comprehensive preventive mental health programmes, and partly because of a lack of understanding of the environmental stresses, including family styles, which trigger relapse, or lead to a deterioration of social functioning. In the United States, there has been increasing pressure on remaining inpatient facilities and an increase in the number of poorly-functioning discharged patients who wander the streets. In Britain, as monetarist policies stretch the resources of the National Health Service and local community Social Services, similar problems are beginning to surface.

A second force has been the steady growth of interest in family therapy amongst mental health professionals, reflected in the proliferation of books on family therapy over the last decade. There have been moves towards a conceptualization of problems in terms of systems theory (for example, Minuchin, 1974), and research has shown that changes made when working directly with families or couples are more persistent and enduring than changes made in one-to-one therapies. For example, conjoint therapy with couples is more successful than parallel individual therapy (Gurman and Kniskern, 1978), and the involvement of a partner in a weight loss programme increases the likelihood of long-term weight loss (Murphy et al., 1982).

A third force has been the scientific work on the relation between family factors and the onset and course of schizophrenia which has emerged from the UK and the US in recent years.

Interestingly, whereas clinical psychologists have been relatively cautious in embracing a family therapy orientation (so that most family therapists are either psychiatrists or social workers), clinical psychologists have been heavily involved in the scientific work on the onset and course of schizophrenia and the evaluation of family therapy treatment programmes with schizophrenia.

There have been two main kinds of studies of family factors. Work in Britain has focused on family factors associated with the *course* of recovery after a patient has been discharged from the hospital. These studies have been conducted mainly at the MRC Social Psychiatry Unit at the Institute of Psychiatry in London. By contrast, longitudinal studies in the United States have focused on family factors associated with the *onset* of schizophrenia and related disorders. Whilst it is important to remember that factors associated with the course of the illness are not necessarily aetiological, it is difficult to:

> view family life as so discontinuous across the life-span that those attributes of the family environment related to the onset of schizophrenia do not overlap with those associated with differential course after an initial episode. (Goldstein and Doane, 1982, p.693)

Course: Expressed Emotion, contact and drug compliance

The introduction of the phenothiazines was a major step forward in the treatment of schizophrenia. They were effective in reducing psychotic symptoms, that is, delusions and hallucinations in schizophrenic, manic, depressive, and organic psychoses. They also significantly reduced the length of hospitalization for acute psychoses. However, 7 per cent of patients' psychotic symptoms were untouched by medication and 35 per cent of patients relapsed within two years, even though they were maintained on the drugs (Leff and Wing, 1971).

A series of naturalistic studies at the MRC Social Psychiatry Unit has examined factors which 'protect' patients from relapse once they have left the hospital (Brown *et al.*, 1958, 1962, 1972; Vaughn and Leff, 1976). These studies suggest that there are three important factors which protect a patient from relapse. The most important factor is low 'Expressed Emotion' in relatives who live with them. Expressed Emotion (EE) is rated from attitudes spontaneously expressed to an interviewer by the relative during a semi-structured interview about the patient, the Camberwell Family Interview (CFI).

The number of harshly critical comments is counted and emotional over-involvment is rated. If either or both measures are high, the relative has high EE. Patients who return to homes with one or more high EE relatives have a nine-month relapse rate of 51 per cent; those who return to homes with low EE relatives have a relapse rate of only 13 per cent (Vaughn and Leff, 1976). This finding has now been replicated in the US by Vaughn *et al.* (1982).

The second protective factor is low contact with the relative, defined as less than 35 hours per week of face-to-face contact.

The third protective factor is whether the patient is maintained on medication. Of these, low EE appeared to be the most important in that the nine-month relapse rates of patients with low EE relatives were low, whether or not the patient was on drugs and irrespective of the face-to-face contact. Nine-month relapse patients with high EE relatives were decreased by drug compliance and low contact, however, showing that they are important factors too.

A problem with this work is that it is correlational and thus could be confounded. It could be argued that the more deviant and disturbed the patient is, the more likely it will be that relatives react with anger, guilt and over-involvement, and the more likely the patient will be to relapse. The alternative hypothesis was answered by Brown *et al.'s* (1972) analysis, which partialled out the effect of behavioural disturbance and previous employment, and showed that these had little effect on relapse compared with the effect of EE. However, whether or not the patients were maintained on medication was not independently controlled and so could be confounded with the motivation of the patient, the attitudes and persistence of prescribing physicians and community psychiatric nurses, and environmental factors including family factors.

In spite of these problems of interpretation, this body of research has had an important impact in suggesting the possibility of a causal effect of the family's attitudes and involvement on the course of schizophrenia.

Onset: communication deviance and affective style

Longitudinal prospective studies can examine whether there are measurable aspects of family relationships which occur prior to the onset of schizophrenia. Because of the low base-rate for the occurrence of schizophrenia, longitudinal studies have selected samples which are presumed to be at high risk for the development of schizophrenia.

A recent study at the UCLA Family Project (Doane *et al.*, 1981) used as a high-risk sample a cohort of 65 consecutive adolescents brought to an outpatient clinic for treatment for a variety of problems. Each family was screened for the presence of both parents and for the absence of psychotic signs in any family members. Amongst various measures of family communication, two have proved particularly powerful in the prediction of 'schizophrenia-spectrum' disorders (Wender *et al.*, 1968) at five-year follow up. The schizophrenia spectrum includes severe personality disorders – schizo-affective, schizoid, antisocial and borderline – as well as diagnoses of schizophrenia: all made according to strict research criteria. One variable, parental 'Communication Deviance' (CD), was measured from stories given to Thematic Apperception Test cards. The coding was developed by Jones *et al.* (1977) from the criteria of Singer and Wynne (1966) for measuring the fragmentedness and amorphousness of communication by counting examples of lack of closure, extreme uncertainty, breaking off mid-sentence, odd word usage, etc.

The other variable, parental 'Affective Style' (AS), was measured from a 10-minute discussion about a conflict-provoking issue between the parents and the adolescent (Doane *et al.*, 1981). This measure was composed of criticisms, guilt induction and intrusiveness. Together, CD and AS predicted with a high degree of accuracy which families had adolescents who developed schizophrenia-spectrum disorders. The study suggests that families with parents who cannot communicate clearly, particularly about emotional material, are more likely to have offspring with schizophrenia-spectrum disorders.

In conclusion, research on onset and course has suggested the relevance in predicting schizophrenia-spectrum disorders of three measures (EE, CD and AS), which presumably relate to the family's ability to cope with the inevitable stresses of life, including internal family pressures. It is not clear why these variables have predictive power; they may reflect the importance of a higher-level construct such as 'enmeshment' (Minuchin, 1974), or they may indicate that communication styles play a direct role in family coping. Nevertheless, they are useful as indicators of family processes, and can point to possible areas of family intervention. The family intervention studies described below have built on these studies of family communication.

FAMILY INTERVENTION WITH SCHIZOPHRENIA

Prior to systematic studies of family intervention with schizophrenia, it was thought that psychodynamic individual psychotherapy on its own or in combination with neuroleptics could improve the outcome of patients. However, a major study reported by May and Tuma (1976) did not support this contention. Random assignment of patients to drug treatment, psychotherapy, drug treatment plus psychotherapy, milieu therapy, or electro-convulsive therapy, showed that an ego-supportive, reality-oriented psychodynamic therapy was neither as effective as medication nor added to its effectiveness.

Meanwhile, the field of family therapy had been developing. Esterson *et al.* (1965) reported the results of therapy aimed at families of schizophrenics. They emphasized the importance of taking psychotic symptoms seriously, of understanding the meaning of hallucinations and delusions, particularly in relation to family communication. They took an existential approach with the patient, and a demystifying approach with the family, trying to unravel the disguised family communication. Bowen (1978) described work in which he hospitalized whole families of schizophrenic patients for observation and treatment. Bowen worked intensively with such families attempting to 'differentiate' family members from 'the undifferentiated family ego mass'.

In the sixties and seventies, the work of Weakland *et al.* (1974) and of Palazzoli *et al.* (1978) focused on the communication of families in 'schizophrenic transition'. They saw the psychotic behaviour of the identified patient as a symptom of a disturbed pattern of transactions in the family. Weakland *et al.* describe the results of 96 cases (only some containing schizophrenics) who were seen for an average of seven sessions, and reported that 72 per cent were significantly improved. Palazzoli *et al.* also claimed success for their methods, in which they see families of schizophrenics about once a month and focus on 'positive connotation' of the psychotic behaviour, and on prescribing therapeutic paradoxes.

Unfortunately, whilst all these approaches are intriguing methods of inducing change in the family system, none have employed randomized assignment designs, or systematically reported outcomes of family therapy.

The new batch of studies is concerned with improving the after-care of patients discharged from hospital, by involving the family in treatment (*see* Tables *1* and *2*). This new focus reflects two trends, one theoretical and one pragmatic. Theoretically, most workers in the field now assume that schizophrenia is a disorder caused by an interaction between a genetically predisposing biological sensitivity and stresses in the environment. Pragmatically, the focus of psychotherapy has moved from 'curing' the patient of psychotic symptoms, to seeing what impact psychotherapy can have on social functioning and resistance to stress once the major tranquillizers have reduced acute psychotic symptoms.

Crisis-oriented family therapy

Goldstein *et al.* (1978) reported the first random assignment study of family therapy as used in after-care. The study grew out of previous studies on consecutive schizophrenic admissions to a mental health centre in California where the average length of hospitalization was 14 days, short compared with Britain. Three major facts emerged. First, the majority of readmissions (31 per cent) occurred within four weeks of discharge. Second, patients did not take the prescribed oral phenothiazines. Third, patients did not use the supportive outpatient therapy offered. So, Goldstein *et al.* (1978) devised a study to examine the impact of a short-term crisis-oriented family therapy after-care programme in combination with various levels of drug dosage.

The sample consisted of 96 first and second admissions who received independent diagnoses of schizophrenia from ratings on the New Haven Schizophrenia Index. Of these, 69 per cent were first admissions and 31 per

Table 1. Summary of family therapy programmes with schizophrenia

Study	Comparison groups	Length of treatment*	Place of meetings	Number of patients	Mean age	First admissions
Goldstein *et al.* (1978)	2 x 2 factorial: low and medium drug dose plus family crisis therapy or not	Six weekly family meetings	Clinic	96	23	69%
Leff *et al.* (1982)	Relative education and group *vs* standard aftercare	18 biweekly drop-in relatives groups plus 6 family meetings (average)	Group at clinic; family at home	24	35	30%
Falloon *et al.* (1982)	Family education and behavioural family therapy *vs* individual case management	Weekly for 3 months, biweekly for 6 months	Home	36	25	36%
Anderson *et al.* (1981)	2 x 2 factorial: relative education and structural family therapy or no therapy; plus social skills training or not	Twice a week during hospitalization, then every 2 or 3 weeks	Clinic	–	–	–

* Note: In the first nine months after discharge: family treatment was continued after nine months for the three later programmes.

cent were second admissions who had all been admitted within the year. The sample had a mean age of 23 years.

Patients were assigned to one of four conditions by a stratified random method. Their premorbid sociosexual adjustment was measured on the UCLA social adjustment scale and median splits were used to stratify males and females separately into good and poor premorbid groups. Then patients were randomly assigned to cells in a two-by-two factorial design. One factor was the presence or absence of family therapy. The other factor was the level of medication. All patients were given long-acting injections of phenothiazines. The low dose group received what was judged a minimally therapeutic dose of fluphenazine (0.25 ml); the moderate dose group received 1 ml.

The family therapy was short-term and very concrete. Based on crisis intervention theory, the main goal was to help the family understand the events around the psychosis so as to improve future coping. Family therapy sessions with two co-therapists were held weekly in the outpatient clinic for the six weeks following discharge. There were four stages of treatment. First, each family member, including the patient, was asked about their experience of the events before and during the patient's psychotic break. This was an important aspect of the programme, which many mental health professionals avoid, thus letting patient and relatives seal over important feelings, or feel shame about the psychotic break. Goldstein and Kopeikin (1981) report that both patient and relatives experience a great deal of relief talking about the breakdown, and also become aware of its serious nature. During this discussion, the therapists helped the family identify stressful events which

Table 2. Results of three randomized studies of family therapy with schizophrenia

Study	First follow-up	Relapse rate in family therapy group	Relapse rate in comparison	Comparison group
Goldstein *et al.* (1978)	6 months	0%	48%	Low dose, no family therapy
Leff *et al.* (1982)	9 months	8%	50%	Normal out patient care
Falloon *et al.* (1982)	9 months	6%	44%	Individual education and case management

occurred prior to the breakdown, and to make links between these precipitating events and the breakdown.

The second stage was to identify the two or three situations which were currently most stressful to the patient. The third stage was the development of strategies for avoiding or coping with these stressful situations. During the week, the family would carry out these methods of coping and report back at the next meeting. The final stage was planning to anticipate future crises and developing stress prevention and coping mechanisms in advance of such crises. Of major importance was the discussion of the possible emergence of psychiatric symptoms. Other topics might be resuming employment, making friends, or future living arrangements. In summary, the family meetings were planned for identifying current and potential stressors, and planning coping mechanisms for the patient and relatives to use.

Results. At the end of six weeks of treatment, 10 of the 96 patients had deteriorated clinically, so that they had to be rehospitalized or have their medication increased dramatically. This was an overall relapse rate of only 10 per cent, considerably less than the 31 per cent found previously. At six-months follow-up, the rate of relapse was 0 per cent for the moderate dose–family therapy group, but 48 per cent for the low dose–no therapy group. The other two groups were in between: moderate dose–no therapy had a relapse rate of 14 per cent; low dose–no therapy was 21 per cent. There was a significant effect of drug dosage (p < .01), for family therapy (p < .05), and the extreme groups differed very significantly (p < .001)

The symptomatic status of the patient was examined using behaviour ratings on Overall and Gorham's (1962) Brief and Psychiatric Rating Scale (BPRS), not the most reliable instrument, particularly with inexperienced raters. The most significant effects were for the family therapy: at six weeks, family therapy had a significant overall effect on symptoms, which was particularly marked for withdrawal, especially 'blunted affect'. Thus, the family therapy seemed to prevent the patient withdrawing socially and becoming less emotionally responsive. At six months, only withdrawal was significantly related to treatment group: the effect of therapy is now only found in the group with the higher drug dose.

Overall, it can be concluded that the six weeks of moderate drug dosage and short-term family therapy had significant effects on relapse rates and social withdrawal up to the six-month follow-up. A long-term follow-up was conducted on those patients still in the area after three to six years. There were no longer any effects. In other words, the effect of the six-week intervention ceased to be significant as its impact diminished in comparison with that of later events.

Subsequent to the publication of this brief family intervention project, the results of two projects with smaller samples but longer-term interventions have been published.

Education, relatives' support group and family therapy

First there is the work of Leff *et al.* (1982,1983), which grew out of the research relating Expressed Emotion (EE) and Face-to-Face Contact (FF) to relapse. To examine whether this correlation was causal, they decided to 'manipulate experimentally' relatives' EE and FF, and examine the effect on relapse.

Consecutive admissions to several London hospitals were screened for the presence of the following:

1.Three months' continuous residence with relatives prior to admission;
2.A diagnosis of schizophrenia according to the Present State Examination (PSE) criteria;
3.A high level of FF (more than 35 hours per week).

Subsequently, each relative with high FF was given the CFI and their EE level assessed. The 24 high EE families were randomly assigned to an experimental group, which received a special intervention package, and a comparison treatment-as-usual group. Both groups received identical assessment at intake and follow-up: a PSE with the patient, a CFI and a structured interview about their knowledge of schizophrenia with each relative. Most patients were on long-acting injections of phenothiazines. The 16 low EE families were also randomly assigned to treatment and comparison groups, but data are not reported because of drop-outs from these groups.

The intervention package had three components (Berkowitz *et al.*, 1981). First, an education programme was given at home to relatives. This consisted of four short lectures covering possible causes, symptoms, likely course, and treatment. Relatives were encouraged to ask questions. The patient's condition was explicitly described as 'schizophrenia'.

The second component was a relatives' group composed of both high and low EE relatives. This was led by two professionals and met every two weeks. It had been observed previously that low EE relatives had more effective coping mechanisms for dealing with their schizophrenic relative, which decreased pressure on the patient and elicited more support for themselves. Thus, the initial hope was that low EE coping mechanisms would rub off on the high EE relatives. This turned out to be overly optimistic because most of the low EE relatives simply stopped attending (an effective way of dealing with EE relatives!). In response, the group leaders became more active in helping the relatives find better coping mechanisms.

The third component, family meetings in the home, was developed to include the patient and deal with family dynamics. The approach was pragmatic, varied and flexible.

Most relatives in the treatment group received the educational component, and attended the group about once a month. Every family had at least one family meeting at home, with an average of five. Nine months after discharge, the PSE and CFIs were repeated.

Results. Only 30 per cent were first admissions, and the sample had a mean age of 35: an older and more chronic group than in the Goldstein study. After nine months, 50 per cent (6 out of 12) of the patients in the comparison group had relapsed, compared with only 8 per cent (1 out of 12) in the treatment group, a significant difference (Fisher's exact p = 0.03).

Looking at the intervening variables which might have contributed to this decrease, it was found that for the high EE relatives who had six or more critical comments initially, the mean number of critical comments made by the intervention group (n=11) decreased from 16.7 to 6.5 (t=3.7, d.f.=11, p < .005), whereas the mean number made by the comparison group (n=8) decreased from 12.0 to 10.7, not a significant difference. A similar analysis of emotional over-involvment showed a trend for decrease in the treatment group but no significant effects. Finally, 6 of the 12 treatment families had lowered their FF below 35 hours, compared with only 3 of the 12 comparison families.

Thus, the mixture of drug and social interventions had an effect on relapse rates at nine months and the evidence points to this being associated with change in the attitudes of relatives, particularly towards holding less critical attitudes towards the patient.

One methodological shortcoming of this study was that diagnoses and ratings were not made with judges blind to the treatment condition, although every effort was made to obtain second opinions with marginal cases. It could be argued, however, that in a follow-up diagnostic interview where patients may be defensive, knowledge of previous symptomatology could be an advantage. Secondly, a statistical short-coming was that the method of multiple *t*-tests was applied to data which could have been analysed more powerfully with an ANOVA with initial levels as covariates. Nevertheless, the study showed that a relatively straightforward programme of social intervention applied by mental health professionals without extensive training in family therapy can significantly decrease the likelihood of a relapse. It also demonstrated how clinical research can be conducted with few resources. Particularly effective aspects may have been the group support, the direct education, and the clear focus in family meetings on a few aspects of family communication.

Behavioural problem-solving family therapy

Falloon *et al.'s* (1982) programme differed from the previous two in several respects. First, medication was given orally and flexibly, at the minimum level possible. This followed findings that long-acting intramuscular medication may impair social functioning more than oral medication (Falloon *et al.*, 1978), despite similar effects on relapse rates. Flexible, minimal dosage may mean a better response to psychosocial intervention.

Second, a short educational programme was given to each family but, in contrast to the Leff programme, the patient was included and made an expert on his or her symptoms by the clinician who played a one-down role, thus unbalancing the status hierarchy in the family!

Thirdly, the main focus was behavioural family therapy in the home, rather than a relatives' group. A problem-solving model was used in which the family was trained to pinpoint a problem, generate solutions, evaluate potential consequences, agree on a best strategy, implement the strategy, and then review results. The therapist taught the model and then coached the family, expecting them to take responsibility for problem-solving between the meetings. The therapist also focused on communication training, encouraging the family to communicate clearly by active listening, being specific about requests, and owning positive and negative feelings clearly. Falloon *et al.* point out that their aim was not to prevent the expression of emotion but to change its expression so that it was more effective.

Thirty-six PSE-diagnosed schizophrenics were randomly assigned either to the family education and therapy programme, or the the individual programme. The individual programme consisted of education about schizophrenia, and then supportive therapy focusing on problems of everyday living. Both treatments were done by the same clinicians, which may have biased the results since all favoured the family approach.

Results. The sample had a mean age of 25, and 36 per cent were first admissions. Psychiatric functioning was monitored by rating three monthly target symptoms initially present, and by conducting a PSE at nine-month follow-up. After nine months, only 6 per cent (1 out of 18) in the family intervention group had had a relapse, compared with 44 per cent (8 out of 18) in the individual treatment group, a highly significant difference (Fisher's exact $p=0.009$). Over two years, family management patients tended to have exacerbations at a much increased rate and with increased intensity.

A feature of this study was the comprehensive assessment of change, particularly in social and family functioning (Falloon, 1984). The previous studies focused on psychiatric functioning. Here multiple outcome measures were used including the Social Behaviour Assessment Schedule (Platt *et al.*, 1980) which assessed both subjective and objective measures of social functioning. Data showed increased social functioning in terms of fewer hospitalizations, less behavioural disturbance, better-reported family relationships and more friends. Informants reported greater satisfactions with the patients social behaviour, and less family burden, both objectively and subjectively. Live observation of family communication using the UCLA confrontation procedure showed the family engaged in more problem-solving and showed less negative Affective Style in terms of less criticism, intrusion and guilt-induction.

Thus, this study documents important changes in social as well as psychiatric functioning as a result of family interventions, presumed to be because of increased ability to solve problems.

Survival skills and structural family therapy

Finally, mention must be made of a large programme at Pittsburg (Anderson *et al.,* 1981), from which results are expected soon. The unique aspect of this programme is the way the education about schizophrenia is provided. A one-day 'survival skills' workshop is convened for a large group of relatives. Lectures on schizophrenia are given and relatives are encouraged to ask questions and speak of their experiences. This has a powerful impact on relatives by decreasing their experience of isolation and shame, increasing their feeling of mutual support, and leading to commitment to the family therapy programme, and also informal support outside. Family treatment is fortnightly and focuses on coping mechanisms and clarification of boundaries and communication. In the second year, the focus shifts to structural aspects of the family.

Preliminary results (Anderson, 1983) show a nine-month relapse rate of 3 per cent and a two-year relapse rate of 24 per cent. This might have been even lower, had there not been a major thrust to improve occupational and social functioning: at two-year follow-up, 87 per cent were either working or students, probably greater than in the other programmes.

COMMON CHANGE PROCESSES

There are a number of features common to all four programmes which may explain their effectiveness in comparison with previous methods. These can be divided into family therapy, education, and drug compliance processes.

1. Family therapy

The family therapy approaches were all gentle, supportive, and concrete. The traditional 'intensive' exploratory feeling-oriented family therapy was not used. Intensive family therapy can be over-stimulating and lead to regression. For example, interpretations of internal motivations can lead to patients thinking the therapist can read their mind. Further, the psychoanalytic stance of an expert who knows what 'really' goes on in people's minds is not a good model of communication in families. Rather, the approaches use some or all of the following processes:

Connecting. Each programme has ways of making the patient and family members feel that their point of view is valued and important. This may partly be due to researchers wanting compliance, and therefore treating relatives with a great deal more respect than in the all-too-frequent cursory psychiatric interview with relatives to obtain diagnostic information.

Further, the CFI and the PSE are research interviews with a model of respectful inquiry: relatives are asked to describe in detail the problems which *they* have experienced in relation to the patient's behaviour. The goal of the CFI is to obtain information about the relatives' emotional reactions, how they coped, and how they reacted. Relatives often report that the interview *per se* was helpful.

Contracting. Partly because of the legal requirement for obtaining informed consent, a clear contract was negotiated at the outset with each family. The aims, structure, and length of the programme were explained fully, including randomization to treatment conditions, and follow-up procedures.

Focus on current transactions. The focus of treatment in all these programmes is on current transactions between family members. Therapists do not focus on the historical development of the family, or on the development of personality, but on present-day coping, on how the patient and relatives deal with stress, and how they react to each other. Very quickly, the focus is moved away from either 'what is wrong with the patient and how can she be cured' at one extreme, or 'what is wrong with the relatives and how can they be tamed' at the other, to an examination of family interaction and coping to see if there are alternative methods of coping which can be used to deal with the inevitable stresses of life more successfully. The UCLA confrontation procedure of asking families to talk together about a conflict provoking issue for 10 minutes often has the therapeutic benefit of helping family members see that the way they talk to each other and solve problems together can be improved, thus easing their transition into family therapy.

Positive connotation. Relatives often feel that their contribution to helping the patient is not appreciated by hospital staff. They may also feel blamed for the patient's problems (especially if they have heard of family therapy or the work of Laing!). They can thus defensively reject any attempt at 'treatment'. Their guilt and anxiety can lead them to behave towards the patient in ways which are counter-productive. Therefore, it is often useful to talk not of 'family therapy' but of 'family meetings', which does not imply there is something wrong with the family. Relatives are often enlisted to help: 'We will help you help (the patient)'.

Once the joining process has taken place, positive connotation can be used to reframe the intentions of relatives and patient. Depth interpretations which can imply criticism and induce guilt are not used. Rather, every effort is made to see the problem from each person's point of view and to reframe intentions. Thus, parents are described as making their best efforts to be helpful, as being 'protective' rather than 'emotionally over-involved', as 'encouraging independence' rather than 'hostile and rejecting'.

Reframing. Reframing is a way of re-presenting problems in a new light, often by punctuating repetitive sequences of interation differently, so that the family can see new cause and effect relationships and come to understand their contribution to maintaining counter-productive transactions. Thus, a problem which may be seen by parents as their child being unable to leave home can be recast as a problem of the parents being afraid to push their child out into an uncertain, hostile world and being unwilling to break away from their child.

Boundaries. A common theme is the clarification of interpersonal boundaries. This is exemplified in the clarification of communication, so that people talk for themselves and do not label the intentions of others, but rather describe their own feelings and other people's *behaviour*. There may also be a focus on helping parents work together rather than at cross-purposes, thus clarifying boundaries between generations.

In summary, a variety of modern family therapy techniques are used in these programmes, which all involve treating relatives with respect and enlisting their help.

2. Education

Each programme stresses the importance of facing the psychotic experience directly, although each treats this slightly differently: Goldstein focuses on understanding the precipitants of the psychotic episode without talking about schizophrenia *per se*; Falloon, Anderson, and Leff all have structured education programmes about schizophrenia which are given to families; Falloon and Goldstein have the patient present, whereas Anderson and Leff do not.

Interestingly, the education, although short, seems to be very powerful and helpful, particularly for relatives of people who have had several hospitalizations over the years. They may continually have asked what is wrong, and received only vague answers from mental health professionals. They may recognize that medication helps but have no idea what it does. They may feel guilty, particularly if ward staff have told them to stay away because when they visit, the patient gets upset. And, perhaps most importantly, the fantasy develops that there is something terribly wrong, fuelled by the vague answers, just as people guess they have cancer from the growing wall of silence around them. Maybe their relative is mad and will only get worse and worse. Maybe they have even got that dread disease, 'schizophrenia'.

The education programme seems to burst this bubble, and leads to relief rather than despair. Knowing at last that their relative has schizophrenia and hearing explanations of its likely course and response to treatment, they feel more in control. They now have a better idea of what they can expect and what is and isn't possible for them to do to help.

3. Drug compliance

It has been argued that family therapy may have a beneficial effect by increasing compliance with medication. Thus, Falloon *et al.* (1982) note that more reliable tablet-taking was found in their family treatment group, and suggest that if family treatment does lead to greater compliance with medication and hence less symptom exacerbation, the family treatment approach is indeed a step forward. However, the results of several studies have suggested that drug therapy alone is not enough to prevent relapses, so family treatment seems to have an effect beyond that of increasing drug compliance.

CHOOSING A PROGRAMME

The four programmes vary in a number of ways. Falloon *et al.* and Leff *et al.* see families at home; Goldstein *et al.'s* crisis-oriented programme lasts only six weeks; the rest are more extensive. What conclusions can be drawn about the appropriateness of the programmes?

Probably the most important variables affecting a family's response to treatment are the number of previous admissions and the length of the illness. Anderson (1983) noted that whereas relatives of long-term patients usually respond with relief to the survival-skills workshop, relatives of recent-onset patients can be shocked by the information about schizophrenia and its likely course; they find the prognosis to be very pessimistic and grim. Furthermore, the prognosis for a one-time admission is much better than for a repeat admission; it is entirely possible that the patient will never have another psychotic break.

Thus, it may be most appropriate, in the case of recent-onset patients, to talk with the family about the 'psychotic experiences' of the patient, possible precipitants, and future ways of coping in the brief crisis-oriented approach of Goldstein *et al.* If further admissions occur, it may then be appropriate to talk directly about schizophrenia and its implications, and have a more long-term programme of after-care.

FUTURE RESEARCH DIRECTIONS

A number of important questions could be answered with new designs and methodological improvements, particularly in the area of the assessment of change.

First, it seems important to learn more about the relative impact of the family education and therapy. Although it is possible to make some independent estimate of the impact of the education from knowledge interviews (Berkowitz *et al.*, 1984), it is difficult to draw clear conclusions without an experimental design which contrasts education and family therapy.

Second, as I have detailed elsewhere (Strachan, 1984), it will be important to include measures which assess social functioning as well as the psychiatric functioning of the patient, measures which assess hypothesized intervening variables of family functioning, and, most neglected of all, measures which assess active ingredients of change in terms of the process. Interpersonal process recall (*see* Barker, this volume) may help elucidate what successful family therapists do.

Third, because of the research component, all these programmes have had extensive involvement of professionals with vested interests in the success of their programmes. It is important to test these methods in real-world situations. It is also important to establish what kinds of family therapy are helpful for families of schizophrenics and which are not. Here's my gauntlet on the floor to strategic and systematic therapists to do some systematic comparative outcome studies.

Acknowledgements

This work was supported in part by National Institute of Mental Health Grant MH 14584 administered through the Family Project, Department of Psychology, University of California at Los Angeles. The work was conducted while the author was a postdoctoral fellow at the MRC Social Psychiatry Unit, Friern Hospital, London.

REFERENCES

ANDERSON, C. (1983) Psyco-educational family interventions: Suggested modifications for specific subgroups of schizophrenic patients. Paper presented at the Max Planck Institute International Conference on Young Schizophrenia Patients, Bavaria, West Germany.

ANDERSON, C.M., HOGARTY, G. and REISS, D.J. (1981) The psychoeducational family treatment of schizophrenia. In: M.J. Goldstein (ed.) *New Developments in Interventions with Families of Schizophrenics*. London: Jossey-Bass.

BERKOWITZ, R., EBERLEIN-FRIES, R., KUIPERS, L. and LEFF, J. (in press) Educating relatives about schizophrenia. *Schizophrenia Bulletin* .

BERKOWITZ, R., KUIPERS, L., EBERLEIN-FRIES, R. and LEFF, J. (1981) Lowering expressed emotion in relatives of schizophrenics. In: M.J. Goldstein (ed.) *New Developments in Interventions with Families of Schizophrenics.* London: Jossey-Bass.

BOWEN, M. (1978) *Family Therapy in Clinical Practice.* New York : Jason Aronson.

BROWN, G.W., BIRLEY, J.L.T. and WING, J.K. (1972) Influence of family life on the course of schizophrenia. *British Journal of Psychiatry, 121,* 241–258.

BROWN, G.W., CARSTAIRS, G.M. and TOPPING, G.G. (1958) Post hospital adjustment of chronic mental patients. *Lancet, 2,* 685– 689.

BROWN, G.W., MONCK, E.M., CARSTAIRS, G.M. and WING, J.K. (1962) Influence of family life on the course of schizophrenic illness. *British Journal of Preventative and Social Medicine, 16,* 55–68.

DOANE, J.A., WEST, K.L., GOLDSTEIN, M.J., RODNICK, E.H. and JONES, J.E. (1981) Parental affective style and communication deviance as predictors of subsequent schizophrenia spectrum disorders in vulnerable adolscents. *Archives of General Psychiatry, 38,* 679–685.

ESTERTON, A., COOPER, D.G. and LAING, R.D. (1965) Results of family-oriented therapy with hospitalized schizophrenics. *British Medical Journal, 2,* 1462–1465.

FALLOON, I.R.H. (in press) *Family Management of Mental Illness: A study of clinical, social, and family benefits.* Baltimore: John Hopkins Press.

FALLOON, I.R.H., BOYD, J.L., McGILL, C.W., RAZANI, J., MOSS, H.B. and GILDERMAN, A.M. (1982) Family management in the prevention of exacerbations of schizophrenia. *New England Journal of Medicine, 306,* 1437–1440.

FALLOON, I,R.H., WATT, D.C. and SHEPHERD, M. (1978) The social outcome of patients in a trial of long-term continuation therapy in schizophrenia: Pimozide vs. fluphenazine. *Psychological Medicine, 8,* 265–274.

GOLDSTEIN, M.J. and DOANE, J.A. (1982) Family factors in the onset, course, and treatment of schizophrenic spectrum disorders. *Journal of Nervous and Mental Diseases, 170,* 692–700.

GOLDSTEIN, M.J. and KOPEIKIN, H.S. (1981) Short and long-term effects of combining drug and family therapy. In: M.J. Goldstein (ed.) *New Developments in Intervention with Families of Schizophrenics.* London: Jossey-Bass.

GOLDSTEIN, M.J., RODNICK, E.H., EVANS, J.R., MAY, P.R.A. and STEIN-BERG, M.R. (1978) Drug and family therapy in the aftercare of acute schizophrenics. *Archives of General Psychiatry, 35,* 1169– 1177.

GURMAN, A.S. and KNISKERN, D.P. (1978) Research on marital and family therapy: progress, perspective and prospect. In: S.L. Garfield and A.E. Bergin (eds) *Handbook of Psychotherapy and Behavior Change: An Empirical Analysis.* New York: Wiley.

JONES, J.E., RODNICK, E., GOLDSTEIN, M.J., McPHERSON, S. and WEST, K. (1977) Parental transactional style deviance as a possible indicator of risk for schizophrenia. *Archives of General Psychiatry, 34,* 71–74.

LAMB, H.R. (1981) What did we reallly expect from deinstitutionalization? *Hospital and Community Psychiatry, 32,* 105–109.

LEFF, J., KUIPERS, L., BERKOWITZ, R., EBERLEIN-FRIES, R. and STUR-GEON, D. (1982) Social intervention in the families of schizophrenics. *British Journal of Psychiatry, 141,* 121–134.

LEFF, J., KUIPERS, L., BERKOWITZ, R., EBERLEIN-FRIES, R. and STUR-GEON, D. (1983) Social intervention in the families of schizophrenics: Addendum. *British Journal of Psychiatry, 142,* 313.

LEFF, J.P. and WING, J.K. (1971) Trial of maintenance therapy in schizophrenia. *British Medical Journal, 3,* 599–604.

MAY, P.R.A. and TUMA, A.H. (1976) The Paul H. Hoch Award Lecture: A follow-up study of the results of treatment of schizophrenia. In: R.L. Spitzer and D.F. Klein (eds) *Psychotherapies, Behaviour Therapies, Drug Therapies and Their Interactions.* Baltimore and London: John Hopkins University Press.

MINUCHIN, S. (1974) *Families and Family Therapy.* Cambridge, Mass.: Harvard University Press.

MURPHY, J.K., WILLIAMSON, D.A., BUXTON, A.E., MOODY, S.C., ABSHER, N. and WARNER, M. (1982) The long term effects of spouse involvement upon weight loss and maintenance. *Behaviour Therapy, 13,* 681–693.

OVERALL, J.E. and GORHAM, D.R. (1962) The brief psychiatric rating scale. *Psychological Reports, 10,* 799–812.

PALAZZOLI, M.S., BOSCOLO, L., CECCHIN, G. and PRATA, G. (1978) *Paradox and Counterparadox.* New York: Jason Aronson.

PLATT, S., WEYMAN, A., HIRSCH, S. and HEWETT, S. (1980) The Social Behaviour Assessment Schedule (SBAS): Rationale, contents, scoring, and reliability of a new interview schedule. *Social Psychiatry, 15,* 43–55.

SINGER, M.T. and WYNNE, L.C. (1966) Principles for scoring communication defects and deviances in parents of schizophrenics: Rorschach and TAT scoring manuals. *Psychiatry, 29,* 260–280.

STRACHAN, A.M. (unpublished manuscript) *Family intervention with schizophrenia: The assessment of change.*

VAUGHN, G.E. and LEFF, J.P. (1976) The influence of family and social factors on the course of psychiatric illness. *British Journal of Psychiatry, 129,* 125–137.

VAUGHN, G.E., SNYDER, K.S., FREEMAN, W., JONES, S., FALLOON, I.R.H. and LIEBERMAN, R.P. (1982) Family factors in schizophrenic relapse: A replication. *Schizophrenia Bulletin, 8,* 425–426.

WEAKLAND, J.H., FISCH, R., WATZLAWICK, P. and BODIN, A.M. (1974) Brief therapy: Focused problem resolution. *Family Process, 13,* 141–168.

WENDER, P.H., ROSENTHAL, D. and KETY, S.S. (1968) A psychiatric assessment of the adoptive parents of schizophrenics. In: D. Rosenthal and S.S. Kety (eds) *The Transmission of Schizophrenia.* Oxford: Pergamon Press.

ATTEMPTED SUICIDE

J. Mark G. Williams

Some years ago I used to do some clinical sessions at a small day unit not far from the university department where I worked. I had recently become interested in cognitive therapy for depression and one of the first patients I was referred was a depressed patient: a 34-year-old woman, former teacher, mother of three children, wife to a rather distant and uninterested husband. The first session was unremarkable – some assessment, some laying of groundwork for later therapy, some explanation, establishing rapport. Two days later the woman's GP telephoned me. She had taken a massive overdose of her tranquillizers and antidepressants the evening after seeing me. How had she been that afternoon? What had we been talking about? How was she when she left? I told him that the session seemed to go alright. We left it there, unexplained. But inexplicable?

Some years later, I read with interest the following passage from Wekstein's (1979) *Handbook of Suicidology* :

> An individual with depression and anxiety may have his lethality intensified in the course of treament, and under such conditions the hazard of suicide may arise or increase. Psychoanalysts are particularly sensitive about giving premature interpretations and attempting to offer insights indiscriminately.

Returning to my patient – did I do something that was ill-advised, or did I *not* do something I should have done. Could I have 'picked up' the suicidal tendencies by careful assessment? Was she a member of an 'at risk' group that I should have known? How would my account have 'stood up in court', had it come to that? (It didn't.) These are important questions to which more and more clinical psychologists are going to have to know the answers. If there are no answers to some of the questions we need to know that too.

Why do we need to become aware of these issues now? Firstly, we need to know because attempted suicide behaviour is on the increase and is posing a great challenge to the health and psychiatric services of which we are a part. (The term 'attempted suicide' is used in this chapter interchangeably with its current synonyms, 'parasuicide' and 'deliberate self-harm'.) Since the early 1960s episodes of attempted suicide have increased from 30,000 a year in England and Wales to over 100,000 a year. This means that in most district general hospitals there will be between five and ten cases of attempted suicide every week attending the accident and emergency services, of which about 70 per cent will be admitted for a short time for medical or psychiatric reasons.

A second reason for knowing more about the aetiology and management of attempted suicides is that more psychologists are now treating patients who are at greater risk for making such attempts. I am referring to the great increase in the use of cognitive behaviour therapy for depressed patients. In times past, when psychologists working with adult patients saw predominantly anxiety neurotics, suicide attempts were a less likely occurence. But many more depressed patients are vulnerable to both suicidal ideas and suicidal acts, some 10 per cent of depressed patients attempting suicide within a year of entering treatment (Paykel and Dienelt, 1971). As the type of patient referred to our clinics shifts, so will the likelihood of patients showing suicidal behaviour.

A third, rather more direct reason for clinical psychologists knowing more about and being more involved with this group of patients in the future is that the Department of Health has recommended that they are so involved. A recent multidisciplinary Working Party convened by the Royal College of Psychiatrists at the request of the DHSS in order to prepare guidelines for the management of patients who attempt suicide by self-poisoning has recommended that:

> there is a need to amend the original recommendation of the Department of Health that all patients who have deliberately harmed themselves should necessarily be assessed by psychiatrists... In some instances referral to another professional worker who has received special training such as a social worker, nurse, or clinical psychologist may be considered more appropriate.

So it will be expected that, where resources are available, the clinical psychologist will have something to contribute to the team.

Clinical psychologists' distinctive approach to clinical problems has always been their combination of skills in assessment, treatment and research. The field of attempted suicide has the same need for an integrated approach. In this chapter, after presenting some of the basic data about attempted suicide, I should like to examine briefly these three aspects, so that the implications for future developments may be more clearly seen.

THE PARASUICIDE PHENOMENON

The basic data about attempted suicide is largely undisputed. Many large-scale studies in Oxford, Edinburgh, Bristol, London and from abroad have found the same range of predisposing factors, the same sex and age distributions and similar repetition rates (varying depending on length of follow-up). These data have been recently reviewed by Morgan (1979), Farmer and Hirsch (1980) and Hawton and Catalan (1982), so will only be briefly mentioned here.

Taking a temporal perspective, five aspects (or phases) of the parasuicide phenomenon may be distinguished: long-term vulnerability factors; short-term vulnerability factors; precipitating factors; the event; and the aftermath.

1. The long-term vulnerability factors could be taken to include all those factors in the person's past or current relationships and living conditions which act as background to the shorter-term crises. Maris (1981) for example, found that 83 per cent of attempters, as compared with 31 per cent of a control group, had experienced either early loss by death or separation (from fathers more often than mothers) or other major traumas within the families, such as alcohol or drug abuse, mental illness, criminality, or a sibling in a foster home. Similarly, Williams and Hassanyeh (1983) have found an association between the occurrence of a suicide attempt which included laceration, and a childhood in which physical violence between the parents had been witnessed.

The more current 'long-term vulnerability factors' for attempted suicide are to be found in the living conditions of the patients. The 1975 report from the Edinburgh Regional Poisons Treatment Centre reported the following types of patients' problems: overcrowding, living alone, criminal record, debt, violence used on others, violence received from relatives, and being unemployed (Office of Health Economics, 1981). In a study of attempted suicide in 13 to 18-year-olds by Hawton *et al.* (1982) 12 per cent had been in care at some time in their lives, over half had problems with school work and relationships with teachers, and three-quarters had difficulty with one or both parents. Indeed, 36 per cent were living with only one parent, and 12 per cent with neither parent. Social isolation was a fairly common background factor. Superimposed on these disturbed social contexts of suicide attempters of all ages, Paykel *et al.* (1975) have found an increase in stressful life events in the six months prior to the suicide episode. These events included both those which could be partly attributed to the patient's state (for example, violent arguments, separations, etc.), and those which were out of the patient's control (for example, serious illness in a family member).

2. The short-term vulnerability factors could be taken to include all those factors in the person's current situation which, against the background of the long-term vulnerability factors, put an additional burden on, or actively reduce the person's coping ability in the month prior to the attempt.

Paykel *et al.'s* study, referred to above, found that whereas both a parasuicide and a depressive group had increased incidence of life-events compared with controls, the parasuicide group suffered a steep increase in events in the month prior to the attempt. Additionally, both this study and other research has found that there is an increased incidence of physical illness (especially in women) in this short-term vulnerability phase (Bancroft *et al.*, 1977; Hawton *et al.*, 1982), though the potentially important role of premenstrual syndrome in exacerbating the physical and psychological symptoms in women has not been satisfactorily studied (Jack, 1984). Given the preponderance of sources of physical and emotional stress it is not surprising that 57 per cent of attempters, including 82 per cent of adolescent attempters (Hawton and Catalan, 1982), contact some helping agency (most of them the GP) during the month prior to the attempt. Many patients are prescribed psychotropic medication at this time, which is subsequently used in the parasuicide episode.

In addition to discrete life-events, investigators have found an increase in disturbance in relationships and work during this phase (Bhagat, 1976). Bancroft *et al.*, (1977) found that both male and female attempters reported equivalent levels of relationship difficulties (68 per cent female, 83 per cent male for marital difficulty; 70 per cent female, 77 per cent male for boy/girlfriend difficulty), though more males than females reported significant work difficulties (16 per cent and 54 per cent respectively). In their study, only 9 per cent of both men and women reported having a current alcohol problem, a proportion which is very much lower than that reported in Bristol (36 per cent in men) and Edinburgh (48 per cent in men). Finally, male unemployment at the time of the overdose varies between 36 per cent (Bristol: Morgan *et al.*, 1975) and 49 per cent (Edinburgh: Holding *et al.*, 1977) but is generally found to be high.

3. Precipitating factors are those events which occur in the few days prior to the attempt. Morgan *et al.* (1975) list several: disharmony with 'key other' person (40 per cent), disharmony with relatives (20 per cent), with anxiety about work/employment, financial difficulties and physical pain or illness accounting for a further 14 per cent. Bancroft *et al.* (1977) found that almost half their female patients had had a quarrel with their spouse or boyfriend in the week (mostly 48 hours) prior to the attempts. Fieldsend and Lowenstein (1981) examined those events occurring in the 48 hours preceding the parasuicide and found that relationship problems predominated: quarrels (39 per cent females; 20 per cent males) separation (5 per cent females; 25 per cent males) and infidelity (6 per cent females, 0 per cent males).

4. The event. Despite the fact that most of the vulnerability and precipitating events have involved both sexes (that is quarrels have involved both the husband and wife, boyfriend and girlfriend, as have separations, physical illness, etc.), the proportion of women to men taking overdoses is between 1.5 to 2.5:1. However, wherever these figures have been examined in relation to age of patient it emerges that the peak for women is in the 15 to 19 age range, whereas the peak for men comes 10 years later, in the 25 to 29 age group. This means that giving an overall sex ratio misrepresents the situation to some extent. The female:male ratio for adolescents is 3.5:1; for late 30s it is 1.1:1. This trend continues into later life, where the sex ratio is much more evenly balanced.

Over 90 per cent of episodes of attempted suicide involve self-poisoning. Self-laceration accounts for under 10 per cent, although lacerators are a more disturbed group (Simpson, 1976; Williams and Hassenyeh, 1983). Current figures from various centres show that minor tranquillizers and sedatives, together with non-opiate analgesics account for the greatest proportion of substances used in self-poisoning. The younger patients tend to use non-prescribed drugs (for example aspirin) the older patients use prescribed drugs (minor tranquillizers and, less often, antidepressants). One fifth of patients take alcohol with the drugs, and some 35 per cent have consumed alcohol within six hours of the attempt (Office of Health Economics, 1981). In most cases the attempt is an impulsive act, with two-thirds of patients not having thought about it for more than one hour beforehand.

5. The aftermath. Both Morgan (1979) and Hawton and Catalan (1982) have observed that it is not the norm for the suicidal act to produce a great change for the better in the person's social circumstances, thus correcting a common myth. A not uncommon finding is exemplified by the following patient, a 40-year-old woman who had planned to marry the man she was living with in a few weeks' time. The invitations had been sent out and other arrangements made. After a rapidly escalating series of quarrels, she took a serious overdose when she found out he had unilaterally cancelled the arrangements and written round to all their friends to inform them. He came to visit her in hospital. To make up? By no means. He stayed only long enough to give her back the wedding rings and tell her that he had packed her belongings into suitcases and left them outside the front door for her to collect. Given such a case, it is unsurprising that up to 25 per cent of patients repeat the attempt within a year (and half of these within three months) of the index attempt.

Bancroft and Marsack (1977) have distinguished three types of repeater: the chronic repeater, who tends to move from one crisis to another; those who make several repeats in a few months extending over a period of prolonged stress, which stops when the stress is resolved; and a third group of 'one-off' attempters, who may occasionally repeat. This 40-year-old patient probably falls into the second of these categories.

These subgroups of repeated attempters outlined by Bancroft and Marsack make a large demand on the health services in general, as well as straining the personal resources of those who would help them. Yet their presence should not blind us to the majority of attempters who do not repeat. Newson-Smith and Hirsch (1979) found that 31 per cent of attempters were suffering a definite psychiatric disorder, with 29 per cent borderline (virtually all depressive) at the time of the episode. But they also found that these percentages had fallen to 24 per cent and 16 per cent one week after the attempt and 8 per cent and 14 per cent three months after. The proportion of individuals reporting nervous tension (on the Present State Examination) in the four weeks preceding the overdose, fell from 75 per cent to 41 per cent and 28 per cent one week and three months afterwards. The corresponding proportions for depressed mood are 73 per cent (before) 37 per cent and 24 per cent; and for hopelessness 61 per cent (before) 33 per cent and 14 per cent. It is clear that for most patients the aftermath is a period of considerable emotional change, although research has not yet documented exactly how this change comes about.

This, then, concludes a brief overview of the five main phases of parasuicide. We turn now to assessment, treatment and research.

ASSESSMENT

There are three main aspects of assessment: the assessment of current hopelessness in a patient who has not attempted suicide (or is between episodes); the assessment of suicidal intent following an episode; and the assessment of prognostic factors for subsequent suicidal behaviour.

1. Assessment of current hopelessness is important because hopelessness is more closely related to suicidal ideas and behaviour than is general level of depression (Nekanda-Trepka *et al.,* 1983). As Beck *et al.* (1979) have pointed out, an individual may be able to live with depressive symptoms, but if they become devoid of hope for the future, they become a suicide or parasuicide risk. Probably the best available assessment scale available for this aspect of mental state is the Hopelessness Scale (Beck *et al.,* 1974). It is widely available (*see* Williams, 1984), has been subject to factor analysis with interesting results (*see* Nekanda-Trepka *et al.,* 1983), and there are British norms available (Greene, 1981; Nekanda-Trepka *et al.,* 1983).

2. Assessment of suicidal intent. Morgan (1979) has reported that some 46 per cent of men and 34 per cent of women said they wanted to die at the time of the attempt. He has also pointed out that by the next day, or soon afterwards, only 17 per cent of men and 10 per cent of women regretted not doing so. Many have pointed out that suicidal intent is indeed an important element to assess, and is best inferred from the behaviour of the patient just before and after the attempt, the expected lethality of the drug used, and whether any effort was made to seek help. Beck *et al.* (1974) have devised a Suicide Intent Scale, a shortened version of which has been used by Pierce (1981) and is reproduced in *Table 1.*

Pierce found that later death by suicide was associated with high scores on his scale, especially for the penultimate suicide attempt, and Kovacs *et al.* (1975) have found a high correlation between suicidal intent and current hopelessness as assessed by the Beck Hopelessness Scale. An interesting repertory grid study has examined the meaning of attempted suicide in relation to suicidal intent (assessed with Beck *et al.'s* Scale) in a group of young attempters (mean age 21 years) (Parker, 1981). The 'low intent' group perceived the overdose as similar to 'being alone and crying' and 'getting drunk'. For the 'high intent' group, however, 'overdose' and 'suicide' appeared to be occupying similar locations in the patients' construct systems.

Bancroft, Hawton and their co-workers have argued that it is important to go beyond merely assessing whether the patient wanted or did not want to die, and to examine the motivations and intentions behind the overdose more carefully. Bancroft *et al.* (1979) offered 41 randomly selected overdose patients various possible reasons for the overdose. Fifty-six per cent said that 'the situation was so unbearable that they had to do something and didn't know what else to do'. Forty-four per cent also said the overdose was 'to get relief from a terrible state of mind'. A slightly smaller proportion said they had 'wanted to die'. Interestingly, when transcripts of interviews with these patients were shown to three independent psychiatrists who were also asked to give their opinions as to the 'reasons', they much less frequently gave 'wishing to die', and much more often said the patient 'wanted to make people understand how desperate they were feeling' (71 per cent), and/or 'wanted to frighten, get their own back, or make people sorry' (71 per cent). This discrepancy between the perspective of patient and psychiatrists may have important implications for treatment, but no one has so far examined whether, for example, widely divergent perspectives predict a worse outcome.

3. Assessment of prognosis has normally been concerned with predicting which patients will repeat the attempt. As has already been seen, the very hopeless patient who obtained a high 'suicide intent' score is clearly vulnerable to later attempts, even fatal ones (Pierce, 1981). Ovenstone and Kreitman (1974) estimated that 23 per cent of the attempters they were seeing in Edinburgh represented those who made multiple attempts despite fairly continuous help from a variety of agencies. Buglass and Horton (1974) outlined what the characteristics of these patients are. They have problems in the use of alcohol; they have at some time received a diagnosis of sociopathy; they have had previous inpatient or outpatient psychiatric treatment; they are not living with relatives; they will have tended to have made at least one previous suicidal gesture before the index episode. Taking the inpatient and outpatient treatment as separate items, Buglass and Horton found that these six items predicted repetition in an additive fashion. The probability of repetition within one year for someone with none of these characteristics is 5 per cent; if five or six are present the probability is 48 per cent. What we don't know is

Table 1: A suicidal intent scale (Pierce, 1981)

Circumstances related to suicidal attempt

1. Isolation	0 somebody present
	1 somebody nearby or in contact (as by phone)
	2 no one nearby or in contact
2. Timing	1 timed so that intervention is probable
	2 timed so that intervention is not likely
	3 timed so that intervention is highly unlikely
3. Precautions against discovery and/or intervention	0 no precautions
	1 passive precautions, e.g. avoiding others but doing nothing to prevent their intervention (alone in room, door unlocked)
	2 active precautions, such as locking doors
4. Acting to gain help during or after the attempt	0 notified potential helper regarding attempt
	1 contacted but did not specifically notify potential helper regarding attempt
	2 did not contact or notify potential helper
5. Final acts in anticipation of death	0 none
	1 partial preparation or ideations
	2 definite plans made (e.g. changes in will, taking out insurance)
6. Suicide note	0 none
	1 note written but torn up
	2 present

Self-report

1. Patient's statement of lethality	0 thought that what he had done would not kill him
	1 unsure whether what he had done would kill him
2. Stated intent	0 did not want to die
	1 uncertain or did not care if he lived or died
	2 did want to die

Table 1. (cont.)

3. Premeditation	0 impulsive, no premeditation
	1 considered for < 1 hour
	2 considered for < 1 day
	3 considered for > 1 day
4. Reaction to the act	0 patient glad he has recovered
	1 patient is uncertain whether he is glad or sorry
	2 patient sorry he has recovered
Actual risk	
1. Predictable outcome in terms of lethality of patient's act and circumstances known to him	0 survival certain
	1 death unlikely
	2 death likely or certain
2. Would death have occurred without medical intervention	0 no
	1 uncertain
	2 yes

Note: mean (N = 500 consecutive cases) = 7.49 (SD 4.9) Seven subsequent suicides – mean (index episode) SI = 10.29 (SD 5.44) but for presuicide attempt: Mean = 13.57 (SD 4.12)

why the other 52 per cent who *do* have five or six of these characteristics do not repeat the attempt. Further research will be necessary to establish what the protective factors are.

TREATMENT

Hirch *et al.* (1982) have recently reviewed treatment outcome studies of attempted suicide. Their conclusions make dismal reading. Firstly, suicide prevention centres do not reduce the incidence of suicide or parasuicide. Secondly, though patients who actually attend for outpatient psychiatric treatment following attempted suicide do show less repetition, they are self-selected rather than randomly assigned, so the effect is probably not due to treatment. Thirdly, behaviour therapy is no better than insight-oriented psychotherapy when administered intensively over a 10-day inpatient period. Fourthly, antidepressant medication does not affect repetition rate.

The only study in which medication has been shown to be effective is that by Montgomery and Montgomery (1982), who have shown what appears to be a remarkable effect with the phenothiazine flupentixol. They found substantially reduced repetition rates in a group of patients who would normally be diagnosed to have personality disorders and who had repeated at least three times. This group of impulsive, hostile, unpredictable and 'characteristically angry' individuals who showed rapid shifts in mood did not respond to antidepressants, but, apparently, responded to flupentixol. This result clearly requires replication, and further studies must also assess other psychological functioning in these patients to ensure that the drug is affecting general psychological well-being, rather than acting as a pharmacological strait-jacket.

Although Hirsch *et al.* are pessimistic about behaviour therapy, the study they cite (Liberman and Eckman, 1981) did show an overall effect of inpatient treatment in a behaviourally run token economy milieu on repetition. All the patients in the study were chronic repeaters (at least two previous attempts). There had been 70 parasuicide episodes in the sample of 24 patients within the previous two years. In the two years following the intensive 10 day treatment there were only 11 repetitions (in five patients). However, it is true to say that within this milieu therapy to which all patients were exposed, those patients randomly assigned to spend time doing social skills and anxiety management training fared little better than those patients receiving insight-oriented treatment. Two other outcome studies may be mentioned. Gibbons (1980) compared 200 patients allocated to task-centred casework (nine interviews over three months) with 200 patients offered routine psychiatric treatment. At four-months follow-up, the casework group evidenced a reduction in social problems. The areas of social functioning assessed were:

- significant personal relationships;
- handling social transitions such as bereavement or divorce;
- general loneliness;
- emotional distress interfering with coping;
- practical difficulties such as work, money, housing;
- problems with formal organizations;
- role performance as parent or wife/husband.

In the casework group, 81 per cent were improved at four months, in the psychiatric group this improvement was 66 per cent. This difference, however, disappeared over 18 months, and type of treatment had no effect on repetition rates. Indeed, Gibbons points out that the high risk-for-repetition cases (who had three or more of Buglass and Hortons' characteristics) showed no benefit from casework.

The other outcome study worthy of note is that by Hawton *et al.* (1981). They compared routine psychiatric appointments with domiciliary visits. The mode of treatment was the same in both cases, the crises intervention approach outlined in helpful detail by Hawton and Catalan (1982). The 'completion of treatment' rate was much greater in the domiciliary groups, but there was no difference in repetition of parasuicide rate between the two groups.

There seems to be remarkable unanimity about the ineffectiveness of various psychological treatments in affecting outcome. But before leaving consideration of treatment, two points are worthy of note. Firstly, there needs to be a more sophisticated assessment of treatment outcome than the presence or absence of repetition in a specified period. Although investigations have attempted to introduce other continuous outcome variables (for example, social problems in Gibbons' study; or depression and assertiveness level in Liberman and Eckman's study), attention invariably falls on the repetition rate. This is understandable, but there may be more helpful ways of evaluating outcome. For example *delay until first repeat* might be routinely assessed, since in cases where repetition is deemed probable, lenthening the time intervals between episodes may be a reasonable target. Secondly, other aspects of the repeat need to be assessed: for example, suicidal intent, lethality, strength of provoking agents. For example, a repeat after two months which is provoked by a minor quarrel and is made with serious intent ought to be judged differently from a repeat following a major upset which is made with less intent to die. Which would one judge to be more a case of therapeutic failure? It is not an easy question, yet it is clear that the different combination of components illustrated by these two cases of repetition do represent different outcomes, and some recognition of this needs to be made when judging success or failure of one's treatment strategies. Thirdly, outcome should never be judged without reference to some probability judgment that repetition will or will not occur within a specified time interval. We need to split groups into levels of risk, so that the way in which our intervention procedures interact with membership of the various subgroups of attempters may be observed. Buglass and Horton's (1974) six characteristics are a start in this endeavour.

Secondly, account needs to be taken of cognitive variables. So far, attention has focused on treating patients' failures to cope with real-life (external) problems. But as Beck *et al.* (1979) have indicated, suicidal patients have a combination of external problems and 'internal' cognitive distortions. Beck *et al.* recommend several strategies for alleviating hopelessness in the suicidal patient, including assessment of the extent to which the suicidal wishes represent a 'communication' to a third party or an 'escape', the listing of 'reasons for living' versus 'reasons for dying'; and the use of more general cognitive therapy techniques, such as reality testing, cognitive rehearsal and the 'search for alternatives' (Beck *et al.*, 1979; Williams, 1984).

RESEARCH

It would not be overstating the case to say that the field of attempted suicide research stands at a crossroads. Indeed, to many it appears to be a blind alley! For example, there seems little more that large scale epidemiological studies can tell us about attempted suicide. It is pointless for more and more studies to tell everyone what they already know! Treatment outcome studies have come up with the same pessimistic conclusions with monotonous regularity. It is perhaps time to do further small scale research to determine more about impulsive acts such as attempted suicide – to focus on the 'why now' question more than the 'in whom'. Secondly, we need to know more about the aftermath of attempted suicide, how do people *naturally* recover (as most do), before we try again to alleviate the distress in those who do not so readily recover. There is surprisingly little research into this aftermath phase. Generally, investigations of patients which gather data while patients are within this phase have been confined to asking them questions about the build-up phase and the event, rather than looking at the aftermath as a phase in its own right. Also, in studying the aftermath we need to assess not only mood and psychiatric symptomatology, but also changes in the internal cognitive distortions which render the (often genuine) external problems such an enormous burden.

There seem to be several central problems on which the overdose research is unlikely to make progress unless it takes account of psychological variables. Of these, we may briefly consider two. The first is why, more generally, people's foreknowledge about where they can turn for help does not help them to cope when the event arises. Little psychological research has been done directly on these issues but it is possible to see areas of literature which may be relevant to the eventual answer.

The first area concerns the multiple attempters. It may be that the association of alcohol problems, criminal behaviour, history of psychiatric treatment, and past diagnosis of sociopathy indicate that this group must more properly be seen as a 'borderline' personality group. The DSM III classification includes two forms of borderline personality, one involving schizophrenic phenomenological experience, the other involving more anti-social, unstable and impulsive characteristics, including suicide attempts. Gordon Claridge and his co-workers at Oxford have recently been piloting the use of a schizotypy questionnaire which assesses both DSM III aspects, (Claridge and Broks, in press) and have demonstrated relationships between scores on this scale and interhemispheric cognitive function. Claridge's theories concerning the nervous typology of schizophrenia and its close dimensional associates make the results of Montgomery and Montgomery using depot phenothiazines with multiple attempters seem less surprising. It provides a psychological model for what might otherwise have become seen as a medical phenomenon.

The second area concerns the explanation of why people don't call for help when in distress. Greer and Anderson (1979) found that 72 per cent of attempters knew of the existence of the Samaritans or an equivalent helping agency. Thirteen per cent had used the Samaritans before. Of course, a proportion would think that helpseeking for a personal problem was unacceptable, and a further proportion would not want help because they either want to die or want to influence others (Turner, 1980). But it still leaves a problem in understanding why intellectual knowledge of how to cope exercises so little control when the crisis occurs. Can psychological research help here?

It is clear that at the time of the parasuicide the mood of depression and hopelessness is dominant. Lloyd and Lishman (1975) were the first to document the effect that depression has on the accessibility of negative versus positive memories; increasing depression and neuroticism are associated with an increasing tendency for unpleasant memories to be relatively more accessible than pleasant memories. Teasdale and co-workers (1980) have proved beyond doubt through experimental manipulation of mood that these effects can exist independently of the actual rates of real-life past unpleasant versus pleasant experiences. The implication is that the mood of suicidal patients, though they may have had contact with helping agencies which may indeed have been helpful at the time, may cause the memories of these experiences to be inaccessible relative to memories associated with past failures. Do the context-specificity effects exist in overdose patients?

In a small pilot study to study the feasibility of assessing autobiographical memory in patients who had taken overdoses as recently as 12 hours before assessment, patients were asked to give memories in response to cue words; some of which were pleasant and some unpleasant. The results of correlating the latency to access a pleasant versus unpleasant memory with hopelessness showed that the memory biasing effects were indeed present in these patients, too. They offer one explanation for the way in which the suicidal act arises often impulsively despite the 'intellectual' knowledge of alternative strategies. Further analysis of patients who are particularly vulnerable to these effects may help to discover the methods of treatment which can more successfully break into the network of cognitive distortions which help to produce hopelessness.

CONCLUDING REMARKS

This chapter started with a clinical problem and has ended with a call for further research. This is a pattern familiar to many! But unlike other fields, the call for research is not because we don't know enough about parasuicide phenomena. In one sense there is a great deal of knowledge with which we can become familiar. It is known what ages and sex are most vulnerable, it is known what the predisposing and precipitating factors are; it is known how to assess current hopelessness, suicidal intent and prognosis fairly accurately. The further research that is called for needs to concentrate more on cognitive variables, intensively studied, and to analyse the way in which some individuals naturally recover from the stress that precipitated the attempt, and the stress of the event itself. Psychological approaches can promise some hope so long as they can avoid the trap of thinking that just because it is a large problem, each research study has to involve a great many subjects in which too few variables are studied in too little depth.

REFERENCES

BANCROFT, J. and HAWTON, K. (1983) Why people take overdoses: A study of psychiatrists' judgements. *British Journal of Medical Psychology, 56,* 197–204.

BANCROFT, J. and MARSACK, P. (1977) The repetitiveness of self-poisoning and self-injury. *British Journal of Psychiatry, 131,* 394–399.

BANCROFT, J., REYNOLDS, F., SIMKIN, S. and SMITH, J. (1975) Self-poisoning and self-injury in the Oxford area: epidemiological aspects 1969–73. *British Journal of Preventive and Social Medicine, 29,* 170–177.

BANCROFT, J., SIMKIN, S., KINGSTON, B., CUMMING, C. and WHITWELL, D. (1979) The reasons people give for taking overdoses: a further enquiry. *British Journal of Medical Psychology, 52,* 353– 365.

BECK, A.T., WEISSMAN, A., LESTER, D. and TREXLER, L. (1974) The measurement of pessimism: The hopelessness scale. *Journal of Consulting and Clinical Psychology, 42,* 861–865.

BECK, A.T., RUSH, J., SHAW, B. and EMERY, G. (1979) *Cognitive Therapy of Depression.* New York: Wiley.

BHAGAT, M. (1976) The spouses of attempted suicides: a personality study. *British Journal of Psychiatry, 128,* 44–46.

BUGLASS, D. and HORTON, J. (1974) A scale for predicting subsequent suicidal behaviour. *British Journal of Psychiatry, 124,* 573–578.

CLARIDGE, G.S. and BROKS, P. (in press) Schizotypy and hemisphere function. I. Theoretical considerations and the measurement of schizotypy. *Personality and Individual Differences* .

FIELDSEND, R. and LOWENSTEIN, E. (1981) Quarrels, separations and infidelity in the two days preceding self-poisoning episodes. *British Journal of Medical Psychology, 54,* 349–352.

GIBBONS, J.S. (1980) Management of self-poisoning: Social Work Intervention. In: R.D.T. Farmer and S.R. Hirsch (eds) *The Suicide Syndrome.* London: Croom Helm.

GREENE, S.M. (1981) Levels of measured hopelessness in the general population. *British Journal of Clinical Psychology, 20,* 11–14

GREER, S. and ANDERSON, M. (1979) Samaritan contact among 325 parasuicide patients. *British Journal of Psychiatry, 135,* 263– 268.

HAWTON, K., BANCROFT, J., CATALAN, J., KINGSTON, B., STEDEFORD, A. and WELCH, N. (1981) Domiciliary and out-patient treatment of self-poisoning patients by medical and non-medical staff. *Psychological Medicine, 11,* 169–177.

HAWTON, K. and CATALAN, J. (1982) *Attempted Suicide: A Practical Guide to its Nature and Management.* Oxford: OUP.

HAWTON, K., O'GRADY, J., OSBORN, M. and COLE, D. (1982) Adolescents who take overdoses: their characteristics, problems and contacts with helping agencies. *British Journal of Psychiatry, 140,* 118–123.

HIRSCH, S.R., WALSH, C. and DRAPER, R. (1982) Parasuicide: a review of treatment interventions. *Journal of Affective Disorders, 4,* 299–311.

HOLDING, T., BUGLASS, D., DUFFY, J.C. and KREITMAN, N. (1977) Parasuicide in Edinburgh – a seven year review 1968–74. *British Journal of Psychiatry, 130,* 534–543.

JACK, R. (1984) Self-poisoning and self-injury in women. Unpublished paper.

KOVACS, M., BECK, A.T. and WEISSMAN, A. (1975) Hopelessness: an indicator of suicidal risk. *Suicide, 5,* 98–103.

KREITMAN, N. (1976) Age and parasuicide ('attempted suicide'). *Psychological Medicine, 6,* 113–121.

LIBERMAN, R.P. and ECKMAN, T. (1981) Behaviour therapy versus insight-oriented therapy for repeated suicide attempters. *Archives of General Psychiatry, 38,* 1126–1130.

LLOYD, G. and LISHMAN, W. (1975) Effect of depression on the speed of recall of pleasant and unpleasant experiences. *Psychological Medicine, 5,* 173–180.

MARIS, R.W. (1981) *Pathways to Suicide.* Baltimore and London: John Hopkins University Press.

MONTGOMERY, S.A. and MONTGOMERY, D. (1982) Pharmacological prevention of suicidal behaviour. *Journal of Affective Disorders, 4,* 291–298.

MORGAN, H,G. (1979) *Death Wishes? The Understanding and Management of Deliberate Self-Harm.* Chichester: Wiley.

MORGAN, H.G., BURNS-COX, C.J., POCOCK, H. and POTTLE, S. (1975) Deliberate self-harm: clinical and social economic characteristics of 368 patients. *British Journal of Psychiatry, 126,* 564–574.

NEKANDA-TREPKA, C.J.S., BISHOP, S. and BLACKBURN, I.M. (1983) Hopelessness and depression. *British Journal of Clinical Psychology, 22,* 49–60.

NEWSON-SMITH, J.G.B. and HIRSCH, S.R. (1979) Psychiatric symptoms in self-poisoning patients. *Psychological Medicine, 9,* 493–500.

OFFICE OF HEALTH ECONOMICS (1981) *Suicide and Deliberate Self-Harm.* London.

OVENSTONE, I.M.K. and KREITMAN, N. (1974) Two syndromes of suicide. *British Journal of Psychiatry, 124,* 36–45.

PARKER, A. (1981) The meaning of attempted suicide to young parasuicides: a repertory grid study. *British Journal of Psychiatry, 139,* 309–312.

PAYKEL, E.S. and DIENELT, M.N. (1971) Suicide attempts following acute depression. *Journal of Nervous and Mental Disease, 153,* 234– 243.

PAYKEL, E.S., PRUSOFF, B.A. and MYERS, J.K. (1975) Suicide attempts and recent life events: a controlled comparison. *Archives of General Psychiatry, 32,* 327–333.

PIERCE, D.W. (1981) Predictive validation of a suicide intent scale. *British Journal of Psychiatry, 139,* 391–396.

SIMPSON, M.A. (1976) Self-mutilation. *British Journal of Hospital Medicine, 16,* 430–438.

TEASDALE, J.D., TAYLOR, R. and FOGARTY, S.J. (1980) Effects of induced elation–depression on the accessibility of memories of happy and unhappy experiences. *Behaviour Research and Therapy, 18,* 339–346.

WEKSTEIN, L. (1979) *Handbook of Suicidology.* New York: Brunner/Mazel.

WILLIAMS, J.M.G. (1984) *The Psychological Treatment of Depression: A Guide to the Theory and Practice of Cognitive Behaviour Therapy.* London/Canberra: Croom Helm.

WILLIAMS, J.M.G. and HASSANYEH, F. (1983) Deliberate self-harm, clinical history and extreme scoring on the EPQ. *Personality and Individual Differences, 4,* 47–350.

GIVING UP ADDICTIONS

Bill Saunders and Steven Allsop

Addiction behaviour is characterized by an individual repeatedly behaving in a way which, although enjoyable and beneficial in the short term, can accumulate adverse consequences for the individual over time. Hence the essential feature of addiction behaviour is the balance between short term rewards and long term adverse consequences.

If this definition is accepted then a wide variety of behaviours can be conceived of as addictions. Obviously the repeated use of opiate drugs, cigarettes or alcohol falls within this definition. But so do some less expected behaviours, such as the ritual checking carried out by a person with an obsessional disorder, the frequent changing of sexual partners, and the repeated climbing of high mountains. For the purposes of this chapter discussion will be restricted to consideration of the role of treatment in the modification of an individual's use of mood altering (psychoactive) substances, but it is relevant to cite the examples above as a reminder that addiction behaviour is a frequent, common behaviour and is not a discrete, abnormal or bizarre form of behaviour exhibited by a minority of peculiar people.

A further proviso is also warranted and this is to stress that addiction behaviour is not necessarily to the obvious and inevitable detriment of the individual. As Russell (1976) has noted there are addictions which are valued in society, of which the total commitment to work, irrespective of any negative consequences to health or family life, is but one example. Therefore the fact of exhibiting addiction behaviour is not of itself a precursor to some form of treatment.

The nature of the problems

If people persist in the frequent and repeated use of a psychoactive substance then they put themselves at risk of accumulating problems from that use. Thorley (1980) has usefully noted that 'drug problems' may derive from three aspects of drug use – from intoxication, regular use and from dependence.

In the main, problems of intoxication are legal or social in nature, for example, drunk driving, drunkenness or familial discord, whereas problems relating to the regular use of a substance primarily concern the physical damage that results from years of drug use. Finally, problems may result from the individual perceiving him or herself as being dependent upon their preferred drug. Definitions of dependence are notoriously difficult, but the term is used here to refer to an individual's difficulty in refraining from drug use. This state may involve the experiencing of withdrawal symptoms and the development of a lifestyle in which the taking of the chosen mood altering substance becomes paramount.

Treatment has a variable role in relation to these three categories of problems. The treatment of intoxication is restricted to the medical response to any life threatening consequences such as overdoses and asphyxiation or trauma sustained whilst intoxicated. Such acute medical responses occur daily in accident and emergency departments in Britain but are not the focus of this paper. Similarly, problems of regular use are predominantly of a medical nature. Sherlock (1982) has recently reviewed the extensive medical consequences of regular drinking and the health damage caused by the use of tobacco is legion and well documented (Royal College of Physicians, 1977). In terms of illicit mood altering substances, the long term damage from repeated use is less certain and less well recorded. In some cases, such as cannabis, or the various substances subsumed under the label of solvents, the evidence about long-term harm is inconsistent and incomplete (Institute for the Study of Drug Dependence, 1982). Again, however, such damage as may accrue is usually perceived as an essentially medical or surgical problem.

Thus the focus of this chapter is on those interventions that are a response to the problems of dependence, that is, strategies which are directed at overcoming the individual's difficulty in refraining from the use of the substance which is deemed problematic.

The nature of treatment

It is necessary to attempt some definition of treatment. Intervention of a psychological or counselling nature can be delivered in various forms and guises, and any assessment of the impact of such intervention on the resolution of a problem behaviour requires that some framework is established to delineate the activity under review.

Thorley (1983) has argued that treatment is an activity which has an individual focus and comprises the use of specific and discrete intervention methods which are applied with the stated intent of removing or reducing identified symptoms or problem behaviours. Treatment is done to passive recipients who may or may not co-operate and who are considered to have some characteristics of illness. Treatment as such is a short term and prescriptive activity. Thorley has contrasted treatment with rehabilitation, with the latter being a more broad spectrum process in which individuals are helped to:

> establish a state...in which they are capable of coping with situations encountered, thus enabling them to take advantage of the opportunities that are available to other people in the same age group.

Rehabilitation is thus a process in which individual responsibility for behaviour is stressed, and emphasis is placed upon the active acquisition of new skills.

The effectiveness of treatment

As treatment is the standard response to addiction problems, any evaluation of the impact of intervention upon alcohol and drug problems is of necessity an examination of the role of treatment in the giving up of addictions. A series of reviews of treatment for the various conditions under discussion here has recently been published. In this section we highlight the conclusion of these evaluations. Though inevitably such summaries omit much detail, the essential message of these major reviews can be encapsulated in the following quotations.

It is helpful to commence with work on the treatment of alcohol problems because, of the addiction behaviours, this is the one that has been studied most extensively and, notwithstanding many methodological criticisms, most carefully. Moos *et al.* (1982) commenced one recent review by noting that:

> In spite of extensive research aimed at evaluating the treatment of alcoholism very little is known still about factors that contribute to or mediate successful treatment. (p.ll20)

Similarly Miller and Hester (1980), in what is the most authoritative and extensive review of alcohol problems treatment to date, concluded that:

> The majority of treatment procedures for problem drinkers warrant a 'Scotch Verdict' of unproved at the present time. Ironically the most widely accepted and commonly used treatment techniques currently fall into this category of 'unproved'. (p.l08)

Perhaps the most terse and succinct conclusion about the current status of the treatment for alcohol problems is that of Mulford (1979) who noted:

> None of the dozens of formal treatments for alcoholism appear to be either necessary or sufficient for recovery. (p.5ll)

Thus it is only too evident that little success has been recorded in the treatment of alcohol related problems. This failure to demonstrate the efficacy of treatment has been variously ascribed – with some authors blaming poor treatment (Clare, 1977), some poor research (Nathan and Lansky, 1978), and others blaming both (Orford, 1980). Whatever the eventual truth of this matter, there is a similar lack of evidence for the effectiveness of treatment of other addictions. For example, Callahan (1980) in his review of the treatment of narcotic addiction was forced to conclude that:

> Treatment of narcotic addiction in the US has undergone rapid changes in mood and content over the past 100 years. In mood the addict has been seen as benign (for example, 1800s grandmothers), alien (Chinese labourers in San Francisco), medically ill, mentally ill and/or dangerous. Content of treatment has ranged from drying out, to clinical substitution, to radical personality change, to working with client assets and deficits. The single consistency perhaps is the usual persistence of the desire to use narcotics. (p.163)

Not surprisingly Callahan ended his review with a call for more research and the development of new, more effective treatment methods.

This acknowledgement of the impotence of existing treatment procedures is also echoed by McFall (1978) in his analysis of the effectiveness of smoking cessation methods. He concluded that:

> Despite the extensive efforts of numerous investigators over many years, cigarette smoking continues to be a major health problem. An efficient, safe, effective treatment for smoking behaviour remains an elusive goal, although progress toward this end seems to have been made in recent years. (p.712)

Comments such as these reflect an essential problem for the scientist-practitioner. The belief that treatment is a necessary and humane response is constantly challenged by research evaluation which fails to demonstrate the superiority of one approach over another, or the impact of treatment itself.

This 'head versus heart' dilemma results in calls for more research, better treatments and the expression of hope that a breakthrough is imminent. However, given these consistent – across the addiction behaviours – findings, that treatment is not a powerful force in the remission process, it may be advisable to call, not for a redoubling of existing effort, but a re-appraisal of the role of treatment.

To be set against these melancholy treatment research data is the over-whelming evidence that drug addicts, problem drinkers and 'smokers' do often terminate their harmful use of these substances. For example, Vaillant (1983) in his extensive longitudinal study of problem drinkers found that over the twenty year follow-up period, 64 out of 110 male problem drinkers had successfully modified their excessive drinking. Similarly, in a study of 128 opiate users who attended drug dependence clinics in London, 31 per cent became non-users over the ten year follow-up period (Wille, 1980). In terms of smoking, there is again considerable evidence that many smokers do successfully terminate their drug habit (Royal College of Physicians, 1977). Here then is an interesting conundrum. Research evidence fails to demonstrate the effectiveness of alcohol and other drug problems counselling, yet people with such problems do appear to relinquish their addiction behaviour. As Chick (1982) has noted, there is much for the beleaguered clinician to learn from investigation of the way in which people give up their addictions.

GIVING UP ADDICTIONS

1. Alcohol: a case study

If there has been one main flaw in the treatment research to date it has perhaps the conviction of researchers that treatment itself is the only – or is the single most powerful – factor in the recovery process. Perhaps the failure to demonstrate the effectiveness of treatment stems from the failure of the employed research methods to tease out subtle treatment influences. This contention is perhaps best illustrated by a single case study, for as Edwards (1980) has sagely noted, when any endeavour is going badly it is wise to go back and re-examine the basic prinicples upon which the endeavour was initiated.

The following case study is derived from an investigation conducted by Ross (1980) who simply went and asked some forty ex-problem drinkers to tell of their recoveries. Originally Ross intended to assess whether people who had attended different treatment agencies would report different aspects of treatment as being beneficial. In the event Ross found that treatment factors were seldom reported by his respondents, who in the main gave an unexpected commonality of reasons for their recoveries. The most frequently cited factor was the individual's vivid recall (often coupled with apprehension about possible re-occurrence) of some disastrous personal crisis which had happened whilst drinking. This feature is highlighted in the following case study – as is the difficulty of gauging the effects of treatment.

In 1978, the respondent in question (J.B.) was married, living at home, employed in a Clydeside shipyard and drinking heavily. His problem drinking career is outlined in figure 1. During 1978 his drinking gradually increased and a number of adverse events occurred. These included a road traffic accident, domestic discord, redundancy and the onset of severe withdrawal symptoms which eventually precipitated admission to the local Alcohol Treatment Unit (ATU). This admission interrupted J.B.'s heavy drinking and the beginning of 1979 was a period of relative sobriety and improved domestic relations. However, by mid-1979, J.B. had re-established his heavy drinking pattern and this resulted in J.B. being ejected from the family home. His spouse initiated divorce proceedings and by the end of the year, J.B. was a member of a small group of homeless, heavy drinkers. After some 6-8 weeks of living rough, J.B. was admitted to the local Salvation Army detox centre, from where he was transferred to a small 'dry' hostel. Having achieved four weeks off alcohol he was moved on to a less well supervised establishment and J.B. took the occasional drink. This move was followed by the somewhat fortuitous allocation of a small council flat and in July 1980 temporary re-employment in the local shipyards. At the same time, tentative contact was re-established with his wife and family. J.B.'s drinking which was already far more controlled than previously gradually attenuated. In 1984 he celebrated three years of total abstinence, is now reconciled with his wife and family and in his spare time is a voluntary counsellor for a local alcohol problem agency.

The effect of treatment in J.B.'s remission is almost impossible to gauge. His initial admission to the A.T.U. interrupted his drinking behaviour to the extent that the first three months of 1979 were domestically harmonious. If the A.T.U. had conducted a three month follow-up in early 1979 then they would have classified J.B. as improved, since he was drinking less and the familial situation was much ameliorated. However, a 12-month follow-up would have shown the reverse with the patient not having worked in the previous year, drinking heavily and living rough. Any temptation to claim that the gains made at first follow-up were due to treatment would logically require the admission that by 12 months the treatment had made the patient worse. Similarly, the impact of 'detox' and the subsequent hostel regime are impossible to gauge. The Salvation Army offer little in the way of sophisticated or intensive treatment, being primarily concerned with providing accommodation.

This problem drinker career highlights the inappropriateness of a 'treatment applied, patient out, follow-up conducted' treatment evaluation paradigm. While appropriate for some discrete and focused interventions that may occur in medicine or surgical procedures (for example in hip replacement) the application to addiction behaviour problems is less appropriate, for factors external to the intervention delivered appear crucial in determining outcome. J.B.'s recovery is consistent with a model of addiction behaviour remission proposed by Tuchfeld (1976). Within this model, treatment effects need to be considered against the background of events that are happening in the addicted individual's life – for example, the quality of his/her interpersonal relationships, the degree of job satisfaction and the advent of positive or negative life events. It is becoming increasingly apparent that factors such as these have considerable influence upon a drinking or drug taking career.

2. A tentative model

Tuchfeld's model of the remission process was based on a careful and detailed analysis of interviews carried out with 51 'spontaneously' recovered problem drinkers. He proposed that recovery is essentially a two-stage process.

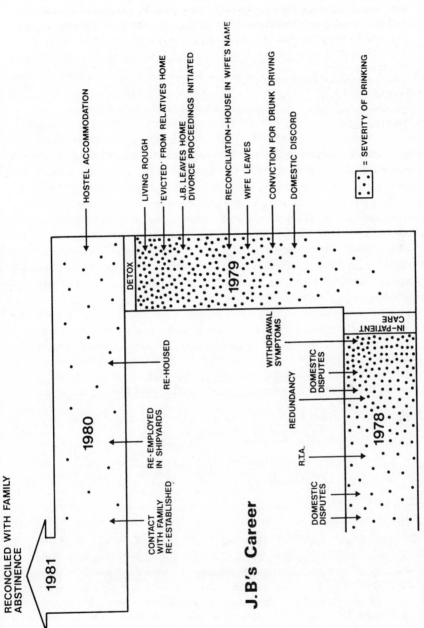

Figure 1. J.B.'s career.

The first stage is concerned with the recognition by the individual that his or her drinking has become problematic. For Tuchfeld, this recognition may be either a gradual or an almost instantaneous process. For those people who slowly appreciate their difficulties it may be that the costs of drinking (for example, hangover, nausea, family and work problems, or withdrawal symptoms) slowly increase and the balance between the short term pleasures of drinking is outweighed by the accumulation of long term adverse consequences. Thus the individual may come to the realization that the addiction behaviour is not 'worth it': the negatives outweigh the positives.

Such recognition however may also occur in a sudden and dramatic manner. Saunders and Tate (1983) in a study of 25 ex-problem drinkers who had improved without formal treatment contact, found that whilst half of the sample reported that their resolution to abstain or curtail their intake was gradually achieved, the remainder made a sudden and often dramatic decision to stop drinking excessively. For this group the decision to stop could be directly linked to what the respondents considered as a critical and meaningful event.

This is illustrated in the following case. A middle aged woman, separated from her husband because of her drinking behaviour, reported that, after ten years of heavy drinking and a myriad of associated social and physical problems, the under-noted events occurred:

> It was Christmas Eve, I was broke and chapping doors in a tenement near where I live begging for money. It was raining, cold, miserable. I asked people for money for the children, but it was for drink. As I got to the top of one tenement, I felt so bad that I swore that if God let me get through the night I'd never drink again. From that Christmas Day I've never had another drink.

Reports such as these are not uncommon in the literature. Tuchfeld's study is replete with similar examples and many other researchers have reported similar findings. For example, Knupfer (1972) in a follow-up study of community-identified problem drinkers found that some had, over the period between interviews, markedly curtailed their drinking behaviour. She noted, however, that:

> the motivation for the recovery is usually to a large extent mysterious. In explaining 'why they quit' respondents often give strangely trivial reasons. One man after 17 years of drinking a fifth of whiskey daily said 'I seen it wasn't doing me no good, so I quit!' Another began going with a woman (his future wife) and was ashamed for her to see him drunk. Another walked into his favourite bar one day and the bartender began telling him about the fancy car he had just purchased. The respondent thought to himself, indignantly 'He's buying that car with my money, goddam it, and what have I got?' Then and there he decided to quit. (p.272)

The above reports tend to arouse conflicting thoughts in psychologists. The apparently superficial nature of the events involved in the decision-making process engenders doubts about the importance of the event, and the validity of the meaning subsequently attached to it. Another question persists as to why, out of the multitude of personally adverse events that most addicts experience, did this specific event trigger off the remission process? To return to Tuchfeld's remission model the examples cited above are illustrations of the first stage of the recovery process in which the individual, via some currently unexplained mechanism, makes a resolution to change. The second stage is maintenance of this resolution. In many ways, this stage is better understood and a number of studies are available in which certain aspects of an individual's life are indicated as being important as maintenance factors. In Tuchfeld's study such factors included the extent to which an individual was able to change his or her daily lifestyle, the development of a sense of control over the drinking problem and the gradual attainment of a sense of psychological well being. Tuchfeld also considered that these factors were themselves influenced by external factors, such as housing, employment, financial situation and relationships, which contributed to the quality of the individual's past-drinking lifestyle.

Tuchfeld's model is consistent with the findings of Saunders and Kershaw (1979). In their study of some 60 ex-problem drinkers detected in the community, it was found that respondents' resolutions were sustained by gradual, though often quite marked, changes in lifestyle. These changes included the establishment of new significant relationships, marriage, new employment, a change of house, or the onset of physical ill health which restricted the ability to drink with impunity (for example, acute pancreatitis). It is pertinent to note that of those respondents who had received formal treatment (seven out of the sixty respondents) the experience of counselling was not considered of major importance. Interestingly, all had had multiple contacts with counselling but it was only when treatment coincided with the onset of a new job or a new significant relationship that sustained progress was achieved.

Perhaps the most authoritative study of the process of giving up alcohol abuse is that of Vaillant and his colleagues (Vaillant, 1983; Vaillant and Milofsky, 1982). In this longitudinal study of 110 problem drinkers, it was found that four factors could be determined as being of major importance in the giving up process. The first of these was the development of what Vaillant terms a 'substitute dependency', whereby the individual's interests become focused upon behaviour which is different from drinking. Such substitute dependencies included meditation, compulsive work or involvement in hobbies and the extensive use of other drugs such as tranquillizers or cigarettes. The second was the occurrence of factors which ensured that drinking either became an immediately unpleasant experience (such as the onset of epilepsy, hypertension or the development of an ulcer) or that the personal costs of drinking were obviously raised, for example by coercive restraints imposed by courts or employers.

Vaillant and Milofsky (1982) also identified two further factors which are similar to Tuchfeld's maintenance factors. These were the discovery of a new source of increased hope, self-esteem and self-efficacy and also the establishment of new relationships which were

> uncontaminated by the old injuries, resentments and guilts that alcoholics inflict on those who care about them. For many, this relationship was a new wife or a special relationship with a non-professional helping person or mentor; for others it was learning to help others who were as troubled as themselves. (p.130)

Thus, from studies which have focused on the recovery from alcohol problems, the picture is that remission is orchestrated by an interaction of personal experience, personal decision-making and commitment to change, and then having the opportunity to alter lifestyle accordingly. This process of recovery is, once initiated, facilitated and sustained by the quality of the individual's everyday existence – his relationships, job opportunities, housing, health and the extent of life stress.

This tentative model of recovery, which places the engineroom of remission within the social milieu of the individual, is made more convincing by the similar findings of independent research in the other addictions. Two studies are of special relevance, one from opiate use (Wille, 1980) and the other from smoking research (Prochaska and DiClemente, 1983).

3. Lessons from other addictions

As noted above, Wille's study (1980) was concerned with the ten year follow-up of a representative sample of 128 heroin users who attended Drug Dependence Clinics in London in the late 1960s. Wille found that over the period of the follow-up, 40 (31 per cent) of his sample became abstinent. The routes to recovery reported by these ex-heroin users closely parallel those reported in the alcohol studies cited above. One case study, that of Bob O., is illustrative. Bob O. started using heroin at 16, and by 18 was being prescribed 120 mg. heroin and 120 mg. methedrine on a reducing script. This failed because Bob O. 'wasn't ready to come down' and his life became increasingly chaotic. Job loss, an overdose, trouble with the police and physical ill-health were experienced. Wille notes that 'he was worried by his physical deterioration, his abscesses and overdoses, the death of his best friend from a barbiturate overdose, the decline of his old drug scene and his mother's illness and her complaints about his way of life' (p.107).

Bob O. then ceased his misuse of sleeping pills and started working regularly, and a gradual reduction of his heroin prescription was begun – this time with his agreement. He noted:

Because I met Ann and I wanted to get married and pack it all in, because I always made a thing in my own head that I would never get engaged or married until I was off drugs; because I knew if I was to get engaged while I was on drugs that I'd still be using today. (p.107-108)

Wille further reports that:

After ten years of heroin use, Bob O. became abstinent...married his girl-friend...completed a government retraining course as a carpenter and started a successful career. He has his own house and car, and...has been abstinent for four years. (p.108)

It is contended that the role of treatment in this remission is very much akin to that of treatment in recovery from alcohol problems. In the case of Bob O., treatment was at best a weak influence, and his decision making and overall recovery were due to an interaction of the adverse consequences of his drug taking, a recognition of the need for change plus the opportunities to establish a new significant relationship, gain employment and establish self-respect. This emerging picture of the remission process is also confirmed and extended by work with cigarette users. In an innovative and most interesting study, Prochaska and DiClemente (1983) interviewed 872 media-recruited people about their smoking habits. Of this sample, 247 were 'long-term quitters' who had achieved at least six months of non-smoking and a further 134 people were 'recent quitters' – that is, of less than six months abstinence. The remainder of the sample consisted of 187 'contemplators'; 108 'immotives' and 196 'relapsers'. The classification of these sub-groups is of interest. 'Contemplators' were persons who, whilst currently smoking, were concerned about their cigarette use and were seriously thinking of stopping. 'Immotives', in contrast, gave no indication that they wished to terminate their use and steadfastly enjoyed their cigarette addiction. Finally, the 'relapsers' were people who had in the past year failed to maintain a resolution to stop smoking.

All subjects in the study completed a Processes of Change Questionnaire designed by the authors to measure ten different behaviour change strategies which earlier investigations had shown are utilized by people to alter addiction behaviour. These strategies include consciousness raising (the seeking out of facts about smoking), self-liberation (I can quit if I wish), self re-evaluation (being annoyed or disappointed about being addicted) and dramatic relief (being upset by health hazard warnings).

The investigators were able to determine that the different sub-groups in the overall sample utilized different behaviour-change strategies. Not surprisingly the immotive group used significantly fewer change strategies; as a group they tended to avoid or ignore information about smoking, did not think about their smoking habit, and were not upset by the associated health hazards. In contrast, the 'contemplators' were concerned about their problem behaviour, alert to anti-smoking literature and emotionally upset by the health risk of their addiction behaviour.

For those who were in the early stage of change, self re-evaluation and self-liberation strategies were frequently utilized, while counter-conditioning (for example, doing something other than smoking in order to relax) and stimulus control (removing smoking cues) strategies were of importance in the maintenance of the no-smoking vow. Prochaska and DiClemente's work is of obvious relevance to any debate of the role of treatment in the giving up process. As the authors noted:

> Rather than assume that all smokers coming for treatment are ready for action, clients would be grouped according to which stage of change they are in. Research with clients applying for therapy indicates that there are clusters of clients in each of the stages of change...Thus, smokers in the contemplation stage would begin with consciousness raising and self-evaluation processes, while smokers ready for action could begin to apply the more behaviourally-based processes. (p.l0)

It is interesting that the authors avoid mention of treatment as a useful strategy for shifting people from an 'immotive' to a 'contemplator' state. In fact, a major implication of their research is that the recognition of a need to change is very much an idiosyncratic event. As a number of the alcohol studies in this area suggest, it may be that the experience of nasty and threatening drug associated consequences prompts a resolution to change. If this is the case, then the chest pains of the smoker, the 'shakes' and 'sweats' of the heavy drinker and the 'busts' of the illicit drug user are of potential value. Vaillant and Milofsky's (1982) research would support this contention for they noted that 'paradoxically alcoholics who were most severely afflicted often achieved the most stable recoveries'. In addition, Chick (1982) has commented that 'treatment may actually make some alcoholics worse by sheltering them from the consequences of their drinking' (p.2).

THE CLINICAL IMPLICATIONS: SHIFTING THE FOCUS OF THERAPY

Earlier it was noted that a conundrum exists. Treatment could not be demonstrated to be effective, yet there was overwhelming evidence that people do move out of inimical addiction behaviour. Perhaps the essential lesson from the study of natural recovery is that our treatment, as currently practised and delivered, fails to take a sufficient account of the social milieu of the individual. This contention is well supported by the research of Moos and his colleagues, who in a series of investigations (Moos *et al.*, 1982; Billings and Moos, 1983; Cronkite and Moos, 1980) have focused on the influence of post-treatment factors upon remission or relapse. In a two-year follow-up study of 113 married, inpatient, problem drinkers, Billings and Moos (1983) found that the recovered patients (n = 55) could be distinguished from the relapsed patients (n = 58) on three indices of post-treatment functioning other than drinking behaviour. The factors were the incidence of life stressors, the nature of the coping skills used in response to problems, and the quality and/or availability of social resources such as friendships, marital relationships and satisfaction with one's employment. When compared to recovered patients, relapsed patients reported twice as many post-treatment negative, and only half as many positive life events. Furthermore, recovered patients were significantly more likely to use active cognitive behavioural problem solving skills whereas the relapsers tended to employ avoidance coping strategies such as ignoring the problem, blaming it on other people or using other drugs to cope. In terms of social resources the successful patients reported greater family cohesion and greater job satisfaction. The importance of Billings and Moos's work is that it implies that the characteristics associated with good outcome – such as familial cohesion, job satisfaction and the use of problem solving skills to counter adverse events, were not the consequence of abstinence but the facilitators of abstinence. From Billings and Moos's work it can be said that the old adage that if one becomes sober everything else will improve is not necessarily true – the attainment of abstinence is itself dependent upon improved family functioning, job satisfaction and the use of problem solving skills. The implications of this work for the clinician are clear: there is a vital need to adopt a broad spectrum approach in both assessment and intervention and to be alert to opportunities to facilitate change in the client's overall pattern of living.

In this regard it is relevant to cite the work of Azrin who can claim to have conducted the only consistently favourable series of treatment studies so far reported (Hunt and Azrin, 1973; Azrin, 1976; Azrin *et al.,* 1982). Azrin's community reinforcement approach is based upon the active restructuring of a client's marital, occupational and social functioning in order that life becomes more satisfactory, contingent on not drinking excessively which in turn becomes less desirable. Considerable energy and resources are spent in this approach in providing clients with sufficient basic requirements so that they can take advantage of opportunities to improve the quality of their lives. Thus, if necessary, patients will be provided with accommodation, transport, job-retraining or 'refresher' courses and introductions to new social contacts. As may be appreciated, this approach is fundamentally different in focus from that normally delivered by the average alcohol or drug dependence treatment unit. The community reinforcement approach involves the manipulation of environmental factors to facilitate and maintain change and this approach has consistently been found to be superior to more individual and psycho-therapeutically focused hospital regimes.

The difficulty for the average clinician is that such broad spectrum and socially focused interventions are difficult to orchestrate from the constraints of the average clinic. Thus whilst acknowledging the need for a keen awareness of the individual client's social functioning what can be legitimately attempted? As part answer it is relevant to cite Edwards (1982) who has recently commented that:

> Therapeutic work is only likely successfully to produce movement when its efforts are in alignment with the real possibilities for change within the individual, his family and social setting. The basic work of therapy is largely concerned with nudging and supporting the movement along these 'natural' pathways of recovery. We need a far more developed sense of people's innate capacity for recovery and the possible dimensions of recovery rather than the belief that we can impose therapies on people who are to be marched along at our dictate. The clumsy therapist is like someone who tries to carve a piece of wood without respect for the grain. The basic work of treatment requires immense respect for the grain, and therapy must always be matched to individual needs. (p.178)

Perhaps then the task of the therapist is one of 'nudging' movement. From the work of Prochaska and DiClemente (1983) cited above it is possible to argue that an early and important task is to determine whether the presenting client is an 'immotive' or a 'contemplator'. If the latter then it may be possible to precipitate an attempt at short term abstention via the use of 'motivational interviewing'. This term coined by Miller (1983) describes an elegant system of interaction with problem alcohol and drug takers which is diametrically opposed to the 'denial–confrontation' motivational stance normally considered as necessary to elicit a change in drinking behaviour. For Miller, a commitment to change is established by encouraging clients to construct their own inventory of problems related to drug taking, expressing concern about them and verbalizing the need to change their drinking/drug taking behaviour. In motivational interviewing the therapist's task is to encourage the client to talk about the problems that they perceive as existing in relation to their drug use, and to re-affirm and reflect the client's view of their problems, encouraging continued discussion about them. There is no requirement to have the client admit to being 'an alcoholic' or 'an addict' and the essential basis of the approach is that the client convinces the therapist that he/she has a problem rather than vice versa. This is a fundamental re-appraisal of the traditional adversarial intervening stance, and one that requires no little skill. Although this approach has yet to be rigorously evaluated, Miller's claim that 'a person is more likely to integrate and accept that which is reached by his or her own reasoning processes' has sufficient plausibility to merit application. The approach is certainly consistent with Edward's demand that therapists pay respect to 'the grain'.

If a commitment to change the drinking behaviour is achieved, then the task of treatment personnel is that of facilitating events within the social milieu of the client, to the extent that is possible from the counselling room, so that the initial resolution to change is maintained.

This opens up an area of drug and alcohol counselling which was until recently sadly neglected. This is the issue of 'relapse' or more usefully 'resolution breakdown'. As Billings and Moos's work has shown, the breaking of a resolution to abstain is often precipitated by a failure to cope successfully with a problem or by the post-resolution period being marred by deep-seated marital or relationship discord and hostility. For the clinician the tasks are to assess such potential precipitants of failure of resolve and to prepare the client against the possibility of renewed problematic alcohol or drug use. The area of resolution failure is currently attracting considerable attention (for example, see Curson and Rankin, in press) and it is pertinent to note that if a client's 'relapses' can be prevented or managed, so that the severity is reduced, then treatment may be deemed as being of value.

It is in regard to the management of resolution failure that the most innovative and theoretically most important work has recently been reported. Working from a social learning philosophy, Rankin, Hodgson and Stockwell (1983) have proposed that 'relapses' involve both the initial breakdown of the resolution (for example, the first or early drinks of the abstaining problem drinker) and the decision to continue to use, with the result that high levels of intoxication are achieved. They argue that there is a compulsion to continue to drink after some alcohol has been ingested. For severely dependent individuals, the 'priming' impact of moderate doses of alcohol acts as a trigger for further consumption, and this separates the problem drinker from his/her social drinking counterparts. Intervention should therefore be focused on reducing the former's feeling of inability to stop once started. Taking note of the successful treatments for obsessional neurosis, Rankin and his colleagues have piloted a cue exposure and response prevention programme for severely dependent problem drinkers. In the latest of their investigations patients were, after a period of detoxification, given sufficient alcohol to raise their blood alcohol levels to between 65–100 mg/%, and then in the presence of alcohol (cue exposure) urged to resist the temptation to drink (response prevention). Patients were told to first look at a glass of their preferred beverage, then hold it, and finally smell the available alcohol whilst fighting down the urge to consume. When evaluated on 'desire for a drink' and 'difficulty in resisting' scales patients, over the six experimental sessions, showed a marked reduction in their feeling of compulsion and the 'irresistibility' of the situation became manageable. Their ability to cope with the task of refusing alcohol once intoxicated was significantly superior to that of a control group who had not experienced the cue exposure and response prevention programme.

Work such as this is of crucial importance for it demonstrates a technique, based on a sound theoretical basis, which may unlock the inevitability of addiction behaviour enshrined in such slogans as 'one drink–one drunk'. It can help both clinician and client understand better, and thus combat, the impaired control over drug use which is the hallmark of drinking and drug problems.

SOME CONCLUDING COMMENTS

The treatment of alcohol and drug problems is currently in a state of transition. The early hopes that intensive and psychotherapeutically-oriented programmes would reduce the prevalence of such problems have not been realised. Instead there has developed a growing awareness that the social milieu of the client has greater impact upon outcome than any strategy devised in the clinic. There has, therefore, been a move back to more simple, advice-giving strategies and an appreciation that the professional's role is one of catalyst of change. Treatment is thus one factor among many in the remission process. Consistent with this view of the reduced importance of treatment has come an acknowledgement of the need for new, innovative responses. The advent of motivational interviewing, resolution maintenance programmes and cue exposure and response prevention strategies are part of this response, as is an increased clinical awareness of the importance of the client's social milieu. The challenge of the next decade is therefore to develop and assess intervention strategies that are consistent with evidence relating to the processes and factors involved in remission and maintenance. Concomitantly, traditional, intensive and expensive interventions must respond to the demand to demonstrate their practical value.

Acknowledgements

Georgina Barr is to be thanked for the provision of a high standard of secretarial skill.

REFERENCES

AZRIN, N. (1976) Improvements in the community-reinforcement approach to alcoholism. *Behaviour Research and Therapy, 14,* 339–348.
AZRIN, N., SISSON, R., MEYERS, R. and GODLEY, M. (1982) Alcoholism treatment by Disulfiram and community reinforcement therapy. *Journal of Behavioural Therapy and Experimental Psychiatry, 13,* 105–112.
BILLINGS, A. and MOOS, R. (1983) Psychosocial processes of recovery among alcoholics and their families: Implications for clinicians and programme evaluators. *Addictive Behaviours, 8,* 205–218.
CALLAHAN, E. Alternative strategies in the treatment of narcotic addiction: a review. In: W. R. Miller (ed.) *The Addictive Behaviours.* New York: Pergamon Press.
CHICK, J. (1982) Do alcoholics recover? *British Medical Journal, 285,* 3–4.
CLARE, A. (1977) How good is treatment? In: G. Edwards and M. Grant (eds) *Alcoholism: New Knowledge and New Responses.* London: Croom Helm.

CRONKITE, R. and MOOS, R. (1980) The determinants of post treatment functioning of alcoholic patients: a conceptual framework. *Journal of Consulting and Clinical Psychology, 48,* 305–316.

CURSON, D. and RANKIN, H. (in press) *Alcoholism Relapse.* London: Logos Alpha.

EDWARDS, G. (1980) Alcoholism treatment between guesswork and certainty. In: G. Edwards and M. Grant (eds) *Alcoholism Treatment in Transition.* London: Croom Helm.

EDWARDS, G. (1982) *The Treatment of Drinking Problems: A Guide for the Helping Professions.* London: Grant McIntyre.

HUNT, G. and AZRIN, N. (1973) A community reinforcement approach to alcoholism. *Behaviour Research and Therapy, 11,* 91–104.

INSTITUTE FOR THE STUDY OF DRUG DEPENDENCE (1982) *Drug Abuse Briefing.* London: Institute for the Study of Drug Dependence.

KNUPFER, G. (1972) Ex-problem drinkers. *Life History Research in Psychopathology, 2,* 256–280.

McFALL, R.M. (1978) Smoking-cessation research. *Journal of Consulting and Clinical Psychology, 46,* 703–712.

MILLER, W.R. (1983) Motivational interviewing with problem drinkers. *Behavioural Psychotherapy, 11,* 147–182.

MILLER, W. R. and HESTER, R. (1980) Treating the problem drinker: modern approaches. In: W. R. Miller (ed.) *The Addictive Behaviours.* New York: Pergamon Press.

MOOS, R., CRONKITE, R. and FINNEY, J. (1983) A conceptual framework for alcoholism treatment evaluation. In: E.M. Pattison and E. Kaufman (eds) *Encyclopaedic Handbook of Alcoholism.* New York: Gardner Press.

MULFORD, H. (1979) Treating alcoholism versus accelerating the natural recovery process: a cost-benefit comparison. *Journal of Studies on Alcohol, 40,* 505–513.

NATHAN, P. and LANSKY, D. (1978) Common methodological problems in research on the addictions. *Journal of Counselling and Clinical Psychology, 46,* 713–726.

ORFORD, J. (1980) Evaluation of treatment of alcoholic patients. Paper presented at the Third European Seminar on Health Policy. Commission of the European Communities, Luxembourg, March 1980.

PROCHASKA, J. and DICLEMENTE, C. (1983) Stages and processes of self change of smoking: toward an integrative model of change. *Journal of Consulting and Clinical Psychology, 51,* 390–395.

RANKIN, H., HODGSON, R. and STOCKWELL, T. (1983) Cue exposure and response prevention with alcoholics: a controlled trial. *Behaviour Research and Therapy, 21,* 435–446.

ROSS, T. (1980) A study of self reported important factors maintaining recovery of remission from problem drinking. Unpublished manuscript, Alcohol Studies Centre, Paisley College of Technology.

ROYAL COLLEGE OF PHYSICIANS (1977) *Smoking or Health.* London: Pitman Medical.

RUSSELL, M. (1976) What is dependence? In: G. Edwards, M. Russell, D. Hawks and M. MacCafferty (eds) *Drugs and Drug Dependence.* London: Lexington Books.

SAUNDERS, W. and KERSHAW, P. (1979) Spontaneous remission from alcoholism: results from a community survey. *British Journal of Addiction, 74,* 251–265.

SAUNDERS, W. and TATE, D. (1983) Spontaneous remission revisited. Paper presented at the 16th Scottish Alcohol Research Symposium, Pitlochry, October 1983.

SHERLOCK, S. (ed.) (1982) Alcohol and disease. *British Medical Bulletin, 38,* No. 1.

THORLEY, A. (1980) Medical responses to problem drinking. *Medicine (3rd series), 35,* 1816–1822.

THORLEY, A. (1983) Rehabilitation of problem drinkers and drug takers. In: F. Watts and D. Bennett (eds) *Theory and Practice of Psychiatric Rehabilitation.* Chichester: John Wiley.

TUCHFELD, B. (1976) *Changes in Patterns of Alcohol Use without Aid of Formal Treatment.* N. Carolina: Centre for Health Studies, Research Triangle Institute.

VAILLANT, G. (1983) *The Natural History of Alcoholism.* Cambridge, Mass.: Harvard University Press.

VAILLANT, G. and MILOFSKY, E. (1982) Natural history of male alcoholism. IV Paths to recovery. *Archives of General Psychiatry, 39,* 127–133.

WILLE, R. (1980) Processes of recovery among heroin users. In: G. Edwards and A. Arif (eds) *Drug Problems in the Sociocultural Context.* Geneva: World Health Organization, Public Health Paper No. 73.

CLINICAL PSYCHOLOGY IN PRIMARY HEALTH CARE

Teresa A. Griffiths

The practice of clinical psychology in primary health care is an emergent but no longer relatively novel area of interest within the profession.

The stimulus for the initiation of primary care services comprised a number of coincidental factors, including the work of Shepherd *et al.* (1966), which indicated that a significant proportion of people who consult their general practitioner have problems which can be labelled 'psychological' and contained the suggestion that general practitioners do not provide adequate treatment for these problems. Also relevant was the increasing involvement of social workers in general practice (Goldberg and Neil, 1972), showing that non-medical specialists have a relevant contribution to make in this area. Then the re-organization of the Health Service in 1974 and finally the specific encouragement within the Report of the Trethowan Sub-Committee (DHSS, 1977) on 'The Role of Psychologists in the Health Services' to develop work with general practitioners, all generated increasing interest in this as a new area of work.

The arguments raised by those in favour of the move were subjective, and centred on the benefits expected to accrue, namely convenience and lessening of stigma for the patient, ready access to psychological expertise for the GP and patients, and increased job satisfaction for the psychologist. All of these have been claimed by several authors (Davidson, 1977; Johnston, 1978; Ives, 1979; Koch, 1979), but the objective evidence of gains for the patient and the primary care team has been less clear (Earll and Kincey, 1982). Also, from the beginning there were fears that if everyone who presented to a general practitioner with psychological problems was referred to a clinical psychologist, there would be a demand which it would not be possible for our small profession to meet and the argument was put forward that it would, therefore, be unwise to open the floodgates by offering a service to general practice. In addition there were fears that the very popularity of work in primary care would lead to an increase in presented morbidity rather than a reduction (Hood, 1979).

So what has actually happened to the relationship between clinical psychologists and the primary health care team over the last 10 years? What, if anything, have we learned from the contact and where should we go from here?

At the outset a few Health Boards established experimental posts to encourage the exploration of the liaison between clinical psychologists and the team in general practice (McAllister and Philip, 1975; Johnston, 1978; Jerrom *et al.*, 1983), but in general it has been done by psychologists operating from a hospital base with a sessional commitment to primary care. It is possible that this strategy contributed to the way in which the service began to develop, which was by providing a direct clinical service to individual patients, and which has since led to some concerns about the effectiveness of a service which assumes that as its dominant role (McPherson and Feldman, 1977; Hood, 1979).

Some attempts have been made to explore other possibilities, although it is also clear that GPs generally expect clinical psychologists to provide a therapeutic service, and are keen to have access to such a service (Eastman and McPherson, 1982). As Eastman and McPherson point out, the image of clinical psychologists as providers of individual therapy is becoming established in primary care and may prove a hindrance to future developments. It is, therefore, important to examine other contributions that might be made.

Much remains to be done if the clinical psychologist in primary care wishes to exploit the setting into which he/she has ventured. The orderly cephalo-caudal sequence of normal development has not applied so far. On the contrary, there has been an element of 'feet first and fingers crossed' about progress, which has not been helpful to the long-term prospects for the co-operation of psychologists with the primary health care team.

CLARIFICATION OF TERMS

There is often confusion between the terms 'community psychology' and 'primary care psychology'. This is because both concepts are relatively new, and therefore fluid, and there is a degree of overlap. Generally, *community psychology* is considered to apply to the interface between the health and social services and the local environment, and so would be concerned with people who are not involved with the health service or who are leaving it, and with facilities such as hostels and day centres for mentally ill and mentally handicapped people. *Primary care psychology* refers to the entry of a person into the health system and to the interface between general practice and the hospital level of the system. It is in this sense that I shall use the term.

Before considering the psychologist's involvment, we should clarify some of the terms commonly used in discussions of primary care.

The *primary care team* is generally thought of as comprising general practitioners, community nurses, health visitors, receptionists and secretaries, with occasionally social workers, physiotherapists, dieticians and clinical psychologists.

The term *primary health care* refers to the first contact between a member of the public and the health services, and to the continuing care that follows from that contact.

It is unlikely that many psychologists will ever be, or wish to be, the first contact between the patient and the health service, although the development of high street 'drop in' centres where people are encouraged to present medical and/or psychological problems may provide opportunities for this in the future. It is, therefore, likely that primary care team members, usually general practitioners, will continue to make decisions about who to refer to clinical psychologists. In this event the education of team members about the skills, training and expertise of the psychologist assumes considerable importance. Undergraduate medical students are now required to undergo a behavioural science course, which usually includes some lectures by psychologists, but this is not likely to increase their awareness of the possible relationship between a psychologist's work and their own. However, vocational training courses for general practitioners provide a more valuable opportunity for such teaching at a stage in the doctor's training when it can be seen to be relevant, and at a time when specific techniques such as interviewing and other communication skills can be taught.

In addition, psychologists must endeavour to learn as well as to teach. If we wish to work effectively in primary care we must do our utmost to match the service we offer to what is required by the members of the primary care team. It is important to pursue the idea of defining the problems with which most general practitioners do not feel competent or confident to deal, and which lie within the area of competence of a clinical psychologist. McPherson and Feldman (1977) began to move along this track when they asked a GP and a clinical psychologist to make independent ratings of the relevance of psychological problems to the presentation of patients observed during surgeries. Having found good agreement, the psychologist carried out home interviews to determine those who would benefit from psychological intervention. It would have been interesting to check whether these were the people that the GP would have considered suitable for referral. The presence of a psychological problem is not the only variable weighed by a doctor in making a referral. The severity of the problem, knowledge of the individual and his/her ability to cope, the total environment in which the patient exists are all examined, as well as the doctor's confidence in dealing with the problem.

Finally, we should be wary in our use of the term 'psychological problem', which is frequently employed in such a way as to suggest that everyone to whom the term is applied is ill and/or requires to be referred to a psychologist. In fact, as Ingham (1982) reminds us, '... the majority of psychological problems seen in primary care consulters are not illnesses'.

He goes on to emphasize that people with normal psychological problems should not be encouraged to consider themselves ill. Johnston (1978) suggested that, when working in primary care, it is more useful to consider for treatment 'those patients for whom a psychological solution might be appropriate', rather than those described as having psychological problems. This is certainly a more realistic and expedient description of a potential target population in primary care.

THE CLINICAL ROLE

During the last 10 years many descriptive, some evaluative, and a few catechetical papers have appeared on the activities of clinical psychologists in primary care.

Judging by the papers which have appeared to date, the psychologists working in primary care have given priority to the development of a clinical service in establishing their role (McAllister and Philip, 1975; Ives, 1979; Koch, 1979; Earll and Kincey, 1982; Jerrom *et al.,* 1983). The explanation for this may be that by providing a clinical service the psychologist is seen to be contributing to patient care and is thereby more acceptable to other members of the primary care team. Individual case work is clearly the area which has received most attention from psychologists so far.

1. Problems referred

There is general agreement about the types of problems which are commonly presented to clinical psychologists in primary care. They are: generalized anxiety or specific phobias; marital and sexual problems; behavioural problems and cognitive difficulties in children or old people or in association with organic illness (McAllister and Philip, 1975; Johnston, 1978; Bhagat *et al.* 1979; Clark, 1979; Ives, 1979). However, in most cases it is not clear to what extent the nature of the problem may be affected by the interests or expertise of the referrer or of the psychologist, who has usually determined the referral policy.

2. Nature of contacts

There is a consensus about the nature of the work with individual patients. Assessment by interview (with psychometric testing when required) and treatment (usually behaviourally-based) or counselling, are most frequently described. The need to employ a variety of techniques has also been emphasized. (Johnston, 1978; Clark, 1979; Ives, 1979). Other aspects of patient contact, such as the number of appointments with each patient and the duration of these have been given some attention. Ives (1979) saw patients for an average of five half-hour sessions, which is consistent with McAllister and Philip's (1975) description, while Koch (1979) spent an average 8.8 sessions of unspecified duration with each patient. The site of contacts, that is, home, work, day care centre, health centre, and whether other people such as family, health care staff, etc. are involved have not been well documented.

It has therefore been impossible to make detailed comparisons with psychological treatment carried out in other settings.

One of the arguments postulated in favour of developing psychology services in primary care was that the patient is likely to be 'less ill' and that his/her problem can be treated more effectively within the situation in which it has arisen, sometimes with the active co-operation of spouse, family or friends, rather than within a hospital environment or outpatient clinic often geographically distant from the person's home. Sufficient evidence is not yet available to draw conclusions on this point.

3. Outcome

Early papers which evaluated treatment outcome in terms of variables such as change in symptom severity, medication obtained, consultations with general practitioners and patient satisfaction with service, found considerable improvements in all measures. Koch (1979) claimed that on ratings of change carried out by the therapist, 73 per cent of the patients had improved and none were considered to have deteriorated during the course of treatment. Following psychological treatment the mean number of GP consultations dropped from 9.27 in the year before referral (this is three times the national average annual figure) to 5.64. Ives (1979) rated the progress made by his patients and reported that 72 per cent could be classified as 'improved'. He also found a significant reduction in the number of GP consultations and of prescriptions issued for psychotropic drugs in the three months before and three months after treatment for the patient group.

However, encouraging as these studies were, they did not include control groups for comparison. Earll and Kincey (1982) described a study which attempted to evaluate psychological intervention in primary care using a carefully selected control group. Patients were over 15 years of age with no evidence of psychotic illness or organic brain disease and were not receiving any treatment for their problems from outside the practice. The general practitioners were given guidance in the form of written illustrations of anxiety and stress problems with which a psychological approach might be effective, and were then free to refer any patient they thought suitable. After making the decision to refer, doctors assigned patients randomly to either a treatment or control group, with the patients in the control group being treated by the GP, and the treatment group referred to a psychologist. No attempt was made to standardize the length or duration of treatment by the psychologist and follow-up evaluation was carried out seven months after referral by another psychologist. Objective measures, including the number of prescriptions obtained, the number of GP consultations, the number of hospital outpatient appointments and time spent as a hospital inpatient indicated no significant benefits as a result of treatment from a psychologist. A similar conclusion was reached on the basis of the results of subjective measures, such as self-ratings by the patients of current level of emotional distress, life satisfaction, and level of personal control. It should be noted that the treatment group in this study included data from several patients who were deemed unsuitable for treatment, whereas in the Ives study unsuitable patients were referred elsewhere or given no further appointments, and the results were calculated on the basis of patients who completed treatment.

More recently France and Robson (1982), in a preliminary report on a randomized controlled trial of a clinical psychology service in a health centre, described results on a small proportion of their patients who had reached the follow-up stage at 34 weeks. Thus far their results suggest that those patients treated by a psychologist are rated by themselves and by their GP as significantly less affected by their symptoms at 14 and 22 weeks after treatment than a control group who were treated within the practice, or by hospital referral where appropriate. This differential effect is no longer significant at 34 weeks post-treatment, but France and Robson argue that as most general practice problems are episodic in nature, the rapidity of the effect of psychological treatment may be more important than its long-term effects.

Overall, the studies of outcome indicate an urgent need for further controlled evaluative research to confirm or refute these findings, particularly in view of the apparent persistence of psychologists in pursuing this single role in general practice.

THE LIAISON AND EDUCATIONAL ROLE

Creating an effective link between the mental health services and primary health care is an important role for the clinical psychologist in general practice. It is necessary, particularly in these times of financial stringency, to ensure that services are not duplicated; so, if a sexual problem clinic or an effective marriage guidance service exists in the area, then a referral should be made to them rather than the psychologist provide the same service. This implies that the psychologist should make him/herself familiar with the facilities and services available.

Knowledge of the local community and its resources is also important, as a psychologist in primary care is dealing with people in the environment in which they live, work and spend their leisure time. Making use of these existing resources, or appreciating the lack of them, can be vital in assessing and treating problems in primary care.

There are a few papers, again mainly descriptive, giving examples of co-operative work between psychologists and other members of the primary care team. Coupar and Kennedy (1980) described a weight control group run by a psychologist and a GP providing dietary advice, behavioural management procedures and group support, which achieved good results in terms of maintenance of weight loss over an 18-month period. Griffiths and McMillan (in preparation) describes a clinic dealing with childhood nocturnal enuresis, which is another problem of concern to members of the primary care team. This was run by the psychologist with a health visitor undergoing tuition in the use of behavioural assessment and treatment methods until competent to manage the clinic with minimal supervision from the psychologist. Training other members of the primary care team in this way has been suggested as a method of dispersing psychological techniques, and is also described by Hambly and Paxton (1979), where a GP uses behaviour therapy in his normal consultations. Preventative activities, such as stop-smoking groups and health education projects such as those described by Gaskell and Watson (1978), also fall into this category, as they involve working with groups on specific clinically relevant topics.

The functioning of the primary health care team provides a further opportunity for teaching in order to improve the organizational skills and maximize the effectiveness of the interaction between different professions in the multidisciplinary primary care team. The British Psychological Society in its evidence to the DHSS Joint Working Group on the Primary Health Care Team (1979) drew attention to the fact that within the profession of psychology there is an extensive body of knowledge about the processes which occur within teams. It suggested that this research could usefully be applied to health care teams, but no reports of such involvement have yet appeared.

Doctors who become general practitioners are now required to undergo vocational training. Teaching on such courses provides an opportunity to give information about the psychologist's training, skills, and expertise, as well as to teach specific communication skills. Over the past few years those involved in medical education both at undergraduate level and in vocational training have become increasingly aware of the importance of training doctors to communicate effectively with patients. Pendleton and Hasler (1983) direct attention to the study of the doctor–patient relationship, and to the attempts to explore and improve all aspects of this interaction.

Health visitors undergoing training are often taught basic psychological theories, but the practical relevance of these principles to their anticipated work is often not specified. Psychology lectures to health visitor students are rarely delivered by applied psychologists, and so in-service courses teaching behavioural techniques to qualified health visitors are often welcomed.

PSYCHOLOGICAL RESEARCH IN PRIMARY CARE

A comprehensive description of psychological research relevant to psychology in primary care would be drawn from an enormously wide area encompassing all of normal development, aspects of abnormal psychology from psychiatry, child psychiatry, mental handicap, neuropsychology, psychogeriatrics, and general medicine, and social systems research (particularly the functioning of teams), as well as general psychological research.

In fact, research carried out thus far by psychologists in primary care has been relatively narrow in scope and limited in range. Much is simply descriptive of a clinical service. However, some research workers have directed their attention to different aspects of patients' behaviour, the behaviour of health care professionals, the interaction between the patient and the health care worker, and the operation of the health care system.

One of the important examples of exploratory work is a series of epidemiological studies carried out by Ingham and Miller (1979, 1982) with general practice populations, which indicate that interpreting the prevalence of symptoms without regard to the severity of symptoms can be misleading. They compared a group of patients attending the GP with a new episode of illness who had one or more of a constellation of symptoms (backache, tiredness, anxiety, headache, depression, irritability and dizziness), although these were not necessarily the main reason for the consultation, with a group of people in the same practice population who had not consulted their GP in the preceding year. They found that both groups had these common symptoms and in both groups the duration of the symptoms was more than seven months. The difference between 'presenters' and 'non-presenters' was in terms of the severity of the symptoms. The later work (Ingham and Miller, 1982) has emphasized the importance of stress, the effects of the illness on the patient's life, social factors (age and sex), and symptom severity as being important in the presentation of symptoms to the general practitioner.

Other studies have attempted to determine the characteristics of people who attend their doctor very frequently – the 'problem patients' – and to speculate about a possible role for psychologists in assisting members of the primary care team in dealing with this group (Broome, 1978).

The behaviour of the doctor in the consultation has attracted the attention of many researchers. Byrne and Long (1976) examined tape recordings of general practice consultations, and identified a scale of seven styles of doctor behaviour (ranging from doctor-centred to patient-centred) which seem to be maintained across consultations regardless of the presenting problem. Others have looked at aspects of consultations such as the patient's satisfaction with the consultation and the quality of the communication in terms of the amount of information given and its comprehensibility (Ley, 1975).

The interaction between doctors and the psychologists has received some attention. Davidson (1977) sent a questionnaire to 145 GPs in the Croydon area, and found that of 76 who responded 59 per cent wanted the psychologists to be involved in the assessment of intellectual ability, with assessment of mental handicap, vocational guidance, and assessment of cognitive deficits in decreasing order of popularity. The largest treatment demand was for sexual/marital problems, with phobic anxiety, addictive disorders and treatment of obesity in that order. It is not clear what, if any, involvement the doctors had with psychologists before responding and therefore what opportunity to discuss or observe a psychologist's contribution to general practice. It is also unclear whether they were able to specify the nature of the contact they would prefer, rather than responding to multiple-choice questions where the alternatives were specified.

The opinions of the general practitioners of the services provided for primary care by psychologists have been described (Blakey, 1983; Eastman and McPherson, 1982), and indicate that although welcomed by GPs, they rate a psychologist's effectiveness as low compared to other groups to whom they refer patients. This is perhaps not surprising, as Eastman and McPherson were asking GPs to rank psychologists alongside nurses, midwives, health visitors, all of whom have traditionally worked closely with doctors. The rank order of practice nurse, community nurse, health visitor, midwife, physiotherapist, community psychiatric nurse, social worker, clinical psychologist and psychiatrist, family therapist and dietician is probably in direct relation to the degree of interaction between GP and the other professional groups.

One of the important findings from the clinical studies is that although intra-subject improvements in symptoms have been reported to be maintained up to 15 months post-treatment by Ives (1979) and Koch (1979), Freeman and Button (1984) suggest that the natural history of patients with 'psychosocial' problems is that of crisis and remission, and that this must be borne in mind when using measurements of change in consultation rate as an indicator of improvement. In fact, the comparisons of a treatment and control group by Earll and Kincey (1982) found no difference at follow-up at seven months post-treatment.

It is necessary now for clinical psychologists who wish to be involved in individual clinical work with patients in general practice to direct further effort towards assessing the effects of the psychological treatments they are using. They must answer such questions as: Do these techniques have an effect on the problems presented in general practice, and is the effect greater than the changes due to the natural history of the illness? Also, does psychological treatment lead to a more rapid change than no treatment, or other treatment, and is the effect maintained over time? Only when we can assure ourselves and our medical, nursing and other colleagues that we are effective will our clinical role in primary care be confirmed.

On the other hand, our role as research workers investigating the primary care team, the nature of illness, and the interaction between patients and health professionals must continue to extend, and to bridge the gap between the theory and application of psychological knowledge.

FUTURE DIRECTIONS

It is interesting to examine the aims of a primary health care team as defined by a panel set up by the British Medical Association's Board of Science and Education (1974). These were summarized as follows:

> To encourage early presentation of problems whether for advice or help. To refer to colleagues as necessary. To support the family as the fundamental unit of the community. To educate on health matters. To gather information on epidemiology. To promote the care of the patients in all settings (home, clinic, day care). To maintain continuity of care. To facilitate communication between team members and between the team and other branches of the health services and between the team and the community.

It is clear that there is an emphasis on the promotion of health and prevention of ill-health, and this area has, as yet, received little attention from psychologists in primary care. However, the interest in the institution and support of self-help groups and the appreciation that working in primary care must involve the psychologist in looking beyond the individual to the total context of his/her behaviour may lead to further developments in this area in the future.

The problems which currently beset clinical psychologists working in primary care have been outlined by Spector (1984). He concludes that the need for careful evaluation of existing and projected roles is of paramount importance to justify the manpower resources currently deployed to primary care. Broadhurst (1977) found that approximately one in seven clinical psychologists was working with general practitioners to some extent, and it is likely that the degree of involvement has at least been maintained, if not increased, despite the several papers which have questioned the efficacy of the individual treatment role generally adopted.

How then can this continuing interest be channelled to maximum effect without reducing manpower to other areas of need? The profession is no longer expanding in the way that it was when primary care jobs were first established and new posts will not become available in the near future.

Perhaps the most satisfactory and generally acceptable format for the future is to see primary care psychology as an area of special interest within a department, with several individuals giving a sessional commitment to local health centres or practices as part of an overall plan to provide psychological services from birth to old age for a defined population. Within such a service there would be various speciality areas such as adult mental illness, psychiatric rehabilitation, child psychiatry, paediatrics, geriatric services, neuropsychology, and general medicine, with individual psychologists spending their time in one or several of these areas. It is not practical to consider 'primary care only' specialists in many places, but it is feasible to develop a primary care service in tandem with other services provided from a hospital-based department. However, some of the specialized posts which exist should be maintaind to explore alternative ways of functioning, and other psychologists should then be encouraged to incorporate these new ideas into practice.

The main requirement is to draw on expertise from other areas. Clinical psychologists will have to draw on the work of medical sociologists, social psychologists, health educators and others to realize the potential of the area. The research of our colleagues in universities and research institutes might be applied to the primary care system, to the patients who enter the system, and to how we and others deal with them within the system. Reciprocally, research psychologists must participate in more applied areas, and collaborative ventures in primary care would be of mutual interest and benefit.

As the field develops, as with all other new areas of work, clinical psychologists in training should be introduced to the ideas, practices and current research, even if placement experience is impractical. As with other areas of special interest in clinical psychology it is impossible to provide adequate training at probationary level with the multiplicity of other topics and skills encompassed in a generic training. It is clear that the psychologists who intend to pursue primary care work will require the wide range of skills and broad base of knowledge acquired from a good generic probationary training. Further, more specialized training should then be available at post-probationary level. Such training would cover all the relevant areas of research outlined earlier, including social and organizational topics related to the functioning of the primary health care team and the application of this body of knowledge in practice. Difficulties which can arise in communication between psychologists and doctors due to differences in the structure of the professions (Hetherington, 1983) and to the different expectations held about primary care psychology (Eastman and McPherson, 1982) must be explored and resolved, both at an individual level and by communication between the two professional bodies. It is important that the psychologist in primary care is experienced clinically and in areas of administration and methodology where professional interests are likely to converge.

If all these requirements can be met and if the profession so wishes, the interest in primary care from psychologists and from general practitioners can continue to develop. Time and further research will enable us to define the elements which are of optimal efficacy and incorporate these into established practice.

REFERENCES

BHAGAT, M., LEWIS, A. and SHILLITOE, R. (1979) Clinical psychologists and the primary health care team. *Update,* February, 479–488.

BLAKEY, R. (1983) General practitioners' opinion of direct clinical psychology services. *DCP Newsletter, 40,* 27–31.

BROOME, A. (1978) A psychologist's view of GPs' work. In: *Psychology and Primary Care.* Proceedings of a joint meeting of the Northern Region Branch and the Scottish Branch of the Division of Clinical Psychology of The British Psychological Society.

BRITISH MEDICAL ASSOCIATION (1974) *Primary Health Care Teams.* Report of the panel on Primary Health Care Teams, Board of Science and Education. London: British Medical Association.

BRITISH PSYCHOLOGICAL SOCIETY PROFESSIONAL AFFAIRS BOARD (1979) *Evidence to the DHSS Joint Working Group on the Primary Health Care Team.* Leicester: The British Psychological Society.

BROADHURST, A. (1977) What part does general practice play in community clinical psychology. *Bulletin of The British Psychological Society, 30,* 305–309.

BYRNE, P.S. and LONG, B.E.L. (1976) *Doctors Talking to Patients.* London: HMSO.

CLARK, D.F. (1979) The clinical psychologist in primary care. *Social Science and Medicine, 13A,* 707–713.

COUPAR, A.M. and KENNEDY, T. (1980) Running a weight control group: experiences of a psychologist and a general practitioner. *Journal of the Royal College of General Practitioners, 30,* 41–48.

DAVIDSON, A.F. (1977) Clinical psychology and general practice: a preliminary enquiry. *Bulletin of The British Psychological Society, 30,* 337–338.

EARLL, L. and KINCEY, J. (1982) Clinical psychology in general practice: a controlled trial evaluation. *Journal of The Royal College of General Practitioners, 32,* 32–37.

EASTMAN C. and McPHERSON, I. (1982) As others see us: general practitioners' perceptions of psychological problems and the relevance of clinical psychology. *British Journal of Clinical Psychology, 21,* 85–92.

FRANCE, R. and ROBSON, M. (1982) Work of the clinical psychologist in general practice: preliminary communication. *Journal of The Royal Society of Medicine, 75,* 185–189.

FREEMAN, G.K. and BUTTON, E.J. (1984) The clinical psychologist in general practice: a six-year study of consulting patterns for psychosocial problems. *Journal of The Royal College of General Practitioners, 34,* 377–380.

GASKELL, P.G. and WATSON, L.M. (1978) Trial of a self-help scheme. *Update,* March, 661–663.

GOLDBERG, E.M. and NEILL, J. (1972) *Social Work in General Practice.* London: Allen and Unwin.

GRIFFITHS, T.A. and McMILLAN, G. (in preparation) Behavioural treatment of nocturnal enuresis by a Health Visitor in general practice.

HAMBLY, K. and PAXTON, R. (1979) The use of behaviour therapy in general practice. *Update,* October, 645–648.

HETHERINGTON, R.R. (1983) Communication between doctors and psychologists. *British Journal of Medical Psychology, 83,* 99–104.

HOOD, J.E. (1979) Psychology and primary care: a plea for restraint. *Bulletin of The British Psychological Society, 32,* 422– 423.

INGHAM, J. (1982) Defining the problem. In: A.W. Clare and M. Lader (eds) *Psychiatry and General Practice.* London: Academic Press.

INGHAM, J. and MILLER, P. (1979) Symptom prevalence and severity in a general practice population. *Journal of Epidemiology and Community Health, 33(3),* 191–198.

INGHAM, J. and MILLER, P. (1982) Consulting with mild symptoms in general practice. *Social Psychiatry, 17,* 77–78.

IVES, G. (1979) Psychological treatment in general practice. *Journal of The Royal College of General Practitioners, 29,* 343–351.

JERROM, D.W.A., SIMPSON, R.J., BARBER, J.H. and PEMBERTON, D.S. (1983) General practitioners' satisfaction with a primary care clinical psychology service. *Journal of The Royal College of General Practitioners, 33,* 29–31.

JOHNSTON, M. (1978) The work of a clinical psychologist in primary care. *Journal of The Royal College of General Practitioners, 28,* 661–667.

KAT, B. (1978) Primary health care: on finding one's place in the team. *Bulletin of The British Psychological Society, 31,* 154–156.

KOCH, H.C.H. (1979) Evaluation of behaviour therapy intervention in general practice. *Journal of The Royal College of General Practitioners, 29,* 337–340.

LEY, P. (1975) What did your doctor tell you? *New Behaviour,* May, 58–61.

McALLISTER, T.A. and PHILIP, A.E. (1975) The clinical psychologist in a health centre: one year's work. *British Medical Journal, 4,* 513–514.

McPHERSON, I. and FELDMAN, M.P. (1977) A preliminary investigation of the role of the clinical psychologist in the primary care setting. *Bulletin of The British Psychological Society, 30,* 342–346.

PENDLETON, D. and HASLER, J. (1983) *Doctor–Patient Communication.* London: Academic Press.

SHEPHERD, M., COOPER, B., BROWN, A.C. and KALTON, G.W. (1966) *Psychiatric Illness in General Practice.* London: Oxford University Press.

SPECTOR, J. (1984) Clinical psychology and primary care: some ongoing dilemmas. *Bulletin of The British Psychological Society, 37,* 73–76.

TRETHOWAN, W.H. (1977) *The Role of Psychologists in the Health Services.* London: HMSO.

TREATMENT MANUALS

Anthony Turvey

Imagine for a moment a group of professionals who adequately validated self help-books and who educated consumers in their proper use. This indeed would be something new.
(Rosen, 1977, p.179)

Since Glasgow and Rosen's review (1978), the number of manuals and the range of problems treated by manual-guided therapy continues to grow. Why has there been such an increase in this approach to therapy? Perhaps most importantly, there is a strong ethos of self-help and, for emotional and behavioural problems, people seek help from a wide range of sources – books, magazine counsellors, self-help organizations – besides the health and social services. For psychologists who recognize that the number of people they see may represent only a small percentage of those they might be able to help (McPherson and Feldman, 1977), there is also a strong incentive to look at alternatives to direct therapeutic work as a possible way of meeting more of this demand. The dilemma of clinical practice, as Hawks (1981) points out, is to meet the demands of a large client population while at the same time allowing time for the detailed assessment and treatment of complex problems that will continue to need therapists' direct intervention.

Self-help treatment manuals represent an attempt to provide effective treatment for certain problems where individuals can select and apply the appropriate treatment to themselves. In their review, Glasgow and Rosen (1978) report on the efficacy of manual-based therapy for such problems as fear, smoking, weight, sexual dysfunction, lack of assertiveness, child behaviour problems, studying and physical fitness. The evidence for bibliotherapy for academic achievement, attitude change, training counsellors, marital satisfaction and self-development is discussed by Schrank and Engels (1981). Other self-help manuals have been produced for insomnia (Alperson and Bigleu, 1979), depression (Burns, 1980) and controlled drinking (Robertston and Heather, 1982). Texts for using psychological approaches generally are also available (for example, Flanders, 1976). Here I intend to look at issues in the evaluation, clinical use, and promotion of manual-based therapy and select specific manuals to illustrate these points.

Bibliotherapy can cover a wide range of uses of written material, for example, giving factual information about the problems being treated or the general nature of therapy, or using stories for discussion groups; here I am concerned with manuals describing how to use treatment techniques, with or without therapist assistance. Tews (1970) traces the history of bibliotherapy from its classical origins to the use of books in a psychoanalytical context to provide insight and catharsis. While there are case reports of the effectiveness of bibliotherapy in psychotherapy, most of the experimental evaluation has been carried out on behaviourally-based treatments. O'Farrell and Keuthen (1983) identified 124 behavioural self-help manuals where some evaluation had been carried out, but this represents only a small proportion of all the treatment manuals available. (Kimbrell 1975 identified more than a hundred books on dieting alone.)

ISSUES IN EVALUATION

While many of the issues in evaluating any treatment approach are relevant to the assessment of manuals, these manuals also present some special points for consideration.

1. Evaluating treatment in the way it is intended to be used

A manual may be written for use as an entirely self-contained treatment needing or requiring some level of therapist involvement. Glasgow and Rosen (1978) distinguished between *self-administered* therapy (no therapist contact), *minimal contact*) therapist acts as a support for primarily manual-guided therapy), and *therapist-administered* treatment (therapist sees client regularly and elaborates on the material in the manual). Assuming that a manual shown to be effective under one condition will be effective under others ignores possible problems of generalization (Stokes and Baer, 1977). An example of this is Burns (1980), where the cover of the American edition describes the book as 'the clinically proven, drug free treatment for depression'. While the treatment it describes – Beck's Cognitive Therapy – has been shown to be effective in therapist-administered treatment (for example, Rush *et al.*, 1977; Blackburn *et al.*, 1981) there is no evidence yet for its effectiveness in a self-administered form. It is only later in the book (p.24) that the author suggests who should seek professional help with treatment.* As well as the specific treatment format, the general context in which the manual is given

---

* While the cover is unfortunately misleading, I have found this book extremely useful and would recommend its use as an aid in therapist-administered cognitive therapy.

may influence its effectiveness. Is the same self-help book, obtained from a high street shop, recommended by a magazine counsellor, or psychologist specializing in that particular field likely to generate similar expectancies of efficacy and compliance to the suggested treatment? Similarly, when a manual is used under therapist supervision, its perceived usefulness may be influenced by whether or not the therapist is seen as having expertise with the particular problem being treated. Robertson and Heather (1982) and Mathews *et al.* (1981) have each developed manuals for different problems (problem drinking and agoraphobia) which are used in different formats – self-administered and therapist-aided – and provide examples of evaluating the manual in the way it is intended to be used. The evaluation of self-help material bought from high street shops raises some difficult problems in evaluation, since any attempt at assessing progress may be much more intrusive than when the clients already have some therapist contact and so may influence compliance and outcome.

2. Understanding the manual

O'Farrell and Keuthen (1983) reviewed the readability of 124 behavioural treatment manuals using the Flesch formula (Flesch, 1948) and found that 35 per cent of the US population would find many of the manuals too difficult to read comfortably.

Ley *et al.* (1976) showed that increasing the readability of instruction leaflets increased compliance to medication. Psychological treatment manuals may include a number of treatment techniques that are more difficult to use correctly than, say, taking medication as prescribed, so the importance of presenting this material as clearly as possible cannot be underestimated. Besides word length – the measure the Flesch formula is based on – the layout of the booklet, categorization of information, repetition of key advice and use of diagrams may all help understanding (Hartley, 1984). While there may be limits in presenting certain treatment approaches as simply as possible, Dow (1980) was able to produce four manuals for sexual problems that could be understood by 75 per cent of the population and Heather *et al.* (in press) report 80 per cent understanding for their controlled drinking booklet. O'Farrell and Keuthen (1983) note that while the American Psychological Association recommended the reading level of self-help manuals be provided when they are distributed to the public, this has yet to be implemented widely.

3. Type of controls in evaluation

In outcome research it is important that different conditions differ only on one variable (Dow, 1982), so it is necessary, for example, to decide whether to assess the same manual under different levels of therapist involvement, different manuals under the same conditions, or to present the same information in different mediums (for example, O'Dell *et al.*, 1982, compared an audiotaped with a written manual for improving parenting skills).

A control group to assess whether any changes are due to the specific instructions in the manual or other factors is necessary. Heather *et al.* (in press) compared their controlled drinking programme with a Health Education Council booklet describing facts about drinking and its dangers to health. With self-administered therapy it is possible for the assessor to be completely blind as to the treatment being given by giving the manuals in sealed envelopes.

4. Subject attrition

Glasgow and Rosen (1978) noted that as many as 50 per cent of subjects starting self-administered desensitization dropped out during treatment, and Heather *et al.* (in press) found only 31 per cent of those who responded to an advertisement for treatment completed the assessment measures. Knowing what proportion of the initial sample start and complete treatment is important for evaluating cost-effectiveness, and identifying why clients do not begin, or else drop out of therapy may be important when trying to improve the overall success of treatment.

5. Process measures

Detailed process measures may help identify how well clients use manual-based therapy and for what reasons they drop out of therapy. However, regular assessment, particularly under self-administered or minimal contact treatments, may influence treatment response.

6. Single treatment or multiple component manuals

Many manuals contain a number of treatment techniques, on the grounds, perhaps, that there will be something suitable for each individual. Detrimental effects of such an approach might be that a longer manual becomes less comprehensible, or people may be less likely to try a number of alternatives (and then follow what they find most useful) than follow one set of instructions. Identification of the crucial variables of a treatment package is of much importance in bibliotherapy, as in any other therapy.

7. Follow-up period

Glasgow and Rosen (1978) recommend a six-month follow-up period as a minimum. The importance of follow-up is well recognized, but is particularly necessary for treatments where the goal of therapist contact maybe to teach skills that the client continues to use after the therapist contact ends.

Mathews *et al.* (1981) found with their manual for agoraphobia that 'about half as much change took place after treatment as during its course' (p.23), and this change over follow-up differed from earlier therapist-directed treatment. In addition, Jannoun *et al.* (1980) also found with agoraphobia that the rate of improvement differed with programmed practice or problem-solving treatment manuals.

8. Cost-effectiveness

Treatment manuals, particularly under self-administered, minimal contact, or when used by other agencies, would appear to represent a great saving in psychologists' time. Also, psychological treatment might be offered – as self-administered manuals – for problems that might not be judged severe enough to be referred for individual therapy, even though effective treatment is available (for example, Frankel and Merbaum, 1982).

Evaluation of cost-effectiveness needs to include assessment of behavioural goal attainment and duration of therapy (discussed in detail by Dow, 1982). Subject attrition and the possible inappropriate use of manuals are other factors to be considered. It may be tempting to over-simplify individuals' problems and suggest self-administered therapy when a treatment manual is available rather than carry out adequate assessment prior to offering treatment.

9. Subject characteristics

Schalhow (1975) showed that subjects with higher internal locus of control scores tended to do best in following a self-administered treatment. Dow (1982) cites further evidence to suggest that personality factors may influence response to self-administered treatment; clearly these factors need to be assessed in relation to appropriate selection of subjects for therapist or self-administered treatment. Since some manuals involve the patient's spouse in treatment (for example, Cobb *et al.,* 1984), the personality of the partner and relationship variables may also be influential in determining treatment outcome.

Jeffrey and Gerber (1982) found that when subjects were offered a choice of treatment for obesity (group therapy or self-administered manual) their choice was related to subject characteristics. For those who actively partici-pated in the treatment they chose, there was no difference in effectiveness of treatment.

Being able to choose a treatment approach may have an influence on satisfaction with treatment and also increase compliance to that treatment. Bornstein and Rychtarik (1983) discuss the assessment of consumer satis-faction in detail and report one study (p.195) where in the bibliotherapy condition for weight reduction subjects felt 'angry and lonely'.

CRITERIA FOR A TREATMENT MANUAL

As well as the factors to be considered in evaluating treatment manuals, it may also be useful to look at what should be considered when writing a treatment manual.

1. Ensure that the manual is easily understood by a large proportion of the public (or of the client group it is intended for) and give some indication of the reading level or schooling required for understanding.

2. Organize the material clearly in labelled sections, with the main points summarized and repeated as often as possible. Longer manuals should have a contents or index page (see also Ley, 1977).

3. At the start, give a clear description of the problem the manual is intended for and how this can be distinguished from any other, similar problem.

4. Describe any factors that indicate that people with this problem should not follow the treatment described in the manual: give advice about how to obtain more appropriate help (for example, Miller and Boca, 1983; Heather *et al.,* in press).

5. Briefly describe any factors related to outcome, and indicate rate of progress with treatment (if known) to help generate realistic expectancies.

6. Summarize, or give references to, any treatment reports (for example, Carruthers and Murray, 1976).

7. Include baseline diaries or other assessment measures, such as forms for clients to record their treatment goals and progress on.

8. Include checks on understanding – regular summary pages, multiple-choice questions (for example, Mathews *et al.,* 1981) or a questionnaire that the client, having read the manual, should be able to answer before starting therapy.

9. Provide background information about the nature of the problem – prevalence, common features, etc., and correct common misconceptions about the problem.

10. Provide a rationale for the treatment being suggested and a description of what factors may be maintaining the problem (Sloane *et al.,* 1975 found

this to be rated as an important part of treatment by subjects in their study p.206).

11. Indicate how much time treatment will take, with suggestions for fitting this into people's lifestyle.

12. Include techniques that may help to increase compliance with the treatment (though check that what you are suggesting does have a positive effect in the type of therapy being used; for example, Barrera and Rosen, 1977).

13. Where appropriate have a section for significant others to increase their understanding of the problem and ideas for how they can help: also, alert them to any behaviours they may carry out that may be maintaining the person's problems. Mathews *et al.* (1981) provide a manual for the agoraphobic's spouse, although Cobb *et al.* (1984) did not find spouse involvement to be necessary.

14. Include a section on long-term maintenance of progress, particularly to help anticipate situations that may be difficult to deal with in the future.

15. Deal with setbacks. Help the person to accept that setbacks can occur, to work out what is causing them and to resume progress. Since some people may fail with self-help manuals it may be useful to include a brief section recognizing this, and suggesting that, rather than give up with psychological treatment, they seek assistance to re-assess their difficulties and possibly carry out a more appropriate treatment with a greater degree of help.

Not all of these factors will be equally important for different problems or level of therapist involvement.

USING MANUALS IN CLINICAL PRACTICE

Psychologists may use bibliotherapy in their own casework. Having assessed the individual, the first decision is whether their problems might be treatable by manual-based therapy. A choice then has to be made regarding the amount of therapist involvement needed. With self-administered therapy, acceptance of the treatment plan by the client and some arrangement for contact, if problems arise, may be the limit of therapist contact. With minimal therapist intervention the therapist's goal is primarily to help the clients to use the treatment manual to work on their own problems. As the client progresses in therapy, the therapist should point them to relevant sections of the manual rather than immediately step in with specific advice, as this may lead to problems of maintenance when the therapist ends his contact. Some people may find it difficult to maintain progress after therapist contact ends, particularly if unexpected problems or additional stresses occur, and the therapist should have a way of providing further advice, if necessary, without fostering dependency.

Therapists may also use manuals as an aid to the direct treatment they are providing. Manuals might be given at the end of treatment to enhance maintenance of treatment. However, since the use of manuals is a skill to be learnt, it may be better to integrate the material into treatment from the start so the therapist can check that it is understood, and that the techniques in the manual have been practised in the sessions. A more flexible approach can be used and the therapist can select articles, or sections from different manuals to give to the client at relevant points as therapy progresses. When giving reading as homework it is important at the next session to go over this with the client, to ensure the material has been understood and also to discuss its relevance to the problems.

Another way in which psychologists may be involved in bibliotherapy is in providing advice and materials for others to use. The main advantage here is that the psychologist may be providing treatment for more people than he could hope to see himself – given that even self-administered treatment should be preceded by assessment. One possible problem, however, is that bibliotherapy might be used inappropriately by the other therapists unless they are aware of the factors determining the effective use of that particular manual. However, advice might be provided in a therapist guide covering such topics as selecting appropriate clients, explaining the treatment approach to them, dealing with any common problems people have in using the manual and, if the person is not able to use if effectively, what other help can be offered.

It is important to ensure that any people intending to carry out psychological therapies should be aware of the time and skills that are needed. For example, when using relaxation techniques it may be tempting for therapists to give clients taped instructions without any practice sessions – to save time – although the evidence suggests that practice is necessary for people who are clinically anxious (Borkovec and Sides, 1979). A longer-term goal when giving away treatment approaches for others to use is the need to keep them up to date with any developments, so such skill transmission might best be done where the psychologist has a clearly agreed role for support and consultation.

INFLUENCING THE CONSUMER

Clients seen by psychologists and provided with 'adequately validated self-help books' (Rosen, 1977) will continue to be only a small proportion of the people using self-help material. How then can the second part of Rosen's wish

– consumers educated in the selection and use of bibliotherapy – be achieved? Passing on skills and effective manuals to others will help, but there is also a need to try and influence the consumers, who often look for self-help material before consulting others. Helping the person who may never come into direct contact with a psychologist select the most effective treatment manual presents a challenge that cannot be ignored.

At the moment someone walking into a high street bookshop may be over-influenced by factors such as prominence of the book on the shelves or in display, jacket design, author's credentials, and price. Even someone looking for evidence of the effectiveness of what they are buying may find it difficult to obtain this at the time they are choosing what book to buy. As individuals, psychologists can seek to guide consumers by the advice they give in the general press and on radio, etc. They may also exercise influence through consumers' organizations (which are taking an increasing interest in health care, for example, Rudinger, 1982), self-help groups, and other advisors by telling them about the most effective treatments available. Also, they have an important contribution to make through research, both in developing new treatment manuals and in evaluating the claims made for those already available. When publishing material it may be possible to include, as an appendix, a summary of research on its effectiveness (for example, Carruthers and Murray, 1976), so that the purchaser can look at this before deciding whether to buy the book. Rosen (1978) notes that most reviews of treatment manuals contain the reviewers' impression of the booklet rather than an empirical evaluation and it will probably be some time yet before all self-help texts are evaluated before they are published.

As a professional body, The British Psychological Society might also recommend self-help materials. One level of endorsement might be given for meeting such criteria as level of readability and consistency with effective psychological treatments, etc. A second level of endorsement could be given for meeting a more stringent criterion of demonstrated effectiveness in independent outcome studies. What would be the advantage of such a system? Allowing the publishers to advertise on the cover an imprimatur such as 'recommended by The British Psychological Society' might influence the purchaser to select the most effective books and reward the publisher with increased sales, as well as stimulating the amount of research carried out prior to publication. Goldiamond (1977) raised legal problems that might be involved in using a 'seal of approval' but recognized that other professions such as the American Dental Association did recommend certain products in this way. In the UK organizations such as the AA (Automobile Association, 1982, p.19) have a similar scheme, and while the issues in evaluating psychological treatment may be more complex than for car products the principle is similar. Lists of recommended booklets could also be made available to people who offer advice.

CONCLUSIONS AND FUTURE DEVELOPMENTS

One major difference between a manual selected by a therapist and one that is self-selected is that the therapist may have much more information to guide his choice of therapy. For those people treating themselves it might be useful to develop self-administered assessment schemes to help them identify their problems correctly. Examples of such an approach are already available in family health books (for example, Smith, 1982). With increasing developments in computer technology, it might be possible for interactive assessment programmes to be available at health centres, or via teletext services to help people identify their problems and decide on appropriate action. This is not to suggest that all assessment and treatment can be standardized, but that screening out people who only need self-administered or minimal contact therapy will allow the limited psychological services to concentrate on problems that need intensive evaluation and intervention (*cf.* Hawks, 1981).

A second possible use of developing technology is that of word-processing programmes. With this, a therapist could quickly modify a standard treatment manual prototype to an individualized handout, with a description of the origin and maintenance of the problem, specific goals, and combination of treatment techniques for the individual. For example, a wide range of treatment approaches may be used in the treatment of anxiety (relaxation, graded exposure, distraction, social skills training, cognitive therapy, etc.) If all possible treatment techniques were included in one manual, with background information, it would be a large document. Instead, it would be possible to select from a series of files the material most appropriate for the individual and to be printed out as a personalized booklet. Alternative forms for each treatment technique could also be prepared, so a choice could be made between a very detailed description for the methods thought to be most important for that individual, with briefer notes for less important skills, or for different reading levels.

The development of bibliotherapy may also be important for therapy generally. It can provide a minimal contact condition with which other treatments can be compared. Next, the results of research into manual-based therapy may, like any other treatment, contribute to understanding of basic processes in therapy. In the Jannoun *et al.* (1980) study one of the two therapists was as effective in treating agoraphobia with a problem-solving manual condition that did not emhasize leaving the house at all as he was with the graded exposure manual. While this does not exclude the possibility that the problem-solving group decided to adopt graded practice of their own accord, there was no increase on their diary record of time spent outside of the house in this condition (*see* Mathews *et al.,* 1981, p.154–155, for full discussion). While this finding needs to be replicated it does support the contention that exposure may not be the only factor necessary for fear reduction (de Silva and Rachman, 1981). Self-administered therapy may also provide a way of separating the effects of the specific treatment techniques from the general influences of therapist contact.

Why should we also be concerned about the promotion of effective self-help material for people who might never come into direct contact with psychology services anyway?

Firstly, because the public is increasingly concerned – quite rightly – about effectiveness, and relevant information should be as freely available as possible. Next, while psychologists can only see a proportion of those people they may be able to help, it is unrealistic to expect expansion of services to be able to meet such a demand completely (Hawks, 1981). A large proportion of psychological therapy will continue to be given by non-psychologists and it is important to provide them with information about the usefulness or otherwise of treatment manuals. If the results of such research are not made as widely available as the manuals themselves, then we may be doing ourselves a disservice. Failure to evaluate self-help therapy and to moderate over-optimistic claims for it may lead to a public reaction against it similar to the response to benzodiazepines. Initially hailed as a cure for many problems, inappropriate use in many cases, and increasing evidence of their questionable effectiveness (McCormick *et al.*, 1983) have turned the public against not just them, but also in some cases against other medical treatments, and the medical profession generally. Could unfulfilled expectations of psychological treatment, which many people may come into contact with only through self-help books, lead to a similar general rejection of psychological treatment which may, in many instances, be highly effective? To avoid such a possibility it is important to devote time and energy to the active promotion of appropriate and effective forms of bibliotherapy, and to increase users' awareness of material that is of proven value.

REFERENCES

ALPERSON, J. and BIGLEU, A. (1979) Self-administered treatment of sleep onset insomnia and the importance of age. *Behaviour Therapy, 18*, 347–356.

AUTOMOBILE ASSOCIATION (1982) *1982/83 Handbook.* Basingstoke: AA Publications.

BARRERA, M. and ROSEN, G.M. (1977) Detrimental effects of a self-reward contracting program on subjects involvement in self-administered desensitization. *Journal of Consulting and Clinical Psychology, 45*, 1180–1181.

BLACKBURN, I.M., BISHOP, S., GLEN, A.I.M., WHALLEY, L.J. and CHRISTIE, J.E. (1981) The efficacy of cognitive therapy in depression: a treatment trial using cognitive therapy and pharmacotherapy, each alone and in combination. *British Journal of Psychiatry, 139*, 181–189.

BORKOVEC, T.D. and SIDES, J.K. (1979) Critical procedure variables related to the psychological effects of progressive relaxation – a review. *Behaviour Research and Therapy, 17*, 119–121.

BORNSTEIN, P.H. and RYCHTAVIK, R.G. (1983) Consumer satisfaction in adult behaviour therapy: procedures, problems and future perspectives. *Behaviour Therapy 14*, 191–208.

BURNS, D.D. (1980) *Feeling Good. The New Mood Therapy.* New York: New American Library.

CARRUTHERS, M. and MURRAY, A. (1976) *F-40 Fitness on Forty Minutes a Week.* London: Futura Publications.

COBB, J.P., MATHEWS, A.M., CHILDS-CLARKE, A. and BLOWERS, C.M. (1984) The spouse as a co-therapist in the treatment of agoraphobia. *British Journal of Psychiatry, 144*, 282–287.

DOW, M.G.T. (1980) A comparative evaluation of 'self-help' and conventional Masters and Johnson treatments for sexual dysfunction. Paper presented at The British Psychological Society Conference 1980, Aberdeen.

DOW, M.G.T. (1982) Behavioural Bibliotherapy: theoretical and methodological issues in outcome research into self-help programs. In: C.J. Main (ed.) *Clinical Psychology and Medicine.* New York: Plenum.

FLANDERS, J.P. (1976) *Practical Psychology.* New York: Harper and Row.

FRANKEL, M.J. and MERBAUM, M. (1982) Effects of therapist contact and a self control manual on nailbiting reduction. *Behaviour Therapy, 13*, 125–129.

FLESCH, R. (1948) A new readability yardstick. *Journal of Applied Pschology, 32*, 221–233.

GLASGOW, R.E. and ROSEN, G.M. (1978) Behavioural bibliotherapy: a review of self-help therapy manuals. *Psychological Bulletin, 85*, 1–23.

GOLDIAMOND, I. (1976) Singling out self-administered behaviour therapies for professional overview. *American Psychologist, 31*, 142–147.

HARTLEY, J. (1984) Current research on text design. *Bulletin of The British Psychological Society, 37*, 116–119.

HAWKS, D. (1981) The dilemma of clinical practice – surviving as a clinical psychologist in the primary care setting. In: I. McPherson and A. Sutton (eds) *Reconstructing Psychological Practice.* London: Croom Helm.

HEATHER, N., WHITTON, B. and ROBERTSON, I. (in press) Evaluation of a self-help manual for media-recruited problem drinkers: six month follow-up results.

HESSAYON, A. (1983) *A Patient's Guide to the National Health Service.* London: Consumers' Association/Hodder and Stoughton.

JANNOUN, L., MUNBY, M., CATALAN, J. and GELDER, N. (1980) A home based treatment program for agoraphobia: replication and controlled evaluation. *Behaviour Therapy, 11*, 294–305.

JEFFREY, R.W. and GERBER, W.M. (1982) Group and correspondence treatments for weight reduction used in the multiple risk factor intervention trial. *Behaviour Therapy, 13*, 24-30.

KIMBRELL, G.M. (1975) Note: diet dilettantism. *Psychological Record, 25*, 273–274.

LEY, P. (1977) Psychological studies of doctor–patient communication. In: S. Rachman (ed.) *Contributions to Medical Psychology, Volume 1.* Oxford: Pergamon.

LEY, P., JAIN, U.K. and SKILBECK, C.E. (1976) A method for decreasing patients' medication errors. *Psychological Medicine, 6*, 599–601.

MATHEWS, A.M., GELDER, M.G., JOHNSTON, D.W. (1981) *Agoraphobia. Nature and Treatment.* London: Tavistock.

McCORMICK, J., EAST OF IRELAND FACULTY OF THE RCGP AND THE DEPARTMENT OF COMMUNITY HEALTH, UNIVERSITY OF DUBLIN (1983) A double blind randomized control trial of diazepam. *Journal of The Royal College of General Practitioners, 33*, 635–636.

McPHERSON, I.G. and FELDMAN, M.P. (1977) A preliminary investigation of the role of the clinical psychologist in the primary care setting. *Bulletin of The British Psychological Society, 30,* 342–346.

MILLER, W.R. and BOCA, L.M. (1983) Two year follow up of bibliotherapy and therapist-directed controlled drinking training for problem drinkers. *Behaviour Therapy, 14,* 441–448.

O'DELL, S.L., O'QUINN, J.A., ALFORD, B.A., O'BRIANT, A.L., BRADLYN, A.S. and GIEBENHAIN, J.E. (1982) Predicting the acquisition of parenting skills via four training methods. *Behaviour Therapy, 13,* 194–208.

O'FARRELL, T.J. and KEUTHEN, N.J. (1983) Readability of behaviour therapy self-help manuals. *Behaviour Therapy, 14,* 449– 454.

ROBERTSON, I. and HEATHER, N. (1982) *So You Want to Cut Down Your Drinking?* Edinburgh: Scottish Health Education Group.

ROSEN, G.M. (1976) The development and use of non-prescription behaviour therapies. *American Psychologist, 31,* 139–141.

ROSEN, G.M. (1977) Non-prescription behaviour therapies and other self-help treatments: a reply to Goldiamond. *American Psychologist, 32,* 178–179.

ROSEN, G.M. (1978) Suggestions for an editorial policy on the review of self-help treatment books. *Behaviour Therapy, 9,* 960.

RUDINGER, E. (ed.) (1982) *Living With Stress.* Consumers' Association.

RUSH, A.J., BECK, A.T., KOVACS, M. and HOLLON, S.D. (1977) Comparative efficacy of cognitive therapy and pharmacotherapy in the treatment of depressed outpatients. *Cognitive Therapy and Research, 1,* 17–37.

SCHALHOW, J.R. (1975) Locus of control and success at self-modification. *Behaviour Therapy, 6,* 667–671.

SCHRANK, F.A. and ENGELS, D.W. (1981) Bibliotherapy as a counselling adjunct: research findings. *Personnel and Guidance Journal, 60,* 143–147.

SILVA, P. de and RACHMAN, S.J. (1981) Is exposure a necessary condition for fear-reduction. *Behaviour Research and Therapy, 19,* 227–232.

SLOANE, R.B., STAPLES, F.R., CRISTOL, A.H., YORKSTON, N.J. and WHIPPLE, K. (1975) *Psychotherapy versus Behaviour Therapy.* Cambridge: Mass.: Harvard University Press.

SMITH, T. (ed.) (1982) *The Macmillan Guide to Family Health.* London: Macmillan.

STOKES, T.F. and BAER, D.M. (1977) An implicit technology of generalization. *Journal of Applied Behaviour Analysis, 18,* 349–367.

TEWS, R.M. (1970) Progress in bibliotherapy. In: M.J. Voight (ed.) *Advances in Librarianship, Volume 1.* New York: Academic Press.

PSYCHOLOGY AND THE PLANNING OF HEALTH SERVICES

Bernard Kat

The National Health Service is a large and complex organization with well-defined procedures for developing the services it provides. After an overview of these procedures, this chapter discusses the issues involved in the planning of clinical psychology services. Some broader psychological aspects of planning health services are then considered.

PLANNING IN THE NATIONAL HEALTH SERVICE

The government's policies and priorities in health care

The National Health Service is the responsibility of the Secretary of State for Social Services, the Secretary of State for Scotland, the Secretary of State for Wales, and the Secretary of State for Northern Ireland, in each country respectively. In 1981, the National Health Service in England was providing health care for nearly 46.5 million people. In order to do so it was spending £11,375 million, approximately 5.5 per cent of the national gross domestic product. It employed over 800,000 people in both hospital and community settings.

The organization of this vast undertaking has inevitably been the subject of much review and change. In 1982 the local organization and administration of the hospital and community health services in England became the responsibility of 14 Regional Health Authorities, 192 District Health Authorities and the 9 Special Health Authorities, which administer the postgraduate teaching hospitals.

The overall pattern of service provided by the NHS is not just the sum total of the individual decisions of all the separate health authorities. Each must make its decisions within the context of national policies and priorities. The most recent statement of these policies was published in 1981 in the form of a handbook for the Chairmen and members of the new District Health

247

Authorities which were then being set up. Entitled 'Care in Action' (DHSS, 1981) the handbook reviews the government's priorities across the whole field of health and personal social services. High priority is given both to the prevention of ill-health and to the better provision of the so-called 'Cinderella' services for people who are mentally ill or handicapped, and those who are elderly.

With regard to the statutory services, the Secretary of State said that he:

> expects authorities to give priority to the further development of services, both statutory and voluntary, for the needs, as locally assessed, of the following priority groups.
>
> (a) Elderly people, especially the most vulnerable and frail. The number of people over 75 is increasing and those who need care have often been provided with unacceptably low standards of service, particularly in some aspects of long-term care.
>
> (b) Mentally ill people. This group is frequently provided with services of inadequate standard and services need developing in more accessible facilities.
>
> (c) Mentally handicapped people. This group also is often not provided with services of adequate standard and many services need developing in more appropriate locations and on a different model.
>
> (d) Physically and sensorily handicapped people. Services to meet the needs of this group are frequently inadequate.

It will be noted that these are all groups of patients with whose care clinical psychologists have traditionally been involved.

The Secretary of State also indicated that he:

> expects attention to be given to the further development, in accordance with local assessment of requirements, of the following *priority services.*
>
> (a) Maternity services and neonatal care. The aim is to reduce further the number of perinatal deaths and handicaps.
>
> (b) Primary care services. These are effective in many parts of the country but the object should be to raise standards elsewhere.
>
> (c) Services related to the care of young children at risk and to the care and treatment of juvenile offenders. As the number of young children increases the emphasis should be on social and health services needed to protect those most at risk, and on services which, by dealing with youngsters in the community, can make a major contribution to the maintenance of law and order.

It continued to be a major policy objective

> to foster and develop community care for the main client groups – elderly, mentally ill, mentally handicapped and disabled people, and children – as well as for the special and smaller groups such as alcoholics...the specific objectives of community care policies are different for the different client groups, but the general aim is to maintain a person's link with family and friends and normal life, and to offer the support that meets his or her particular needs.

These overall objectives are given additional weight by annual guidelines, such as those published in HC(84)2 in January 1984 (DHSS, 1984).

> Ministers wish to see authorities place an early emphasis on the development of services for elderly people – assessment, rehabilitation, longer-stay and community – and the development generally of community based services, but especially those for people with mental handicap or mental illness. Within the acute sector, there is a special need to develop services for renal failure, coronary artery surgery, joint replacement and bone marrow transplantation. Specific targets will be set for renal failure services in discussion with Regional Health Authorities.

The government not only defines the broad policies which govern development in the NHS, it also determines the method for allocating the resources to carry out those developments. The basic principles are set out in 'Sharing Resources for Health in England: the Report of the Resource Allocation Working Party' (DHSS, 1976). An attempt is made to match the amount of money each region gets to run its services (its revenue allocation) to the need for services in that region. Need is estimated by means of a combination of indirect measures. Each region's share of the total NHS budget is calculated by means of a formula which incorporates the size and age/sex structure of the region's population, its standardized mortality ratios (SMRs), standardized fertility rates, and patient flows across the regional boundaries. Additional amounts are given in recognition of the extra costs incurred by teaching districts within the region. Some Regional Health Authorities use the same principles in deciding how much money to allocate to each District Health Authority in the region.

The RAWP approach has been criticised. For example, SMRs, which are based on deaths, do not provide a satisfactory indicator of morbidity (illness), especially given the changing pattern of ill-health in the community. However, routine data on morbidity has often been criticised on grounds of incompleteness and inaccuracy.

Other approaches to defining need have been explored. Acheson (1978) suggests that it should be defined in relation to the procedures available to meet it and the resources available to permit those procedures to be used.

The government's control of resources allows it to introduce incentives to concentrate on particular kinds of development. Thus there are special funds available for community care projects jointly planned between the Health and Social Services (DHSS, 1983) and projects focusing on the needs of deprived inner city areas, to mention but two examples.

The NHS planning system

Within this overall framework, each District Health Authority has to decide what hospitals, other health facilities, staff and equipment are needed in their district. The procedure governing the decision-making process is the NHS planning system and it is described in HC(82)6 (DHSS, 1982) with some modifications in HC(84)2 (DHSS, 1984).

The system has three components. Every five years, authorities must undertake a comprehensive review of all their services and formulate a *strategic plan* covering a forward period of 10 years. The strategic plan is seen as a snapshot of the continuous process of research and evaluation which results in long-term goals and policy decisions.

Every year, authorities must prepare and publish an *Annual Programme* setting out their proposals for carrying forward their district strategy over the next two financial years. The Annual Programme is a statement of the decisions which are about to be expressed as financial estimates, budgets and operational targets.

Each year each District Health Authority meets its Regional Health Authority and each Regional Health Authority meets Ministers at the DHSS for an *Annual Planning Review*. These reviews provide an element of accountability in the system.

Where do the plans come from? Each DHA will establish a number of district planning teams composed mainly of senior officers and professional staff of the authority, each team having the task of developing plans for particular client groups or services. The work such planning teams need to undertake has been described in a number of places, for example, Health Advisory Service (1982) and Hunt (1983). Clinical psychologists, particularly those in the more senior grades, are often, but not invariably, members of district planning teams, and thus have an opportunity to make a distinctive psychological contribution to the planning process.

Data for planning purposes

Epidemiologists and planners have developed methods and terminology applicable to their task.

Because they are concerned with the needs and characteristics of populations the data they use are often either proportions or rates. Disorders or illnesses which occur in an unusually high proportion or at a higher rate than usual may become the subject of special investigations. Proportions are usually expressed in terms of a standard size of population, such as 1,000 or 100,000 persons. Percentages could be used but would give rise to awkward numbers – compare the ease of talking about a disorder which occurs in 25 per 100,000 population with talking about one which occurs in 0.025 per cent of the population. Rates are another common form of data, since the frequencies with which various events occur – births, deaths, admission to hospital, etc. – are important. Typically, a rate is expressed as the number of events in the standard population in a specified unit of time, such as a year.

The *prevalence* of a disorder is the *proportion* of the population who suffer from the disorder at a particular moment in time (the point prevalence), or during the course of a particular period of time (the period prevalence). The *incidence* of a disorder is the *rate* at which new cases of the disorder occur. It is usually expressed as the proportion of the population who develop the disorder in the course of a year.

Incidence and prevalence data are used to help judge the needs of the population. Another kind of data, also expressed in terms of a standard size population, refers to the quantity of services provided. These data are called *norms*. Authorities will ask themselves 'are we very badly off for this; not too badly off for that?' Some sense of standards is required. Not uncommonly reference is made to norms. Comparison with a norm therefore provides a rough and ready form of service evaluation.

The following table, taken from the White Paper 'Better Services for the Mentally Ill' (Cmnd. 6233) illustrates some norms for provision for the mentally ill.

Table 1. Rates per 100,000 population

	Facility	Beds	Day places
Hospital services	District general hospital psychiatric unit	50	65
	Accommodation for the elderly severely mentally infirm	30–40	25–40
	Units for the 'new' long stay	*	
Local authority services	Hostels	4–6	
	Long-stay accommodation	15–24	
	Day centres		60

*Still to be determined

Taking the above example, a typical health district with a population of 250,000 which has significantly less than 60 day places for the elderly severely mentally infirm will consider whether the services that it is providing are adequate.

However, the existence of norms can have a stultifying effect on thought.

They tend to focus people's attention on the exact size of the population to be served and whether the number of beds or day places which can therefore be justified by reference to the norm are too great or too few. Attention is not directed towards creative consideration of the kind of service, or the characteristic strengths and preferences of the local population.

Since norms are nonetheless still widely used, it is worth noting that there are several different types, and that norms are based on assumptions which may not be appropriate to a particular application (DHSS, 1978).

A norm may refer to:

- the 'ideal service', in other words a long-term target.
- a policy – the level of provision desired by a certain date and which it is intended to reach.
- a minimum standard – the level below which provision must not fall.
- the 'good practice' norm – typically, the average level of provision across the country as a whole.
- 'if then' norms – if the workload is x cases and staff can handle y cases a day, then there should be z staff.
- the Whitley norm – for example, a psychology department with at least two senior grade psychologists warrants a head of department graded at top grade.

Adding the financial dimension to planning gives yet another set of issues and associated figures or 'indicators'. Fenton Lewis and Modle (1982) propose that indicators should be categorized into one of two groups, depending on the elements of an input/output model to which they refer:

$$input \longrightarrow activity \longrightarrow output$$

Stage 1 indicators are those used to compare the relative efficiency of two activities (treatments, methods of management, etc.). Input refers to the resources which produced the planned activity. The ratio of activity to input gives a measure or indicator of the unit cost of the activity, and this can be used as the basis for comparisons of two comparable activities. In other words, the activities being compared must be known to be identical in quality, that is, they confer similar benefits on the patients.

Whether they are indeed similar in quality may be determined by the use of Stage 2 indicators, which relate output to activity.

Activity A may be more efficient than activity B in the sense of having lower unit cost (Stage 1 indicator). However, if activity B is more effective than activity A in the sense of producing the desired output more frequently or more reliably (Stage 2 indicator), then the comparison of A with B in terms of efficiency will be invalidated. They are not identical activities in terms of their benefit to the patient. Of course, the activities in question must be known to produce the output predicted – the effect on the patients must be due to the treatment, not placebo effects, for example.

Fenton Lewis and Modle also propose a distinction between output measures and outcome measures.

> An *output* measure implies a causal relationship between the output and the activity related to it. Furthermore, it is important to measure only output that is causably related in this way. Often, of course, it is not possible to claim a causal relationship; in such a case we would define the *outcome* measure as the total change seen (in the individual patient or in the population) that appears to have some causal relation to the activity but where the extent of it is unknown or at best only partial.

For example, one might consider the activity consisting of a psychologist seeing patients at a health centre. The input would be the cost to the NHS of the psychologist's time, travel, additional training, etc. The *outcome* might well be a certain number of patients whose condition improved. Whether their improvement was the *output* of the psychologist's sessions might still remain in question, unless the activity was part of a clinical trial to demonstrate its effectiveness.

A wide range of methods for relating costs and outcomes (defined generally) have been developed:

Cost utility analysis contrasts estimates of the cost of different treatment options to estimates of the outcomes that would result from implementing those options;

Cost benefit analysis contrasts the monetary costs of a particular treatment programme to the monetary value of treatment outcomes referred to as the benefits;

Cost-effectiveness analysis contrasts the monetary costs of a particular treatment programme to *non*-monetary measures of outcome;

Cost accounting refers to comparisons based on treatment costs alone, with no outcome measures taken into account. The interested reader should consult Yates (1980) for details.

THE PLANNING OF PSYCHOLOGY SERVICES

Clinical psychology within the system

Many District Health Authorities have appointed a district psychologist, one of whose jobs it is to formulate plans for the development of the psychology services. The district psychologist will do this on the basis of his or her own judgements and in consultation with colleagues. If the district has organized its services in accordance with the recommendations of the Trethowan Report (DHSS, 1977), each of a number of different fields of work may have a senior psychologist responsible for making recommendations concerning the development of that section of the service.

But clinical psychology services are not planned and developed in the abstract. Indeed, they normally develop only as an element of a much larger development such as the opening of a day hospital for the elderly, or the creation of a community based team for the support of the mentally handicapped. The plans for the psychology service will be part of the authority's Annual Programmes and Strategic Plan.

Trethowan on manpower

How many clinical psychologists should there be in a district? This question has the same answer as 'How long should a piece of string be?' – 'It all depends'.

Section 5.7 of the Trethowan Report has been so widely misquoted, that it is worth quoting it here and pointing out what it does *not* say:

> 5.7.2....We have referred in paragraph 4.30 to the estimates of manpower requirements which were put forward in the evidence we received, giving a ratio of one clinical psychologist to between 30,000 and 60,000 population. This represents an approximate range of 830 to 1,640 clinical psychologists for England and Wales. A ratio of one psychologist to 25,000 population (which was suggested by The British Psychological Society as a long-term target) would represent a total of about 2,000 clinical psychologists...
> 5.7.4...It would, however, be unrealistic for us in the absence of a detailed study of the question to suggest precise long-term manpower targets or a precise timescale for achieving them. There is a clear need for such targets to be developed – not least so that decisions can be taken on the level of training facilities – and we think that a full study of manpower needs should be undertaken as soon as possible by the Department of Health and Social Security.

No such study has been undertaken. The British Psychological Society, amongst others, had recommended an 'ideal service' norm of 1 psychologist per 25,000 population. But the assumptions on which this recommendation was based were not made explicit and the Trethowan Committee itself did not recommend any such target.

Even The British Psychological Society's recommendation was unacceptably vague. Would a service consisting of four newly-qualified psychologists for a total population of 100,000 people be equivalent to a service consisting of four principal grade psychologists serving the same population? Would it matter if they were generalists or specialists? Does the denominator of 25,000 refer to the total population? Or does it mean 25,000 people outside regional secure units, day hospitals for the elderly mentally ill, wards for the severely handicapped, for all of whom additional psychologists might be required?

Clearly, the continuing implementation of two of the Trethowan Committee's main recommendations – the development of district psychology services and of specialist sections within those departments – means that norms cannot yet be used to answer the question of how many clinical psychologists will ultimately be required by the health service. And since there are no norms, they cannot be used for planning at local level.

How can one plan psychology services?

The government's priority areas for development are those in which psychologists have traditionally been involved. But the work of the profession has also diversified into many new fields since the publication of the Trethowan Report in 1977.

Districts differ widely in the range of services they themselves provide or are dependent on neighbouring districts to provide. That alone will result in a different pattern of psychology services in each district.

However, certain issues will need to be considered in relation to every district psychology service.

The priority fields of work. Because of the national emphasis on developing community care for the elderly, the mentally ill and the mentally handicapped, and improving the quality of hospital care for those groups, there are likely to be pressing demands for psychological services to those groups. The response to these demands needs to be balanced against the legitimate needs of the specialist services for children, neurological patients, and also newer services such as pain control clinics and counselling in relation to termination of pregnancy or still-birth.

A balance of routine services and innovation. On the one hand one may ask, if it isn't the job of clinical psychologists – highly knowledgeable and highly skilled – to provide psychological services, then whose is it? On the other hand, there are many reasons why clinical psychologists might be better seen as a resource for service development rather than service provision. The profession is so small that it would be swamped by a serious attempt to provide a wide range of routine psychological services. Since all health professions are concerned with the care and management of people, all have a psychological component to their work; perhaps psychologists are better seen as a resource to them. Finally, psychologists' skills as applied scientists, in research and development, are lost to the health service if they concentrate on the provision of routine services.

The evolution of the district service as an organization. Broadly speaking, a District psychology service is a distinct element of the services provided by a health authority, the ultimate development of which cannot be foreseen since it will be an adaptive response to the needs of the population served. That concept of a service implies that certain work – over and above the provision of patient-oriented services – needs to be done. The assessment of what would be the most efficient and effective service to provide is one example of such work. The provision of professional support, guidance and training to the staff of the service, especially with regard to changes they may need to make in their practice in the light of that assessment, is another. The work takes time, and provision needs to be made for it.

Feasibility of implementing service developments. The question which must be answered in relation to planning at district level is 'could we really do that here?' There is a world of difference between a report of a successful innovation under research conditions, and the use of those methods routinely under ordinary working conditions. The latter requires not just a conceptual model but also a clear description of, amongst other things, the facilities and equipment that will be required, the caseload that could be managed by the staff who will be available, the policy for responding to cases of non-compliance with the new methods, and the cost of introducing and maintaining the new service. A treatment which could be given to large numbers of people, would be beneficial half the time and harmless otherwise might be more satisfactory in practice than one which was almost invariably successful but could only ever be given to small numbers of people.

A career pathway for psychologists. The growth of clinical psychology depends almost entirely on newly-qualified clinical psychologists. There is no significant pool of qualified, experienced clinical psychologists outside the NHS which can be drawn on in order to extend the quantity and range of services provided. To a certain extent, movement of psychologists from one district to another to gain promotion is a healthy way of ensuring that they gain a broad experience of the health service and that innovations are transferred from district to district. However, too much and too frequent movement is disruptive. Particularly where new services are being developed or profound changes in the organization of services are being attempted, the time-scale for bringing about developments must often be measured in years. This needs to be taken into account when first establishing posts, by ensuring that they are not undergraded (as a result of which the individual would begin to seek promotion before doing the job required), and by ensuring adequate support for their development as a psychologist.

Where the money is. Developments occur as a consequence of the allocation of additional funds ('betterment monies') to districts by RHAs, as a result of the revenue consequences of capital schemes (RCCS), and as a result of a multitude of special schemes designed to implement a government priority (regional secure facilities; transfer of long stay patients to community care, etc.). Developments do not always occur as a result of systematic planning at local level; priorities *are* affected by where the money is.

A more detailed account of the options for the overall organization of clinical psychology services can be found in the paper by Ovretveit (1984). That paper also provides some general principles for the planning of psychology services. However, the search for a rational approach to development may have intensified, but for the foreseeable future, a pragmatic, even opportunistic approach will remain the order of the day.

SOME PSYCHOLOGICAL ASPECTS OF PLANNING HEALTH SERVICES

The clinical psychologist in planning

Whilst it may seem self-evident that psychologists should have a substantial role in the planning of their own services, the case for their participation in the planning of health services generally may be less obvious.

In the eyes of many people, psychologists may be primarily involved in the planning process because of the contribution of their own services.

The White Paper *Better Services for the Mentally Ill* (Cmnd. 6233) commented that the mentally ill:

constitute only a small proportion – in practice those with psychotic illness – of the total numbers of those who are currently seeking and receiving help from general practitioners and psychiatrists for psychological problems of various kinds, from severe depression, and phobias, through a whole range of sexual, marital and other human relationship problems.

But what proportion? How can decisions be made about the nature and scale of services to be provided in the absence of sound quantitative data about the incidence and prevalence of these problems?

What constitutes a case for the purpose of planning mental health services is a substantial area of research (Wing *et al.,* 1981). On the whole, psychologists have been conspicuous by their absence from the epidemiological study of problem behaviour. Goldberg and Huxley (1980) review the field in relation to adults. Rutter *et al.* (1975) report a study of psychiatric disorders in children. Lambert (1980) discusses the issues from the point of view of a general practitioner.

But psychologists should not confine their interests to the epidemiology of psychological problems *per se.* The need to prevent and control chronic disease, which has replaced the acute infectious illnesses as the major form of ill-health in the Western world, gives rise to a whole area of epidemiology and interventions to which psychologists have a special contribution to make.

An examination of the statistics of disease and of the changes in our social and physical environment indicate the four main groups of health problems which face us today; those concerned with the ageing of the population, with an unhealthy life-style, with mental health, and with environmental hazards. (DHSS, 1976, p.91)

Sexton (1979) refers to the study of the behavioural determinants of health status as 'behavioural epidemiology'. In view of the increasing importance to the NHS (not to mention the population itself) of diseases related to the lifestyle of the individual, this is an area of research warranting psychologists' attention.

There has been an almost explosive growth of practical applications of psychology to health care – categorized according to the conceptual scheme of the book or journal in which they are reported as 'Medical Psychology', 'Health Psychology' or 'Behavioural Medicine' (*see*, for example, Rachman, 1977; Pomerlau and Brady, 1979; Bakal, 1979; Oborne *et al.*, 1979). Are clinical psychologists willing or able to feed such new developments into NHS planning? It is of interest that some of the major concerns of psychologists in health care are not so much with new technologies as with ideological bases for services, such as normalization (Wolfensberger, 1976) reality orientation (Holden and Woods, 1982), and mental illness as an adaptive response to unmanageable social stress (Cochrane, 1983). In their own eyes, it may be psychologists' research and statistical skills which justify their involvement in planning, especially with regard to service evaluation. However, this is neither a unique contribution, nor one that clinical psychologists have yet emphasized in their work. Although the Trethowan Committee emphasized the psychologist's role as researcher, it seemed to be more concerned with maintaining high academic standards and the avoidance of intellectual isolation (op. cit., paragraph 5.10.1), than with the incorporation of psychological research findings into the planning and delivery of health care.

Yet there has been some psychological research and theory building which could be valuable to the design of services in any aspect of health care, for example how people monitor and care for their own health, the way they use health services as an aid to self-care and how illness behaviour may be modified. In such a brief chapter, it is possible only to touch on such issues, and no reference will be made to such other important topics as the psychology of planners and the planning process (Adler and Milstein, 1979), or to the assessment of the population's wishes and preferences for kind of services (Neuber *et al.*, 1980).

The subjectivity of need

Although health services are usually considered to be provided for those who 'need' them, people only receive services when they express their 'need' as 'demand' and seek help. Only services which are used can be effective.

Unravelling the relationship of 'need' and 'demand' for health care is potentially one of the most interesting aspects of psychology in relation to the planning of health services. The essential subjectivity of 'need' is being recognized in the development of new indicators of health, models of why people use health services, and in a developing analysis of the experience of ill-health as distinct from the bodily phenomena associated with ill-health. Concepts appropriate to these questions are illness behaviour (Mechanic, 1962, 1966) and health belief (Becker and Maiman, 1975). Gaining an understanding of the population's illness behaviour and, indeed, learning how to manage it, is an important area of research because, as Mechanic (1962) explained:

> The realm of illness behaviour falls logically and chronologically between two major concerns of medical science: etiology and therapy. Variable affecting illness behaviour came into play prior to medical scrutiny and treatment, but after aetiological processes have been initiated. In this sense behaviour even determines whether diagnosis and treatment will begin at all.

Referring to psychiatric care, Goldberg and Huxley (1980) neatly summarize:

> the selection processes which operate on psychologically disordered individuals which determine which of them will seek care; having sought care, which will have their disturbances detected; having been detected; which will be treated in a primary care setting and which will be referred for psychiatric care.

Table 2. The pathway to psychiatric care: five levels and four filters (based on Goldberg and Huxley, 1980, *Figure 1*)

Morbidity in random community sample   (250 per 1000)

FILTER 1 _____   Patient's illness behaviour _____
Total psychiatric morbidity, primary care   (23 per 1000)
FILTER 2 _____   Detection of disorder by GP _____
Conspicuous psychiatric morbidity   (140 per 1000)
FILTER 3 _____   Referral to psychiatrists _____
Total psychiatric patients   (17 per 1000)
FILTER 4 _____   Admission to psychiatric beds _____
Psychiatric inpatients   (6 per 1000)

Although Goldberg applies his filter model to people with psychiatric disorders, it should not be assumed that people with physical disorders seek help purely because they experience symptoms. Indeed, many people with significant medical abnormalities receive no treatment, either because their needs are not recognized by themselves or their doctors, or because they make no demand on the health services.

Research on illness behaviour has produced results which contradict the idea that many people use health services with only minimal reason.

There have been a small number of studies which have been done on people who have not visited their doctor for a long time (for example, Anderson *et al.*, 1977; Kessel and Shepherd, 1965). Kessel and Shepherd found that patients who had not visited their doctor for at least two years perceived themselves as healthy, although they had just as many recent symptom episodes as a matched group of people consulting their GP. The non-attenders were less likely to self-medicate and their self-image of healthiness was considered the most important determinant of their non-response to symptoms.

Other studies of illness behaviour (for example, Banks *et al.*, 1975; Wadsworth *et al.*, 1971) have provided evidence of the infrequency with which symptom experience leads to seeking medical help.

The much quoted study by Wadsworth *et al.* (1971) surveyed a random community sample of approximately 2,100 adults, concerning their state of health in the previous fortnight. Although one-third of the sample assessed their state of health as 'perfect' and another third as 'good', only 5 per cent reported being totally symptom-free. Of the other 95 per cent one-fifth did nothing about their symptoms. One of the commonest actions amongst the other four-fifths was self-medication. Medical help seeking was infrequent – only about 12 per cent of those experiencing symptoms went to their doctor.

The study by Banks *et al.*, (1975) led to similar conclusions. One hundred and ninety eight women aged 20 to 44 completed questionnaires on anxiety and on their social characteristics, kept symptom diaries for four weeks and were monitored for their usage of their GP over a period of 12 months. Other work using symptom recall methods suggests that adults experience symptoms on about 7 out of every 28 days. Using diaries for recording, these women reported symptoms on about 10 out of every 28 days. However, there was, on average, only one patient-initiated consultation for every 37 symptom episodes. There were some interesting variations in the extent to which various types of symptoms were presented to the GP.

Table 3. Ratio of symptom episodes to consultations (Banks *et al.*, 1975)

Changes in energy	456 : 1
Headache	184 : 1
Disturbed gastric function	109 : 1
Backache	52 : 1
Pain in lower limb	49 : 1
Emotional changes	46 : 1
Abdominal pain	29 : 1
Disturbed menstruation	20 : 1
Sore throat	18 : 1
Pain in chest	14 : 1

Hannay (1979) reports findings which suggest that 'the iceberg' of undetected and untreated illness (Last, 1963) represents a more common form of inappropriate illness behaviour than the unnecessary use of services. On the basis of interviews with a random community sample of 1,344, Hannay found that 77 per cent of those with physical or mental symptoms involving severe pain or disability, or which the person thought serious, sought professional help appropriately, whereas the remaining 23 per cent inappropriately sought no help or only lay help.

In contrast, of those with physical or mental symptoms with no pain or disability, or which the person thought were not serious, 91 per cent appropriately sought no help or only lay help, whereas only 9 per cent sought professional help inappropriately.

If it isn't just the experience of symptoms which determines help seeking, what does? Two studies by Ingham and Miller (1976, 1979) looking at seven common symptoms (backache, tiredness, anxiety, headache, depression, irritability, dizziness) investigated the extent to which variations in consulting behaviour can be accounted for by variations in symptom severity. Though they found that the prevalence of these symptoms amongst non-consulters varied between 2 per cent and 33 per cent depending on the symptom and type of sufferer, when account was taken of the severity and chronicity of the symptoms, and of previous but non-recent consultations, the symptoms reported by non-consulters were, on average, less severe than those reported by consulters. However, Ingham and Miller also concluded that whilst the severity of the symptom had probably increased the likelihood of the consulters consulting, the symptom was not so much a precipitant of the consultation as a background factor.

Two recent health measures, one developed in Nottingham, the other in Dundee, emphasize the subjective dimensions of health. Thus, they encourage the identification of subjective need for health care and may lead to a more accurate prediction of demand.

The Nottingham Health Profile (Hunt and McEwan, 1980) consists of nine statements referring to emotional reactions, eight to pain, eight to physical mobility, five to social isolation, five to sleep and three to energy level. Respondents are asked to answer 'yes' or 'no' according to whether or not they feel the item applies to them 'in general'. An example from each set:

- I have trouble getting up and down stairs or steps (physical mobility)
- I'm tired all the time (energy)
- I lie awake most of the night (sleep)
- I'm in constant pain (pain)
- I feel there is nobody I am close to (social isolation)
- I'm feeling on edge (emotional reactions)

Hagart and Billington (1982) describe the Dundee Health Status Profile. Using factor analytic methods, they constructed a questionnaire incorporating perceptual methods which attempts to measure health, rather than illness. The scores obtained are effective discriminators between criterion groups.

> The elements often having the strongest relationships with a variety of dependent variables (age, coronary heart disease, etc.) were purely perceptual factor scores, that is, those based on general perceptions of health, rather than the more objectively defined constructs such as social and physical health. (Hagart, 1982)

CONCLUSION

Planning is a practical activity. The questions 'What shall we do?' and 'How shall we do it?' are practical questions, especially since they must be answered within the bounds of the answer to the questions 'How much can we spend now? – next year? – over the next ten years?'.

Nonetheless, it is an important activity. The kinds of services that are provided and the way in which they are provided reflect not just technical capabilities but ideologies, beliefs about health, illness, disability, and people and their needs, not to mention social, political and moral judgements of the most far-reaching kind. It is also of great interest psychologically because concepts like 'need' and 'demand' have an irreducible subjective element. It is to be hoped that clinical psychologists will consider the planning of health services worthy of their time and effort.

REFERENCES

ACHESON, R.M. (1978) The definition and identification of need for health care. *Journal of Epidemiology and Community Health, 32,* 10–15.
ADLER, N.E. and MILSTEIN, A. (1979) Psychological perspectives on health care and planning. In: G.C. Stone, F. Cohen and N.E. Adler (eds) *Health Psychology* San Francisco: Jossey Bass.
ANDERSON, J.A.D., BUCK, C., DANAHER, K. and FRY, J. (1977) Users and non-users of doctors – implications for self-care. *Journal of the Royal College of General Practitioners, 27,* 155–159.
BAKAL, D.A. (1979) *Psychology and Medicine: Psychobiological Dimensions of Health and Illness* London: Tavistock Publications.
BANKS, M.H., BERESFORD, A.A., MORRELL, D.C., WALLER, J.J. and WATKINS, C.K. (1975) Factors influencing demand for primary medical care in women aged 20–44 years: a preliminary survey. *International Journal of Epidemiology, 4,* 189–195.
BECKER, M.H. and MAIMAN, L.A. (1975) Sociobehavioural determinants of compliance with health and medical care recommendations. *Medical Care 13,* 10–24.
COCHRANE, R. (1983) *The Social Creation of Mental Illness.* London and New York: Longman.

DEPARTMENT OF HEALTH AND SOCIAL SECURITY (1976) *Sharing Resources for Health in England: Report of the Resource Allocation Working Party.* London: HMSO.

DEPARTMENT OF HEALTH AND SOCIAL SECURITY (1977) *The Role of Psychologists in the Health Services.* (The Trethowan Report.) London: HMSO.

DEPARTMENT OF HEALTH AND SOCIAL SECURITY (1978) NHS planning: the uses of staffing norms and indicators for manpower planning. (Issued with Dear Administrator letter ref N/M242/022 dated April 1978.)

DEPARTMENT OF HEALTH AND SOCIAL SECURITY (1981) *Care in Action.* London: HMSO.

DEPARTMENT OF HEALTH AND SOCIAL SECURITY (1982) Health Service Development: The NHS Planning System. Circular HC(82)6.

DEPARTMENT OF HEALTH AND SOCIAL SECURITY (1983) Health Service Development: Care in the Community and Joint Finance. Circular HC(83)6.

DEPARTMENT OF HEALTH AND SOCIAL SECURITY (1984) Health Service Development: Resource Distribution for 1984–85 – Service Priorities, Manpower and Planning. Circular HC(84)2.

FENTON LEWIS, A. and MODLE, W.J. (1982) Health indicators: what are they? An approach to efficacy in health care. *Health Trends, 14,* 3–8.

GOLDBERG, D. and HUXLEY, P. (1980) *Mental Illness in the Community: the Pathway to Psychiatric Care.* London: Tavistock Publications.

HAGART, J. (1982) How should we measure health? Paper presented at The British Psychological Society's London Conference.

HAGART, J. and BILLINGTON, D.R. (1982) Towards an understanding of health status: perceptions of health status dimensions. *Journal of Community Medicine, 4,* 12–24.

HANNAY, D.R. (1979) *The Symptom Iceberg.* London: Routledge and Kegan Paul.

HEALTH ADVISORY SERVICE (1982) *The Rising Tide: Developing Services for Mental Illness in Old Age.* Sutton: Health Advisory Service.

HOLDEN, U.P. and WOODS, R.T. (1982) *Reality Orientation: Psychological Approaches to the Confused Elderly.* Edinburgh: Churchill Livingstone.

HUNT, L.B. (1983) Community Services for community care: Notes on joint planning for community physicians. *Health Trends, 15,* 77– 81.

HUNT, S.M. and McEWEN, J. (1980) The development of a subjective health indicator. *Sociology of Health and Illness, 2,* 231–246.

HUNT, S.M., MCKENNA, S.P., MCEWEN, J., BACKETT, E.M., WILLIAMS, J., and PAPP, E. (1980) A quantitive approach to perceived health status: a validation study. *Journal of Epidemiology and Community Health, 34,* 286.

INGHAM, J.G. and MILLER, P. McC. (1976) The concept of prevalence applied to psychiatric disorders and symptoms. *Psychological Medicine, 6,* 217-225.

INGHAM, J.G. and MILLER, P. McC. (1979) Symptoms prevalence and severity in a general practice population. *Journal of Epidemiology and Community Health, 33,* 191–198.

KESSEL, N. and SHEPHERD M. (1965) The health and attitudes of people who seldom consult a doctor. *Medical Care, 3,* 6–10.

LAMBERT, H. (1980) Problem behaviour. In: J.Fry (ed.) *Primary Care.* London: Heinmann.

LAST, J.M. (1963) The Iceberg: 'completing the clinical picture' in general practice. *The Lancet, July 6 1963,* 28–31.

MECHANIC, D. (1962) The concept of illness behaviour. *Journal of Chronic Disease, 15,* 189–194.

MECHANIC, D. (1966) Response factors in illness: the study of illness behaviour. *Social Psychiatry, 1,* 11–20.

NEUBER, K.A., ATKINS, W.T., JACOBSON, J.A. and REUTERMANN, N.C. (1980) *Needs Assessment; a Model for Community Planning.* (Sage Human Services Guide 14.) London: Sage Publications.

OBORNE, D.J., GRUNEBERG, M.M. and EISER, J.R. (1979) *Research in Psychology and Medicine.* London: Academic Press.

OVRETVEIT, J. (1984) *Organising Psychology in the N.H.S. A Health Services Centre Working Paper.* Uxbridge: Brunel University Institute of Organisation and Social Studies.

POMERLAU, O.F. and BRADY, J.P. (eds) (1979) *Behavioural Medicine: Theory and Practice:* Baltimore: Williams and Wilkinson.

RACHMAN, S.J. (1977) *Contributions to Medical Psychology, Volume 1.* Oxford: Pergamon Press.

ROSENSTOCK, I.M. and KIRSCHT, J.P. (1979) Why people seek health care. In: G.C. Stone, F. Cohen and N.E.Adler (eds) *Health Psychology.* San Francisco: Jossey Bass.

RUTTER, M.L., YULE, B., QUINTON, D., ROWLANDS, O., YULE, W. and BERGER, M. (1975) Attainment and adjustment in two geographical areas: III Some factors accounting for area differences. *British Journal of Psychiatry, 126,* 520–533.

SEXTON, M.M. (1979) Behavioural epidemiology: In: O.F. Pomerlau and J.P. Brady (eds) *Behavioural Medicine: Theory and Practice.* Baltimore: Williams and Wilkinson.

WADSWORTH, M.E.J., BUTTERFIELD, W.J.H. and BLANEY, R. (1971) *Health and Sickness: the Choice of Treatment.* London: Tavistock Publications.

WING, J.K., BEBBINGTON, P. and ROBINS, L.N. (1981) *What Is a Case?* London: Grant McIntyre.

WOLFENSBERGER, W. (1976) *The Principle of Normalisation in Human Services.* Toronto: National Institute of Mental Retardation.

YATES, B.T. (1980) The theory and practice of cost-utility, cost-effectiveness and cost-benefit analysis in behavioural medicine. In: J.M. Ferguson and C. Barr-Taylor (eds) *Comprehensive Handbook of Behavioural Medicine, Volume 3.* Lancaster: MTP Press.

SUBJECT INDEX